a great fan of Don Bachardy's work. Of course I met him because his close relationship with Christopher Isherwood, with whom I had emi-close relationship from afar. But I was honored to be a part of brilliant *Berlin Stories*, which were adapted into the film *Cabaret* and orded me the opportunity to bring the character of the Emcee to the ge and screen, which would not have been possible without him. So m forever grateful to both gentlemen."

—**JOEL GREY**, TONY AND OSCAR-WINNING ACTOR

ave liked and admired Don Bachardy ever since I first met him in s Angeles in the early 1970s, together with Christopher Isherwood. It came immediately apparent that one was in the presence of not just single but two extremely creative artists, and that they comple-nted each other in a subtle and remarkable way.

"My wife Pat and I were delighted when Don asked us to sit for him d were even more pleased with the results, samples of which hang our home to this day. At that time, Don employed a more classical rm of draftsmanship, consisting of intense observation yet allied to ability to put his subject at ease. Later his style changed, becoming ore free-form and relaxed, and often executed with color, but it re-ained equally intense.

"We used to love going to their canyon-hugging house in Santa Mon-a for dinner, where we would be served tasty home-cooked food as un-etentious as they were. Eventually they became an amalgam of each her, with voice and even handwriting remarkably similar. They collab-ated on artworks and screenplays, but perhaps their greatest collabora-n are the portraits of Christopher that Don made as his partner lay ing. They have a Goya-esque intensity and are unforgettable.

"We feel privileged to have known them—theirs was a legendary rtnership.

"This groundbreaking oral biography reveals its multitalented sub-ct in multifaceted detail, providing fresh, intimate insight into the gendary Bachardy-Isherwood partnership."

—**MICHAEL YORK**, FILM AND EMMY-
NOMINATED TELEVISION ACTOR

"A fascinating book! Anybody who has a much younger lover should read this book to learn how to negotiate the chasm between Youth and Experience, which Chris and Don did with patience and a hands-off tolerance. They became a legendary gay couple when all other gay celebrities were closeted. This book is a paean to Don's love for Chris and his enthusiasm for life.

"Don calls himself an artist of personality, and he certainly met and drew all the Hollywood stars of the day, from Charles Laughton to Natalie Wood—and all the literary personalities from Tennessee Williams to E. M. Forster."

—**EDMUND WHITE**, LEGENDARY GAY NOVELIST, MEMOIRIST, AND BIOGRAPHER

"I was thrilled and very honored to be asked to sit for a portrait by Don Bachardy, and to experience that private moment with his enormous talent. I'm very proud of the drawing that he did of me. This book wonderfully captures the very special experience of being in Don's intimate company, listening to his spellbinding stories about his extraordinary life with Christopher Isherwood and as a portrait artist in Hollywood."

—**ROBERT WAGNER**, EMMY AND GOLDEN GLOBE-NOMINATED ACTOR AND AUTHOR

"Don Bachardy captures the outer likeness and the inner life of his subjects. He is genuinely interested in them and sometimes seems to actually love them."

—**SIR IAN MCKELLEN**, TONY-WINNING AND MULTIPLE ACADEMY AWARD AND EMMY-NOMINATED ACTOR

"In his own words, Bachardy leads us through a thorough and compelling journey of his life, gently guided and provoked by Michael Schreiber's spontaneous, well-researched questions. This is an intimate autobiography that unfolds seamlessly, revealing a complex personality, riveting and deep."

—**TINA MASCARA**, AWARD-WINNING FILMMAKER

"I had the great fortune to sit for a portrait with Don. It was an incredibly personal thing as he seemed to look right through me. Don's eye misses nothing. In the end, he was unhappy with the picture and much to my chagrin, he destroyed it. He did, however, complete a beautiful portrait of Richard Buckley, who was my life partner for thirty-five years. It hangs in a prominent place in my bedroom.

"*Don Bachardy: An Artist's Life* is a captivating read. I have always been struck with how comfortable Don Bachardy is with himself. I think that this is perhaps one of the reasons that he and Christopher Isherwood were daring enough to live the open life that they did long before it was conventional or even safe to do so. Their love story is one of beauty, and is an inspiration to all who have ever felt trapped by convention."

—**TOM FORD**, FASHION DESIGNER AND ACCLAIMED FILMMAKER

Don Bachardy

Don Bachardy

AN ARTIST'S LIFE

An oral history by

MICHAEL SCHREIBER

with forewords by

SIMON CALLOW AND JAMES IVORY

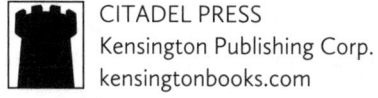

CITADEL PRESS
Kensington Publishing Corp.
kensingtonbooks.com

CITADEL PRESS BOOKS are published by

Kensington Publishing Corp.
900 Third Avenue
New York, NY 10022

All Kensington titles, imprints, and distributed lines are available at special quantity discounts for bulk purchases for sales promotions, premiums, fund-raising, educational, or institutional use. Special book excerpts or customized printings can also be created to fit specific needs. For details, write or phone the office of the Kensington sales manager: Kensington Publishing Corp., 900 Third Avenue, New York, NY 10022, attn Sales Department; phone 1-800-221-2647.

10 9 8 7 6 5 4 3 2 1

First Citadel hardcover printing: November 2025

Printed in the United States of America

ISBN: 978-0-8065-4379-6

ISBN: 978-0-8065-4381-9 (e-book)

Library of Congress Control Number: 2025937909

The authorized representative in the EU for product safety and compliance
is eucomply OU, Parnu mnt 139b-14, Apt 123,
Tallinn, Berlin 11317; hello@eucompliancepartner.com

"I am a camera with its shutter open, quite passive, recording, not thinking. Some day, all this will have to be developed, carefully printed, fixed."

—CHRISTOPHER ISHERWOOD, *GOODBYE TO BERLIN*

"The truth is, to me, the real beauty. The Hollywood loveliness is a lie, and the truth is far more exciting—and far more tragic even than your most tragic Hollywood film."

—DON BACHARDY

Contents

Foreword

BY SIMON CALLOW

Simon Callow, 1986. © DON BACHARDY

WHEN I STARTED writing about Charles Laughton, in 1985, I knew that I needed to talk to Christopher Isherwood. At the time of Laughton's death, the great actor had been working with Isherwood on an adaptation of three of Plato's *Dialogues*, a project very dear to Laughton's heart. This, I thought, was a unique opportunity to discover something both about Laughton's attitude to his sexuality, a subject on which he was—publicly, at any rate—in complete denial, but also about the cast of his mind; Isherwood, master observer of gay lives within straight society, would surely have much to tell me on the subject of his old friend.

By happy chance, just before I planned to go to Los Angeles, where he lived, I was working with Isherwood's friend Claire Bloom. She gave me his phone number, but said, very firmly: "Speak to Don first. He'll smooth the way." I knew, of course, who Don Bachardy was; knew all about him—his romance with Isherwood, the extraordinary gap in ages between them, their writing collaboration on the dramatization of A Meeting by the River. He and Isherwood were an exceptionally rare example of an openly gay couple; his elegant, exquisitely refined drawings adorned the covers of most editions of Isherwood's novels, and his drawings of the stars of John Osborne's eagerly awaited brace of plays, A Hotel in Amsterdam and Time Present, had advertised them on the programs and posters at the Royal Court Theatre in London. He was a star in his own right.

The day I arrived in Los Angeles, I called the number Claire had given me. "Hello," said a crisp English voice.

"Oh, hello," I said. "Could I speak to Don Bachardy?"

"Don's not here at the moment. This is Christopher Isherwood. Can I help?"

"Well," I stumbled, "My name is Simon Callow. Claire Bloom gave me your number."

"Oh, how is Claire?"

"Well, very well. The truth is, Mr. Isherwood, it's you I want to talk to. I'm writing a book about Charles Laughton, and—"

"I don't want to talk about Charles," he said, crisply.

"I assure you," I burbled, "I'm not interested in anything prurient."

"I don't want to talk about Charles," he continued. "I can give you Mrs. Laughton's number."

I knew, as he must have done, that Elsa Lanchester was long gone in Alzheimer's, and accepted defeat as graciously as I knew how. "Thank you," I said, pretending to note down the number. "You've been very helpful."

I had taken care not to mention my Isherwoodolatry; I sensed it would only make things worse. I did the only thing I could do: Claire had given me Isherwood's address, and I took a cab to Adelaide Drive in Santa Monica, where he lived, just down the road from the Laughtons' house, and pushed a copy of my first book, *Being an Actor*, through the letterbox. I inscribed the book: *To Christopher Isherwood from Simon Callow. In no sense an inducement to talk about Laughton, simply a very small token of profound admiration and gratitude.*

I never spoke to him again. Some months later, his death was reported, and I realized why he hadn't wanted to talk: he died of cancer, exactly what Laughton had died of. Time passed; nearly a year. I was asked, before the book came out, to make a television documentary about the great actor. This involved going to New York to interview people who had worked with him—Rex Harrison, Peter Ustinov; wonderful. But I still regretted the absence of an interview with Isherwood. Then it suddenly occurred to me that Don Bachardy must have known Laughton almost as well as Isherwood did, so I called the number I had called before.

"Hello," said a crisp English voice—Isherwood's voice.

Bewildered, I stuttered, "Could I speak to Don Bachardy?"

"This is Don. Who am I speaking to?"

"My name is Simon Callow. I'm a British actor, and—"

"I know exactly who you are. Christopher was, uh, uh, reading your book for the second time when he died."

"Goodness."

"He found it, uh, fascinating." He laughed. "How can I help you?"

I told him about the documentary. Would he talk?

"Uh, uh, I don't know what I'd say."

I suggested that we could discuss it when I came to Los Angeles the following week. When I called him from New York to make arrangements, he said, quite abruptly, "I don't want to talk about Charles. He was an enthusiasm of Christopher's I didn't share."

"Oh," I said.

"I'm very sorry," he continued. "But may I ask you an odd thing—would you, uh, uh, allow me to paint your portrait?"

"Goodness. Well, of course I would."

As soon as I got to Los Angeles, I made my way to Santa Monica. Don was smaller than I had imagined, but compact and powerful in his white wifebeater and gray jeans. There was a fierce gravity about him, disrupted by sudden gurgles and gasps of laughter. And he spoke with the unmistakable accents of the upper middle-class Englishman with whom he had lived for over thirty years. "I know I talk like Christopher," he said. "I don't care."

The house was hung like a laundry, with large sheets of paper, filled with images in rough strokes, gray and black, a mixture of Japanese brush and black acrylic paint. The images were unmistakably of Isherwood, in pajamas, mostly, sometimes naked. I had seen innumerable images of the writer, many—perhaps most—by Don, but this was something altogether different: the writer's habitual spryness and quizzicality, sexy and elfin, replaced by something almost monumental, the face contorted with pain, but occasionally almost blank, the body sometimes clothed, often not, his *membrum virilis* dangling in the foreground, slack, majestic, redundant. Here was Isherwood awake, Isherwood slumbering, Isherwood locked in pain, Isherwood dying, Isherwood dead.

"I embarked on this, uh, uh, sequence during Christopher's last illness. It was something I knew had to be done. He was in great pain, but I insisted. It was very difficult for us both."

Seeing the drawings at such close quarters, in the house in which Isherwood had lived and died, was overwhelming, the experience both intimate and impersonal, being suddenly taken to the heart of this exceptional relationship, admitted into his confidence by a man I had only just met, describing, in his searching way, some pretty deep truths not only about Chris, but about what it is to be so viscerally connected to another person.

It was all the more extraordinary that these profound truths were coming from the mouth of someone who, though his hair was becoming silvery, was still slim-hipped and bright-eyed, almost boyish. He expressed his hard truths with something like joy, the joy of having precisely nailed experience. Silence fell. He laughed, a sort of private laugh, reflecting on what he had lived through. "Shall we do the drawing?" he said, brightly.

He put me next to a window that looked out over the Santa Monica Canyon. I quickly sensed that he preferred not to talk, so we sat together for nearly two hours in that strange intimacy that exists between subject and artist: who else apart from a mother or a lover—or perhaps a doctor—looks at one with such penetrating scrutiny? "It's done," he suddenly announced. "You're a very good sitter."

"The silence was wonderful," I said.

"Yes!" he cried. "I only recently realized that the reason I paint portraits is because it's the only way I can get that silence."

After finishing a portrait, Don famously asks his sitter to sign it, as if he or she were somehow its co-creator. When I went to put my name to the one he had made of me, I was taken aback: he had drawn a sort of double portrait of me and Charles Laughton—as if Laughton and I had had a child together. I pointed this out. He said, "Oh, really? I never know what I've done. I rely on people to tell me."

As if all that were not enough, as we were making our farewells, he suddenly, unprompted, started talking about Laughton, how pompous he was, and how he failed to relate to Don at all. And then, with wonderful precision, he talked about the relationship between Charles and Elsa. "They tormented each other—that was their whole life's work—and they were, uh, uh, perfectly innocent that this was what they were doing." In ten minutes of sustained and brilliantly observed analysis, he told me everything I needed to know about them in these later years of their life. I understood then that Don's portraitist's eye went far beyond the surface.

I left him having been brought abruptly closer to my literary hero, Christopher Isherwood, and my biographical subject, Charles Laughton. Not bad for three hours that also produced an extraordinarily striking image of me as I had certainly never seen myself. I wasn't sure where our acquaintance would go after that.

As it happens, I was summoned a day or two later to the Hollywood mansion of Tony Richardson, the cavalier English film director, whom I had never met but who had, he said, a wonderful new play in which he wanted to direct me. When I arrived, he told me that he had found out that Don and I knew each other and that he would be arriving at any moment, which was delightful to me. Then Richardson, with what I knew from other people was entirely characteristic behavior, told me that he wanted me to read the play there and then. I was reluctant to do so at pistol point, so to speak, and told him that I'd read it overnight and call him first thing in the morning. This did not please him.

At this point, Don arrived, and Tony left the house huffily, urging us to avail ourselves of the contents of his drinks cabinet and instructing me to call him the following morning *without fail*. So there Don and I were, in someone else's house, sitting on the floor—there being, for unfathomable reasons, no chairs to sit on. We got drinks and started to talk. Don was somewhat subdued; inevitably, our conversation turned to Christopher. I ventured that of all his books, the one I was least able to connect to was *My Guru and His Disciple*—a highly enjoyable study of his discipleship with Swami Prabhavananda. As an account of pupil and guru, it was entirely compelling. The difficulty was trying to connect that aspect of Isherwood's life with all the rest of it.

"It was, uh, uh," said Don, "the only area of him of which I couldn't be part."

I said that I could see how that might be so. There was, however, I said, one exchange in the book that I found infinitely touching.

At one of their first meetings, Isherwood had asked Prabhavananda whether his being involved in a sexual relationship with a young man was an obstacle to his spiritual development. After briefly sighing, Prabhavananda had replied, "You must try to think of him as the Lord Krishna."

When I said this, Don's face broke up, and he wept. "I'm sorry," he said. "It's still so fresh."

I hugged him—we were still sitting on the floor—and I said, "What you're feeling is unimaginable. So many years of being intertwined."

He said, "I think we'd better go to supper."

I was meeting friends; he joined us. Over the meal, we talked about everything but Christopher; Don drank a great deal and laughed a great deal, as did we all.

Since then, I have seen him pretty well whenever I've been in Los Angeles. I've seen him in London, and in Berlin, where I read from the collection of his and Christopher's letters, *The Animals*; oddly, at his behest, I read his letters and he Christopher's. Later, at the Metropolitan Museum in New York, Alan Cumming read Don and I Christopher, which seemed a better fit.

I have rarely traveled so fast and so deep into friendship as I did with Don. The odd circumstances—the last drawings of Christopher in the house, the intense portrait session, our abandonment by our host in Hollywood, his sudden access of grief—seemed to take us very rapidly to a position of great frankness and emotional freedom. I have since discovered that all his friendships are of this order. He is an uncommonly present individual. It is impossible to imagine him having a casual friendship, or indeed a casual conversation. He brings the entirety of his being to whatever he's doing—painting, talking, writing. There is always about him that sense of discovery, of nailing, or doing his utmost to nail, a particular truth. To be with him is to join him on that exhilarating and unending voyage.

Foreword

BY JAMES IVORY

Ismail Merchant, 1974. © DON BACHARDY
(Photo of the artwork by Seth David Rubin, courtesy of James Ivory)

WE KNOW HOW it happened. An eighteen-year-old boy on a California beach, with an engagingly cute gap between his two front teeth, captivated a famous English author thirty years his elder. So much so, that they lived happily together for the rest of Christopher Isherwood's long life. *Don Bachardy: An Artist's Life* exactly tells us the story in the words of the boyfriend, Don Bachardy. Why, then, am I providing another foreword to that famous love story? In the opening pages of this book, there is already an excellent introduction by Michael Schreiber. The need for another is that Michael Schreiber never knew Christopher Isherwood, who died several decades ago. But I did know him, as well as Don Bachardy, in the mid-1970s, when we all became friends—the "all" here including my partner Ismail Merchant, the film producer.

We met Christopher at a luncheon party in a Beverly Hills restaurant in 1974, given by Dorothy McGuire and her photographer husband John Swope. Ismail and I were about to start shooting a new film, *The Wild Party*, a '20s Hollywood story. We planned to make our film in Riverside, California, which is about a hundred miles east of Los Angeles. Merchant Ivory had never before worked under the noses of the powerful motion picture guilds of Hollywood—those representing directors, writers, and actors— and we were not members, or signatories, as production companies are called. At the luncheon party, somebody warned us that the Directors Guild could become upset because *The Wild Party* was not to be directed by one of its members, especially as we were about to cast members of the Actors Guild—and already had: the film's two leading stars, Jimmy Coco and Raquel Welch. I replied at once, "Well, I'll just join the Directors Guild."

Someone else said, "One doesn't just 'join' that guild; one has to be introduced by another member."

Then Christopher spoke up: he knew George Cukor very well; he offered to call him and put us together. Surely that grand old veteran would second me? The call was made, and a day or two later, I went to meet Cukor at his beautiful house in Hollywood. He was mourning the death of his old dog, but he said he would be happy to recommend me to the Directors Guild. He'd liked *Shakespeare Wallah* very much.

I don't recall meeting Don Bachardy at that lunch, but I soon did, if not, and liked him at once. Though no longer that cute teenager in a bathing suit with a "mouse face" who first attracted Christopher Isherwood, he was a little humming and electric personality who could never sit still, was full of ideas, and was for sure most attractive. But the clipped way he spoke was unexpected.

Sometimes over the telephone to them, I was unsure who had answered: was it Chris, or was it Don? The speech of Americans who spend a lot of time in England does alter. Mine did. Today, when Don and I speak, I can hear the echo of Christopher, long gone.

After Dorothy McGuire's luncheon party, Chris and Don invited Ismail and me to their Santa Monica home. I remember it, and also very much liking how it was furnished. I can see their living room to this day: the contemporary art on the walls, and being struck by a set of stylish Robsjohn-Gibbings chairs with bright pink upholstery. You had to park well above, then make your way down a lot of stairs to the house, pinned on a steep hillside. There were fine views towards the Pacific, and once safely inside, lots of books that you wanted to examine. Ismail and I would go back again and again to that house. Not for meals or to dinner parties; I think neither of them much liked to cook, though maybe they did. We always ate in restaurants nearby that Chris and Don liked.

We were often in Los Angeles in those days during and after *The Wild Party*, and we were always welcomed. They must have enjoyed our company, and the four of us went places together, often to film screenings. Once I remember driving Chris home to Santa Monica. Instead of sitting up front next to me, he lay stretched out flat, face up, on the back seat of our rented car; Don must have been at work in his studio that day. Did Chris suffer from car sickness? I didn't like to ask, and anyway, I treasure this memory.

Ismail and I decided we would make a documentary film about the most famous gay couple in America. We planned to show Chris and Don at home, mainly in their Santa Monica house, with Don in his studio, where all sorts of famous people came and went. But we intended to put Chris's relationship with his spiritual advisor, his guru, Swami Prabhavananda, whom we never met but to whom Chris often referred in conversations, out of our minds—and thus, out of our film. That side of his life, oddly, was of little interest to us. Both Ismail and I had had by then too much experience in India of gurus. Merchant Ivory had even made a film about that subject, called *The Guru*, though in our film, the guru had been a great musician, and his disciples were his pupils learning to play the sitar. But we had met too many Western, mostly enervated disciples of Indian spiritual gurus; had visited their ashrams, had eaten the horrid food there, and been told about the holy men's sometimes unholy behavior. We intended, if Chris would let us, to draw a curtain across all that. There are for sure Indian gurus who are enlightened souls, doing great good amongst their disciples. Probably Swami Prabhavananda was one of those; had he not been, Christopher would have seen that, and left him. We could not have made an authentic film with Christopher Isherwood if we had not included Swami Prabhavananda at the very center of his life—almost another partner in it, like Don Bachardy, both intellectually and emotionally. I never asked myself, what must Don make of all that?

American Public Television at that time was making a series called *American Masters*, and we went to them for possible financing. We told them that shooting our film would take only a month or so to complete. Our idea was turned down, however, without any explanation. Was it because Christopher Isherwood was not a native American, and purportedly had left England with the poet W. H. Auden during World War II when things got bad there? Or was it because he and Don were "America's Most Famous Gay Couple"? This was in the mid-'70s. We could give Chris and Don—who were encouraging us to make our film, and were going to find the time to do it with us and permit a film crew to enter their house—no reasons why we suddenly seemed to have dropped the idea.

Sometimes the four of us would get together in New York, where Don was to meet the often tiresome, and often mean-spirited, grandees of New York letters, music, and dance. Don has a lot to say about some of these people in this book. He drew Ismail's and my portraits in our apartment on East 52nd Street. As

I sat there opposite him, I remember I was very aware that my face had its good angles, as well as less good ones. All movie directors become sensitive to this aspect of most faces as we appraise our actors and actresses early on, deciding which are their "best angles." And I knew—I'd tested it many times—that when I viewed my face from the left, I could slightly lengthen it to become more handsome if I did not relax my jaw. So I did that, as I sat there for the artist. Don, who had doubtlessly drawn the jaws of hundreds of vain persons like myself, must at once have noticed how I had "enhanced" my profile, but carried on. I looked very odd in the finished drawing and not at all myself, but I signed and dated it anyway, which Don always makes his sitters do. Ismail, posing next in that same room, in the same bright daylight, sailed home triumphantly, and exactly, just as handsome as in life.

Somewhat later, the three of us who at first made up Merchant Ivory were approached by the National Portrait Gallery in London. They wished to include us in their collection of notable men and women in the arts, though the origins of each of us were far from British. One of us was Indian, Ruth was German, and I am an American from Oregon. We were to choose a photographer, or artist, who could come up with the portraits, and we chose Don Bachardy. He came to my house in Upstate New York at Claverack and spent a summer weekend making sets of three paintings of each of us. He asked us not to linger too long observing while he painted any of us. That time I didn't stick my jaw out, while Ismail tried hard not to disrupt his sittings by being on the phone— though Don ought to have painted Ismail talking on the telephone, which was practically an extension of his body, of his entire being. During Ruth's sittings, I have no doubt that though mostly silent, she was thinking of many, many things.

About that time, Don did a series of handsome, nude, sexy-looking men, which was later published. He told me once that getting sexed-up over any male sitter always destroyed any possibility of working. But sitting with him sometimes in that quiet intimacy for many hours, one's thoughts could easily run to sex, and possibly—quite often—to sex with him. Could he tell what I was thinking, in that uncanny and all-seeing way of his? When I stuck out my chin that time, was I flirting with him?

Introduction

DON BACHARDY: A PORTRAIT OF THE ARTIST

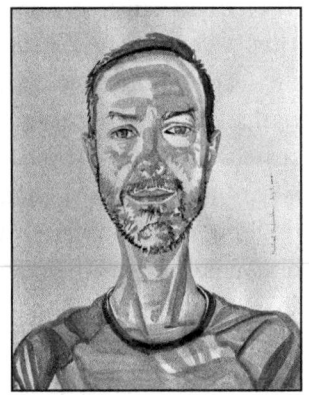

Michael Schreiber, 2018. © DON BACHARDY

I'VE NEVER SAT so still or so silently, and for as long, as I have during my portrait sittings with Don Bachardy. I've never been so intensely looked at, either, by *anyone*, or felt so deeply looked *into*, so thoroughly *seen*.

In his preferred work uniform—colorfully paint-spattered shorts, tank top, and sneakers—Don could lie perfectly camouflaged across the equally paint-spattered floor of his studio. But even starkly framed against the room's sunlit white walls, he seems in moments to almost disappear. So total is his absorption in recording his subject—*me*—it's as though he has somehow absorbed himself *into* me.

The resulting portraits are more than just accurate likenesses of me. They're *ghosts* of me, with my essence *also* nakedly captured on paper in vibrant colors that almost palpably radiate. They're the me from the outside looking in, yet also the me from the inside looking out. It's truly an eerie experience, to say the least: looking at a mirror image of oneself, yet from it also *feeling* oneself from outside of oneself.

But mine are not unusual among the thousands of portraits Don has channeled through his skilled eye and hand over the past sixty years: through just an economy of brushstrokes, time and again he captures in his work both the physicality and the energetic imprint of his subjects. Whether they be of celebrities or "everyday" people like myself, Don's portraits reveal the extraordinary in even the most ordinary of faces. Indeed, throughout his long career, he has sought to indiscriminately portray the tremendous variety of humanity, drawing and painting people of diverse racial, gender, sexual, and generational identities in an effort to demonstrate what binds rather than separates us as fellow humans. While American society and its politicians and judges continue to debate the equal inclusion of all of its citizens and their stories in its fold, Don's portraits offer an accurate, celebratory inventory of just how richly diverse and storied that society truly is. The occasional famous face in the mix has been a professional necessity, he points out, explaining that as a portrait painter, "it's no good to do just portraits of people who aren't going to be recognized by the public. How else can they know that I can get a good likeness if my subject isn't somebody they've seen?"

Don readily attributes his success as an artist to the early and continuing nurturing and encouragement he received from Christopher Isherwood, the renowned English writer, whom he fatefully met on a Santa Monica beach some months before their official coming together on Valentine's Day in 1953. Although Don was then just eighteen and Isherwood some thirty years his senior, their unlikely romantic pairing not only survived, but thrived—both domestically and creatively—over the next three decades. Isherwood and Bachardy became a legendary couple in literary, artistic, and Hollywood circles, while separately and collaboratively crafting written and visual character studies that adroitly recorded their astute observations of humanity.

As Isherwood had observed in his semi-autobiographical 1939 novel, *Goodbye to Berlin*, which later inspired the blockbuster Broadway musical and movie *Cabaret*, "I am a camera with its shutter open, quite passive, recording, not thinking. Some day, all this will have to be developed, carefully printed, fixed." This famous quotation has often come to mind over the past decade as Don and I have intimately discussed his own remarkable life and career, his fabled relationship with "Chris," and their courageous, pioneering advocacy as a fearlessly openly gay couple in a fearfully buttoned-up mid-twentieth century America. "They are the most famous gay couple who has ever lived," Christopher Harrity boldly declared not long ago in *The Advocate*, while conceding that perhaps only Gertrude Stein and Alice B. Toklas might also lay claim to that title.

Like Stein and Toklas in their time, Isherwood and Bachardy knew just about "everybody who was anybody" in their own, counting among their closest friends a host of household superstar names from the worlds of American and British art, literature, music, and theater. But for Don—a lifelong movie fan who had daringly gatecrashed star-studded Hollywood premieres as a teenager in the early 1950s—Isherwood's added status as a studio screenwriter opened doors into the intimate worlds of movie stars and moviemakers. In time, Don's own celebrity capital as a rising art star grew to match Isherwood's literary fame, making them a Hollywood power couple in their own right. Chris and Don routinely found themselves as guests at A-List celebrity parties, on movie sets visiting famous friends "in the business," or in their

Santa Monica home, casually hosting a glittering guest list of their own. In 2021, that iconic house and studio were designated a combined Historic-Cultural Monument by the City of Los Angeles, but both the extraordinary and the everyday of Don's life and career carry on unabated within, some six decades after he and Chris first made it their home, and now nearly four decades since Chris's final departure from it.

I made my first pilgrimage to that famous house some twelve years ago, approaching its front door with the hesitant step of a latecomer. After all, with so much of the Isherwood-Bachardy legend already recorded—much of it by Chris and Don themselves, across published volumes of Chris's diaries, their love letters, and Don's Hollywood portraiture—what could possibly be left unasked and untold? But I was then in the waning days of a magical friendship with the nonagenarian artist Bernard Perlin, who had encouraged me to "look up Donny" on a vacation trip I was taking to Los Angeles. Although never really friends, Bernard and Don had intersected many times across many years, beginning with Don's first trip with Chris to New York in 1953. Now, exactly sixty years later, I expected a brief but thrilling (for me) encounter with a cultural icon who was gracious enough to humor the curious young friend of an old acquaintance.

Truth be told: I was rather starstruck by Don, little realizing then how perfectly fitting it was that I had discovered him in the movies. Through a screening of Guido Santi and Tina Mascara's spellbinding, aptly titled 2007 documentary film *Chris & Don: A Love Story*, the Isherwood-Bachardy story had magically unfolded for me and instantly, irretrievably folded me back up into it. But I was even more mesmerized by the film's teller of that real-life Hollywood fairytale: Don Bachardy himself. As Chris had described an eighteen-year-old Don just several weeks into their relationship, "There's a brilliant wide-openness about his mouse face, with its brown eyes and tooth gap and bristling crew cut, which affects everybody who sees him. If one could still be like that at forty, one would be a saint." At then nearly eighty, that same "mouse face"—now slightly wizened and white-haired—welcomed me into his wondrous world with a wide, gap-toothed smile and a devilish laugh that punctuated the disarming candor of his storytelling about himself and others, thus belying Chris's earlier prophecy about Don's potential sainthood.

If not quite an angel, Don is proudly a lifelong and diehard Angeleno, a fact not easily betrayed by his distinctive Mid-Atlantic, Katharine Hepburn-like accent—the lasting result of his early unconscious mimicry of Isherwood's British-English. "A young man's life is largely governed by the myths he has made about himself," Christopher Isherwood once told an interviewer. "One of the most attractive myths for a young man is the myth of himself going out to distant lands to find some treasure or truth. But of course, it was all right there where he'd started out from. It was a matter of finding the key to open the door and the door flew open and there it all was in one's own closet." A person, not a disappointed return from a distant place, held that key for Don: from the moment of what Chris described as their "fated, mutual discovery" of each other on a California beach, Chris "opened doors for me that never would have opened," Don told me during our own first meeting. "I wouldn't have even had a chance to know what the doors were without him!"

Little did *I* know, when Don warmly greeted me at his front door on that first visit, that further doors were about to be opened for *me*. But our own first meeting proved in itself to be something of a fated, mutual discovery: of each other as unadulterated fellow fans of the Golden Age of Hollywood. That I could easily keep up with Don's references, no matter how obscure the film or star, and he could in turn with mine, swiftly sealed our friendship. But whereas I thought that I "knew it all," Don had actually intimately *known them all*. Over the past eighty years, he has engaged with sundry stars and star-makers, either fleetingly (as a teenage autograph seeker), socially (in the company of Christopher Isherwood), or professionally (as the venerated Hollywood portrait artist he has become). But he long ago ceased being just a fan, for he has remarkably become one of their own: one of Norma Desmond's "wonderful people out there in the dark" who long ago crossed over into the spotlight as an art star and Hollywood celebrity in his own right.

I first approached Don not as a reporter seeking a scoop, or as a literary or art scholar seeking to do a treatise, or even as a Hollywood screenwriter looking to do a treatment of his very cinematic life story, but just as a curiosity seeker, one with passionate interests in midcentury movie history and matters of the midcentury queer heart and experience. My equally passionate interest in his process and product as a portrait artist only added to the teeming list of questions I had for him—all of which he answered unflinchingly. As Don candidly, compellingly, and often comically recounted both familiar and previously untold stories of his intimate life with Chris—and of his encounters and creative collaborations over the past seven decades with legendary Hollywood, literary, and artistic figures—I realized that I was privileged to be hearing material that was wonderfully supplementary to, but in no way could supplant, all that has already been fixed in print and on film about the Isherwood-Bachardy story. But remarkably, Chris and Don's is *still* an ongoing story: one of a love so profound that it is *still* fueling the richly inspirational life that Don continues to actively live in exploration and expression. He remains as collaborative with his past as he is creatively engaged with his present and future.

Don is certainly an "open book," but in opening *this* book about Don Bachardy, readers should be aware of its inherent conceit: that our conversations about his life were actually conducted chronologically, as they are presented here. As Eve Babitz observes in *Slow Days, Fast Company: The World, the Flesh, and L.A.*, "You can't write a story about L.A. that doesn't turn around in the middle or get lost." This holds true with a spellbinding raconteur like Don:

the tantalizing tales he told me often tumbled down rabbit holes into wonderlands of further fertile terrain. But over hundreds of hours across eight years, my trusty voice recorder faithfully followed the winding flow of our conversations, which I then transcribed, edited, and loosely sculpted into the ready-made outline of Don's remarkable life story.

It should also be noted that the vast majority of our interviews, which began in the spring of 2013, occurred well before the interruption of Covid-19 lockdowns in early 2020. When I was able to return to Los Angeles in the summer of 2021 on a delayed Andrew W. Mellon Foundation Fellowship at the Huntington Library, which I had been awarded in support of this project, Don and I reunited for a few sessions just to tie up loose ends with the manuscript, and to discuss my research in his and Christopher Isherwood's papers at the library.

While he repeated many of the stories we had already covered, some of his new retellings and answers to follow-up questions contained some inaccuracies which now revealed, as he called it, "the encroachment of age/brain deterioration." These new responses ultimately needed to be vetted, further questions respectfully scrapped, and the entire manuscript carefully critiqued by outside eyes for repetitions and accuracy. Edits were made accordingly.

What has emerged is, fittingly, a *portrait* of Don Bachardy, taken from his later life—or, rather, three intertwined portraits of Don's three distinctive yet intrinsically interconnected identities: as a lifelong movie fan; as Christopher Isherwood's legendary boyfriend; and as an acclaimed portrait artist.

Each of the three has found and lived his own extraordinary love story.

Don Bachardy

CHAPTER 1

I was just waiting to be told who I was

Don at eighteen, photographed by his
brother Ted, 1952. © DON BACHARDY

*If anyone's life story can be likened to a fairytale, it's yours, Don. And
it all began for you, quite literally and fittingly, just within reach of
Hollywood.*

On Casitas Avenue, the last street in Atwater, which is part of
L.A., then the railroad tracks were behind the houses across the
street from us, and beyond those, it became Glendale. The big en-
gines, when they were going full force, made a lot of noise and
shook the house, but I loved it! It was exciting to me. Oh, the

wonderful nights I spent listening to the trains, the whistling and the stopping and starting again jerks: it was all very full of sound, and I loved it. To me it was the most glamorous sound; it just swept me away. When I was really little, I dreamed of one day being on one of the trains that I'd been listening to. We used to have people visiting, and we took them to the train station, and it always seemed so exciting to be departing or even meeting somebody that would get off. Yes, I still think it's so much more glamorous than plane travel, but even plane travel seemed exciting when I was young.

Did you ever have the opportunity as a boy to get on a train and travel somewhere?

Yes, to Cleveland, Ohio, to visit my grandparents with my mother and brother in January 1942, and I loved it. The train trip itself was just the height of glamour for me at that age. after all those years of listening to the trains, to suddenly get on one and to be going somewhere, going into *snow* country? I'd never seen snow!

It would have taken you two days to travel by train from Los Angeles to Cleveland. Did you have a private room, or sleep in berths?

No, we took the coach car. My mother sat up in a coach chair all night, and Ted and I slept on the floor. They brought us pillows, and there was some kind of carpeting that we slept on. We arrived very early, the first or second or third of January, but it had been a very unusual winter so far: not a flake of snow! But that night, as my brother and I were going upstairs, our grandmother opened the front door to see something or other, and there was *big* excitement: the first dusting of snow on the front porch! I'd been so disappointed when I'd heard "no snow yet" by early January, and the next morning, it was a winter wonderland!

As though ordered by Hollywood just for your benefit!

Yes, just at exactly that time!

So unlike you and your brother, were neither of your parents native Californians?

My mother grew up in Cleveland, and my father was born in New Jersey, into a very poor family. I did meet his mother when she was out here staying with my uncle, my father's older brother, and she was the oldest woman I've ever seen in my life. My mother's father, whose name was Deland, was the captain of a Great Lakes boat. Somewhere along the way, I remember very clearly a photograph of him in his official uniform, with a hat and looking very official. So one summer, my mother and her sister Donna were guests on his boat, with parasols and lots of frills, and from the bridge my mother first spied my father, from under her umbrella. He was working in the hold, but was on deck doing something, carrying something into the hold or bringing something up, stripped to the waist, and looking pretty good to her! But of course, that was frowned on madly by her father, the captain, because he considered those laborers very low-down. He was dead set against the marriage, and she had never crossed him in her life, but she would not yield.

And evidently, she won out.

It didn't matter to her! She wasn't thinking of *class* at that moment!

She certainly had a great eye for genetics, given the two beautiful offspring she and your father would co-create.

Yes! I think I look more like my father than my mother, partly because she had very clear, pale blue eyes. Ted got my father's brown eyes, and mine are officially hazel, which I assume is a certain mixture of the brown with the blue.

What had brought your parents out to Los Angeles?

It was all because my mother was intent on coming to California and seeing Hollywood, seeing stars in the flesh. So my father first went to work at Lockheed in 1928, I think. My brother Ted was born in 1930; I was born in 1934. Our house, all of the time the four of us were in it, was incredibly dignified by a giant palm tree right in the center of the front yard; it gave the house such character. I guess we were in that house on Casitas until 1950. Until then, that was all I remembered of my only experience of home, and then my mother and my father separated, and she and Ted and I moved to Hollywood, to an apartment off Western Avenue. And then it was early in 1953 that I got together with Chris, and I never looked back. A hell of a lot has happened since then!

Indeed it has, but looking back now, if you will, to your young life before the momentous advent of Christopher Isherwood in it, what are your earliest memories?

Of being taken to the movies by my mother. The first film that I have a vivid image of is called *The Mad Miss Manton*.

A 1938 screwball comedy-mystery starring Barbara Stanwyck and Henry Fonda.

When I thought I was seeing it for the first time in the '50s, I wasn't aware of having seen it before until suddenly there was an image on the screen that had a very deep reverberation inside me. I can't even fit it into any kind of storyline in the film, but it's a woman on a dark street at night, and there's a detailed shot of her gloved hand reaching down and picking up some kind of sparkling piece of jewelry—probably a diamond bracelet—off the sidewalk. That's the first image I can identify in a movie, and that was in 1938, so I was no more than four.

So you were being taken to the movies at that young an age?

Oh, sure! Yes, it was always by my mother. My brother Ted and I were her filmgoing companions. Her companions in general, but especially for films. My mother loved movies, so I was seeing movies when I was three and four years old. My mother and brother and I were a real trio. During World War II, while my father was slugging away at Lockheed Aircraft, we were downtown watching movies, sometimes going to three different theaters in a row. He went off early every day and didn't get back until late at night. My mother would even occasionally take Ted and me out of school if she wanted to go downtown to a movie and didn't have anyone to go with!

That sounds like heaven!

Heaven, yes! Oh, I had a wonderful childhood. And it was exciting, too, because my mother didn't want us to let on to my father what we'd been doing, so it was secretive, which made it all the more fun!

Were there particular film genres or movie stars that she favored?

It was particular movie stars. That was a major draw for her: seeing particular movie actors that she liked in whatever films they were making at the time, but we saw so many that she couldn't afford to be particular about the kinds of films. We saw all kinds, and there was no fooling around with movies for children. We saw *everything.*

Who were your first favorite movie stars?

Oh, Bette Davis and Alice Faye, they were my two favorites in those very early years, in *Jezebel* and *In Old Chicago* and *Alexander's Ragtime Band.* And of course, they were favorites of my mother's, and so they became favorites of both Ted's and mine. Paulette Goddard was very popular with Ted and me especially, but her forehead was too high for my mother!

Although you were just five years old in 1939, you were already an avid moviegoer during what is now considered "Hollywood's Golden Year."

Let's see: *Rose of Washington Square,* which is the best of the later Alice Faye movies, was in 1939, and Bette Davis was in *The Old Maid, Dark Victory, Juarez,* and *The Private Lives of Elizabeth and Essex.*

Would you have also seen The Wizard of Oz *during its first run that year?*

Oh, definitely. It was something to remember and a key film, and a special event when I was taken, but Judy Garland didn't then have any sway over me like Bette Davis and Alice Faye did.

How about Gone with the Wind, *the biggest movie event of that year?*

Oh, sure, yes, I loved it! It was my idea of *super* glamour, being taken to a nine A.M. screening of it downtown at the United Artists Theatre! We were really the Three Musketeers in moviegoing.

Were you three likewise devoted readers of Photoplay *and other then-popular movie magazines?*

We lived in them. Yes, there were always movie magazines, and they had a particular palpable attraction to me: the colored covers, the typography of the magazine titles, are still very vivid in my memory.

Would you save and savor those magazines, or perhaps clip photos from them?

Oh, yes. Following my mother's example, we did keep a collection of movie star clippings. She was very particular about not really sharing *hers* with Ted and me; they were off bounds for us. We, of course, knew where she kept her scrapbooks, but we were forbidden to inspect them without her, and she was very reluctant to share them with us. That's peculiar, but not if you knew my mother. Partly it was that we were still young enough that we couldn't be trusted to handle them, but I think she was a little bit shy about her own fascination with movie stars and clippings. I suspect that she felt it was childlike of her to hoard those clippings.

Did you then follow your mother's example and keep scrapbooks of your own clippings?

No, because it ruined my clippings to put glue or paste on them, and because the other side of them was so often of interest to me,

I didn't want to hide the back of some of them forever in a scrapbook. I liked handling them. To this day, there's hardly a one of them that has a tear or is damaged in any way. They're all stored in a filing cabinet in my carport. I've actually still got all my movie stills, too, because I had a later period of raiding the movie studios, going to their still departments.

So you would actually get yourself onto movie studio lots? How did you manage to do that?

Oh, yes, yes. The stills department in all the studios I visited was open to the public, and you could get the numbers of the photographs and then, like I did, order prints from New York or wherever that were of particular interest to me. And you see, it was a good cover for getting onto the lot, because I would dutifully go to the still room, which is what my visit was specifically for, and then I would come out and could roam the studio! Imagine wandering around on all the sets and watching movies actually being made, and without anybody giving me a "what are you doing here" look? It was such a different time, that at the gate you could just tell them that's where you were going, and they would let you in.

So was it from such studio photographs, either obtained as stills or seen reproduced in movie magazines, that you first developed an interest in portraiture?

Yes, we started copying movie star portraits from the magazine pictures. Yes, indeed. My brother, who was four years older, had a real skill.

What compelled that activity?

I guess making them more vivid to ourselves: entering into the pictures more completely by studying them closely in order to copy them and to get a likeness. That takes great skill and great powers of identification. But certainly that kind of identification in other forms was also going on—very much, I think—with both Ted and me, and with my mother, too.

Were there certain stars who held particular visual appeal for you?

Both Faye and Davis made period films, so particularly their hoop skirt period—Davis in *Jezebel* and Alice Faye in *In Old Chicago*—that made them peculiarly attractive to Ted and me. Well, *Jezebel* was my first female obsession. The long curls, full skirts, and a dress that's supposed to be bright red, and she goes to a ball where all the virgins are in white! I had lots of pictures of her in it.

What would you do with those early sketches? Collect those in scrapbooks, perhaps?

Oh, those would have been with pencil and crayon. No, I never made scrapbooks of them or a collection of them. Of course, I did them in school, too: I used to do portraits of my classmates. Mostly girls; I think only exclusively girls, and I think I was quite popular in second grade, doing these portraits and passing them around.

So that truly was the beginning of your career as a portrait artist!

Yes, yes, but the identification with these movie people expressed itself as wanting to be an *actor*, rather than an *artist*. Drawing from those pictures was just a more intense way of identifying with them, and the objective seemed to be exactly *like* them: to appear in movies, and probably, preferably, in hoop skirts and long curls!

Did you also solicit autographs and photos of Hollywood stars by writing them fan letters?

Oh, yes, I wrote letters with my brother Ted, a lot of fan mail. It was so exciting to find in the mailbox a 5x7 envelope! MGM always sent out only signed pictures that were *in* the photographs, not on them, but everybody at 20th Century Fox always had real ink autographs. But oh, I was so disillusioned when I found out that 20th Century Fox had a whole squad of forgers! And some of them were just so lazy that they didn't even bother to imitate the real signature. Often I knew the signature—sometimes from having gotten it at a premiere—that I could tell when it was nowhere near, but then some of them were pretty good forgers. I was very tuned into that at the time.

You and Ted soon started sneaking into Hollywood movie premieres, attempting to get even closer to the stars you admired.

By the time Ted and I were in our teens, we were going on our own, but we were first taken to premieres in the '40s by our mother and father. He was necessary because he was the only driver among us, so he would take us to Hollywood premieres, mostly at the Carthay Circle or the Grauman's Chinese or the Egyptian. I think maybe the first one was in 1942. I would have been eight, and Ted was four years older. To get a seat in the bleachers outside, you had to be there by three or four in the afternoon and sit it out until eight or eight-thirty. So we sat with our mother in the bleachers, watching the stars arriving in their cars. Some of them would even come over and sign autographs. Most of them would at least come within good sight of the people in the bleachers.

What was the film that was being premiered?

The Pied Piper with Monty Woolley and Anne Baxter, and Roddy McDowall is in it. Our first real infiltration, but only of the events outside the theater, was at the opening of *Since You Went Away* at the Carthay Circle Theatre, which no longer exists, in 1944. This was before we actually got bold enough to sneak inside, as we learned how to do later. All kinds of stars were there, and that was my first encounter with Jennifer Jones, getting her autograph, and years later she became a very close friend to Chris and me. And then Danny Kaye's first movie, *Up in Arms*, had a big opening at the Pantages. That would have also been in '44. *That* was the first time that Ted and I got inside a theater. Imagine! It was so very exciting

to be actually in the lobby rather than outside in the bleachers!
And the lobby had almost emptied—the film was about to begin—
when Alan Ladd arrived. He was the first male movie actor that I
kept magazine pictures of, because I thought that he was so stunningly handsome. He was. He was late, and he was by himself and
in a hurry to get into the theater—the film was just beginning—
but I ran up to him with my autograph book. But instead of being
irritated, he stopped and couldn't have been more charming to me,
and talked to me. So it wasn't like just getting a signature from a
star who was moving on; he really showed pleasure to be doing it.
And I remember him being just a little bit taller than I was—and
I wasn't tall!

You were all of ten years old!

It was the first time a Hollywood actor of either sex *really*
showed pleasure at being accosted. I mean, he was in a hurry, but
he stopped. It was the first time I heard that wonderful voice of
his: that deep, velvety voice. Oh, I would have loved to known him
better, but that first encounter with him really was like for the first
time feeling for a man what I felt for women.

How so?

I felt a connection with him like a connection I'd naturally felt
with females. I was not nearly so interested in getting the autograph of somebody like Gregory Peck. But speaking of Peck, when
Duel in the Sun opened at the Egyptian Theatre on Hollywood Boulevard in '46, Ted got in without me. I guess it just hadn't occurred
to us that it'd be much more fun going together, but very soon after
that we started going together, and never either of us did it singly
again. Well, I never did it by myself; it was always under Ted's leadership, but he did that one alone: there was some reason why I
didn't or couldn't go, otherwise I certainly would have, because Jennifer Jones was one of our most beloved of that period. *Duel in the
Sun* started our obsession with her: we loved that film, both Ted

and I. Afterwards, there was almost a full-page photograph in a movie magazine of Gregory Peck at the premiere, with Ted coming up behind him! In some of the magazines, with the cutting at the top of the picture, Ted's eyes were cut into, but we looked at many issues of the magazine at many different stands, and we found some of the pictures of him that actually cut into his forehead, showing all of his eyes. There were, I think, at least two magazines later that we found a picture in of *me* getting autographs.

I'm sure you and Ted were the envy of fans across America who saw those pictures in movie magazines. You were doing what no other fans were able to do.

Yes, we really were the most inventive and the most determined fans, and it was always under Ted's leadership. He had corrupted his little brother: he was very sly and tricky, and yes, I learned a lot from him!

How would you work your way inside?

Well, Ted, being four years older, was the instigator of our stealthiness. We would dress up in our best clothes—I was often in the suit which was bought for my graduation from junior high—and get onto the streetcar dressed up in our ties; then at the premiere, each of us would choose a middle-aged couple who could be our parents, and do our best to look like we might belong to them. We never had tickets, ever, so we would follow behind them closely as they walked in—close, but just behind, so that they were not aware. There was usually one ticket taker on either side of the door, so each never knew whose ticket the other one was taking. We never had *anyone* come anywhere near saying, "What do you think you're doing?" So it was very easy for Ted and me to get inside, and once inside, we brought out our autograph books and went to work. Eventually, Ted started bringing along his little Brownie camera, just a perfectly ordinary little camera with a flashbulb attachment. So soon we were photographing the actors, too.

The kind of easy access that you and Ted were able to connive and contrive to those star-studded events would be unheard of nowadays.

Oh, it would be impossible now. That was a golden era of just about barely ten years, if even that. The whole setup is changed and gone forever, and it will never return. It was a much more innocent world then, and it's much, much different now. But it was dangerous then, too, because of all the police watching and protecting the stars from exactly what we were! You know, in all those years of slipping into premieres, we could have been arrested! The fan world really created these two very daring, inventive lawbreakers—reckless lawbreakers who snuck in and asserted themselves and made the movie stars obey! It seems to me like nothing else: a real, almost hysterical version of fandom. I would be surprised if you could ever find another movie fan with quite the collection of memorabilia that I've got! Well, you know, all of my collection of those snapshots, I have not only listed the movie and the theater the premiere took place in and the dates, but I still have the programs of the premieres, with the various autographs on them that I was getting. I don't have enough of my pictures of Ted, but I have a complete set of his pictures of me, because he gave them to me. If I'd had my head screwed on toward the end of his life when I knew he was failing, I should've thought of that and got from him all that material that would've been valuable to me, because I know it just probably got thrown out by one of his last partners.

I marvel at how you and Ted unwittingly became junior film historians, so conscientiously documenting that golden era of Hollywood stars!

Imagine, in my teens still, behaving like a little historian! In our amateur career, we knew our subjects, knew how to chase them, and knew how to make them divvy up! Imagine Ted and I pushing in with our camera, and doing such an enormous job of confronting and recording all these people, these two little unknown creatures asserting their will and their mission and their adoration? How many other movie fans were so well-equipped?

Would you try to get inside early, as the stars were also coming in?

No, we waited, because once the stars started arriving, everybody waiting for them was then paying attention to getting them into the theater and showing them to their seats. But it took a *long* time to get all those people in the theater, so the early arrivers then had to sit sometimes for more than an hour, and that really made them vulnerable and bored, I'm sure, just sitting there waiting. Meanwhile, all of the lights and action and movement was on the outside: the limousines arriving; the fans in bleachers, usually on two sides and screaming and carrying on.

While those stars already inside became sitting ducks for you and Ted!

Yes, once they got into the theater, there they sat, sometimes for an hour or more, like sitting ducks for Ted and me! And because all the lights were on, we could identify them all, and that made it all possible for Ted and me to cover the whole downstairs audience. We were so in tune, it was real teamwork; and we were indefatigable and devoted. It was such a genuine expression of passion that we shared. We were like two halves of the same person.

Were you at all discriminating in whom you sought out?

Of course, we picked out our particular favorites. For our first really in-depth photographing assignment, our objective was Marilyn Monroe at the Academy Awards ceremony at the Pantages Theatre in 1951. Now that was a good two years before she became an official star with *Gentlemen Prefer Blondes*, but we had already been tracking her since the late '40s, from her first starring role in a B movie called *Ladies of the Chorus*. And then we had seen her in all kinds of walk-on parts, like a Dick Powell/June Allyson movie called *Right Cross*: she has just one scene in it.

And were you successful in your quest to "capture" her, so to speak?

Yes, we have a variety of pictures of her with her acting coach, with whom she attended the Oscars, and we have pictures of her by herself; and toward the end of the evening, actually after the ceremony, we have pictures of her with each of us: of Ted standing almost surreptitiously next to her, and of me, too. I have a picture of her looking into Ted's camera lens with me standing beside her in full grin. I've got it framed, and it charms me every time I look at her face, at her expression! She was wearing a black evening gown. And then we had another encounter with her at a radio show at CBS on Sunset Boulevard, wearing her bright fuchsia pink dress from *Niagara* and looking so delicious. She might have even been making that film at the time, but she wore that dress a lot in public. I saw pictures of her at other events wearing it. But again, this was before she was an official star, right before *Gentlemen Prefer Blondes*, which without question was her star-making appearance.

You encountered her that second time at a taping of The Edgar Bergen and Charlie McCarthy Show *in October 1952, just as she was about to begin production on* Gentlemen Prefer Blondes.

The radio show didn't matter at all to Ted and me! I guess it was announced that she was going to be a guest on the show, so we went. It was outside the theater that we got that picture of her. She had made *Don't Bother to Knock* and got star billing, but *Gentlemen Prefer Blondes* was really the official declaration of her stardom. She couldn't have been sweeter to both of us on both occasions.

Your photos reveal that she had hairy arms!

Yes, indeed! The studio retouchers would have seen that and taken care of it.

You're both positively beaming in these candid shots.

She was a real pro! It just tells so much about her, and what a good person she was.

You mentioned also encountering Monroe at a radio show. So your stalking of stars wasn't just limited to movie premieres?

No. Before that, it was through going to the racetrack with our parents. When I was really not even ten yet, I'd seen people like Betty Grable, Andrea Leeds, George Raft, and Fred Astaire at the racetrack.

Would this have been at the Santa Anita Racetrack?

Santa Anita and Hollywood Park, too. My parents—my father particularly—were trying to make money by betting. He never really got the knack, but they did go a lot to the racetrack, and Ted and I would sneak into the Turf Club and get autographs. Betty Grable and Harry James were regulars—they were real racetrack aficionados. I remember she was very friendly, very nice, but I was really a kid then. Well, and so was Ted. Harry wasn't friendly, but she was. And Fred Astaire was often at the racetrack, but I just didn't pay attention to him. I was so devoted to the women, mostly. I also remember going on a Sunday morning to the *Lux Radio Theatre* and getting Linda Darnell's autograph. Monday night was the performance night, but my brother and I knew they rehearsed Sunday mornings, so sometimes when we found out what show they were rehearsing on Sundays, we would go.

Was Linda Darnell gracious when you approached her?

Oh, she was very sweet. I remember she'd already started signing her name when I said, "To Don, please." So what did she do? She did something nobody else had ever done: she finished writing "Linda Darnell," put an apostrophe-s: "Linda Darnell's best to Don."

Have you held onto your autograph collection through the years?

I still have the programs, and they're autographed, but I gave away the precious autograph book to somebody I hardly knew, because his name was Don! I just had a new life with Chris, and I felt that that was my past: that was kid stuff, and it had really had no significance compared to life with him. But I've regretted it ever since. Oh, the priceless autographs in that book! Marilyn Monroe was in there, and all kinds of people. I probably could have gotten a pretty penny for it!

The Lux Radio Theatre *was a long-running, popular radio anthology series that presented hour-long adaptations of films, featuring some or all of the original cast members. What was Linda Darnell there performing in?*

She was doing *Fallen Angel*, but instead of Alice Faye, who was also in the movie, they had Maureen O'Hara. Almost anybody would've been better than Faye in that. I think it's a terrific film; it's one of Linda Darnell's best, but Alice Faye, whom I have a soft spot for, sinks it. Well, she had real blame for Darryl Zanuck, regarding him as the villain who cut down her part in that film in order to ruin her career, but he also destroyed a perfect picture.

Although Faye was a major star at 20th Century Fox and ostensibly the lead in Fallen Angel, *studio head Zanuck had ordered many of her scenes drastically cut from the finished film both to sabotage her and to build up rising star Darnell.*

Everything else about it is so good: Anne Revere, Dana Andrews, John Carradine are all good, and the tone of it. Yes, it has lots of atmosphere. Well, Darnell was always so good, but particularly in those bad-girl parts. I'm crazy about Linda Darnell. That wonderful voice: I can hear it in my ears now. And then Faye comes on, and she's just at sea. It was so wrong for her, and she was even the wrong age and the wrong look for it, with that blond hair. And she plays a virgin: an old virgin!

It's like Oscar Levant's famous quip about having known Doris Day before *she was a virgin!*

Here she's supposed to be a kind of spinster, a young spinster with bleached-blond hair, which she braids and puts on over her head. Incidentally, that was my mother's hairdo, her most classic hairdo even before Faye had it in *Fallen Angel*. All of my drawings of my mother are with her braids on her head, with one exception because I asked her especially to leave her hair down for one sitting. But it's braided in all the others, and it really did suit her better than any other hairdo. But my God, how awful Faye is in *Fallen Angel*, and really so wrong for it!

And the film is ironically and prophetically titled, for it did indeed spell Faye's fall from stardom. After it, she walked away from her career and was effectively blackballed by Zanuck.

Yes, indeed. Her '40s career hardly existed. There were those Carmen Miranda movies, which were in color, and, what, *Fallen Angel*, and what were the other color ones? Awful pictures. *Hollywood Cavalcade.*

She later reemerged to co-star with her husband, the bandleader and comedian Phil Harris, in their own eponymously-titled radio program.

I saw one of them in real-life broadcast.

You were there in the audience?

Yes, I saw one of those shows she did with Phil Harris, and I have a picture of myself with her. It was the night of the broadcast that Ted and I went, and we waited afterward at the stage door.

What was that experience like, being in the audience as one of those now-classic radio programs was being performed live and recorded?

Well, since my two childhood fascinations had been Bette Davis and Alice Faye, she always had a claim on my attention. She looked great. She had very blond hair, much blonder than ever in movies, and long, and it was kind of built up on top as well as having lots down. I guess she was still in her middle to late thirties, but to my eyes, which were very searching, she still looked very good. I was hypersensitive to aging actresses, and she passed muster for quite a while.

Were they just standing on a bare stage with their scripts and a radio crew?

Yes, a kind of spare production, but still it was very amusing. Just the nearness of the real creature was exciting. I thought it was so damaging to her and undignified for her to be doing it, but I don't think she really knew or cared. I think we all felt it was a debasement of her, but she was allowing it because she was married to the guy.

Phil Harris was quite funny in small doses as part of the ensemble on Jack Benny's perpetually popular radio program, but carrying a show himself was something else entirely. And Faye was there in support, mostly just to play foil to his buffoonery.

And we sort of cringed for her, having to put up with this rather embarrassing husband! And Phil Harris was looking *so* kind of overripe!

One of your more audacious escapades to see a star up close in the flesh involved a particularly beautiful one—although one laid out in an open casket in a cemetery chapel?

Oh, Carole Landis, yes! Hers was the first dead body I'd ever seen. Wouldn't you know it would be a movie star?

Although she was also a popular pinup girl and intrepid USO performer during World War II, Carole Landis was unlucky both in love and name. After four failed marriages, she committed suicide at age twenty-eight in 1948 over a failed romance with the married actor Rex Harrison. Meanwhile, the Hollywood star whose name she had modeled her own after, Carole Lombard, had tragically perished in a plane crash just six years earlier.

The death of Carole Lombard was one of the major events of my early life. Oh! How could a major movie star like her die, except in a movie? And we would often see a new Carole Lombard movie. But believe me, those events gave those two actresses *so* much glamour and interest. I used to see all of their films. But yes, Carole Landis was just there at Forest Lawn in Glendale, in an open casket for viewing, and *crowds* came. There were long lines, but Ted and I learned when the best times to go were, to get a really good look at her; otherwise, you had to wait an hour or more. But that was an early feast, yes, and the first dead person I had ever seen. I wouldn't have recognized her. I mean, she looked perfectly alright, and you could see it was the body of somebody very good-looking, but Carole Landis? I could never have identified her if I'd never identified her before, and I had already very sharp recognition equipment from going to premieres and racetracks and spotting the Hollywood figures I wanted to chase after. And she had actually been a favorite of my brother and me because of seeing her in *One Million B.C.*: we loved that film, and *Hot Spot*, too, which was retitled *I Wake Up Screaming*, with Betty Grable and Victor Mature. It was all about Carole Landis for us; Victor Mature didn't interest us much! She was the singer, and she gets murdered.

And ironically, that's how you ended up seeing her in "life"—as a beautiful corpse!

Yes, but she didn't look at all like Carole Landis to me! I would never have guessed who it was, but still the image is implanted in my mind, because it was such a daring thing for us to do!

Indeed it was, just as your stalking of then-living stars ultimately evolved beyond just getting an autograph to also getting yourselves photographed with them. Were Hollywood stars gracious about your approaching them at these events?

Oh, it was a different time. In the older days, it was easier, I guess just because the people were less on their guard then than they've become. Yes, it was easier then to meet big Hollywood stars than it certainly became very soon. But I remember Hugh O'Brian, who played the lead in a very popular TV show, *Wyatt*

Earp, wasn't so gracious. Ted and I were photographing his escort, the woman he was with—I forget who it was—and we weren't paying attention to him, so he started making disparaging remarks about us that we were meant to hear, and did hear. But yes, we almost without exception had encouraging experiences with most of these people. They were very friendly, obliging; graciously signing autographs, "To Ted," "To Don." The early times were in autograph books, but then on the premiere programs because the title of the movie was on the program, and that was a good reference that was visible in the photograph. Yes, we were very insistent. And as with Monroe, we concentrated on particular favorites, and eventually got ourselves with both Bette Davis and Alice Faye.

Your childhood idols, both of whom would later sit for portraits by you.

Yes, to get Bette Davis to sit for me was a major accomplishment of my life as an artist: I could have stopped there! Alice Faye also sat for me. What a lugubrious creature she was!

We'll get to the delicious stories of those sittings later on, but what was that first encounter with Davis like?

The premiere of *All About Eve* at Grauman's Chinese had been a must for us, because Bette Davis was such a big favorite of ours, and we *really* were hoping to see her in the flesh. We never had, and we knew she would be coming, but somehow or other, she got into the theater before Ted and I realized it. We were *so* deflated that we knew she was inside, but we hadn't quite the nerve to sneak in; we hadn't yet devised our entry. So our encounter happened at the preview of a movie called *Decision Before Dawn*. Imagine giving that picture a premiere? The decision before dawn should have been: don't bother seeing that movie!

Decision Before Dawn *was a war film starring Davis's then-husband and* All About Eve *co-star Gary Merrill, with a screenplay by Peter Viertel, the son of Christopher Isherwood's friends Berthold and Salka*

Viertel. But those behind-the-scenes names would have meant little to you then.

And we would never have *dreamed* of going, except that Gary Merrill was Davis's husband, and we thought it was a pretty good chance to get at her, and how right we were. She was indeed with Gary Merrill, but of course we didn't bother to photograph him. You can imagine us being a little bit afraid of Davis, with her movie image, but she was gracious. I'm not sure she even knew we were being photographed together.

Just as you were unaware, until recently, that a photographer for the Los Angeles Examiner *had unwittingly captured you and Ted positioned behind Davis and Merrill on the sidewalk outside the theater as they arrived for that preview screening in December 1951.*

My God, it's supernatural! It's like magic time-traveling, seeing that photograph! That your sleuthing turned up that still, that picture that I had *no* idea of at the time, *stunned* me! There we are, so clearly visible, and there the two of them are, and there's such a distance between us, and yet the two couples are the focal point of the photograph! We're as important as Davis and Merrill in that photograph! I have no memory of realizing that the photographers were using their cameras in a way that could even include Ted and me. We were certainly watching the photographers photographing Davis and Merrill, but I had *no* idea that we would ever be included in a film or a photograph taken by anybody else. That's what's so almost inexplicable: to come up with that photograph, it just seems supernatural! The way we're poised, and the distance between the two couples—it's a kind of spooky picture, and that it involves Bette Davis, who was just one of the most spectacular performers of that movie era? What a surprise that was! It was fascinating and pleasing just for me to see it.

It's an extraordinary documentary photograph, capturing you with your autograph book in hand and Ted with your camera, both of you with eyes locked on Davis and Merrill, sizing up your opportunity to swoop in.

Yes, as they should be, like hunters in the African wild! And we *did* swoop in! For one of the pictures, we followed her out of the theater, and she was just getting into their car when we called out to her, and she turned around and gave us a perfect picture, with Ted standing behind her. I was proud of that; it's the best snapshot of the whole event. And she was even looking pleasant!

On another deep dive into press archives from Hollywood premieres of that period, I found an equally extraordinary photograph of you getting Susan Hayward's autograph at the opening of David and Bathsheba *at Grauman's Chinese Theatre.*

Yes, that's a real treat to me, too! I love having that. I look at that picture a lot. It's framed on my desk now, and it goes with its twin that Ted took of me.

Ted must have been standing almost next to the photographer for the Sydney Morning Herald *who captured that press image: Ted's snapshot catches Hayward in the act of signing the autograph for you, but the press photographer catches the moment after, as she hands your autograph book back to you with a gracious smile and you both lock eyes, while Hayward's then-husband, actor Jess Barker, looks on.*

Jess Barker's aloofness was probably that I crossed his male ego! He made a lot of films, but she was somebody that Ted and I followed almost from the very beginning of her career, after seeing her in *Sis Hopkins*, a Judy Canova film, and we felt we'd really discovered her, practically.

As such devout movie fans, those first experiences of actually meeting these stars you so revered must have been thoroughly thrilling.

Well, you can imagine, we were supremely excited. We were associating with gods and goddesses: they were just true, lighted creatures for both of us. We were intoxicated: it was a real adventure. I have vivid memories of those premieres and encounters. And of course, everybody was in evening dress, and ourselves in ties and jackets. Yes, it was very exciting being in the presence of these amazing people in the flesh. Some of them I had never seen in Technicolor: there were more black-and-white films than color then, and a few of those people had never made color films.

Your photos read like a veritable who's who of the greatest women of the golden era of Hollywood: major personalities like June Allyson, Claudette Colbert, Jeanne Crain, Irene Dunne, Greer Garson, Kathryn Grayson, Betty Hutton, Dorothy Lamour, Ann Miller, Eleanor Parker, Rosalind Russell, Ann Sheridan, Claire Trevor, Vera-Ellen, and Jane Wyman, among many others. Most are captured in the act of autographing your program, with some pausing to pose with you. Some, like Janet Leigh, are looking up at Ted's camera in total surprise.

Well, it was Ted calling her to look up, and then it was always, "Janet!" Not "Miss Leigh!" We were very cozy!

It's astounding to also consider some of the historic Hollywood events you and Ted snuck into, an inventory that includes the premieres of many films that are now considered classics, like All About Eve, A Place in the Sun, An American in Paris, *and* Singin' in the Rain. *You were also photographed with Marilyn Monroe after her only appearance at an Oscars ceremony, and at another Academy Awards with Lauren Bacall and Humphrey Bogart the night he won the Best Actor award for his performance in* The African Queen.

Well, there can't be anything like it, can there? I mean, I was a devoted movie fan who then *actually* got to meet so many of the people that I worshipped as a kid! And we had nothing to justify ourselves, to distinguish us from just the lowest class of moviegoers. In fact, we were so low, we were willing to break the law! And you see, we were living alone with our mother by then. If my mother hadn't started divorce proceedings, my father would have entered into the picture, and neither I nor Ted was on good terms with him then.

If he had been a more active part of your homelife then, do you think he would have disapproved of your shenanigans and might have impeded them?

Oh, certainly.

Men are also mostly absent from your premiere photos. Besides Bogart, only a few other male stars appear in them, given your focus and fascination then with female stars.

Gregory Peck and the other actors I did bother to get autographs from or take pictures of were only after I'd worked all the females, yes. Like Clifton Webb: he was a time filler! It must have been a meager premiere, or we still had some film left. Oh, let's go get Clifton Webb!

Other movie men are included only as the escorts of the women you were actually targeting, like Fernando Lamas, seen accompanying Lana Turner to the premiere of An American in Paris, *and Lex Barker, pictured with then-wife Arlene Dahl as she signs an autograph for you. If you'd have caught up with that foursome again at a premiere just a few years later, you'd have found them with swapped partners: Turner would now be married to Barker, and Dahl to Lamas.*

Yes, but not that the men would have been of interest to me even then!

Just as when you got to Ava Gardner, who coincidentally shared an ex-husband, Artie Shaw, with Lana Turner. Gardner was already in her seat at the Egyptian Theatre for the premiere of Pandora and the Flying Dutchman *with her then-husband, superstar Frank Sinatra, beside her, though he's mostly cut out of Ted's photograph of you getting an autograph from his movie star wife.*

Where he belongs, yes! Yes, it's all about Gardner! Gardner is making a face of surprise, and Sinatra . . . oh, yeah! He was on the other side of her!

I imagine there were some favorite stars who ultimately eluded you at these premieres?

Oh, yes. Gene Tierney was one. She was certainly a favorite by that time, and I would have been very keen to see her in the flesh. I'm sure she would've looked stunning. If we'd seen her at any of those premieres, we would've really hounded her, but I don't think she went out much. I do have a bag of my magazine clippings of her still, and there are very few nightclub pictures even of her and Oleg Cassini, when they were married.

Besides Bette Davis and Alice Faye, many of the other stars captured in your fan photos later sat for portraits by you.

I did get to draw Jan Sterling, and oh, she was charming. She was totally unpretentious, very easy, very relaxed, and didn't hurry me; didn't look at her watch. Oh, she was very nice, and really utterly relaxed, just as though it was beyond her to assume anything calculated. There was nothing deep about her, but I liked her, both personally and as an actress, and she was wonderful to work with because she liked being looked at, and she liked performing for me, and that made me like her. We had at least two, if not three, sittings. I also got several sittings with Lizabeth Scott. She was great, too. Really, we could have been friends: she was very, very nice to me. I had a particular thing about her in her early films, and almost none of them were any good! But she had that smoky voice—she must have worked on that, day in and day out! She was so artificial in her sort of sympathetic charm, but it really seemed like charm. And I assumed without any information at all that she was lesbian?

She never identified herself as such, and publicly dated many men, although she never ultimately married. She sued the tabloid magazine Confidential *in the 1950s over a sensational story that purported to "out" her by characterizing the female company she supposedly kept*

as being fellow Hollywood "baritone babes," a euphemism the maga-
zine used to identify lesbians.

I think somebody had brought me to that conclusion years before, and her voice was so practiced, to have those male tones. I
adored that calculated personality of hers in all her early films, and
the way she pouted with her lips sometimes, and then the voice
got even lower! It was so artificial, but she believed in it with her
whole heart! She was very sincere.

Another star with an inimitable voice, Diana Lynn, was also a subject
of both your early premiere photos and your later portraiture.

Diana Lynn—now, that's somebody I admire, and I got to know
her fairly well. She was so *sly*, and that voice of hers! With a kind of
wryness in her speech, in her tone: everything kind of had a funny
edge to her, but it was friendly; it wasn't nasty in any way. She was
accommodating herself to you with this kind of wry sound that she
made. I think I could probably recognize it out of fifty other sounds:
oh, that's Diana Lynn. It's like she's telling you something secret
that she wouldn't tell everybody. She was the right kind of artifici-
ality in her theatrical personality, but she was using something that
was very genuine in her: it wasn't just about the theater, it was also
a little bit about how she felt, and so that made her seem sincere.
She always wanted to entertain you, and to kind of curl her lip a little bit and say something funny. She taught me. I liked her a lot in
films, but I liked her even more in person, and she liked me.

Even as a juvenile performer, she always seemed wiser and much more
sophisticated than her young years, as showcased to delicious effect in
Preston Sturges's The Miracle of Morgan's Creek *and Billy Wilder's*
The Major and the Minor. *She certainly also outshines both future Pres-*
ident Ronald Reagan and their chimp co-star in the much-lampooned
film, Bedtime for Bonzo.

I think that was a real sophistication with her, so she wasn't
afraid of society because she'd found a personality that could wig-

gle through it, and still be herself. And it was a genuine character, and that's how she could be a raw teenager and also a sophisticated performer years later, and they're all of a piece.

And she was accommodating enough toward you to sit several times through the years?

Yes, and one of them is one of the biggest black-and-white drawings I've ever done, and it's the best of all of them. That's very tough to do: it's on a bigger sheet than I usually use, and the head must be almost life-size. But I had a lot of fun doing it. We were communing in the very *best* way, from my point of view. She was so natural that I just took her likableness for granted, and that made me relax with her. She wasn't afraid to show me all of her artifice, and how she maneuvered herself in society. It was all her own concoction. But I came across that big drawing not long ago, and it really pleased me. It was a surprise: it was almost as though I'd never realized how good it was, because it was so like her. And I would say, without any quandary, that we liked each other—and that's something I don't often feel with my sitters: that they're actually liking me. But she felt in some way comfortable with me, and that made working with her fun and like we were both enjoying ourselves. She didn't make me feel like she was getting tired or trying too hard; it came naturally. She was confident about giving me all of her secrets as a personality, because she knew I could appreciate them, and that was flattering and gave me an extra entrance into her personality. Oh, she was very wry, very funny, really one of the smartest of those women I have ever encountered. And she married a millionaire, and she was very pleased with herself for having snagged one! She bragged about it, yes!

Leslie Caron, whom you photographed at the premiere of An American in Paris, *in which she had made her star-making debut, also ultimately became a good friend of yours.*

Yes, she's really one of the very few major stars who became a close friend, and still is. I remember very well the first party Chris took me to at Salka Viertel's: I forget whom Leslie was with, but they were at the front door—they were guests, too—and that was the beginning of our friendship. I can't think of any sitter as famous as she was whom I have as many drawings of, but it was because she was more available for sittings, and I knew that she was pleased to do it. That helped a lot, but also, she was a very good sitter. I noticed early on, when I was commissioned to do a portfolio of the New York City Ballet, that most of those dancers were really first-rate sitters, because it's a physical command of the body that they have that just made it so much easier for them to be still. And so Leslie, being a trained dancer, was always a good sitter, too. We had many sittings, and they were spread out, so I got probably the only Hollywood personality—or one of the few—of whom my pictures have a real range in time and hairdo and mood. But she was relaxed enough and trusted me as a friend enough to not worry about all that, and not to be disturbed with my results in any direction. And through the years, in a way she got more and more beautiful. It took that wonderful little girl quality away from her, but it really turned her into a true beauty, as beautiful in life as she was in the films. Yes, she's really the one I've known best of them all, besides Gloria Stuart.

Gloria Stuart first found fame in Pre-Code films of the early 1930s, then dedicated herself to artmaking and book design before returning to the limelight late in her long life, playing the 100-year-old Rose in James Cameron's 1997 blockbuster film, Titanic.

Yes, she was a very dear friend. Of all the movie women I knew, she and I were much the best friends, and she lived very near. She was also the most intelligent of all the Hollywood actresses I knew personally. She adored Chris. It wasn't nearly mutual, because he was a little edgy with women, but he knew how much I adored her, and so he always preferred I saw her alone.

Her renaissance as an actress must have been wonderful for you to witness.

Yes, it was *so* joyful to participate in it with her! I mean, just to hear her talk about what she was doing and how *fulfilling* it was for her, it was just really a *dream* situation for her. Oh, and to hear her talk about how good Cameron was with her! They had a really good relationship, and he widened her role, they got along so well. But to hear it all firsthand from her, and how excited she was about it, having that kind of revival at the end of her life, after so many years of very little if any work at all—and what there was, was just occasional television. But she knew *always* what to do with her time. She was always busy: painting, printmaking; had lots of friends, was very social; gave dinner parties for often eight, ten people.

You would find another friend and sitter in Shelley Winters, whom Ted photographed signing an autograph for you at the premiere of A Place in the Sun.

Yes, she became a friend, and she was likable—but to me, tiresome, too. It was just that she was a kind of slob, but sometimes very good in films if she was cast well—there are some really very interesting performances by her, but a little of her goes a long way. There was something that was kind of sloppy about her in a social situation, too. But she was *very* sweet-natured, and a much better friend to Chris and me than most of our movie friends, because she was fun and she enjoyed seeing us, and that made it easy to see her. I did quite a few drawings of her.

Your photographs from the premiere of An American in Paris *reveal another first encounter with an actress whom you would ultimately come to know: Nina Foch, Leslie Caron's co-star in that film, which would beat out stiff competition from both* A Place in the Sun *and* A Streetcar Named Desire *to win the 1951 Academy Award for Best Picture.*

Oh, I liked her. I had a more personal relationship with her, but she was a very theatrical personality. She felt she was getting away with showing herself interested, sympathetic, but she was always thinking something else—at least when she was with me. But she was a very good friend of a good friend of mine, who was also an actor—and actually somebody I was sleeping with occasionally for a brief period, and I'm certain he told her about our clandestine meetings—so that made her kind of *sly*, you know, talking to me in a kind of way as though she were taking me seriously, with a kind of worldly, almost forgiving behavior. But also, she was her acting persona: she'd created it carefully, and she thought she was good. And occasionally, she interested me: as a kid, when I was around ten—and in fact, it was from her very first film—both Ted and I were interested in her. But she was too hearty, with a kind of, *oh, I know all about the business*, and she really fell for her own performance.

She became an influential acting teacher for forty years at USC's School of Cinematic Arts.

Oh, I can just imagine what those classes were like, and how phony and theatrical a really smart actor would have judged her, because her idea of herself was that she loved humanity, and she was a good pal. But she just seemed to me, under it all, very neurotic, falling for her own act. Oh, she was an actress, through and through. She'd be so frustrating to live with, because I can't imagine her giving up the phoniness, even in the middle of having love made to her! I can't look at my portraits of her without seeing something phony in her, but it wouldn't be a good likeness if that weren't there.

Who are some of the other personalities from your fan photos who later sat for you?

Alexis Smith was a perfect example of a good-looking sitter: she was a handsome woman, but she had nothing in her face to hang onto. She was beautiful; there was no feature that was wonky or inadequate, but there was something very cold and impenetrable about her. It was all kind of flat across her attention; nothing behind it. It was all blank good looks. Cyd Charisse was also totally cold. Everything about her—her smile, her movements—was calculated; her physicality was so theatrical. I want to say that she seemed dumb to me, in that she showed me what she thought she was getting away with when she would take a pose and kind of hit an expression that she thought would be appropriate, but with no humor at all. She was somewhere else.

As though she couldn't turn off being a dancer, even choreographing her own personal behavior?

Yes, she was *utterly* professional, and that's where it stopped. She'd drained everything out of herself that didn't work in her career as an actress, and so you were dealing with everything that she gave you in her films. Once you took away everything that was Cyd Charisse the movie star, I can't imagine what would be left, because it was all calculated, tested, found to work, and as cold as could be. She was totally unspontaneous. And as a dancer, when she walks across the room in a movie, it's all about what she learned as a professional. It's an intelligent emptiness.

Was Jane Powell, another top star of MGM musicals whom you captured in a premiere photograph and in later portrait drawings, just as vivacious in person as in her on-screen personality?

No. She sat for me twice, and was very serious and very kind of *hurt* by life, sort of disillusioned by life. Odd, coming from her. Oh, she was such a wounded creature, and so suspicious, as if she was thinking, what new hurt are you going to inflict on me? And not understanding what I could possibly want from her, or how I could possibly find her interesting enough to keep going. Both times she sat for me, I had just that feeling about her.

Which is so interesting, given her screen persona as the effervescent, sparkling girl next door who loves life and loves love and, surprise!

*loves the boy next door—although it's slightly complicated—so let's
sing about it!*

Yes, always pert, and it never gets too thick to bear, somehow.
I don't enjoy her singing at all. When she'd been performing for
fifteen years or so, I think she really hit a bump that stymied her,
and I could just see the suffering in her, and the doubt. How could
you be interested enough in me to go on with what you're doing?
That kind of wonderment at my concentration, as though how
could she possibly be inspiring it? By the end of each sitting we
did, she'd run out of juice, because the mystery was so profound
that it had tired her. She couldn't think why I'd go on so long looking at her.

*Speaking of the girl next door, how about Jean Simmons, another sub-
ject of your premiere photos and later portraiture who ultimately became a neighbor of yours?*

Yes, she lived just up the road from here, but we didn't warm to
each other. She was very low-key. Some actors are like that. But
she was dear friends of other friends of mine: she was friendly with
Joyce Howard, a British actress from the '40s who lived nearby on
Ocean Avenue Extension, and with Gavin Lambert—but of course
he knew everybody connected to the movies, anyway. I never met
Stewart Granger, her first husband, but we did know her second,
Richard Brooks. But living so near, she was distant, though she did
sit a couple of times for me. I thought she really disliked me, but
when she sat for me, it was kind of like a long pout: she was still,
not complaining, not moving, just waiting for it to be *over*. I always
felt, in some way, that she was suspicious of me, or she endured
me: that nothing I could do could ever convince her that I was a
likable human being. I thought the first drawing was a failure, so I
didn't even ask her to sign it. And because I was dissatisfied, we actually had another sitting, and it was even *less* satisfactory. She did
sign the one from the second sitting, but I got great resistance from
her. I'd had dire expectations, and I was right. But it's just like her.

It's a masterful portrait, but that experience pales in comparison to the much greater duress that many other Hollywood star sitters put you through.

Well, Joan Fontaine—well, you know!

She proved to be one of your prickliest sitters—another tale we'll get to later on!

Oh, the toughest of them all. Esther Williams also turned out to be a very unpleasant woman. Joanne Carson was a good friend, and at one of her parties I asked Esther Williams to sit for me. But when I called to make a date, she had somehow got word that I was an "operator"—that I was a *movie fan* rather than an *artist*—so nothing doing. She didn't say those words, but oh, her nose went up right away. She was really nasty to me, but that was fine by me: I could do without that. She's only included in our photos because she was famous, not because she was a favorite!

Whereas I imagine that Joan Crawford, seen wide-eyed and wide-smiled as she signs your program, was characteristically charming with a fan?

She was always gracious. Chris knew her, so later I met her at the beach house of his agent, and eventually we visited her on the set of one of her movies, *Female on the Beach.* She couldn't have been nicer. Of course I was with them every minute, but I was just on the sidelines watching them talking, watching her performing for the camera, then sitting with Chris. She was very gracious to him, and charming to me. The studio photographer took a picture of her with Chris, sitting on the entrance step to her dressing room trailer on wheels, but since it was a studio picture, all the photographs of stars had to be retouched.

So they not only retouched Crawford, but Chris as well?

No! So the result is that Chris looks perfectly natural and like a real human being, sitting next to this wax dummy with glaring eyes and a big mouth! It's unmistakably Crawford with those features, but as though she'd come from another planet. She looks freakish: she's swept up clean! Chris howled when he saw it!

Whereas a star who apparently needed no retouching, as evidenced by your candid photo of her, was Elizabeth Taylor.

That was at the premiere of *Quo Vadis* with another Taylor, Robert. He was icy, very unforthcoming, and he looks it in the photograph.

Was Elizabeth Taylor as stunning in person as she was on screen?

Breathtaking! Her dress was a cherry red, and lush beyond belief. She looked just breathtaking. She was at the peak of her beauty then. At the screening of *Royal Wedding*, which was before we started taking our camera to the premieres, she was there with Jane Powell and a group of people. That theater has a long forecourt, and I remember Ted and I following alongside them as they were walking in the theater. She was all in black. It wasn't a formal gown, but she looked just better than she had ever looked in a movie.

Ted also captured several charming poses of you with Debbie Reynolds, apparently from different events?

Yes, she went to the same premieres Ted and I went to!

She looks quite besotted with you in one of your photos together!

Looking at me really as though she were admiring me, yes! Yes, I know that picture.

She was still a teenager herself then, so perhaps had you not been gay...?

Yes! Well, we were close in age. She was one of the few who responded like that. It was very seldom that any of them took any personal interest in either Ted or me, but of course when they observed the routine—being photographed signing my program or autograph book, and then a few minutes later, having the same experience, signing autographs for Ted. . . . It always surprised us: we were four years apart, but people often said we looked almost like twins.

Several of the other stars you were targeting were then just as young as you and Ted were, like Leslie Caron and Piper Laurie.

Yes, I don't know why I'm so swept over by Piper Laurie being a few years older than me. Even though she was a movie actress, she seemed older and more experienced, certainly. In our picture together at a premiere, while I'm standing next to her getting her autograph, there's a hand on her shoulder which looks like it could be my hand, because I was between her and her escort, and our heads are so close that that hand on her shoulder looks like it could be mine! It was one of my favorite pictures: me and Piper! She was never a favorite of mine, but I have a nice impression of something that happened between the two of us, but I can't remember what it is.

Montgomery Clift locks both eyes and hands with you in one of the most remarkable of your fan photos.

Oh, yes! And turning back at me to smile? In the photograph, I have the pencil he returned to me in my hand, and this was not only our first meeting, but I got a goodbye smile, too, from a Hollywood star?

Perhaps there was a little something more to that smile?

I never heard he was any kind of chickenhawk, but I was looking very haveable, I think, in profile!

And it would prove not to be your only encounter with Montgomery Clift.

Yes! During one of my first dinners with Chris here in town— I forget now what restaurant it was—we were in the middle of our meal when I suddenly said, "Chris! Montgomery Clift just came in! Montgomery Clift!" And I kept looking at him, not wanting to miss a move he made, and he came closer and closer and closer and finally said, "Hello, Chris!"

You must have been thunderstruck!

He adored Chris! They hadn't seen each other in a long while. Boy, that was quite a dramatic moment!

How had they come to know each other?

Because Chris was a friend of Fred Zinnemann, who directed Clift's first film, *The Search*, he was often on the set, and he and Monty got along very well. Zinnemann lived right down here on the street below, but they were very reclusive, he and his wife.

Did any of those stars remember you when you encountered them again years later, either socially or during portrait sittings?

Oh, no, there's no way any of them could have remembered me. I mean, we were just fans, although we were particularly assertive fans. We knew of no other movie fans who could present photographs of themselves with these beloved creatures like we could, and we laughed to ourselves: in the movie fan world, *we* were the stars, from our point of view! None of the other movie fans we knew had pictures of themselves with these people. But you know, Jane Russell is the only one of my sitters to whom I ever showed a photograph taken with in those years. There were several people I was photographed with then that I later got to know, like Deborah Kerr and Natalie Wood and all kinds of people, but I never showed them. It was only Russell, and why is that? Because she was *very* friendly, very nice, and I liked her when she came to sit for me, and I already had that picture of her framed by the front door.

What was her response to seeing it?

Oh, she was amused by it, very interested, not at all disapproving, but it was right at the end of her life, and she was already not responding fully. I think I might have gotten more out of her about it a little earlier—or maybe she was just playing down her interest because it surprised her that I had come from such a lowly habit! But she was barely a year from her death, and I wasn't the least surprised. She was tired out: the inside was just going on automatic. I liked her right away, but felt that she already lost her way; she didn't know what was keeping her going. But she was wonderful, and so she's the only one that I showed the photograph to when she came to sit for me. No, there was one other person: Leslie Caron, yes. I showed her one of us together at the premiere of *An American in Paris*, which was at the Egyptian Theatre on Hollywood Boulevard. She looks like a little pixie: sort of wide-eyed and with those bangs, she looks really like a little girl almost. Well, she was. When I showed her that picture she just *screamed* with delight! We *both* look so young in it! She *howled* when she saw it!

In the documentary film Chris & Don: A Love Story, *Leslie Caron remembers you, with "round cheeks and bright eyes," as "one of those young kids who would ask you to sign an autograph, come next to you while you would sign, and his friend would take the picture." The film shows a framed copy of that picture proudly on display in her home. Why didn't you later show any other stars your fan photos of them?*

You know, I was too busy trying to justify myself as an artist rather than just another movie fan, so I didn't let any of the others know, because I thought it put my reputation as an artist at risk to be *also* a movie fan. Movie fans were not highly thought of in those years, so I was so shy of showing myself as a Hollywood fan around Hollywood people. But I'm sure Deborah Kerr would have been delighted. She appears at least twice in the premiere pictures, but I don't think I ever told her—and I know she wouldn't have immediately put me in a lower class. She was so kind and generous a personality.

And she ultimately became a friend of yours?

Yes, because oddly enough she married Peter Viertel, the son of Chris's very close friend, Salka, and I hardly didn't like him at all. He was a son of a bitch—really the worst kind of male attitude—and I wondered how Deborah could bear him? I knew him for years without realizing how much I disliked him. He was so pleased with himself, so sure of himself. All that Hemingway guff.

Peter Viertel, who was said to be the inspiration for Robert Redford's character in The Way We Were, *was a writer best known for his novel* White Hunter Black Heart, *a thinly veiled account of his experiences working in Africa with John Huston during the filming of* The African Queen. *His book was later adapted into a movie directed by and starring Clint Eastwood.*

She wanted him to sit for me, but he had to be actually forced. He was so embarrassed by the experience. I think Peter Viertel was one of the most unlikable men I've ever met. But she sat for me several times, and now I've been seeing some of her films again, and I'm nursing my sudden fascination with her by disciplining myself not to look yet at those drawings, to see if I can see in them any of the respect I have for her now.

Was your mother aware that you were sneaking into premieres?

Yes, we would share the photographs with her. I'm sure we urged her to sneak in with us, but she would never have been properly dressed for it, and she was smart enough not to take a chance.

What was her reaction to your photographs?

There was, every once in a while, an air of doubt or caution: were we really doing something *too* assertive? But in most of those pictures, both Ted and I and the actors we were with were all smiling, so I think she was encouraged to believe that we weren't doing anything *too* naughty!

Would you then stay for the movie that was being premiered?

Yes, eventually. There were always unused seats at every premiere. We only once had a near disaster, at the premiere of *A Place in the Sun* in 1951. It opened at a very tiny theater on Wilshire Boulevard called The Fine Arts. It was real snobbishness to open in a tiny theater, because that made it more exclusive and made it run much longer—it ran for months. So it was a very distinguished premiere, but a *very* tightly controlled operation: there were far fewer people and so far fewer no-shows. There were always empty seats in the big movie palaces where most of the other premieres were held, so we had no trouble making our selection. But at the *A Place in Sun* premiere, we had to move twice when the people with the tickets for our seats showed up, until finally we were sitting in the last two empty seats in the house, in the first row. Can you imagine seeing that film for the first time, looking at it gigantic above us? It was really the most important film of the period, and that made it grander, being in a small, elegant little theater rather than a big one. But if the people had come with tickets to those two seats, we would have been exposed and would have had to leave, but we didn't think about the ugly consequences that could easily have resulted.

The potential threat of which must have made those adventures even more fraught with tension and excitement. Were you able to then concentrate on watching the film, or were you too distracted by ogling the stars in the audience all around you?

Oh, yes, sure, we were experienced moviegoers. We always watched films very concentratedly, in our enraptured state.

You mentioned that you fantasized about becoming a movie star your-self. Did you take any steps toward potentially realizing that dream, like taking acting classes?

Ted, at a certain point, signed up for acting classes in his late teens/early twenties, but like our mother, we were innocent of the world. How to do anything practically about preparing ourselves for movie stardom, that was beyond us. The extent of our invention and cleverness was getting ourselves into the proximity of movie actors, but *becoming* movie actors, that would belong to another world, and our mother couldn't help us, couldn't encourage us there, because she was a very retiring, very reclusive personality, and we just had no know-how how to connect ourselves in a practical way that would lead to some kind of involvement in the movie world. The extent of our careers was as fans, and we got as far as we could, but we were so outside the movie world. We were with them, looking at them, standing next to them, without *being* them. That was a major step that we just didn't know how to take.

CHAPTER 2

A fated, mutual discovery

Don and Christopher Isherwood in photos taken of each other in Monument Valley, Arizona, in May 1953. *(Courtesy of the Christopher Isherwood Papers, The Huntington Library, San Marino, California)* © DON BACHARDY

What was high school like for you?

Oh, a breeze! I was drawing all these pictures of movie actors usually, and I had lots of girlfriends who loved my drawings, so I

was a success. The boys didn't like me because I had access to all
the girls they wanted to go to bed with. *I* didn't want to go to bed
with them!

When were you first aware that you might be gay?

When I was eleven and he was fifteen, Ted was already seeing
all kinds of guys. He was a great beauty and had more boyfriends
than he could handle. But Ted was a whole education in himself,
because he was also a manic-depressive schizophrenic. He had regular breakdowns every other year, sometimes every year, and they
were really killers. I already knew we were both queer, but it also
taught me that I couldn't rely on Ted anymore. He was a great
older brother: he took real good care of me—until he would have
a nervous breakdown, and then he just was a manic nuisance. He
got arrested and hospitalized and the whole routine, many times.
But my acceptance of my own queerness was a foregone conclusion. It was all my business. I didn't need to come out to anybody.

What were your early sexual experiences like?

I had a couple of awkward sexual encounters. There was a
young man named Paul, and I had a Mexican friend, Alex Quiroga,
who was a cameraman.

*Alex Quiroga was then a television lighting director, but later became
the manager of technical operations at NBC, pioneering the use of
color broadcasting in the late 1950s in the highly successful television
series* Bonanza.

I was seeing him when Chris and I got together. Naturally,
Chris always wanted to know what I was up to, and I told him
about Alex. So I was so pleased when, after we had been together
a couple of years, we were having dinner at Musso and Frank's in
Hollywood, which was a restaurant we both liked, and there was
Alex with his current young man. I introduced him and Chris, and
they were very polite with each other; it was a very nice encounter.

When we left the restaurant, Chris said, "Wow!" He thought Alex was just dynamite, which was very pleasing to him, that I had dumped him for Chris!

How and when did you first get to know Christopher Isherwood?

I really got to know him in early '53, because the fall term of '52 was my first term at UCLA, at the campus in Westwood. That was really one of the biggest endurance tests of my early life, that first term at UCLA. In my innocence of programming, I stuffed my schedule with all of these hardcore classes: algebra and language classes and civics, all those horrible subjects, so I worked like I had never worked before. The homework was just daunting. Oh, I hated it; it was just horrible. But when the term ended in late January, I was off for nearly a month, and that was when I got to know Chris. We had already been introduced at the beach a couple of years earlier.

What do you remember of your first encounters with him?

We lived in Atwater, which is practically Glendale, on the last street in the L.A. city limits. So it was on the edge of L.A., but we couldn't have been more young L.A. men than we were. Ted and I used to ride the Red Car trolley for two hours on Saturday and Sunday mornings from the Atwater District to Santa Monica. We would arrive around ten, when the sun is usually coming out. The streetcar used to let us out on Ocean Avenue, where Santa Monica Boulevard ends. I was sixteen and wondered at first why Ted was determined to walk probably a good mile north to the beach right down below this house here, the Will Rogers State Beach. Of course I soon knew it was the queer beach: Ted being a popular beauty, whenever we arrived together, there was right away a crowd around him of admirers. Ted was always greeted by a coterie of men. He knew them all, and they certainly knew him, and among them was Chris. But while the others were looking at Ted, Chris was looking at me, with those bright, flashing eyes.

Were you and Ted open with each other by this point about you both being gay?

I used to go to movies with Ted and whichever boyfriend he was spending the evening with. We would maybe sometimes have dinner before or after, and then Ted would usually drive me home and then take the boyfriend home to wherever he lived. Ted was very careful not to corrupt his younger brother. For a couple of years when we went to the beach—again, say, when I was six-teen—he would always do an aside to his friends to keep it down: "Don't spoil my cover. He's too young to know." Of course, I wasn't too young to know. I knew perfectly well what was going on, and I was getting a pretty good look at all the young male bodies I was meeting, but I played it a little bit slyly until I was sure I wanted to admit it to Ted. As close as we were, and this was certainly from the age of seven or eight, I think by mutual agreement we realized that the squabbling we were prone to before then was really of no use. We were both united in our adoration of our mother, who never, ever played the two of us against each other. From the ear-liest time, she made it clear—and I remember her repeating it time after time—"I love you two boys. I love both of you." There was never any question in our minds that we had to compete for her attention: we realized that there was no reason for it. And we were already, both of us, keeping massive collections of movie star clip-pings, so we had everything in common, but he had a sense of re-sponsibility for a younger brother, so he didn't tell me anything about his queer activities. But I knew I was queer a couple of years before I let on to Ted, until I realized, what was the point? I knew he was queer and I knew I was queer, so why shouldn't we unite our energies instead of any pretenses? And the two of us slept in the same bedroom for, what, twenty years nearly, so we knew each other very well. Amazingly, we never became physically intimate: we knew each other so well, and yet we never made anything more of that; we never had sex with each other, ever. It would have been out of the question for both of us. We almost never even saw each other nude—isn't that weird? And yet, I had to declare to *him* that I was queer.

You did?

Yes! Certainly not to either of my parents, and it took me awhile before I decided to let Ted know, but we did everything together anyway that it seemed silly not to admit that, too. I pretended to be innocent until it was finally around the time that we were going to these premieres together that I came out to him, and then we became so much closer, because our pursuits were so similar. Then we could confide in each other about our sexual experiences, and he could take me to the queer beach without having to warn his friends to be discreet in my company. And I met a lot of them, and among them was Chris. As I said, he had the brightest eyes, and he was such a charmer. Not charming just for seduction, but I always noticed it in later years that his charm was at its utmost when he was talking to a young man—and preferably still a teenager.

Your first intimate encounter with Chris, at a party in October 1952, might more accurately be described as a collision, with some passionate kissing resulting in the shattering of a window?

That was at the apartment of an actor named Richard and his friend Leslie, on Gower Street in Hollywood. They had Chris to dinner, and Ted and I were invited as dessert. We were sitting up with the three of them late at night, by which time I was certainly drunk, and I wasn't used to drinking. I came to, as it were, being kissed by Chris, standing up in the middle of the living room, and we lost our balance and did some damage. And I suddenly, as it were, realized how scandalous I was being, from my point of view: such reckless behavior in the middle of the living room! I'm sure the setup was that Ted was invited for the night, but when I suddenly realized I was drunk, and here I was being kissed by this older man, I said, "Ted, I must go home." Luckily, my mother lived in an apartment very nearby, so Ted dutifully drove me home. It would have been after midnight, certainly, and he must have been as drunk as I was, so it was very dangerous, but it was only a few blocks away. And then I'm sure he went back and spent the night with Richard and Leslie. I believe Chris spent the night, too, but I don't think there was any sex involved. Maybe there was a foursome, but Chris never told me that, so I assumed he just went to bed rather than drive all the way back to Brentwood, which would have really been dangerous, and he had the sense to stay the night. But I bet you Ted went back and had a threesome with Richard and Leslie.

Meanwhile, you were in the midst of having your own first sexual and emotional relationship, with Alex Quiroga.

Well, he was certainly my first experience of somebody who wanted to screw me. Alex was already a cameraman working on movies, and he was very attractive: attractive enough to make me consider letting him screw me, but I'd never been screwed; never even considered why I didn't hanker after it. I was afraid; it didn't appeal to me. My sex with Alex, I think, had been perfectly satisfactory, but I knew he wanted to screw me, and I knew if I kept refusing him, I'd probably lose him.

And then came the fateful day when you and Chris finally got together.

By then, Ted had his own car, a coupe with a rumble seat. We were on our way to the beach, it was a Saturday morning, and in the middle of the trip from Hollywood, Ted announced, "Why don't we stop and have breakfast with Chris?" Without any preliminary call or any notice, Ted just drove into the Hookers' driveway up to Chris's garden house.

Chris was then living in a small garden house on the property of his friend, Evelyn Hooker, and her husband Edward. She was a psychologist noted for her pioneering work in the 1950s disproving that homosexuality is a mental disorder, as it was then classified by the American Psychiatric Association. Indeed, her findings led to that institution finally removing that classification in 1973.

There was a mini orchard in front of their house, so their house was completely hidden from the street, and behind that was another little garden house that Chris had built for himself. We could see him through the window, sitting up at his typewriter. But instead of being cross to be interrupted in the middle of work—mornings were always sacred for work—he put everything aside and made breakfast for us.

Had Ted been there before?

Oh, yes. Ted and Chris had already had a brief fling. I wouldn't even call it a romance, but Chris often said that Ted had a pair of the most beautiful legs he had ever seen. He was queer for legs: in a young man, they meant a lot! If they were really well-shaped, that was a test. Ted had better legs than I did, but Chris of course *never* said that to me. It was just something that I knew.

So Chris was receptive to your impromptu visit?

Such was Chris's charm that Ted just instinctively knew that he would be kind to us, and he was. In fact, he enjoyed breakfast with us so much that he decided to take the day off and come to the beach with us. And the next day, Sunday, he did the same thing. And the weekend was such a success that the three of us said, let's do it again next weekend, and we did. The next weekend, Saturday was Valentine's Day, and that night, we were all a little bit drunk, but decent, and Ted was driving, but he was very reliable, and when we were dropping Chris off at his little garden house at the Hookers'—I was in the back seat, and Chris in the front—I made the announcement that I was getting out to spend the night with Chris, without any word to Chris. He was really quite surprised! I was only eighteen—imagine!—and I wasn't an assertive personality at all. It was my drunkenness that loosened my tongue. But Chris didn't make any objection; it was *Ted* who was so surprised. He might have minded that I was usurping one of his man friends, but he had such a coterie of them that I knew he could spare one. So that was the first night we spent together, and ever after, Valentine's Day was our anniversary. Valentine's Day was also my mother's birthday.

Was there an element of surprise in yourself, too? In your boldness to do it?

Well, I was a little bit drunk and not used to being drunk, but I was trusting my instinct about people. And what else did I have, really? It was an instinct about people which was developed by going to the movies; being taken by my mother, both Ted and I, at very early ages. That was my interest in life: people and the way they looked. I'm sure it all came from those giant close-ups in movies, just that romance of movies. And Chris had it, too: that was Chris in *his* teens. He, too, was a devoted moviegoer.

Chris described your meeting as having "the strange sense of a fated, mutual discovery."

Yes, predestination, whatever you call it. I've long since felt that it was fated. It was so out of my experience. I wasn't thinking of having an affair with an older man. Chris was a year older than my father! But such was his charm and his availability and his efforts to amuse Ted and me. Oh, how he made us laugh! He was wonderful with young men—that raised his natural charm to its highest expression. Of course, I was a little bit tipsy. I think all three of us were, with Ted driving us around in his car: he was a reckless driver *without* any drink. Maybe, actually, alcohol calmed him down. But I had never done such a thing with Ted before, making an unpremeditated suggestion that I wasn't going home. He already had a boyfriend that he was going to spend the night with, and I knew it. But he was going to drive me home to my mother's apartment first, as usual, and then he would go to his friend's house, which was also in Hollywood. But that night, Ted didn't drive me home. He was surprised as hell, and Chris was surprised at first, too: he couldn't think what had come over me.

And little could you know in the moment how significantly that impulsive act would impact the rest of your life.

And how can I feel anything but such luck and gratitude—to meet Chris so early, and to have enough sense to realize that he was somebody really unusual, and that his attention to me was like no other I'd ever had? And what was I, in 1953? I was almost nineteen, and I had known him for a year or more, slightly: I'd met him at the beach, and my brother talked about him and had been to bed with him a few times, but nothing in my experience could explain how completely I trusted him, almost immediately. And what brought us together? Of course I was drunk, and I was relaxed and feeling a little bit racy, so I told Chris that Alex wanted to screw me, yet I just couldn't face it. And then it occurred to me, why not try it with Chris? See if *he* could do it, because I trusted him. He was my friend. I knew he'd be gentle; he wouldn't hurt me. We really were physically tuned to each other. And so I asked him, would he be interested? And so we did it—perfectly, gently, and enjoyably—and it wasn't bad at all! It was fun; I liked it! And I was so proud to go back to Alex and announce, "Alright! I'll do it now!" And it was even better with him than it was with Chris! It brought us together as we'd not yet been—and yet, something made me know that Alex wasn't Mr. Right. And so if *he* wasn't Mr. Right, who could it be? Alex would've been probably in his early thirties, and it worked beautifully with him, but here I was, sleeping with Chris already, who was somebody years older—more than thirty years older than I was—and I loved being with him.

What were the most immediate repercussions? Was there jealousy or resistance on either Alex's or Ted's part to your burgeoning relationship with Chris?

Oh, I'm sure Alex was shocked. Ted told me later *he* was stunned, and just couldn't understand it, that *I* was going to spend the night with somebody he'd already rejected. He didn't know for sure that Chris and I had been to bed together, but that made it clear from then on. But as I said, Ted was a great beauty, and had all the beaux he could handle and more—so many beaux, he didn't have time for Chris, but I sure did. He preferred guys his own age, and Chris was way beyond that, from his point of view, and even from my point of view. But still, Ted just couldn't get over it, that I was taking up a cast-off of his, and Chris a year older than my father. If you had asked me when I first met Chris, "Can you imagine living with this man for the next thirty-two years?" I would have said, "You've got to be kidding." But then I didn't know Chris, and I got to know him *very* well, and he improved with knowing. Anyway, right away, Ted went into a nervous breakdown, and I was very upset. I was hoping that he'd finished with that routine, but he hadn't. He was my big brother, and he was very good to me, when he was rational, but impossible when he was crazy. So Chris started inviting me to movies, and that's how it began. I knew more about the movies than anything else, and when he was a teenage boy, what was *his* fascination as well as educating himself, but going to movies? He loved going to movies, and went constantly. So we started going to movies together, and we became a perfect moviegoing pair: we were astonished moviegoers together. It was odd to go from the heavy moviegoing with my mother and brother, then meet Chris and go into another heavy moviegoing period. Chris was just as infatuated with movies as I was, so that really cemented our early years. And he began educating me immediately, but yet so gently, so entertainingly, telling me really what the movies were all about; giving me books to read that I could still understand, and I found myself capable of reading far more intelligent literature than I'd ever been presented up to that point, and I enjoyed it! And that just spurred Chris on. Oh, he could tell me *everything* I wanted to know—and finally, my education for life began, and I had the perfect teacher who made it fun, who made it exciting. It was the birth of my curiosity. I hadn't been really curious about anything, except moviegoing, until I met him. And so he took it in hand to educate me, which was an education that lasted all of thirty years. And we laughed together all the time: he made me laugh like nobody else. Just being with him was an education. So Chris didn't have to seduce me: I seduced *him*. It was just right from the start, and we were just, both of us, so stunned that we didn't even talk about it. And then when my break from UCLA came—I think it was three or four weeks before the spring term— that's when I really started up with Chris. I gave up seeing Alex and became Chris's boyfriend, and we lived happily almost forever after. Imagine having success with Alex, but rewarding Chris? Well, it was fated; it had to be. Chris and I were born for each other. We had so much to give each other that each of us wanted. And so that's how it all began. Our honeymoon was spent in Monument Valley, which he had always intended to go to because he had seen it in all those John Ford westerns.

You're both radiant in the photos you took of each other on that trip.

Oh, yes, each of those pictures is just heaped with significance for me.

How was all of this received by your parents?

They were separated, but my mother was a very good woman. She didn't want me to leave the nest, but Ted was still in the apartment, so it was easy for me to get out. But she sulked for a few weeks. My mother, who was painfully shy, always felt awkward with people, with strangers, but when she met Chris, she was all smiles. She recognized him immediately; she just knew who he was. I had never seen her react to anybody else like she did to him: she was so delighted to see him, and we used to take her out to the movies with us once we started being together. She adored him. My father would have made trouble if he could have, but he couldn't. My father and mother had separated just before I met Chris, and that made it much easier for me, going off with a queer man. My father would have made it uncomfortable, but he was in no position to, because I was living with our mother. Anyway, I was eighteen! But he refused to meet Chris for fifteen years, because it was the '50s. So over the years, Chris was not to be mentioned when we had family dinners. He thought it was part of his parental duty to disapprove.

What finally shifted that dynamic?

My mother revealed to me that every time there was an article about Chris in the newspaper, my father flew to the newspaper. Every time Chris was interviewed on the radio or TV, my father knew about it and just soaked it up! So I knew it was all an act: he was supposed to be this fierce father, but in fact, he liked Chris! He just felt that that was his idea of what a father was: a disapprover of anything that society still thought was wrong. Homosexuality was wrong, so it would be wrong of him to allow respect of my partner. I never imagined that he could accept Chris, but he did anyway, even though he tried to kid himself. But imagine: he robbed himself of a friendship which would have cheered him up to no end! If my father hadn't taken such an absurd position, Chris would have been a very good bosom buddy to him. He just thought that it was expected of him to disapprove. All he was doing was depriving himself. When he finally let himself meet Chris, of course he knew who he was because he had been watching him on television. He was quite fake and had boned up on Chris. And Chris was such a charmer that our very first evening together, *years* later, he was eating out of Chris's hands!

Did any sort of closeness then develop between them?

Really in my father's last years, and that was a real boost. He immediately liked Chris, as of course I knew he would, but I didn't have anything to do with it—I didn't push it in any way. And I really didn't do anything about it earlier, because I thought, as regrettable as it was, he brought it on himself. But then it was enough right at the end, and it was established that the four of us could have meals and have quite a good time, and my father enjoyed it as much as the three of us. *I* knew my mother loved it, too. That has always made me have a whole different attitude toward her, because I thought she was so introverted, and yet she recognized Chris immediately. She never read anything he'd written; it was just the human contact with him. And my father, within weeks of that first dinner we all had together, was coming out to Santa Monica to repair Chris's car. He was a very good mechanic— he worked at Lockheed Aircraft. He loved automobiles and their motors and was a whiz at fixing things, and he had Chris's car, whatever it was, just humming for the rest of his life. Chris always remarked how amazingly his car responded after my father had a hand in it.

It must have been satisfying for your father to feel that he was needed in some way, that he could do something for you and Chris.

Yes, it really had a kind of symbolic underview that none of us referred to, because it was enough in itself. Thinking of those first encounters of my mother and Chris, she was grinning from ear to ear after one or two meetings, and pushing her face forward to be kissed. It was such a revelation to me, and I think it surprised her, too. You see, she was always wary of people. She'd had polio when she was five, and it left her with a lame foot and a big inferiority complex, so she was very hesitant to meet new people. But she recognized in him instantly who he was, and that he wasn't threatening. And by "who he was," not that he was famous, but that he was a good, sweet man.

And as a result, how easily she could allow herself to accept your relationship?

It thrilled me that she could feel that way about him. But of course, we had our life out here in Santa Monica, and then I was so busy making myself into an artist. And eventually, after both Ted and I left the apartment my mother was living in, in Holly-

wood, my father, because he hated paying for two apartments—
one for himself and one for her—moved into hers. They had been
separated for years, but even though they never got along together
before, since both Ted and I had left, neither of them had anything
better to do. They were both shy people, socially awkward, so it
was inevitable they would be together again once Ted and I were
off the scene. My mother had started divorce proceedings but
imagined that they hadn't been really divorced, just because she
had never picked up the divorce papers.

Did their relationship fare any better the second time around?

It was better, but the moment they were together again, my
mother was complaining exactly the same way she had complained all through Ted's and my childhood. But they wouldn't
have known how to live without each other. Well, that's just the
way things were. And eventually, I think, she felt so isolated that
she went into senility long before she should have, but that's
another story.

*You've spoken about your mother being an acute reader of people, an
ability you clearly inherited.*

Yes. I think again it was all about moviegoing. You can't love
movies without loving the people in them, and you learn about
people from movies, from actors in such close contact, such intimacy, alone in the dark with those big faces. It gives you intuition
about people. I know that it helped me—and my mother and
Ted—to read people in a kind of way that we ourselves were unconscious of, and so we found ourselves liking the same people
for the same reasons!

*And your mother ultimately allowed you to "read" her by sitting for
drawings by you?*

Yes, my mother sat for me reluctantly several times, and why
reluctantly? Because the first time she sat, I unwisely . . . well, I was

still at school on that first sitting, and I hadn't even started asking my sitters to sign and date the pictures, but I guess I would've had to have shown it to her, and she took *huge* exception. She even thought that I was intentionally making fun of her. She was very unsophisticated in terms of something like that. She herself had good draftsmanship ability for drawing, but I really hadn't learned to draw properly yet. I always had a kind of natural inclination for it, but it took me a long time to be really in control. Also, I was used to drawing art school models, so there was no effort even to make them look prettier than they were. But my mother really flipped when she saw those first drawings of her and swore she'd never sit again, and so I had to give her a talking-to. I said, "Your own son? And he's becoming an artist, and you won't support him and even sit?" And so I cowed her sufficiently that I got this agreement that, OK, she would sit for me when I asked her to, on the condition that she would never see what I did. And I welcomed that, but then, very soon, I decided to have my sitters sign and date everything I did, and so we agreed I would cover the drawings of her I had done, and just leave one corner free for her to sign. So I've got lots of pictures of her, and they're all signed and dated, but oh, those first ones! I came across them the other day, and they *are* pretty shocking in their crudity, but I was using her like I was using the models in art school. They looked enough like her that she recognized herself, but they were unnecessarily crude. But it was settled finally, and finally she was really relaxed sitting for me, and I did some charming pictures of her, I think. I mean, pictures that were really her at her best.

You included a few of them in a recent show dedicated to your portraits of women.

I had two of her in it that were representative of her two major moods: one with a sweet and charming and open expression, and the other a gloomy, kind of moody, almost mournful look. She was a very split personality.

Did your father ever sit for you?

I only have *one* drawing of him, and it's a very good one—it looks exactly like him—but how *odd*. By the time I did that drawing of him, I'd done lots of sessions with my mother. He was almost eager to sit, which surprised me, and I did this one drawing, very quickly, very easily, and it looked just like him, but I never asked him to sit again. I'm sure he would have. But of course, it's not odd at all that I should have carried that habit so late into my life: there was just, I guess, an early estrangement between us. Well, I say early: it was *throughout* my childhood, and by the time I hooked up with Chris, I'd really kind of grown out of that childish attitude toward him, and we got on, but we were always embarrassed together, because when Ted and I were little, he was very distant, because he was very working class. He was uncomfortable socially, even with his sons. Occasionally, once or twice anyway, I saw him with other men his own age, and even then he seemed to me very artificial. He couldn't relax, and so he put on a kind of gregarious behavior that didn't suit him at all. He was, by nature, kind of gloomy and shy and quiet, and if he tried to be hearty, oh, it was painful. But he did try, and in his innocence, he thought he could bring it off, but he just couldn't. At least Ted and I knew him too well to be fooled.

Certainly under your mother's influence, you and Ted had received a far worldlier education from the movies than anything your father might have taught you.

My father was just a lousy father, but Chris was made for it. He became my father, and just everything else—my *education*: I'd had *almost* no education whatsoever before I met him, except from the movies, and my father hardly participated in that at all. We had one official moviegoing night in which the four of us went to the movies, and that was Sunday night. But Ted and I were instructed by our mother very early on to keep quiet about the fact that by the time we saw movies with him, Ted and I had already seen them all with her! She'd taken us downtown and paid first-run prices to see them. But we, from the beginning, were mum whenever he was present not to *ever* refer to the fact that we'd already seen all of the movies that we went to with him. Well, not all of them: occasionally he would want to see a film that the three of us would *never* have paid to see!

Not as dedicated and discerning cinephiles! So would you have protested his choices at all, or was there just quiet acquiescence among the three of you to go along with whatever he wanted to see?

Yes, because we were putting on a show: it was hard to object to the one we hadn't seen without letting on that all the others, we *had* seen!

As your father was the sole breadwinner for the family, how was your mother able to hide all her extracurricular spending on moviegoing from him?

Well, she was the maker of "the list," writing down the weekly expenses, so she would try to pad them here and there. I can remember my father on Friday evenings, after he would ask to see the weekly list, yelling out, "GLADE!" The poor man, he didn't have a chance with the three of us. My mother had really constructed it, without intention, but just naturally: she made her two sons her confidants, and that locked him out completely. He was bad, anyway, at playing the role of a father; and having a mother who had completely taken over, he didn't have a prayer with his sons. No *wonder* we were both queer, Ted and I: we were queer in the cradle!

And then both of your already embraced identities—as a movie fan and as a gay man—found their ideal counterpart beyond Ted in Chris.

Yes, because it was immediately a language that we completely understood. There were a number of people then who laughed at Ted and me for being so movie-conscious, but it was *exciting*. I remember if we went to parties—and they were certainly queer parties—if we talked movie talk, the other queers were often superior and made fun of us. We were kind of laughable from their point of view. But we were genuinely enthusiastic, and I do think that's what counts. I think you're only really educated when you are paying that kind of attention, because *something* emotional is going on, and *any* interest is better than just a bland kind of acceptance of education, no matter how highbrow it might be. It's that passion of caring about participating that educates you. And then in Chris, I was lucky enough to have a teacher, a mentor who identified with me, just because I'm sure he could remember himself being so excited by movies when he was my age.

As I would suspect they were for Chris, for you the movies provided a profoundly impactful education in reading people, in truly examining the great variety of the human experience.

And that I'd actually then seen these icons in real life, at these movie premieres we'd sneak into? And all the photographs we took of each other with them: the daring of it, the genuine enthusiasm? Yes, that was an education in itself. It really *was* my education. Even before I met Chris, I was always an A student: from grammar school to junior high to high school, if it wasn't all A's, I was indignant! But it seemed to me I had learned nothing. What I *had* learned was how to get an A, and once I realized what it was all about, it was very easy. Very easy. I was the kind of student in school who, when given questions to answer about books, I read the books just until I came to the answer to the question I was looking for, and then I would skip ahead until I found where the answer was to the next question. So I wasn't reading the book. I hardly read *any* book all the way through. But I knew the system of how to get A's, because being a veteran moviegoer, I had to save enough time to keep the movies up. Books were much less fun than the movies! It was Chris who finally told me what education was all about, why it was useful. It just seemed a *task* until I met Chris, and having learned how to get an A, I dismissed what in fact I had learned.

So the knowledge you had actually accomplished was overshadowed by the achievement of having earned the high marks?
Right.

But what a teacher you then unexpectedly found in Chris!
Yes, by making me realize what nobody else had to that point: that reading was a wonderfully entertaining occupation! In fact, they had never told me that in school, and the approach was so flatfooted that I thought I wouldn't have believed them if they *had* told me. Chris was the *best* teacher on the planet, from my point of view. You know, it sounds silly, but from the movies, I got the habit of imitating them, of identifying with movies, and Chris taught me how to identify with book reading. He showed me how I could have a real part in it to play, and like I lived the movies I saw, I started living the books I read. And before very long, I was reading Virginia Woolf, and of course asking Chris questions, all of which he could answer—and he knew her! And told me what she was like! Oh, he created the *glamour* of reading and of knowledge for me; he made it so exciting, what it could do for me. And of course, he was right. My best idea of life, up until that time, had been baseball and movies, more than anything else, and it was *just* my last chance: another six months, or a year, I would've been lost. On the road I was going, if I hadn't met him then, my life wouldn't have . . . well, who knows. Ted's life never amounted to anything worthwhile. Yes, I never gave the movies up, nor did Ted, but if he ever read a book right through, he never told me. I felt so lucky to rediscover reading when I knew what I was reading. And I had somebody who would tell me *all* the background, all the information related that would help me understand it.

And he was somebody who had the patience and the grace to nudge you toward thinking for yourself.

Yes, Chris treated me like a grown-up, and told me what life was all about, and he was determined not to keep any secrets from me. My literature education really came at a wonderful time, at really the right age. Well, he was *right* for a young man. He imagined somebody maybe ten years older than I was, and he probably would've found him, but since I was so available and so curious and such a good moviegoing partner for him, he decided to take me in hand, and he led me to the magic. I had never *ever* read for pleasure, and suddenly Chris was giving me a book or two to read every week, and then was discussing it with me and helping me understand what I didn't, and he was probing to know if I could find what there was to learn in the book. And I did better than I ever would have imagined. Searching for those answers in high school must have given me *some* experience of the reading of literature.

When you were first getting to know Chris, were you aware of his celebrity as a writer and his own association with the movies?

Oddly enough, the previous fall, the road company of *I Am a Camera* came to the Biltmore Theatre downtown here, and Ted and I went to see it. We went on the opening night. In fact, we must have had tickets, because you must have tickets for a play. I knew about Julie Harris from *The Member of the Wedding*, but Christopher Isherwood I'd never heard of, and why should I? The name didn't cut any ice with me; I only knew about movie actors. I wasn't the least bit aware of writers or what their names were. I only realized who he was because in the bathroom at his garden house, over the toilet, was a poster of *I Am a Camera*, with a René Bouché drawing of Julie Harris. I was a great disciple of René Bouché. Bouché was employed by *Vogue* and doing celebrity drawings for most of their issues at the time. I still have a whole envelope of my clippings of his drawings. It was probably my first exposure to a portrait artist who got wonderful likenesses of people I knew from the movies, and even the people I didn't know, who weren't movie actors, I could tell from the drawings that they were done from life. That was a real turn-on for me.

Do you think that Bouché's example made real for you the possibility of translating what you had always done—drawing portraits of movie stars—into a real profession?

René Bouché was a big inspiration for me as a portrait artist. Well, he was the first artist who was doing portraits of contemporary people—contemporary to *me*—and I always combed *Vogue* for his work. I've still got them all saved, all the ones that really whet my appetite. It was probably on my very first trip to New York by myself when a friend, Marti Stevens, who knew Bouché, set up a meeting for me to go to his studio and show him my portfolio. I was in art school by then. It was very exciting for me, going into the actual studio of the master. There was a long corridor leading to his workroom, and on the wall were framed drawings, some of which I had seen in *Harper's Bazaar*. That was really exciting for me. He was very kind to me, and I knew that he was impressed by my work. He praised especially a drawing I had done of Mary Ure, because Tony Richardson had become a good friend of ours.

Tony Richardson had directed Mary Ure in both the play and film adaptation of John Osborne's Look Back in Anger.

I did several drawings of her, but the one that I think is really good is the only portrait I've done of a professional actor with her eyes closed. That was done here by the pool at a house that she and Tony Richardson were living in in Westwood with Wyatt Cooper. Wyatt Cooper later married Gloria Vanderbilt. He rose to the heights. Eventually, he arranged for me to do a sitting with Gloria. She was one of my first sitters in the studio here in '62.

Actor and author Cooper and heiress and fashion designer Vanderbilt are also noteworthy for being the parents of CNN anchor Anderson

Cooper. Let's go back to your emergence as a professional portrait art-
ist. Were you drawing from a young age?

I started drawing when I was three or four, and I drew all as a
child. In the beginning, when I was really young, I just made up
people, made up faces. And in grammar school, some of the other
kids used to ask me for my drawings, so I made myself popular by
drawing. It was always of people. When I got older, I started working from photographs of people, usually movie actors, because I
thought I knew them from seeing them in their movies, so I could
bring something extra to the photographs. Imagine, because those
movie actors were like gods and goddesses! But the drawings I did
weren't interesting as drawings. I don't think any drawing done
from a photograph can be interesting, because it's not *live*. It's
what I call photocopying. But what I was doing, without realizing
it, was developing the accuracy of my eye, because my drawings
were very recognizable. When we first were getting to know each
other, Chris asked me how I spent my spare time? I told him I
sometimes copied pictures of movie actors from movie magazines,
and he asked to see them. I showed him probably a dozen, and he
recognized every one of them. Among them, I remember, was certainly a drawing of Bette Davis, based on portraits of her for *All
About Eve*, and I remember also showing him a drawing of Montgomery Clift and a couple of others. He was impressed and praised
them, and then asked, "Well, have you ever worked from life?" I
said no. He said, "Well, you should try," and in fact, proposed himself as a sitter. So I took him up on it, and I did a little drawing of
him, which was my first from life. It took me at least an hour or
more. He sat very still. When finally I was finished, and he got up
and came around and stood behind me to look at what I had done,
there was a long awful moment of silence. Here was his young
lover doing a picture of him, and it *did* look unmistakably like him,
but as an old man! It was the *oldest* version of him I ever did, including all the last drawings of him and even the drawings after
he was dead, of his corpse, because I had trained myself to put in

everything I could see in the photograph of the movie actors—but of course, photographs of movie actors were all invariably retouched. But in Chris's face, there was so much more going on. Chris was only forty-eight, and sensational-looking at forty-eight, still a great beauty, but nevertheless, there were lines here and pouches under the eyes and crow's feet.

It was a real face.

I put in everything! Everything lovingly rendered, just sparing nothing, every detail, because it was fascinating! I put in, meticulously, every single age indication, yet it looked exactly like him at the same time. So there was almost with an audible gulp before he said, "You know, it's good!" *Phew!* Then once we were getting together, he continually urged me to try art school, but it took me three years, because I was scared of failing, so I kept putting it off and putting it off. Chris was urging me the whole time.

Had you taken any art classes in school prior to that point?

You know, I didn't really have much art experience in school. In my grammar school and junior high, and even in high school, there was just one day a week that was supposed to be an art day, but that didn't have any effect on me; there was no real seriousness about it. I don't think I'd even been to any art museums at all before I knew Chris, so I felt actually lucky not to have any preconceived ideas of the experience when I wouldn't really have been nearly as interested as I was when I finally *did* go to art museums. And then, I remember in New York and London, a couple of times I closed the museums after hours, *hours* inside. In London especially, that was a really wonderful experience for me: I loved doing it. I was just soaking up all of the atmosphere, and loving it. Yes, that was good.

And eventually you relented to Chris's urgings about trying art school.

Yes, finally I relented, and in 1956, very dubious, I signed up for a six-week summer course at the Chouinard Art Institute, which was the best art school here, downtown in Los Angeles, and before the end of the first week, I realized I had found my vocation. I was in my third year at UCLA with a very academic routine of classes. My introduction to UCLA as a freshman was the nadir of my life so far, but at the end of it, I met Chris. It went from the worst to the best almost overnight.

Why do you say it was the nadir?

I took an absurd schedule of classes, all of them heavy, but I got a B average in my freshman year. That was maybe the hardest thing I've ever done, because I hated every moment of it. So I signed off at UCLA and signed up for the full course at Chouinard. I knew I had to have an identity of my own if we were going to stay together, and Chris knew it, too. But if Chris hadn't just patiently prodded me, I would never have had the nerve to do it. I would never even have gone to art school without him. It was way beyond my means, and beyond my idea of myself. I also could never have afforded it, going to art school, and he couldn't even afford it at the time. It was expensive, and he didn't have jobs often. It was his movie studio jobs that really paid for several of our first years together.

What had you been studying at UCLA up to that point?

Languages, because I couldn't think of anything else. Oh, it was an awful program. I had never before been up until two and three in the morning doing homework. I'd spent the first two years doing all the heavy solids, getting credits, and then when it came to deciding, I'd studied Spanish since junior high, but Chris suggested German because he could help me, and he did. I was told by my German teacher that I had the best accent in class, because Chris was tutoring me. I'm a mimic anyway, so I had a natural knack for languages. My mimicking of people is unconscious. After nearly a year with Chris, people were already remarking that I sounded like him—and of course, people who met me thought

I must be doing it consciously. People who knew me before I knew Chris thought I was becoming awfully affected, with what sounded to them like an English accent. They thought I was putting on the dog—and of course I *was*, too!

That accent has stuck to this day.

Yes, it horrified me, because I couldn't hear it myself. I didn't really know what I was doing; it just came naturally. And it got to the point where if I answered Chris's phone, people often didn't know whether it was Chris or me.

Your natural ability for mimicry should come as no surprise, given your similar talent for embodying and expressing the essence of your sitters in your portraiture. Being introduced to working from life must have been such a transformative experience for you.

Drawing from life every day in class, with largely people of my own age! I'd done a drawing of my brother and certainly a drawing or two of my mother, but I don't think I'd *ever* really worked from life before. It was just so exciting, and it was so much easier and more exciting drawing people I didn't know. Yes, I was in it: I was dedicated to art school. I'd found what I wanted to do, and it was such a *relief* to know that yes, truly, I really wanted to be an artist, and I knew I had the capacity for it. But without Chris's encouragement, and of course the financial backing, everything, I would never, *ever* have become an artist. So I went for four years to Chouinard—and I didn't just go there; I practically lived there. I drove all the way downtown from Santa Monica five days a week for the nine-to-four day, and then I'd drive all the way back. Because my parents lived in Hollywood, some days after the four o'clock class ended, I would go and have an early supper with them, and be back for the seven-to-ten class. Or if I wasn't having dinner with them, I would maybe go to a movie, and then go back for the evening class. And I didn't go for any certificate; that didn't mean anything to me. Having learned from college the drudgery of just

taking the classes that were necessary to get some kind of degree
or certificate, I just took all the classes with a live model. Whatever
the teaching was, if there was a live model, I was there drawing
and painting because it was so exciting for me, and I made progress *very* quickly. The rest of the beginners in class were astonished, but all that copying of photographs had trained my eye, so
when I applied that to live sitters, not only did it allow me to be
accurate, but it was even *more* exciting, more demanding. I just
loved it; I couldn't get enough of it. I'd found my vocation. Of
course, Chris was hoping, nudging, but so carefully. Gosh, he was
so good to me. And then it took! And I couldn't leave it alone.
Chris paid for the whole thing, and it was expensive! In those days,
it seemed to me just a luxury, beyond luxury, but he never said—
and in the first year we were together, his savings amounted to
less than a thousand dollars. But of course, some of his friends
were still determined to think that I was a fortune hunter.

Some fortune!

But it was a fortune that they could not possibly imagine. What
really mattered was when I came home after a long day at art
school, he'd say, "Let me see what you did," and we would go
through the pictures, drawing by drawing, and we would really
share in discussing them. "Oh, my life," he would say, "you're getting better and better, and so fast!" Even *he* could see it. That was
just golden. Neither of my parents was capable of that kind of intuitive encouragement. My mother sometimes helped me. Well,
she drew, so she could tell wherever she thought I'd failed in some
of my drawings, but she didn't have an artist's dedication and had
given it up, really. But she encouraged both my brother Ted and
me, if only by just looking at the drawings we did and realizing
and saying that they were perfectly accurate likenesses. But Chris
was the real encourager. It was just wonderful coming home and
having him participate in what I had been doing all day long, because it gave me impetus to keep going. And he was so subtle, be-

cause he understood everything about how to handle a young man, and encourage him without being overbearing. Just, you know, that gentle urging.

Nudging you along on your own path, without overtly prescribing for you what that path should be.

Yes, making it seem like all my idea! And sitting for me *endlessly*, starting with the very first drawing I ever did from life! My belief now, and a long-held belief, is that no work by a portrait artist can really be of any real interest if it's not done from life. Doing pictures of people from life has been the *absolute* definition of all of my work since I began.

And some seven decades later, you're still passionately engaged in that work.

Well, it had to have been in the cards. Chris and I were *exactly* what the other wanted, and he made it all possible. He was just the mentor, influence, partner *supreme*. He couldn't have done it more beautifully, and it wound up pleasing us both. Not *wound* up: *pleasing* us both from the very beginning. It's really one of the accomplishments I'm proudest of. It seems silly even to say it, but what fool wouldn't have latched onto him? That at eighteen, I realized that he was not just an admirer, a lover, but he really had my *very* best interests at heart? And then he made *everything* possible. I was an A student all through school, but oh, the education I got from him! What's considered standard education or even pretty good education was *nothing* compared to what he gave me.

Your own creative passions must have been fueled not only by Chris's example and encouragement, but also by your sudden heady immersion in his intimate literary and Hollywood circles.

Yes, well, without consciously realizing it, I knew I had to find a vocation for myself if I were going to stay with Chris. I just instinctively knew. I was just bursting with a need for a vocation, without really knowing where it might be. I still imagined I might want to be an actor—and by actor, of course, I meant *movie* actor, and by movie actor, I meant movie *star*—so I had to get that out of my head.

Nevertheless, it's fascinating to consider how profoundly the visual language you both learned early on from movies then impacted your ultimate careers: his as a writer and yours as an artist.

And he realized that subtle distinction. I had also been wondering if I could be a writer, but Chris so delicately played up my ability to draw. Unconsciously, I had been developing the accuracy of my eye with all of the copying of movie magazine portraits of actors. When I applied that to real-life people, I instantly made advancements in all of my classes. The other students my age were eventually standing behind me, watching me draw, asking to see the pictures I was doing, and that was exactly what I needed—that kind of encouragement to be regarded as special, not only by Chris, but by people my own age. I couldn't get enough of that.

And in a sense, you were on your way to becoming a star after all, only not one in the movies.

Yes! Of course without Chris, I could have never made it. I had to find him to bring it out. You see, when I settled down with Chris, I was in the home of inspiration, because by his own example, he was teaching me about being an artist by his dedication to his writing. And so there I was, starting art school and coming home to somebody who took real interest in my progress.

Yet, were you still holding onto your fantasy of breaking into the movies? Through Chris's Hollywood connections, you were now having opportunities to socialize with film producers and directors. Indeed, you made a cameo appearance in the 1955 film adaptation of Tennessee Williams's The Rose Tattoo, *the movie for which Anna Magnani won the Oscar for Best Actress.*

Oh, well, I can't be seen in the film. I was just in the back seat of a car. There were four of us stuffed into this little coupe, and I was one of the two in the back of it. It was very shy-making for me: it embarrassed me, and I knew I wasn't really going to be seen by the camera. Oh, the humiliation of it! But how importantly I treasure that experience, because it made me know, *uh-uh*, not for me: starting at the bottom of a movie career that hasn't begun yet, and having to endure that kind of acute embarrassment? It really amounted to humiliation. Yes, I've always blessed that experience, because it was the final death of my ambition to be a movie actor.

Had you hoped that it might be your big break in movies—the first step to becoming a movie star yourself?

We were seeing Tennessee every day. Of course, being with Chris, I met Danny Mann, the director, and Burt Lancaster and Anna Magnani. I had a movie camera with me, and I was able to photograph both Lancaster and Magnani at one of the press interviews— take real close-ups of the two of them. By that time, I even had illusions of maybe becoming a movie director. I was upping my status. Then, what, in a couple of years I was going to art school, so I was taking another path.

I imagine that when Chris was working on various movies in Hollywood, you had the opportunity to visit the sets?

Oh, yes, indeed. I went often to lunch with Chris at MGM. Of course I went onto the set of *Diane*, which he wrote, and met Lana Turner and Roger Moore and Marisa Pavan, and of course that was hugely exciting for me, making real contact with these people, touching them.

Did visiting film sets take any of the magic out of the movies for you?

It made it much more glamorous. That was really inside the movie world. In the first year with Chris, I had more or less given up the premiere-crashing with Ted. When I had shown Chris those pictures and told him how Ted and I were maneuvering, he was very against it. Well, he was just afraid I'd get arrested, and Ted and I were certainly asking for it: the premieres were crawling with uniformed cops. But because of his disapproval, and because of my own understanding of how right he was, Chris saved me from what seemed to be an inevitable fate. And what a dangerous fate I could've met if I'd kept going with Ted, and getting bolder and bolder until I'd found myself in juvenile hall or jail or somewhere equally horrible. How I avoided that fate was just a miracle, as far as I'm concerned, and the miracle worker was Chris. Happily, I met him just in time, and that was the beginning of my real education—the education that mattered, the education that would keep me for the rest of my life: to be a decent human being, instead of a sneaky little movie-crazy fan, under the influence of my even crazier and more dangerous brother, who wound up in *endless* institutions, endless hospitals for people with real mental problems, which he had. I was so lucky that Ted and I didn't *both* find ourselves in mental institutions, or jails, or both. It would've ruined my life. I would have never recovered, because Ted never recovered. Well, it ruined *his* life. But Ted and I were certainly both culpable in our slyness and in our sneaking into situations just to photograph these people, and it so worried Chris that I would put myself in a situation where I could so easily get arrested. He was perfectly right and I knew it, and so I stopped the gate-crashing almost immediately, but there were two or three more occasions. One of them was at the Academy Awards ceremony of early 1954, and Ted and I were there with our camera. Of course, I didn't lie to Chris about where I was going, but he, quite reasonably, disapproved and didn't encourage me to go on with it, so I was moonlighting. And of course, at that final awards ceremony, who was there but Elia Kazan, whom I'd already been introduced to on two or three occasions. So for the first time sneaking into those premieres with my brother, I *knew* one of the celebrities, and in fact, Kazan said, "Hi, Don!" and I said, "Hi, Gadge!" I even knew his nickname and used it, so that seemed pretty classy for me! But suddenly I was shy, because there was Elia Kazan, and I realized that somehow it was different. I had already met him socially, so I didn't really belong at the Academy Awards ceremony. I had been so guilty of sneaking in, and if I had been caught being there without a ticket, it would have been shaming to have been arrested in front of somebody like Kazan. So that was my farewell appearance. The next movie premiere I went to, I had tickets with Chris. An important transition had been made.

Beyond the risks involved, do you think Chris also objected to your gate-crashing because, through him, you were on your way to becoming much more than just a mere fan, but indeed a peer of these people?

Yes, of course. He was already tutoring me, and he didn't want me doing anything underhanded: nothing stealthy, no creeping around, no pretense. I was being taught by Chris to take real responsibility for myself as an adult. He knew that's what I needed, and he knew it far better than my parents. By that time, my mother and father were separated, and my mother was just a movie fan like Ted and me. Chris realized I needed some real teaching: how to be grown up and responsible and to be somebody with a vocation who could do something in the arts, not just devour them. Yes, and meeting these people socially robbed me of my life as a fan. I mean, I could admire them, but I wasn't trailing them. I was no longer intruding into their world; I was meeting them socially. That was something quite different. And Chris was preparing me for that. So that was all part of my very unsentimental education, because he was teaching me to take responsibility for myself and to be somebody, rather than worshipping somebody.

CHAPTER 3

Everybody wanted to meet me

Don and Chris at a party at the beach home of playwright Jerome Lawrence in 1954. (*Photo by L. Arnold Weissberger, courtesy of Anna L. Weissberger Foundation and the Christopher Isherwood Papers, The Huntington Library, San Marino, California*)

At the end of your first year together, Chris took you to New York.

Yes, I had a two-week-long Christmas vacation from UCLA. I'd never been to New York and never been on a plane, so that was very exciting for me. And for the occasion, before we left, Chris took me to a tailor in town and had a suit made for me: an all-black suit, because he said when he was my age, he had a black suit and wore a white shirt and a black tie with it. He knew that that was the most flattering costume for a young man, because there is nothing to look at, really, besides the young man!

As with a woman in a classic little black dress.

Yes, because nothing distracts from looking at the face of whomever is wearing it! So he wanted me to have that experience, too, and I sure did, yes.

The suit, with you in it, was evidently a tremendous success, for your presence in New York created quite a stir among Chris's many illustrious friends there.

Oh, wild enthusiasm! A serious rumor went around town that Christopher had brought a twelve-year-old boy with him from California, so of course they were all panting to see us together!

You did look almost prepubescent still at nineteen.

Yes, I did look young for my age, and it lasted me a surprisingly long time. It seemed to extend my youth, yes. But those two weeks in New York, we were going every which way: we had breakfast, lunch, and dinner, tea and drinks, and late-night parties. Everybody wanted to meet me, and hardly anyone was left out. It was endless! It was just as glamorous and exciting as it could be for any nineteen-year-old! I can't imagine a more exciting introduction to New York.

And not only to New York, but also to a really high gay society.

Yes, a dazzling variety of participants! With Lincoln Kirstein masterminding everything, taking us to the ballet and giving a party for us. There were all kinds of parties. It was wonderful for me, but I'm sure it was not something Chris particularly enjoyed. Well, he enjoyed showing me off, of course, as he would, naturally. That was a pleasure, but he wasn't a partygoing personality, really. But those were two wonderful weeks we spent, yes.

You two were fêted by a pretty rarefied crowd, with the impresario Lincoln Kirstein—a wealthy patron of artists and the co-founder of the New York City Ballet—at its epicenter. But that trip to New York seems like it awakened you in many ways, providing you with a dizzyingly intensive immersion in the arts, along with introductions to an astounding array of Chris's celebrated friends.

You know, New York was so entirely a different place then. It's changed so, from my first views of it. Those two weeks were just so exciting and magical, really. All the theater, and all these distinguished people I was meeting, that was very heady! And to be presented in my brand-new black suit to all of these people, and just seeing New York for the first time, was so incredible. I loved it. I couldn't wait to get back.

Among those distinguished people were Chris's longtime friends, the poet W. H. Auden and his partner Chester Kallman.

Oh, definitely, yes, that's when I met Wystan. I don't think I'd met him before New York.

Chris and Wystan Hugh Auden, who was publicly known by his first initials, had maintained an intermittent sexual and collaborative friendship from the mid-1920s until they sailed together for New York in January 1939. Chris soon left to take up permanent residence in California, where you and he ultimately met, but Auden thereafter remained a New Yorker.

There was no way Chris could live in New York. So that's why it was easier for me to go alone to New York, because he really didn't want to go. Wystan took to New York immediately and got perfectly along there. Chris always marveled at his ability to adapt so completely. Chester, of course, was such an indigenous New Yorker. He knew everything about being queer in New York. But seeing that apartment Wystan and Chester lived in—oh, boy, that was an eye-opener, a real shocker. It was incredibly messy: they were both slobs. And they were so startling-looking themselves:

Wystan with all of his wrinkles, and Chester with his loose look. He was wonderful to draw. They both sat for me a few times. I always marveled that Chester had such a reputation for being a good cook. We were told that by the Stravinskys, as well as others, because they'd all been cooked for by Chester.

Among their other collaborations, Kallman and Auden co-wrote the libretto for Igor Stravinsky's 1951 opera, The Rake's Progress.

Personally, neither Chris nor I thought Chester was as good a cook as he was cracked up to be. I thought it was just terrible, but I kept my mouth shut. And even later, I once visited Wystan in Germany, at his house in the country, and I remember spending the night, and *he* cooked a good dinner for me. It wasn't fancy, but it was good. Chester otherwise always managed the cooking in the New York apartment, but as I say, his cooking didn't impress us much.

I don't imagine that you stayed with them on your trips to New York?

We stayed at the George Washington Hotel. In later trips, we always stayed with Julie Harris and her husband, Manning Gurian, way over on East 40th—I think it was 450 East 40th, just half a block from the river. We had our own bedroom together, with twin beds, but we always slept in one of them. Eventually, they had their son, Peter. There's a lot of footage of him as a baby in our movies.

I've seen the home movies you and Chris shot of your first European trip together, taken a few years after your first New York trip. You again stayed with the Gurians prior to sailing from New York, and then again on your return from Europe.

Oh, yes. We came back and stayed with Julie and Manning, yes. She was doing Joan of Arc then, so her hair was cut very short.

She won her second of a record-setting five Tony Awards for her portrayal of Joan of Arc in The Lark. *Her first Tony had been earned for her performance as Sally Bowles in* I Am a Camera, *the play based on Chris's* Goodbye to Berlin.

That first trip to New York was the first time that I met her.

Did you get your first taste of New York theater on that trip?

Yes, we went to the theater almost every night, and sometimes went and saw a matinee as well on Wednesdays and Saturday. Among the plays we saw was *Tea and Sympathy*, because I was a devoted movie fan, and it was a big thrill to see Deborah Kerr in the flesh. And Chris, because he knew how movie-struck I was and that it would please me, said afterwards, "Well, we haven't met, but I'll trust that she's an Englishwoman. Maybe she's heard of me; maybe she'll see us." So we went to the stage door after the performance, and the stage door man, an old man, was very rude. "Oh, yeah? You want to see Deborah Kerr? Haha!" But Chris wrote a note and said to him, "Would you take it to her, please?" The old man was very skeptical, but came back and led us to the door of her dressing room. It swung open, and there she was! "Oh, Mr. Isherwood, I'm so thrilled to meet you!" She was a real lady, and just was so *thrilled* to meet Chris! And of course, at nineteen, I was all agog, just staring at her. Oh, she couldn't have been more charming. She was still in her stage makeup, but she'd changed into her dressing gown. It was pale blue, two shades of blue, which was wonderful with her red hair. And that was the very year I'd thrilled to her like I never had before at the movies, because that was the year *From Here to Eternity* was released, and that opened up a whole new career for her. She was so good in it, playing an American woman, a blonde: a totally different personality. I don't think I've ever missed a film of hers, but it's only really in the last few years that I've really begun to realize just how good she was always, how reliable. Yes, she was really the best kind of actor, and I feel almost guilty about my late discovery of Deborah Kerr. I took her for granted for so many years.

The play you had seen her in, Tea and Sympathy, *was considered daring at the time for even delicately broaching the then-taboo topic of homosexuality.*

Oh, very much so. Chris and I rather snorted at that! Oh, it was so tame! Tame and apologetic, and we were more advanced!

But of course you were! The tormented young protagonist of that play is ultimately "set straight" by an older woman's rather twisted version of gay conversion therapy. What were some of your other early New York theater or theater-related experiences?

We even went to a hotel where William Inge was living. He and Chris had never met, and we had an afternoon with him. He was very kind and opulent-looking, with his clear blue eyes. Yes, he was very handsome still, and very kind to us. We spent at least an hour, an hour and a half with him, and then later I got to know him, and eventually I got to do some sittings with him.

Inge's play Picnic, *for which he won the Pulitzer Prize for Drama, was then enjoying tremendous success on Broadway, and would soon thereafter be adapted into an all-star movie. And of course, in that incestuous gay midcentury New York society where interconnections were rampant, Inge's then-assistant, John Connolly, was the young lover of another of Chris's friends, the novelist Glenway Wescott.*

Yes, we knew John. He was really helpful to us. He squired us around town in '53.

Glenway Wescott and his longtime partner Monroe Wheeler, a director at the Museum of Modern Art, had previously lived for many years in a ménage à trois with the photographer George Platt Lynes. For one of your early exhibition catalogues, Wescott wrote: "I have known Don Bachardy since he began to be the closest friend of an important friend of mine. He was a sprightly figure, fraught with friendly though uneasy smiles. I once saw an infant squirrel taking its first steps down a steep branch, clutching, eyeing the air on either side. In Don's early look, unlike the squirrel's, there was neither hunger nor fright, only something of a wild creature's concentration. He seemed to like every bit of life around him, above him, beneath him; and his own life was a venture, not just an adventure. Especially when his talent started; it challenged him."

Yes, that was very sweet of him. I was very fond of him. I have drawings of Glenway—and Monroe, he sat for me too, but he and I agreed not to know each other any better. What little we knew of each other was perfectly present and perfectly sufficient, but he wasn't any more forthcoming than I was. But I like that drawing I did of him, and I think he sincerely liked it, too. But Glenway, we always got along together. I don't remember ever any suspicion between us on either side. I would always have avoided any discussion of writing or literature with Glenway, because I discerned that we had a kind of non-literary relationship: there was no reason for either of us to talk literature to the other. I liked him, and I did an early sitting with him and then a late one. Both sittings were a success, from my point of view, but in the last sitting, I did one of my very best pictures, I think, of anybody. It would certainly be considered for any retrospective of my work. The best drawing of Glenway and the best drawing of Monroe were both done not on the same day, I don't think, but on the same trip to New York: it was one of my objectives on that trip to do a proper sitting with each of them. I had a suspicion that I could do a very much better drawing of Glenway, and I was right: I'm very pleased with the drawing that I then did do. I think that it's very much like him, and it even includes both sides of his nature in one drawing, his outward and inward self. Lincoln accused him of envy, and I recognized it in Glenway. I don't think I named it envy when I first saw it; I didn't characterize it as that, but then I thought about it and thought, OK, if you want to call him envious, I suppose it was a perfectly good face for him.

Upon receipt of a blurb Wescott wrote for Chris's family memoir, Kathleen and Frank, *Chris noted in his diary that apart from some "faint
praise dressed up in verbiage," most of Glenway's piece was instead
about himself. You observed in the moment that his envy of Chris had
crippled his ability to write anything favorable.*

And you see, a writer probably would always be able to see that
in Glenway better than I ever could, because there was nothing
that Glenway could be envious of *me* for, except my youth.

What were the circumstances of your first meeting George Platt Lynes?

I think it was quite late in the two weeks we were in New York,
probably close to New Year's. We met at a party, a night party. I
forget who gave it, but George was there, and there was another
guy there who had a whole set of pictures that George had taken
of him. They were nudes, beautiful pictures, and I was so envious!
Oh, it was so exciting to see them! I was hungry to think of being
photographed by him. George and Chris hadn't seen each other
in a while. They knew each other: they weren't good friends, but
Chris had certainly met him before, probably on one of his trips
with Bill Caskey, who certainly had known George.

*William Caskey, also a photographer, and Chris had ended a tempes-
tuous six-year relationship just a year before you and Chris first connected. George Platt Lynes had photographed Chris on one of those
previous New York trips.*

Yes. So then, at that same party, after we'd talked for a while,
George turned to Chris, not to me, to ask *Chris's* permission if he
could photograph me!

Doing his due diligence?

Yes, and Chris knew that he couldn't possibly refuse! Even
though we hadn't been together a year, and that was something
to trust me in the lion's den! I did say to Chris later at the party

that of course I wouldn't let him take my clothes off; that I would sit, but I promised I wouldn't take anything off. I remember saying to Chris again, at breakfast the morning I was due at George's, "Even if he asks me to take off my clothes, I'm not going to." But George was very attractive and so suave and so utterly sophisticated; there was really no question of not surrendering!

So it truly wasn't a matter of if, but when!

You see, the whole photo sitting was about lovemaking. Photographing for him was like drawing and painting are for me: it's all lovemaking. And so, after more than an hour of being told how beautiful I was, when George in passing suggested I might take my clothes off, off they came without a moment's hesitation, and I'm so glad that I surrendered! I would hate to think I had missed that. Oh, yes, he was Mr. Charm himself—and of course, he knew exactly how to handle eager young men!

Were you alone in the studio with him?

Yes. I think particularly with young men, he wanted to be by himself, because it probably often turned into sex at the end of it—because what is more of a turn-on to a young gay man than being photographed nude or practically nude?

And by an adoring, famous photographer who also happened to be stunning-looking himself? Had he told you beforehand what to wear, in advance of being then instructed to get out of those clothes?

No, he had just made a request: white sailor pants. So an hour before I was due at his studio, I went running around to Army/Navy surplus stores. I think I was seeing George at ten at the latest, maybe earlier, and some of the stores weren't open. But I did find one, and found a pair of white bell-bottoms that would fit. Even so, George had to pin them tight at the back before he photographed me. I can't remember whether I had the white shirt with

me or got one that morning, but I did get the white sailor pants.
The setup was all his idea; I just did what I was told. I can't remember how George prepared me, how he shot me, what he
asked for. I have no idea where that kind of dangerous, sultry look
came from.

*It's quite a performance you gave Lynes's lens, going from a smiling,
fresh-faced boy to a smoldering Hollywood hustler.*

Well, it was George prompting me, directing me, telling me
what he wanted.

*He posed you among crumpled newspapers on his studio floor, and
also framed within a large paper cutout.*

Yes, that was all ready to go. The newspapers seemed so corny.
Was I a kind of defrocked newsboy?

Right? Or a young sailor on the make?

And why, why? But then the '50s, and particularly of another
queer age, maybe wasn't the best period for photography. The profiles, I think, are the pictures I like best. I can't think of any other
photo session I've done that I would say I like the profiles best. If
even they happened.

*Lynes's seduction of you went well beyond his camera lens. He sub-
sequently became infatuated with you, and wrote you indiscreet letters.*

Well, we exchanged letters for months, George and I, secretly.
I've never shown them to anybody, and I kept it a secret from
Chris. I was so complicit that George sent all of the letters to me
to my *mother's* address. How's that for betrayal? In those early
years, imagine being so sly! How secretive, how disloyal! But I
was. I knew Chris would worry if I had any kind of friendship
with George, because George was a notorious seducer, and so I
kept it quiet.

Well, but you were also just nineteen and enjoying a little flirtation with an admirer.

That argument would not have made the least impression on Chris! And what was I doing in New York, behaving like this? Who had paid for my trip, introduced me all around, and the moment I was alone with a notorious seducer whom I *vowed* not to succumb to? We wrote to each other, but didn't see each other again for more than a year, not until January '55, when we made a trip back to New York especially because Chris had been told that George was dying of cancer. That was very good of Chris to do that. He invited George to have lunch with us at Le Pavillon, just the three of us, and it was a very nice occasion. You wouldn't have known George was sick from looking at him: he was still very handsome and very charming, as he had been, but he was dead within a few months.

So apart from those brief encounters, your relationship was conducted only through your correspondence?

I was sly and naughty enough not only to know I was writing secret letters to him, but I kept copies of my letters. Well, in those days, I didn't trust myself to write spontaneously, so I always wrote a rough letter and then honed it and then wrote a final copy. And George praised my letters for being good and smart and so forth, but then, as I said, he was such a charmer. He always knew how to flatter! I say "always knew"—what, I knew him barely a year, meeting on that trip to New York in December '53, and then seeing him again at that lunch in early '55.

Do you think Chris ever suspected?

No, I don't think so. I'm a very good liar! But OK, I was sly enough to keep it from Chris; Chris was sly enough to have found it out later one way or another, and keep it from me that he knew. You can never be sure about those things.

Well, one thing he did find out about, when George sent you both a set of the photographs from that session, was that your clothes had come off!

George sent us each a whole set of about twenty-five prints of all the photographs he approved of, and of course we came eventually to a nude one—discreetly only a bare-ass pose, but that's one detail I hadn't told Chris. Chris's remark was, "Oh, you naughty thing!" And what could I say? He was just wonderful. He was so funny, always: such a charming, educated man. But still, George didn't dare send any of the frontal ones to Chris!

There were frontal pictures?

Yes, yes. And at first when I saw that he sent all these copies of so many, but he didn't send those? I thought, "Gosh, was he disappointed?"

Or just being discreet?

He might have been worried about Chris's ire, not that Chris would have really cared. But I couldn't talk it over with Chris!

Of course not, or you would have shown your hand—or in this case, another appendage entirely!

Especially having promised him—or promised myself in front of him—I wouldn't drop my pants! But after I was with George for the first hour, when he suggested taking my clothes off, down they came without a single protest! Not even a whimper! Ah, well, he was a real professional!

Ah, the best laid plans! Beyond his reaction to the bare-ass shot, what was Chris's opinion of the photos?

Chris thought it was so chichi—the newspapers, and particularly the Napoleonic hat George stuck on my head, Chris really objected to that. He thought it was so faggy. It *is* faggy beyond belief, and on a *teenager*? He did that to a teenager? I kind of *groaned* internally when I saw that hat. I didn't want to put that hat on! I never had such a thing like that on my head in my life! Really, how queeny! I felt silly in it, too, but I didn't really make an objection to it. Chris thought the pants were kind of faggy, too! Chris, of course, was very strict—and a good thing, too, because he kept me from my own worst excesses. Faggoty clothes would have been much more my style!

After having been so desirous to be photographed by George Platt Lynes, what was your opinion of the results?

I was disappointed by that awful texture!

Lynes was experimenting during that period with using paper negatives, which then mottle the prints, making the images grainier, almost impressionistic.

It was a new fad, using paper negatives, and even his own devotees of his work disapproved. You know what beats well-lit sharp focus? Nothing, I don't think, and George was a master of it! I was just unlucky to hit him in that phase. What I loved about his photographs was that velvety beauty of them—*that's* what I imagined was going to happen to me. So I was *very* disappointed when I saw the effect of the paper negative that he used. But of course I wouldn't have told George. I did tell Chris I was disappointed. Yes, oh God, I would rather have had the classic Lynes photograph, but you know, why quibble? I was nineteen, so it didn't matter. I could even survive the scratchy-looking technique.

You, in turn, captured George Platt Lynes in a portrait of sorts, shooting what is believed to be the only existing movie footage of him, from shortly before his untimely death from cancer at age forty-eight in 1955.

Like all people who buy movie cameras who aren't moviemakers, we photographed everything —but way too little! Just snippets here and there. Why we didn't just let it run for ten or twenty minutes? It's just so brief, most of it. Yes, it was just one glimpse of George. We had a camera that took magazines of fifty feet of film. Back in those days, I forget even what they cost, but it seemed awfully expensive to me, and so I was mostly behind the camera, trying to save Chris money. But if you want to save money, don't get a movie camera! But considering the opportunities we had, it's a shame we weren't more extravagant. But at least a glimpse is a glimpse, and it's better than nothing.

You similarly captured home-movie "glimpses" of other well-known friends, but in Lynes's case, indeed it's better than nothing.

And George, I realize now, was vain enough not to have wanted to be photographed. That was very near the end of his life, and maybe he thought he was already looking not his best, but he was a good sport. I thought he still looked wonderful, amazing. I filmed him with Chris on the sidewalk outside Le Pavillon, when we took him to lunch. Well, Chris took him to Le Pavillon, which makes it even better! But that footage is so brief! Oh, it's heartbreakingly brief. We had the wonderful occasion to photograph him and other people, and we shot just moments! The briefest moments—they flit by; then before I can say, "That's George Platt Lynes," it's gone!

Which also aptly describes George Platt Lynes's brief but impactful presence in your life.

Yes, it does.

You were later photographed by such other art star photographers as Robert Mapplethorpe, Mary Ellen Mark, and Duane Michals. However, more widely reproduced today is a portrait taken of you on that first New York trip by Carl Van Vechten, a writer and prolific portrait photographer notable for his bold patronage of the Harlem Renaissance and his close friendship with Gertrude Stein.

He took the most terrible photos of Chris ever taken, and in two different sittings! He missed almost everything about Chris, but he was such a kind, sweet man, and because one loved him, the pictures he took mean something. Carl sat for me in 1964, and I have a drawing of him I'm very pleased with. And so did Miss Marinoff: I've got a good one of her, too.

Van Vechten was married to the Broadway and silent film actress Fania Marinoff for fifty years, despite his frequent affairs with men. While you were still a few years away from professionally embracing your own style of portraiture, were you exposed to any art on that trip that had any particular impact or influence on you?

What fascinated me art-wise was Lincoln's collection of Paul Cadmus's *Seven Deadly Sins*. I saw them on that very first trip to New York with Chris, and that was long before I had any idea that I would ever fasten onto the idea of being an artist myself, but oh, I was sure interested in those pictures. Lincoln had them downstairs in his hallway, and I pored over them endlessly when I stayed in the house on a couple of occasions.

What was it about that Cadmus series that so captivated you?

I was nineteen when I first saw them, and I'd never heard of Paul Cadmus. I didn't know anything about other artists. But his work was so of interest to me because he was such a good draftsman, and he could really draw. He must have been one of the last of the draftsmen, because it doesn't seem to me like anybody nowadays has that kind of skill. Either there are people who can draw well and they're just not showing it, or maybe they're just not even bothering to do it anymore. And also, his subject matter: illustrating each of the sins, and finding some grotesque or horrific way of expressing it. For instance, *Lust*: I just couldn't stop looking at it.

Lust is depicted as an inviting and certainly lascivious figure whose curled fingers join to form what looks to be either a brilliant diamond in front of her vagina, or a lighted pathway into it.

Yes, yes, with an abyss, and with the armpits also being hot vaginas! And *Envy*, with the fix of his mouth, and the kind of false invitation! Yes, yes, I remember that very well. *Pride* is one of my favorites.

Cadmus became renowned for his gritty, often grotesque depictions of urban life, and for paintings that daringly objectified the male figure and satirically challenged the social mores of midcentury America. He was classified a "magic realist" alongside his friends and former lovers Jared French, George Tooker, and Bernard Perlin, all of whom were a part of Lincoln Kirstein's inner circle.

I saw lots of paintings and drawings by Bernard Perlin and George Tooker, and George Platt Lynes photographs, and of course all the Cadmus drawings, and I was fascinated. Well, I think that was all preparation for me eventually deciding to try being an artist myself, yes.

As those artists were all intimately connected with Kirstein, did you meet them all?

Oh, I would have met Paul right away. He was around a lot at Lincoln's, and I met Tooker a few times, and I certainly know his work, but there was some kind of unbreakable enclosure that he seemed to be in, from my point of view. It was partly that he was very quiet, and almost mouselike in his avoidance of contact. And I did know Bernard. We were never really close friends, but we were certainly in the circuit together, but it was never anything more than that.

Chris's 1957 diary opens on a subsequent New York trip, with mention of a New Year's Eve party that you and he had attended at Bernard Perlin's apartment, after which you became depressed because, as Chris wrote, you felt you "had no identity." Did being among Chris's high-profile friends in the arts serve to further compel your desire to finally start art school and pursue your own creative identity?

Oh, sure it did, but just knowing Chris, yes, I wanted to be a member of the art world, certainly. And since our very early dealings with each other, he had expressed this interest in my own work and encouraged me to go on with that. That's what really got me going; that's what made the idea of becoming an artist realer than it had ever been before.

After your triumphant introduction to Chris's famous New York friends, you would return two years later to again be fêted, prior to departing on your first trip to Europe, with a star-studded "bon voyage" party thrown for you and Chris by your mutual friend, the writer John Blair Linn Goodwin. Among the attendees were Truman Capote; Tennessee Williams and his longtime partner, Frank Merlo; Chris's ex-lover Bill Harris; Bernard Perlin and his boyfriend, the fashion model Ed Newell; and Paul Cadmus. Newell, there like you among a bevy of other beautiful young men, has told me that John Goodwin greeted his guests at the door with a live ocelot draped over his shoulders!

Yes, I remember that party still! But I feel certain that if I'd seen any ocelot, I would remember it—I think the ocelot must have been either before or after Chris and I were there, and must have been put back in his basket or wherever he came from—but I can imagine John being outrageous like that. He had the rich man's audacity to flaunt it. We really had a genuine friendship, he and I. It was something totally separate from Chris, and I had the sense to keep it separate. I never even told Chris much about my relationship with John, because I didn't want him to really even have an opinion about it. All my most memorable encounters with John were always the two of us alone together. He and his last partner, Anthony Russo, were always people I saw on my single trips to New York, and I also stayed with John on Fire Island. Oddly enough, I never asked him to sit for me, but Anthony sat for me, and I really adored him. I was very impressed by him. He had a natural kind of human kindness, which was remarkable. But yes, I do remember a very friendly, good, warm feeling about that party. Chris and I were on our first trip to Europe and to England together. We had been together more than three years, but we hadn't been to Europe yet, because Chris had had such traumatic experiences getting his German boyfriend into England, out of Germany, so we waited until I was twenty-one before we traveled out of the country!

Chris had fled Nazi Germany in 1933 with his young German lover, Heinz Neddermeyer, who was then refused entry into England. Their ensuing nomadic search for a tolerant safe haven ended with Heinz's 1937 arrest by the Gestapo for draft evasion and "reciprocal onanism"— in layman's terms, for engaging in mutual masturbation. Miraculously, he survived both the forced labor and military service to which he was sentenced. So it's little wonder why Chris was hesitant to take you on any international travels until you were fully legally of age!

Yes! He wasn't about to take any chances!

A remarkable souvenir of your first epic European trip survives in the form of that amateur filmmaking with which you and Chris were experimenting during that period.

There were two reels, according to me, and I think I'm right: there was the European trip, and there was another reel which was all these little snippets and snappets from over the early years. Chris bought the camera for me very early in '53, because when I met him, I still had my dreams of becoming an actor, which meant, in translation, a movie star. But Chris gently nurtured the idea of perhaps being maybe a photographer, then finally announced I should be an artist. I would never have imagined it. Even so, as I said, it took me three years before I finally responded to Chris's nudging and urging to start art school, because I was afraid of failing.

Nevertheless, your films are now historically important, not only for their documentation of your intimate life with Chris, but again also for the many cameo appearances made by notable friends like W. Somerset Maugham.

I used to be terribly embarrassed by a swimming performance I put on: I did my Esther Williams! Even *she* looks absurd! I spliced all of the films together—it was about an hour of home movies—and it was the first piece of film on the reel. I remember I had to grit my teeth every time we showed it to people. Having opened it with that, I could've shot myself! Why did I *ever* put it as part of that reel, that footage of me being Esther Williams? Oh, I died over and over! I was very fond in those days of that kind of performance. I used to mimic records, too!

You lip-synced?

Oh, yes! But Maugham, well, he was adorable. We'd filmed him and Alan when we'd stayed with them for a week at the Villa La Mauresque.

To borrow a phrase from Gertrude Stein, "everybody who was anybody" made the pilgrimage to Maugham's longtime home on Cap-Ferrat in the south of France, which he shared with his secretary-companion, Alan Searle. You and Chris were received on the same hallowed ground upon which the Duke and Duchess of Windsor, Winston Churchill, H. G. Wells, T. S. Eliot, Virginia Woolf, and other literati and glitterati set foot.

Yes! We were there for a week, and I've even got movie film that Chris took of me in bed, in our bedroom at the Villa La Mauresque. There's a brief shot of me on a French telephone in bed, taken by Chris, just because of the French telephone and the fact that we were in the Villa La Mauresque, and we were delighted to have proof that we'd been there! But the footage of them is on that visit to the house: we went out for walks with Willie and Alan, and we took the camera on one of them.

What do you remember most about Maugham?

Oh, just that he flattered me, and he not only seemed like the oldest creature I'd ever met, I think he must have been! All dressed up in his hat and wool scarf and overcoat, and of course, his stammer was *major*. If he wanted to say something, it went on and on and on. It was really something, and I remember I was so surprised the first time, I thought, my God, I can't keep a straight face, but I knew I *had* to. I just couldn't fail to keep myself under control when he was clearly, absolutely unable to help himself.

E. M. Forster, the acclaimed author of A Room with a View, Howards End, *and* A Passage to India, *also appears in your films of your first continental tour. He was nominated for the Nobel Prize in Literature in sixteen separate years.*

I loved reading so many of those novels. Wonderful stuff. They were just the perfect kind of fodder for me. Gosh, those two writers who were so *exactly* right for me at that time of my life, and to actually meet them and be intrigued enough to then really follow it up by getting involved in their work—and there was so much of it from both of them—it was really a *feast* for me. Auden was a little more difficult one for me, because even now, my poetry reading is very scant, so I read *about* him more than I read him. But also, Chris knew many of his poems by heart, and once you heard him reading the poem, that was it; it was just cemented in my memory. In a way, I felt I was ashamed to be so ignorant of literature, except it was so wonderful to be awakened to it by Chris, and then he introduced me to these writers in a way that pleased them as well as they pleased me.

What about Forster as a character? Was he as flattering of you as Maugham was?

Oh, yes, very differently from Maugham, but he was such a sweet man. I was very shy with him, much shyer than I was with Maugham, because Maugham, and especially his friend Alan, treated me like a gorgeous young man, and that made it fun being with them! But there was no nonsense like that from Forster. No, he wouldn't have *dreamed* of bringing up my attractiveness to him, whether it existed or not. But he and Willie and Alan, too, they were so good to us, and I know Chris was so relieved that it was working: that not only I was so thrilled to be there, but the reports he kept getting from them about me were so encouraging: "Where did you find him?"

Another longtime friend of Chris's who appears in your home movies is Dodie Smith, the author of I Capture the Castle *and the children's classic,* The Hundred and One Dalmatians. *You were evidently behind the camera that day, as Chris joins her in the footage along with her husband, Alec Beesley, and, fittingly, one of their beloved Dalmatians.*

Oh, I loved Dodie and Alec, and that was a dear little cottage they had. She was such a weird little figure: I mean, about that high! She could hide it when she was young—she'd had enough vanity earlier in her life to carry it off—but of course she knew as an old lady, she was very vulnerable. I remember really sensing her resistance to all the photography. She was really one of the strangest people I had ever met up until then, and Alec was just as. I had the nerve to get her to sit for me, and I knew even before I began how touchy she was about her looks. I realized her own confidence in herself, at her age then, was vulnerable, and then doing a drawing of her and being the artist that I am, being so accurate with every detail, whether it be flattering or not...?

What was her response when she saw what you had done?

I know she was taken aback, but she couldn't admit it. Alec helped. He really was very good, because he understood her *and* the two of us, so it was OK, but my hand was trembling at the next drawing. And of course, the first one was much the best, and what a preparation it was for the rest of my life as an artist: my sitter having seen and survived the shock of the first drawing I did, when we started the second one, I could see her turning up the corners of the mouth, and the sweetness just melting away. And

I had to draw it—I couldn't avoid it—and that was even more dangerous than drawing her like she really looked! But that's my territory, because that's where even a camera dare not go.

During that first trip to England, you also spent time with Sir John Gielgud, who would become as close a friend to you as he already was to Chris. He later appeared in the films The Loved One, *which Chris co-scripted, and* Frankenstein: The True Story, *which you and Chris co-wrote.*

Oh, yes, he would come out here, and we saw a lot of him on our trips to England usually. He was such a sweet man, and being queer, it was just no trouble at all: he was always very sweet to me. He loved Chris, so there was no hesitation, no reserve: a friend of Chris's was to be treated with equal respect by him. He was a very good man, and very witty and funny, too. Such wonderful stories!

Just a few years earlier, Gielgud, by then already a revered stage and film actor, had remarkably survived the near-ruinous scandal of being arrested for cruising in a public lavatory.

Well, it all came out, really, and the London press is just the worst. But I think Gielgud was really beloved, and I don't think it hurt him badly—that scandal, the arrest.

His very next appearance on stage, in Liverpool, was met with an astonishing standing ovation—an extraordinary showing of public support for a gay celebrity in the 1950s.

Yes, yes. He told us about that himself, and how moved he was. Yes, that was great. Good that they did that.

You'd set sail on that trip from New York for Tangier, via Gibraltar. Chris's iconic character Sally Bowles acquired her surname from his longtime friend, the writer and composer Paul Bowles, the ultimate American expatriate who lived for over fifty years amidst the intrigues of Tangier. Indeed, an evening of unexpected intrigue awaited you in Bowles's apartment, where he and his painter friend Ahmed Yacoubi introduced you to hashish?

Oh, it was absolutely one of the great adventures, that night of the hashish, and Chris allowed it! We were like two total innocents: we had no idea what we were getting into. I'd always felt that it was very sinister of Ahmed and Paul, that whole set-up, but then that was probably mostly due to the hashish. I hadn't had anything like that, and neither had Chris; that was long before marijuana or anything. Ahmed was hot for me, I was convinced, which might all have been a complete purple invention of mine, but I thought they were setting me up for a big rape, and that Chris had been dismantled: that somehow, they'd fixed it so that the effect of the hashish had a completely different effect on me than it did on him. He was becoming befuddled, and I was seeing myself in some kind of jeopardy. I was scared to death, and just couldn't get out of there fast enough. Now, that might *all* have been the hashish. I mean, this was '55: I was just twenty-one, but I felt it was stacked against me. So I went to Chris and said, "We've got to get out of here *right now*. I want to go." It was the most sinister place I had ever been in my life. I didn't like Paul; I didn't like Ahmed. I thought they were very dangerous, and I was having fantasies then going into the depths of fear, of madness. *Madness.* It went from the ecstatic to lights going on in my head. It was both the scariest and most sublime experience I've ever had in my life. But it was way, mega, mega too much for a night in that apartment in the high-rise, so I insisted on going, and they both tried to stop us, to stop me. I said, "No, Chris, we've got to go, we've got to go, get me out of here." I wouldn't even let Paul get in the elevator with us. We got in and went down to the lobby, which was empty. It was a glassed-in lobby with a glass door. I went straight across to the door, and it was *locked*. I turned around to the elevator, and the arm was coming back down. They were coming to get us, to drag us back to the apartment and kill us both! Out came Paul, and I really had a fit. But Paul was just bringing the key to the front door to let us out! I just couldn't get out of that building fast enough, and in the cab back to our hotel, oh, I was so relieved! And Chris hadn't really any idea what was going on with me, and that was so unlike him, because I knew he was very watchful and very cognizant of any situation that I might feel endangered in. But he wasn't available to me; they'd kind of dismantled him in some way. He, of course, supported me, and we did get out of their apartment and into the elevator, but it was embarrassing for us both the next day, as you can imagine, because we were there for the weekend, and we couldn't pretend now that we wanted to see Paul! But how could we get out of seeing him? And so there was an awful lot of embarrassment, at least on my part, but I never doubted that I was right to leave, and that what I was sensing was something that was against Chris, and dangerous to me. But I saw Paul and Ahmed on different occasions, and in fact, Paul sat for me later, two if not three times, years later. He stayed at the Shangri-La here and was here for a while, so we had him to the house and entertained him a couple of times. But that was really a night of adventure like no other that I've spent, and it's very clear: I've never in my life been as scared as I was that night. Well, it was like a bomb going off in my head. What a remarkable but thankfully once-in-a-lifetime experience! And I will never believe that it was just my own personal invention. I know there was something up. I think Paul was always very kind, very nice, a fascinating personality, but also a little bit scary. I hadn't read anything by him at that time, but I did read several of his books later, and nothing ever shook my own view of that night. I had to get out of there, and it would have ended badly for me if I hadn't. I think both Ahmed and Paul were very scary people. I think there was some kind of a bargain they'd made with the devil somewhere along the way. It sounds so silly!

What an awful experience that must have been for you!

Well, it shouldn't be regarded as awful, though it had its awful aspects, because it was a very dramatic and significant experience for both Chris and me in many ways. As scared as I was, it brought us together. I'd never been scared like that in my life up to that point, and even now, I shudder at the fear I experienced. I was going through such incredible mental experiences, and losing my mind and really scaring myself to death. It was really something to cope with, and my life hung on it; my sanity. I don't know what I would've done if Chris hadn't been there to help me, comfort me, assure me. Oh, if Chris had been scared, if I'd not been able to be reassured by him . . . well, it was my sanity that was up for grabs. It was, without Chris. I couldn't trust it.

What a remarkably confirming moment that must have been for both of you in how deeply rooted your mutual trust was.

Oh, it was profound. Very, very long-lasting seeds were planted that night, and Chris's steadiness and assurance and talking me out of it, until finally I began to get through it, that was really something. I wasn't able to tell him nearly all of my horrors that I was going through, but it was certainly a memorable evening.

Happily, that harrowing misadventure didn't curtail your lifelong pursuit of adventure. You've told me there is nothing much that you dreamed of as a child that you weren't ultimately able to experience or achieve—and certainly much of it with Chris by your side or with his support. Beyond the great fulfillment you found in your relationship with him and certainly in your artistic career, you've also been an inveterate explorer of the world.

The older I get, the less I want to leave here. It's really a wrench to get oneself onto that plane. I'm glad I did a lot of traveling when I was young, and I think that's the time to travel, because it's such hard work! Oh, such hard work! Chris was so good about wanting to show me England, and then taking me around the world and all of that, but now my essential nature is that of a homebody. I'm a Taurus, and Tauruses are always very closely related to the houses they live in. That's part of why Chris and I got along so well: he was another earth sign, a Virgo. But you know, when you're young, you want to see the world, and I did: I did travel a great deal with Chris, and also without him. And also when you're young, it's natural to want to show your young, good-looking body to as many people as you can find, really!

CHAPTER 4

I was all eyes

Don, photographed on his first trip to
New York by Carl Van Vechten, January 1954.
(Photo © THE VAN VECHTEN TRUST, courtesy of Don Bachardy)

It must have been especially exciting for you knowing that Chris was so intimately connected to the movies: writing for them; working and socializing with movie people.

Yes! And blessed my movie past, because that's what engaged me with Chris. When he was my age, he was obsessed with movies, and he had a scrapbook that he kept. They were mostly clippings from *Photoplay* magazine, which he got in England. But that's how we got to know each other: going to movies together. We started living together early in '53, and then by the beginning of '54, January, he had the job at MGM writing *Diane*, so I used to hear every evening how Lana behaved!

Lana Turner played the title role in that MGM production.

They did make friends and talked a lot on the set. Of course, I think probably Chris pursued it more than usual, because he knew I was waiting at home for the latest stories! I think he took more trouble over her than he would have otherwise. But a few years later, he was offered another job, and she was already cast in the film. And he said, "Oh, well, that's a sure thing then, because we know each other, so that will cinch it." But it was the reverse: as soon as she heard that they wanted to hire Chris, she said, "Oh, no! He wrote one of my worst movies!" Because *Diane* had flopped, of course blame the writer! But if Ingrid Bergman had been cast in the movie as Chris hoped and was promised, then it would have been a totally different movie. With a talented director, it probably would have been a success, the reverse would have been the outcome, and Ingrid would be saying, "He wrote one of my best movies!"

Did you ever get a sitting with Lana Turner?

I got Turner on the phone, and she was very *cutesy*. At one point, I said something and she interpreted it as it might be a suggestion that she sit *nude* for me, and she got very cute about it, but we made a date. But then her assistant, who was my connection to her—he was queer, and had set it up for me—he called the next morning and said it was canceled because they got drunk together the night before and they had a quarrel, and she said she wouldn't sit for me, to punish him. It sounded very Lana Turner to me.

Whereas your first of many encounters with Ingrid Bergman was nothing short of magical.

It was early in the morning, being picked up on a corner in Paris, and then a whole hour to the studio in a car with Ingrid with a kerchief over her head, no makeup on, laughing, telling stories. I was in seventh heaven.

She and Chris had worked together in 1941 on his first Hollywood film, Rage in Heaven.

Rage in Heaven, yes. It's shown occasionally now on Turner Classic Movies. It's a good film. W. S. Van Dyke directed it. He had directed *San Francisco*, and was considered one of MGM's classier directors. He and Clarence Brown got the sort of hallowed properties, and this was a James Hilton novel, so it was considered pretty good. It was Ingrid Bergman's third Hollywood film; she was considered a hot actress then. Her next Hollywood film was a star-making appearance in *Dr. Jekyll and Mr. Hyde*. It's maybe my favorite performance of hers. She's so gorgeously photographed by Joseph Ruttenberg: he took real trouble over those close-ups in the dream sequences that Jekyll has before he turns into Hyde. It's a perfect example of a star-making appearance: one that turns an actor that people have already seen in movies before suddenly into a major personality, and you see how it's done: you see the magic that is really inimitable. That's what makes someone a star. It's not easy to be an Ingrid Bergman, because it's an unknown formula that has created this new personality. When we were in Paris in '55, we knew that she was making a film with Jean Renoir, which in Europe was called *Elena and Her Men*, but *Paris Does Strange Things* here. Her co-stars were Mel Ferrer and Jean Marais. So it was arranged by phone that we were to be picked up on a street corner of Paris at six in the morning to go to the studio. In the car was Ingrid Bergman. She and Chris hadn't met since *Rage in Heaven*. Somehow, it was even more exciting at six in the morning. She was in a snood because her hair was going to be done at the studio, and makeup and costuming and everything. I don't think filming began until late morning or even early afternoon, because it took so long getting into camera-ready condition. It was a long drive outside of Paris to the studio, and I was witness to Chris and Bergman in conversation.

When you would encounter a movie star like Bergman while in Chris's company, would you likewise participate in their conversation, or hold back as an observer?

I was all eyes. I had the intelligence to keep my mouth shut and not get bored, you see, because I was looking at Bergman. I was listening, of course, but I couldn't reproduce her dialogue to save my life. Maybe right after the event, I could have given a pretty good account of how it was listening to her. I was looking at her, and that's what kept me alert. And why Chris and I were such a good balance together was that I *did* have an art of my own, which was based on looking. His was essentially listening. He could also be a very sharp observer. For instance, if he were having trouble describing a character, he would always come to me to try to find out how I would describe a face. I knew why he was asking me: I could tell in his descriptions of people sometimes that he wanted a certain quirkiness of observation, which I certainly had. I notice things that other people don't notice. Chris was always so impressed when we would go out and meet friends of his, particularly women, how I would always notice if they changed their hairdo—or a man, too—whereas Chris wasn't as fast as I, particularly with women. Maybe with men, he would be a bit more observant, but with women I always noticed a new hairdo or clothes or color or change of nail polish. I was quicker than Chris to observe. That was very useful to me. He learned how to plunder me visually, as it were, to get that essaying of observation that he knew he wasn't as sharp as I was at getting. And of course that spurred me: it excited me to have someone as appreciative as Chris was.

What in particular did you observe during that encounter with Bergman, for example?

Oh, that was just the kind of experience that made me giddy with disbelief, that I could be so close to Ingrid Bergman! And she was laughing and talking and being so friendly! She was just one of the most lovable of all the Hollywood people I met. She was like nobody else; she was so full of vivacity. What was almost the first thing she said to Chris when we got into the car? "Oh, you've gotten so old!" And then I watched her face, and there was a moment when something came over her. She was thinking, "If *he's* gotten so old, what about *me?*" And she looked wonderful! She still looked exactly like herself. She was still in scandalous eclipse in Hollywood. *Anastasia* hadn't been even spoken of yet.

At the height of her stardom, Ingrid Bergman had scandalously become pregnant from an extramarital affair with the director Roberto Rossellini, for whom she left her husband and their daughter—and her Hollywood career. She would make a triumphant Oscar-winning return in Anastasia.

That followed immediately after the Renoir film, in '56. Then, arriving at the studio, we met both Ferrer and Marais. While Bergman was being made up, we were with Mel Ferrer as he was making *himself* up. He was very friendly. Audrey Hepburn had just married him. That same trip, while we were in Paris, we spent an entire Sunday with him and Hepburn. We went to the movies with them to an early morning showing of that wonderful film by Max Ophüls, *Lola Montès.*

How did that extraordinary double date come about?

Chris had gotten to know her because while *I Am a Camera* was in New Haven, where New York productions tried out before Broadway, she was there in rehearsals for *Gigi.* Anita Loos was already a good friend of Chris's, from Anita's Hollywood days here.

Anita Loos was a Hollywood screenwriter and playwright whose satirical novel Gentlemen Prefer Blondes *inspired both the hit Broadway*

musical starring Carol Channing, and its classic film adaptation,
which starred Marilyn Monroe and Jane Russell. Audrey Hepburn
starred in Loos's 1951 play adaptation of Colette's Gigi.

Chris had told me about a Sunday he had spent with Audrey
Hepburn during which they had driven around New Haven, and
she had hung out the window pointing out, "Oh, look at the lovely
boys!" Being probably very ingénue, as part of her training for *Gigi*.
But by late 1955, she had gotten married to Mel Ferrer, and in fact,
it must have been Mel Ferrer who arranged the morning with Bergman, because he was in the film with her. We had visited the location of *War and Peace*, which Hepburn was appearing in, but not in
the scenes that we saw being shot. I remember Mel Ferrer was a
part of a couple of the scenes we saw. On that first trip to Europe,
Chris had chosen Italy because he had never been there, either. All
of the other places we were, he'd been to before, so he thought we
would start with a place neither of us knew. He and King Vidor
didn't know each other before we met at a party in Rome, and
when we said we were planning a trip up north, he said, "Well,
come visit the shooting of *War and Peace*." And so we went to the location and spent the day with King Vidor, and had lunch with him.

King Vidor was a veteran Hollywood film director whose credits in-
clude such silent classics as The Big Parade *and* The Crowd, *the early*
all-African American musical Hallelujah, *the Kansas sequences in*
The Wizard of Oz, *and the Western* Duel in the Sun—*the premiere*
of which your brother Ted had infiltrated.

He was an adorable, charming man: a very, very kind, sweet
man. In his late years, he was still attractive: really such a handsome man, and sweet-natured and charming. I even have some
drawings of him: he was an early sitter of mine. Of course, that was
much later—it must have been in '62, and it was '56 when *War and
Peace* was being filmed. I was disappointed not to meet Audrey Hepburn then, but I'm sure Mel Ferrer, who was also in *War and Peace*,
promised her in Paris. That's how it happened with Bergman.

What was your experience like with Audrey Hepburn?

It was wonderful, and before she got really spoiled and kind of uppity. Of course, she was full of stories of how wonderful it was making *War and Peace*, and how sweet King Vidor had been to her. I think she had already finished most of her filming, if not all of it, by the end of '55. *War and Peace* was released in '56, and Bergman was making *Anastasia* by '56, and of course Bergman won the Oscar for it.

Chris had written Diane for MGM with Ingrid Bergman in mind. The studio, meanwhile, floated the idea of casting Greer Garson for the title character, or potentially trying to lure Greta Garbo out of retirement?

Chris suggested Bergman, but of course Hollywood was still quaking at the scandal. The producer, Edwin Knopf, was far too weak-willed to insist, and MGM was scared of the idea of Bergman. What an opportunity they missed! Had Bergman played in *Diane*, it would have been a major production, and she would have been so wonderful in it! She would have been perfect for it, just perfect for it.

Chris also proposed that Julie Harris play Catherine de' Medici to Bergman's Diane. That would have been quite a dynamic pairing.

Oh, that would have just been a resounding production! What a disappointment for all three. Bergman and Julie and Chris would all have had a great success with *Diane*, I'm sure. You see, all of the attention that *Anastasia* got because Bergman was making her return, that could have been for *Diane*. And they were both released within a year of each other. Gosh.

Instead, Diane *was made with Lana Turner and Marisa Pavan in those roles.*

When Chris first heard that Turner had been cast in it, he said, "Then we'll have to change the title to *The Revenge of the Pig People!*" because he had no opinion of Turner at all as any kind of actress.

The role really required stage-trained acting, and of course Bergman had all of that, as well as all of her filmmaking experience in Sweden.

And Diane *was such a major opportunity for Chris, because he was given carte blanche in fully crafting the script, whereas previously he had been just one of many writers working piecemeal on various studio films.*

Yes, it was partly Knopf's weakness as a producer that he gave full leeway to Chris to write the kind of script that he wanted, but I think that it's a wonderful invention. And contrary to the assumption of all kinds of people in Hollywood—even friends of Chris's, who assumed that Chris took his screenwriting lightly, that it was just a breeze for him or camp or something that he didn't give his best effort to   well, he didn't know how to give anything *but* his best, whatever it was he did. That's one of the major things that he first taught me: that you don't do anything without giving it your absolute best. What better thing can you teach a young person? That's what an artist is: he cares so much for what it is that he does that there's no question of doing anything concerning it that isn't the best he can do. And a script is written: Chris just would not write a sloppy sentence; he didn't know how to. That's why he gave everything he did six or seven drafts, more! Endless drafts, before he knew it was right.

Was the collaborative process a challenging one for him? Again, often he was but one of many writers on a film.

No, not really. There are strong traces in *Rage in Heaven*. I know there are lines that just had to be written by Chris, and there, he only shared credit with one other writer, Robert Thoeren. Chris also worked on *A Woman's Face*.

A melodramatic 1941 Joan Crawford programmer, directed by George Cukor.

He's not given credit, but he was one of at least six writers. Occasionally, movies of that period at MGM would have four or five writers listed. It was always something that the Screen Writers Guild would decide: if there was any arbitration, they always decided who deserved credit and who didn't. Of the pictures that Chris got credit for, *Rage in Heaven* is the one that's most recognizably his. He also worked on a Shirley Temple movie, which was originally called *Judgment* but had several titles until finally they settled on *Adventure in Baltimore*. I think I can ferret out a few signs in it of what's preserved of what Chris had done.

In that 1949 film, Shirley Temple plays a budding feminist and art student whose painting of a bare-chested hunk creates a scandal at the turn of the twentieth century. Whereas Chris shared a "story by..." credit on that film, that same year he was listed as the co-screenwriter of The Great Sinner, *an adaptation of the Dostoyevsky novel* The Gambler *that starred Gregory Peck and Ava Gardner.*

He had quite a bit to do on that, and in fact, Christ's lines at the end of the film are spoken by Chris: "They parted their garments among me and cast dice for my robe." You can hear Chris. It's distant, it's been toyed with, but you can hear him. Chris and I used to meet Gregory Peck at parties, but he was kind of funny towards Chris afterwards.

Why? Because that film failed both with critics and at the box office?

Yes, as though he blamed him in some way.

Chris is also listed as one of the twenty-two writers on Forever and a Day, *a film that was structured sequentially under seven directors and with a large cast of British film stars. Do you know if he wrote one particular segment?*

I haven't seen it since it was new. It was an all-star film, and all the stars have mostly cameos. It's told in sequences, like an amalgam of short stories. Yes, I suppose I could distinguish the one that he wrote if I knew the film better, but even for that single sequence, Chris shared the credit with somebody else, so it wouldn't be all his. *Diane* is far and away the script that is most recognizable of all he did.

What was his opinion of the finished film?

Oh, even after that ungracious title change he suggested, Chris got along with everybody.

Chris had conceived of Diane as "high camp." What was his definition of high camp?

Writing wonderfully beautiful lines to be spoken by an actor with great theatrical emphasis. And *Diane* is full of it, if you read the script with that in mind. Between Diane and Catherine, there are wonderful lines both of them have. But of course, Turner didn't know how to deliver that kind of line, and she was so full of herself. She just seemed so plumply conceited, rather than stylish. It was beyond her. She was charming in other parts when she was young, but she was one of the people who, when she became a star, she lost her talent. She became grand in a kind of phony way, and it just didn't suit her kind of sweetly pretty sexuality. And then when she started looking middle-aged, she took cover in this pretentious personality, and she just didn't know how to carry it. Before long, Chris's friend Ivan Moffat—also a movie writer, British, younger, and very funny and straight—did imitations of Chris drunkenly saying, "Oh, she's not so bad! You know, old Lana, she can do it!" He was talking himself into giving up Bergman and accepting Turner.

Ivan Moffat was Oscar-nominated for co-writing the screenplay adaptation of Giant, the 1956 epic that starred Rock Hudson, James Dean, and Elizabeth Taylor. Meanwhile, Diane, released that same year, was a critical and commercial failure. But Chris was ultimately able to accept Lana Turner in the role?

In fact, they were friends during the filming, and Chris always came home with stories about how he and Lana had had laughs together. She would ask him to say her lines for her. How should she say them? Where the emphasis should be? And they got along very well together. The upshot of that was that Chris was then considered to write a movie for Lana Turner about Suzanne Valadon!

To play the French painter and artists' model in a film?

Can you imagine a proposed movie about Suzanne Valadon, and Turner had agreed she would play it? And would be as wrong for that as she had been for *Diane*! Chris was being considered as the writer. At that time, he had very little money in the bank. I remember Auden came to town and stayed with us, and Chris said that he was working at MGM because he wanted to make some more money. He had only something like nine hundred dollars in the bank account, and that was it. Auden was shocked, and said, "I always worry when the bank account drops below ten thousand dollars!" Well, nine hundred dollars is a far cry from nine thousand dollars! And Chris had a young boyfriend who was going to school! So what did Turner say at the mention of Chris? "Oh, no! He wrote one of my worst movies!" Just because it hadn't gotten good reviews—and largely it hadn't gotten good reviews because *she* was cast in it. Wasn't it her last MGM film? Yes, I think it was. But Knopf wouldn't have been given it if Ingrid Bergman had been cast. He was a lesser producer, and Turner was leaving and they knew it, and that's why it happened.

At about the same time that Diane *was going into production, a film adaptation of* I Am a Camera *was being made in England.*

Yes, by Henry Cornelius.

Did Chris's commitment to Diane *prevent his participation in that 1955 film version of* I Am a Camera? *Or was it already long out of his hands, since the play adaptation had been written by John Van Druten?*

I don't think that was all done by Van Druten, because you see, the deal was a sixty-forty one. Chris was the forty percent. He always thought it was ungracious of Van Druten to take that extra ten percent, since they were friends. It was their mutual friend, Dodie Smith, who got Van Druten to write the play, because Dodie and Chris had discussed it, and I think Chris and Van Druten had discussed it, but Van Druten had said, "I don't see how to do it."

Van Druten was an English playwright best known prior to I Am a Camera *for his successful Broadway plays* The Voice of the Turtle *and* I Remember Mama.

Yes, and so Chris and Dodie had talked about it, and Dodie had said, "Let me see if I can do something." So without telling Van Druten that she and Chris had discussed it, what Dodie did was to tell John Van Druten, "I hear there's discussion of making *Goodbye to Berlin* into a play. I think it's a terrible idea! There's no way of doing it." She knew well enough how competitive Van Druten was, and her having said there was no way of doing it only whetted his appetite. He said, "I think I can do it." But he didn't have the graciousness to make it a fifty-fifty. So it all gets back to Chris, having had no part in the negotiations with Cornelius and the British production. That was a done deal. Though they did use Julie Harris, but part of the disaster of that film is . . . have you ever seen it?

I have. Spoiler alert: they changed the ending!

I was so hideously disappointed when the film was released in '56. There was no real know-how in it. Well, it's sunken into absolute ignominy, hasn't it? Who's ever heard of it, and why should they have? We had seen Cornelius's *Genevieve*, or "GeneVIeve," as Chris Wood always said. Do you know him? He was a British friend of Chris's, and with that oddly resonant name, Chris Wood, rather than Chris *Isher*wood. He called it "GeneVleve." We saw it with him, and we all enjoyed it and thought, well, Cornelius would have just as much success with *I Am a Camera*. And John Collier, the screenwriter, was a sweet man. I met him long after he wrote that. What a shame he didn't do a better job. But it was probably Cornelius's idea to really make the Laurence Harvey character the lead role, and Laurence Harvey wasn't appealing, at least not to Chris or me. We got to meet him, and he was a very likable, charming guy, but Chris thought he was just as *wrong* for the part as he could be! But somehow the emphasis was taken off Julie, and that really left a kind of emptiness in it. It didn't work somehow. Even Julie seemed off her mark. She was wonderful on stage.

And she would become as good a friend of yours as she already was of Chris's?

Well, she and Chris were great friends because of their proximity on the original production, yes, and she stayed here when she came to do *East of Eden*. It was my first experience of having a movie star not only in the house, but spending the nights there! During the week while she was filming, she had a motel room very near the studio, and then we would pick her up on Friday evenings and deliver her back on Sunday night, all the weeks she was out here working. I hadn't seen *East of Eden* in years, and it was just shown the other day, and she looks much better in it than I remembered. She wasn't conventionally pretty, but then she was determined not to be. I think it was partly her conviction that she was not a Hollywood beauty, not a camera beauty, and so she was only comfortable playing a character like Frankie in *The Member of the Wedding*. I think she psychologically decided to make herself physically unattractive whenever she appeared in front of a camera, because that's the only way she felt comfortable. Julie was always so hesitant even to think about movie work. She was very New York in that kind of way: she had that suspicion of Hollywood. She knew in the theater, no matter how close you get to the front row, there's still a distance between you and the audience, and you can use your voice and your movement and everything else to carry the day, to make a star of yourself. And that wonderful voice of hers is really so distinctive. Every time I just hear a few words in her voice, right away everything about her rushes in. She knew she could do that in the theater, but she didn't think she could in film. I think if she had been helped a little bit, she might have had more success looking better in movies, but after *East of Eden*, she was always cast in ugly duckling parts. I guess her best film work is *East of Eden*.

And certainly in her first Oscar-nominated film role, recreating her Broadway success in The Member of the Wedding.

I didn't see it on stage, but I actually saw the film just a few months before my first real encounter with Chris. It played at the Beverly Canon Theatre in Beverly Hills, I remember. It was a kind of art house where it opened, and I saw it with my brother long before I knew Julie.

Because of her, you and Chris actually got to visit the set of East of Eden?

Oh, yes, we went on the set a few times. Yes, whenever I see that film, it brings so much back, because we watched several key scenes from it being filmed. Julie was very sweet, and she loved Chris, so that made it all possible. Just to be on the sidelines and looking and listening, it was just heavenly for me. We saw the scene on the Ferris wheel. Well, we had to see it from below; they wouldn't let us on the crane, but we did see a great deal of that, and we met Lois Smith, who was playing the barmaid. It was her first movie role. We saw the James Dean scene with her at the bar, and a wonderful scene with Jo Van Fleet.

You also had the incredible opportunity to watch in real time as Elia Kazan—a co-founder of the influential Actors Studio and one of the

foremost theater and film directors of that period—shaped their per-
formances.

Oh, gosh, this was a real Hollywood production, with Kazan just demanding respect. Hollywood always groveled in the presence of New York directors, and he was at his ultimate. He hadn't even done *Cat on a Hot Tin Roof* yet: that's what he was rehearsing at the time. Yes, he was just as hot as can be, so there was a hush-hush on the set. And then as I said, on the weekends, on Friday afternoon, we used to pick Julie up in Burbank and bring her out to Santa Monica to stay with us for the weekend, and then take her back to Burbank on Sunday evening.

Would she relate her experiences to you about working on the film?

Yes, we were in on all the intimate events of the film, because we were seeing her regularly. Before we saw any of the filming, she had told us, "I have the most extraordinary young man playing opposite me. He's going to be a great star." And this was in the beginning of filming; I think they had just been rehearsing together. So of course we said, "Julie, let us at him. Let us see him." So she had a little party in her motel room, very close to the entrance at Warner Bros., and there were several other people there. We were so keen to meet this young actor who was going to be a great star, and she finally did introduce us, but she didn't say that this was the young man she'd been talking about. We asked her afterwards, "Which one was he?" She told us, and we said, "Julie, that scruffy-looking creature hulking in the corner? *He's* going to be a great star?" Well, he was doing all that Actors Studio stuff: slouching and sulking and being aloof and shy and wordless, and really over-doing it. Chris and I were dubious, so we said, "*Julie!*" But she said, "No, you're wrong." She held to it: "Oh, wait. He's going to be a great star." But Julie, she knew, and of course she was absolutely right. She was very trained in the theater, so we knew her judgment had to be right, because she wasn't fooled by amateurs.

And then you got to see for yourself, long before moviegoers did, James Dean in his star-making performance.

Yes! Certainly he came to life in front of the camera, and we did realize. He was just madly affected and really just not turning on any lights, like a dark closet, until the bright lights of the set and Kazan paying scrupulous attention to him, huddling him. I remember Jo Van Fleet telling a story that after one of Kazan's huddles with Dean, she and Dean got together for a scene and before the camera started rolling, Dean whispered into her ear some obscenities, probably at the suggestion of Kazan, because he wanted some kind of fury out of her. And she immediately said, "None of that crap! Don't you play those tricks on me! I'm an actor; I can produce my own motivation! Don't you put me on that level!" And really, Julie told us, made a big scene with Kazan, so both he and Dean had to back off. Can you imagine playing a cheap trick like that on her? And how right she was. Julie took Van Fleet's side. How traitorous of Kazan. But then, everything was riding on Dean in that film. Kazan had his way with the casting in every other part, and Dean was his doing, too, but he would trade Jo Van Fleet's faith in him as a director for Dean's. But they both had to back down.

Did you ever speak directly with James Dean?

Oh, yes, we had separate encounters. He was shy, but Chris knew just how to get him out of it and make him smile and relax. Chris was just terrific with people like that. He did open up some, but he carried the shy, *aw shucks* thing too far. But it was just dynamite for his career. The Actors Studio was just the ruin of Hollywood, but it was very hot then. I remember a long evening with Julie and Dean, going to a premiere at Grauman's Chinese, the four of us. We were in the limousine with them, going to the opening of something, but what could it have been? I have to look it up. It didn't matter what they were screening!

I'm sure it was thrilling enough just to be in Dean's and Julie's company, going to a premiere!

Yes! Oh, it was not a premiere: it was a very private and first screening of the film at Columbia, even though it wasn't made by Columbia; it was made at Warner Bros. That always seemed so peculiar to me. But this was just the most "in" and sought-after event: it wasn't a public screening; it was a screening solely for Hollywood people, so Marilyn Monroe was there! Bogart and Bacall were there! So you can imagine my ecstasy: I mean, every other person in the movies was there! The whole joint was full of them, and that was, of course, very pleasing! But if only I'd written my impressions down then! I've missed the opportunity to record *so* many exciting experiences I've had that I know would have interested so many people, and I didn't do it, and I wish I had.

But you were living it in the moment.

I was living it and loving it and lapping it up. And in a way, I think I didn't want to write it and spoil it. I would have written about it if I hadn't been in a close-at-hand situation with them as part of the invited audience. If it had been at a premiere, it would have been so much easier to record it, but not after actually participating as an invited guest.

Did you ever cross paths with Marlon Brando?

Yes. Chris was a good friend of Fred Zinnemann, who directed *The Men*. He was on the set of that film over and over, and had lots of encounters with Brando. Oddly enough, we went to the premiere of *On the Beach* in Hollywood with Tennessee, Brando, Chris, and me all in the back seat of a limousine. Brando was chastising Tennessee for being such a whore, because when we stopped in front of the Chinese Theatre and there were these bleachers with cheering fans, Tennessee was soaking it up much more than Brando.

But neither of them likely as much as you must have been. Just a decade earlier, you would have been one of those fans in the bleachers.

Yes, and as I said earlier, to get a seat in the bleachers, you had to be there by three or four o'clock in the afternoon, and sit it out until eight or eight-thirty!

Do you ever think back in sheer amazement at how, after having idolized movie people from behind the ropes at such events, you would ultimately be walking the red carpet in with them?

To me, they were gods and goddesses. That was my life, my education up until I was eighteen, and then Chris took me in hand. A little late, but not too late. Oh, but what a charmed life I've had so far. Imagine! It was just tailor-made for me: I learned to draw from life, and in no time, they were my sitters. It was just magic to have *Chris* and all that access to the art form that I dedicated myself to for so many years. Chris had such fun lining them up for me, then watching my eyes feast on them—and eventually getting them to come and sit for me. If he was in contact with somebody I wanted to draw, he would always make an effort, and that's how I snagged so many of them.

Just as he engineered other extraordinary opportunities for you, such as bringing you to Hollywood parties or onto movie sets, like East of Eden*.*

And Chris was the first person at Warner Bros. that Kazan showed the rough cut of *East of Eden* to, and Chris insisted on taking me. Kazan would have liked to say no, but he didn't dare! And so I was all eyes and ears, and smart enough to keep my mouth shut.

In a letter I found among Chris's papers, Kazan thanks him for his candor regarding Kazan's Broadway production of Cat on a Hot Tin Roof*. He writes, "I feel I have a good friend in you, Chris, and that I can always rely on you for the precise truth as you see it. I knew you* *were a good friend when you told me that you didn't like what I had done with CAT and I didn't feel any resentment or rancor at all. A lot of people I wouldn't take it from."*

Ah, we flew to the first preview performance in Philadelphia just to see it, yes.

He seemed to rely on Chris's judgment?

Kazan was very open, because Chris was a bona fide writer—he was very snobby about writers, especially British ones—*and* Chris was very shrewd about movies. Of course, I heard it all fresh, because he insisted on taking me with him to all the screenings he went to. But Kazan really listened to him and did a lot of editing at his suggestion. In fact, Chris helped him with a suggestion about the script for *East of Eden*. Chris hated ending it all in that gloomy bedroom with dreary Raymond Massey dying in bed.

What did Chris suggest to Kazan about the ending?

It was already in the can, but he was very frank with Kazan and told him, "Gosh, you know, keep it as short as you can." And Kazan listened to him. *I* even participated in some of those discussions about how *East of Eden* should end, but he didn't pay me the *slightest* attention! Every time I was with him and Chris, he was completely blind to me. His contempt was just so complete, I might as well have been invisible. But I learned a very important lesson, yes: to keep my mouth shut! But oh, that was very exciting, seeing that movie alone in the screening room with Kazan, just the three of us, and at the last minute, just as the movie was beginning, a door opened. It was in the middle of the morning, and a bright shaft of light came in, and some creature rushed in and sat in the first row. It was the first time James Dean was seeing the film, and that made it doubly exciting! And then to be so impressed by his performance! By the time the film was over, it was clear to both Chris and me what Julie had been assuring us of the whole time. But when the film was over, almost immediately he got out of his seat and rushed out, and Chris chased after him and caught up with him because he was so impressed by him, and he just had to tell him how terrific he was, how sensational he thought he was. And he told me that Dean gave way and started smiling and was shyly so pleased! Imagine having this middle-aged Englishman chasing after him to tell him how good he was?

And that Julie Harris's prophecy had indeed proved true! But then she also delivered a memorable performance in that film.

Yes, but I was very reluctant, to even somebody I knew as well as I knew Julie, to praise her work, and she was impossible anyway to praise, because she was always so down on herself—down really to an irritating point. But yes, the film holds up—except dreary Raymond Massey, but even then he wasn't on my mind! Dean was far more a draw for me than Raymond Massey, yes! And Richard Davalos was very nice, and we did see him quite a bit, but he was so outshone by Dean. Dean was the real attraction. He had the excitement and knew it.

For his performance in East of Eden, *James Dean became the first actor in Academy Award history to receive a posthumous nomination for Best Actor, while his co-star Jo Van Fleet won the Oscar for Best Supporting Actress.*

She was great in the film, and we were very keen to meet her. She came to a couple of parties we gave, and we got to know her quite well. We thought certainly she was going to be a regular movie performer, but she never had such a success in films again; never parts of any significance. *The Rose Tattoo* and *I'll Cry Tomorrow,* those are the only two I can remember. Oh, and she plays in another Kazan, *Wild River.*

From 1961, featuring Montgomery Clift.

But after the accident, the poor broken creature Clift became. I think that's how I got my sitting with him: it was after the accident. You see, I think he of course knew—he must have seen it in his films and in photographs—but maybe he hoped that an artist could restore the beauty. But he chose the wrong artist.

Clift's face had been disfigured in a car accident at the height of his stardom, but although plastic surgery had somewhat restored his looks, his chronic drinking and heavy painkiller use thereafter contributed to what Chris described as "a ghastly, shattered expression."

And of course he had to go on making films, but I think he was already resisting being photographed, just for stills, publicity photographs.

Yet he hauntingly sat for you in 1964, just two years before his untimely death at age forty-five.

Yes, and it was easy and relaxed, because he and Chris knew each other. As I mentioned earlier, they had met on the set of Clift's first film, *The Search*, because Chris and the director, Fred Zinnemann, were friends. Chris and Clift had got along very well, and that made it easier for me to do a sitting with him, because he liked Chris and he was pleasing Chris by doing his best for me. He was *so* changed, but being the kind of artist I am, I just have to draw everything I can see; I can't pick and choose. So I did a first drawing, which was OK, it looked like him, but it wasn't really interesting. And then we really got into it. He had his hand up to his face, and kept it and focused on me. His eyes were just big and really not just being still, but seeing me, as though. It was intimidating as well as extra exciting, working with him. But he had already had the car accident, and I know he was hoping from an artist, a sympathetic artist, that I could better restore his beauty than a photographer could, and of course I couldn't. It was only after I'd finished the drawing and got away from it for a few days that I saw how it was so good that it really revealed *all* the changes that the accident had caused. There was something about his eyes that got bigger and more vulnerable, and his mouth loosened and even slurred his speech. Oh, it must have been so painful for him. Well, it ruined him, his looks, and he knew it. He just kind of took the first drawing in his stride, but that second one was really probing. The memory of it is painful, because I know it hurt him.

I don't imagine, though, that you shied away from honestly and accurately drawing every detail of the transformed face that you saw in your sitting with him?

I couldn't do anything else, because I knew that was the basis of my talent. I really *saw* him, and I could record what I saw. So many portrait artists have ruined themselves by *always* wanting to do a likeness that will please the sitter. I didn't have that choice. It was everything I could see and get into the picture before my sitter collapsed, just from the strain of it, and I couldn't do anything but my best, all-out effort. I remember he was very close to me, and *really* looking at me, and *really* disappointed by that second one because it was *too* good; it was too accurate. The way he looked at me, I know he was hoping to see the beautiful Clift again, and instead he saw what he hoped he wouldn't see. But that already had become a familiar experience for me in my sittings, because I just have to record what I see, diplomatic or not. It's something I've thought about, really, over and over again.

That which differentiates you from the typical portrait artist?

What the difference is between me and the term *portrait artist*. We all think of it—even I think of it—in the same way: what we really mean by a portrait artist is what a Hollywood studio does for their actors. They've had the photos retouched until they're appealing. What I do are portraits of people as they look under extreme tension—which is created by sitting still for an hour and a half without moving, and having some mad creature demanding eye-to-eye contact and scrutinizing every detail of your face. How are you going to look when that's being done to you? Are you going to look like a retouched Hollywood portrait? No! You're going to look in a way that even you don't recognize. Maybe you recognize it first thing in the morning when you get up, but you're not going to look like that in what we all assume a portrait artist is going to present: a lovely likeness like Queen Elizabeth got in England. To me, the whole experience of working from life—and it's so hard being raised on movies and being so scrupulous in my demands for how the actors look on screen—is that I then tell the truth about them in life, because that's what life is. I guess movies taught me, but what the excitement of life is is what I can't see in the movies, but I can see in reality: everything that the screen really can't show you or won't show you. Anyway, the truth of the experience for me, even though Clift in my portraits doesn't look like he looks in his early movies, is that the difference, in a way, makes it more exciting. It makes it different from what I've seen in the movies, and I find out what it is that makes him look different. I find out that it's age, it's discouragement, it's loss of beauty that have made his eyes sad. I must get that look of sadness. Of course, I don't say to myself, "Capture a look of sadness." I say, "It's a different look, and what is it?" By looking closely enough that I can reproduce it, I find out, "Oh, it's a look of sadness." But I only see it once I put it into the drawing. It was so exciting to have a creature like Clift, whom I only knew through the movies and maybe a brief encounter or two with Chris, whom Clift adored. So he was a sitting duck for me, and he couldn't really hide from me once he agreed to sit. And so I disappointed him with a likeness of him that he was hoping would correct what the studio photographers couldn't. He was unlucky to find me as the portraitist.

But how lucky for you.

How lucky. I don't think that would have soothed him, nor would it soothe anybody. What do I hear most often as the first comment out of my sitter, when they see their portrait? "Oh, I look so sad." Why? Because I see them under this extreme stress that is unavoidable, trying to be still for an unnaturally long time in front of somebody who is looking at them as though with a microscope. I've had to face the fact that my role as a portrait artist is similar to that of an executioner: I tell the truth, and that truth is death of all hope of looking lovely. The truth is, to me, the real beauty. The Hollywood loveliness is a lie, and the truth is far more exciting—and far more tragic even than your most tragic Hollywood film.

CHAPTER 5

The right kind of beautiful young man

Don, photographed by George Platt Lynes in New York, December 1953.
(Photo © THE ESTATE OF GEORGE PLATT LYNES, courtesy of Don Bachardy)

Despite the idyllic private world you created for yourselves, you and Chris very much remained men of the world. And as gay men in the 1950s and '60s, you certainly faced risks from multiple fronts: societal disapproval, professional discrimination, and even—with frequent police raids on gay establishments—possible arrest, public condemnation, and physical danger.

Oh, yes. In our early years, in the '50s, I'd already been to gay bars with my brother. They wouldn't let me in unless it was really an after-hours, illegal operation: parties in the basement of some down-town building. There were various gay bars that would suddenly go up overnight like mushrooms, and last maybe for a month or six weeks—maybe two months at the most—and then they'd be raided inevitably. But my Chris kept me out of gay bars, and by that time, my relationship with my brother had changed, and he had his own domestic routine, so I didn't go out to gay bars. And I realized it wasn't a deprivation: I really wasn't all that interested in it. If any-thing, I'm more embarrassed by making a pass at someone in a gay bar than I am in a straight one. So I knew going out to gay bars just wasn't necessary, even on my trips to New York. Of course I heard about the gay bars there and was curious enough to go maybe once or twice, but I almost never remember going home with somebody I met in a bar. If I wanted to meet young men, I didn't use bars for it. It's just something I suppose I got from Chris: he was never much of a bar-goer, and I guess I just assumed his attitude.

Like other young American men of the 1950s, coming of age for you meant also becoming eligible for possible compulsory military service. Chris's psychologist friend Evelyn Hooker provided some guidance, but how did you handle the daunting prospect of appearing before the draft board, when your summons inevitably arrived?

She was very helpful to me, yes, and she advised me, but I had to face the music, and I learned to stand up for myself. So I defied all their suppositions: I told them I was queer. I remember being badgered by the old men who were the physical examiners—and that was just horrible, those physical examinations—and one of them, an old, kind of sour man, asked me, "You mean if you saw a naked young man standing in line waiting for a physical exami-nation, you couldn't keep your hands off of him?" And my answer was, "Not if he was attractive!" That kind of surprised him, and si-lenced him. He didn't have a comeback for that!

And that probably sealed your dismissal!

That was really the end of the examination, yes! He wasn't prepared for that answer. And I was pleased with myself, because it was only a few years of being with Chris that taught me to at least remember his example.

And to proudly and boldly assert who you were.

Yes, but I was scared. Oh, that would have just been the *end* of me if I'd had to go into the service. That would've just been a ruination of me, because I'd had enough of it in high school and early college, all that gung-ho stuff. It just would have devastated me. And I didn't want to leave *Chris.* Well, it was very important to me. I knew being drafted would be utter disaster for me, so I was just determined to keep out of it at any cost. And also I had an older brother who was a mental case. Ted went to see Evelyn Hooker, and oh, she agreed with me. She thought that it would be terrible if I got drafted.

Potentially problematic not only for you personally, but I imagine also for your parents for you to be absent, given the demands of Ted's mental health challenges?

Evelyn was very helpful, a very good woman. Yes, I got every bit of help I could get. Oh, thank God I got out of it.

Yours, unfortunately, is not dissimilar to the experience of many other brave yet rightfully fearful gay men of that time who outed themselves before the draft board, hoping to secure their exemption on the basis of the American Psychiatric Association's then-classification of homosexuality as a "sociopathic personality disturbance."

Sure. Yes, if that's what you want to call it, then yes. However they wanted to phrase it, I wasn't going.

In later years, you and Chris became very publicly known as a couple, but in those first years together, how were you introduced to his colleagues in Hollywood?

Chris didn't make a secret of who he was. He didn't suppress his queerness, and he never escorted women to public occasions. Even with Bill Caskey, they went places together in a way no other queer couples in Hollywood had done. The other queers were outraged by Chris. They didn't see him as a pioneer in their cause; they saw him as an invader of polite manners: that if he showed up at a party with a man many years younger than he, they felt that was betraying our society; that was telling on us as queers, what should only be kept in private with our own kind. He really was a pioneer in that sense. Very early, once we were living together, he was taking me to the Huxleys and the Stravinskys—and what higher society? Those were the ultimate reaches of snobbism—in his world, certainly: to share Igor Stravinsky and Aldous Huxley with a boy of eighteen or nineteen was the ultimate that Chris could achieve. It was several months before I was taken to Vedanta to meet Prabhavananda.

Christopher Isherwood was a longtime pupil of Swami Prabhavananda, who was an Indian monk, philosopher, religious teacher, and founder of the Vedanta Society of Southern California.

That was a much trickier undertaking. Why? Because it meant much more to Chris. I mean, he was gambling a friendship, an intimate friendship; a love, really. He loved both the Stravinskys and the Huxleys, but he loved Swami in an even deeper way. Swami's significance for him ran deeper even than the significance of Stravinsky and Huxley. He was afraid, you see, that a snub from Prabhavananda to me might be just an unconscious carelessness, but he was wrong, of course. He didn't take into consideration how important *he* was to Prabhavananda. He was Prabhavananda's prize pupil, but he didn't want to trust it, so it had to be just right. And he had to be sure of *me*: sure that I would be able to behave, even with all the good credits I had up until that point. So it did take longer. I don't think I have ever voiced that before. It is the fruit of long pondering by me that it suddenly drifted into my view: that knowledge that it took him longer to introduce me. But of course, that was much more intimate to Chris.

And was the introduction successful, when it ultimately came about?

Of course it would be, because Prabhavananda would have the sense to know that Chris was queer. He might have been deeply shocked inside because he was, after all, heterosexual in his outlook. Though he was a monk, and a scrupulous monk, it was women to him that were the natural sex objects. To afford a man that kind of feeling would have taken a great deal of extra effort from him. People are trying to say that Stravinsky had a queer streak, too. I never observed anything of my own in Stravinsky that would lead me to question his heterosexuality, except the presence of Bob Craft in his house.

Robert Craft was a conductor and writer known for his intimate professional relationship with Stravinsky.

One night, after a long evening with the four of us, Bob Craft saw Chris and me up to the front door of our house on Sycamore Road, and I followed him back to the gate, and he suddenly startled me by pushing me against the wall and giving me a firm kiss on the mouth—and it was more than a goodbye kiss, with a real kind of almost roughness of unintentional intent. I never told Chris. It was one of the few things I never told him about someone we knew personally, but I think that earmarks my sensitivity as somebody who doesn't indulge in the stirring of the pot just to see what happens, just to see if it would change his attitude toward Bob as an intimate friend. I just thought, why take the chance? And also, it would be drawing attention to my charms to say, "Oh, well, I have a nice little tidbit to tell you about Bob."

Nor did you tell Chris how truly intimate your photo session with George Platt Lynes had been.

No. I still don't know that he didn't guess.

The resulting photos may have suggested it.

Something whispers to me that he might have had a sense, but then as I knew better than to cause trouble between him and Bob, he knew it was best in his relations with me not to know too much about my personal experiences. He wanted always to be able to speak to me intimately, but not to tread irresponsibly on my own private whatever it was.

Did you also ultimately become a practitioner of Vedanta?

Oh, I was initiated a full-blown Vedantist, and from the lips of Prabhavananda. You can't get any closer to Vedanta than that. Of course, Chris didn't wait *too* long to introduce us, because he knew that if he let the gossips get in there too early and too long, they would make it more difficult. And it never was: I went to the weekly dinners at Vedanta Place with Chris, and I was fully accepted. I was initiated by Prabhavananda, so I'm a real, honest-to-goodness Vedantist. I already knew it all from Chris; there was nothing Prabhavananda needed to tell me, but I was just so willing and pleased to know that he took me seriously enough to do it for me and initiate me. He was very respectful of me.

Vedanta is an ancient Eastern philosophy and meditative practice based on a belief that God—or Brahman—exists in all beings; the only purpose in life, therefore, is to search for self-knowledge, to connect with that inner divinity.

Chris was a walking advertisement for Vedanta: I mean, he was *formed* by Prabhavananda and that belief. He was *desperate* before he got to Prabhavananda, and then he knew that it was what he had been looking for all along, and gave it everything he had, and that was considerable. And Prabhavananda adored him, treasured him. He was one of his disciples he was proudest of.

And essentially, Chris became the spokesman for Vedanta.

He wrote about it. Those books are wonderful. They were so helpful to me as introductions to what Vedanta is and how to handle it. They're so clear, so unpretentious: no mystery, no voodoo.

Just tools you've found to be helpful in navigating your life?

Yes! I've taken it for granted for so long that I even forget how important it is, because it's given me so much help. Well, it's been terrific for me, because it really has worked. It's my only religious experience, and I'm very grateful for it. It's all I've needed; I don't need anything else. I'm really not kidding when I say that. What Chris taught me is just fine with me. I learned it very early, and I knew that that was the end of any kind of search I might worry about making for help with my life, and it's never disappointed me. I'm still a faithful Vedantist, and I'll be faithful to the end, I know it, because I need it and rely on it, and of course, it's kept alive by Chris himself.

Indeed, you're still prolifically working, thereby following a Vedantic principle that Chris taught you: "Work for the work itself, not the fruits thereof." Consequently, rather than selling much of your portraiture, you've held onto most of it—a now quite extensive body of work that you ultimately plan to turn over to The Huntington and other art museums?

Yes. In my early years, I always felt it was my responsibility as a kind of act of appreciation for my sitters—that is, if they didn't absolutely loathe what I did—that I had a professional photographer friend who would come here periodically and photograph my work, and I would send people 8x10 prints. I did that for years until my friend was no longer available to me, so I stopped doing it.

You mentioned that Chris introduced you to Aldous Huxley early in your relationship. Huxley was the author of the seminal dystopian novel Brave New World, *and, like Chris, was also a Vedantist and*

English expatriate living in California. What were your interactions like with him?

Chris loved Huxley. They were very good friends, but Huxley was heterosexual and really so much more an intellectual writer. Chris had great respect for him, but he stood for something that Chris thanked his gods that he wasn't: an intellectual like him. But Huxley was so kind: he was *wonderful* to me, and Maria, his first wife, was a very impressive personality. I only had one sitting with him, but he was so good to me that I did four drawings, and they were all good, and Chris was so proud of me because he knew they were good, and he knew how important they were to me.

How did you fare with Chris's former schoolmate and lifelong friend, Edward Upward? They were fellow members of "The Auden Group," as journalists then dubbed a collection of innovative 1930s British poets and writers that centered around Chris and W. H. Auden, and also included Stephen Spender, Cecil Day-Lewis, Louis MacNeice, and Rex Warner.

Yes, yes. He was very kind and very intelligent, and we got along, but that was, in a way, a much more important and personal relationship that Chris had with *him*, because they were young writers together, and he was very much rooted in Chris's whole history.

What was the experience like for you of going to Hollywood parties, of being among Chris's colleagues? Were they welcoming, or just merely politely accepting of your relationship?

Yes, always. I sensed it at the time. Well, of course I had to be observant: we were the only queer couple. In a house full of Hollywood movie stars at the Selznicks', we were the only two men together, and there was this wide discrepancy in our ages, which made it even worse. And everybody had to know: if they knew anything about Chris, they knew about his queerness, because he didn't hide it, and I knew that *I* was marked because of my own queerness and age and size and voice. But I'll tell you one thing: it was so important to Chris to support us that though Eddie Knopf and his wife Mildred invited Chris several times to dinner at their house, which was right here in Brentwood, he never took me with him, and didn't tell them about me or our domestic life.

Edwin H. Knopf, the brother of publisher Alfred A. Knopf, was the producer at MGM who oversaw the production of Diane, from Chris's screenplay.

We entertained on our own from a very early time, and we invited friends to dinner and cooked for them here in the house. We had both the Huxleys and Stravinskys here, and either cooked for them or hired a woman to cook for them, but he never invited the Knopfs to the house. Because if Chris shocked Eddie, or, more importantly, Mildred...

It might have risked his further employment at MGM and elsewhere in Hollywood?

They were square, you know. They weren't aficionados of any kind of gay circles. The gays would have found them dreary, and they would have been embarrassed in a largely male party. I understood it, and I knew exactly why Chris excluded me: because he was supporting us by working at MGM.

So you never took offense at this?

No, I just knew it.

Did you ever face outright homophobia in Hollywood?

Oh, yes. Joseph Cotten was overtly rude to me at one of the Selznicks' parties. He made loud comments within my earshot, calling us "half-men"! That was what Joseph Cotten deplored: "Half-men! Disgusting half-men!" Oh, yes, he went out of his way.

And Cotten had stature then both in Hollywood and at that party, having co-starred with Jennifer Jones in four movies produced by her husband, David O. Selznick. A longtime associate of Orson Welles, Cotten had made his Hollywood debut in Welles's Citizen Kane, *which many critics rank as the greatest film ever made. He then went on to become a popular leading man of the 1940s.*

And there were other instances, but on the whole, people's respect of Chris in social occasions prevented them from making any overt acknowledgment of the fact that they were scandalized. But as I say, it was the other queers at the Selznicks' who would have been outraged more than the straights. And oh, boy, in our early years together at movie star parties—and they were movie star parties like nowhere else on the planet—we were the only openly queer couple *ever!* Rock Hudson and all the rest of them avoided us like the plague.

Guilt by association—was that their worry?

I think he just assumed that we would disapprove of him.

Because he remained closeted, while you and Chris were so daringly out?

Perhaps, but disapprove? Not at all! He was a handsome, attractive, gorgeous man whom I would have loved to have done a sitting with. And imagine that he was the biggest queer movie star, and I never got a sitting with him? And all the straights I worked with? My own kind provided the biggest resistance. I got to Tab Hunter; didn't catch Rock Hudson.

Hunter ultimately sat for you, but much later in his life.

Much later, yes, and even then with suspicion. Yes, suspicion, as though I were a doctor rather than an artist: a surgeon kind of looking for a facial disease. But being queer and knowing that the other was queer, you would have thought it would have facilitated, but it always made it much more difficult.

Why was that, do you think?

Well, for actors, and particularly Hollywood actors, it was the one reputation that you simply could not afford to develop. And even though it was almost always known or suspected, it was just the big bugaboo. Any whiff of queerness: uh-uh. I only got at Tab Hunter late in his career.

He eventually outed himself in a memoir, as did Farley Granger, although very late in their respective lives, and after their movie careers had ended.

But it was common knowledge. I mean, if you were in the line to receive gossip, intimate gossip, it was something everybody knew.

Did you ever get to Granger?

We knew him slightly, but somehow I was never in a position to ask him, and I was pretty good at measuring my chances. After the first years, I guessed who would be easily available, who would be difficult to pin down, and finally, the ones who really might say, "Yes, of course" and never do it. And that was with Chris working on my behalf with each one, too, trying to facilitate it.

In his book Behind the Screen, *William J. Mann wrote that "once, spotting Don Bachardy and Christopher Isherwood at a party, Tony Perkins grabbed his children and moved across the room—'for fear we'd pinch his ass or something,' Bachardy said, 'as if we were the high priests of queerdom.'"*

Well, I was madly in love with him, but like a fan. It was very short-lived: I suddenly realized who he really was. I never got a sitting with him. He was leery of me, and he was a slippery character, very sly. But oh, he was so attractive in the flesh. Wonderful coloring, yes.

It's come to light in recent years that he and Tab Hunter were lovers at the height of their movie popularity.

Yes, one of the best things that either of them ever did was to become a couple!

Another closeted actor, Roddy McDowall, who was quite literally a life-long movie star, did become a sort of friend of yours, and as a fellow movie fan helped facilitate some introductions for you to various Hollywood personalities he had also cultivated as friends.

Oh, he was a pure movie bug. He knew them all, knew all about their careers, and did a lot to help them if they needed money. He was really a Hollywood historian by instinct, and he was very right to regard Hollywood from the historical point of view, and how important that was. He was a very gracious, enthusiastic movie lover. We saw quite a bit of him because, of course, Chris was somebody to him, but I was less than somebody to him, so he was very kind of phony with his kind of pretended fondness of me. He photographed Chris a lot, and even took some photographs of me, but just to please Chris, or not to make trouble with his relationship with him. And he sat for me several times, but always sat so badly.

How so?

Because it was intentional: he was always moving, to sabotage me! Even with his hand to his head, which I thought would maybe force him to keep his head still, he was still *consciously* making it as tough for me as possible. Yet he was particular about his behavior in his movie career and his movie personality, and was a very professional photographer and in everything else he did. I had at least three sittings, if not four, with him, and he did them all badly. He'd get so funny sitting for me, as though he were embarrassed. Nothing could embarrass that guy; it was all just showing me *exactly* what he thought of me, and it wasn't friendly. And the better the drawings of him I did, the less he liked me. I did drawings of him that were exactly like him, which means they revealed everything that was lacking in his social personality. But I never showed any of them, because I figured, well, for some reason or other, he didn't want me to get anything good, and I thought that was just contemptible.

Why do you think that was?

It might have been, you know, queer reasons: maybe I was too much younger and better-looking than I should have been for his tastes, and yet his partner at the time was a beautiful young man. I don't think he would have had anything to do with me if it weren't for Chris. He really had the sense to respect Chris very much, so all the phony actorliness in him came out when we were all together, but especially the farther away Chris got from the two of us, he could show me in so many delicate ways how he had contempt for me. And it wasn't even contempt; it was just natural superiority. When we were with another actor or somebody in the business, oh, he was just twisting with charming talk, and turning his back on me whenever he could. He was difficult for me, I think, just because he couldn't help regarding me as competition. Perhaps he was thinking, "Oh, if only Christopher had found somebody like *me.*" But I think it was just almost like a professional jealousy, because he was a photographer as well as an actor.

And, like you, he was also pursuing celebrity sitters.

Yes, but I mean, the pursuit? They just fell into his lap! They were there! Oh, he really squeezed all of his experience dry and used it and developed it and encouraged it. When he was taking pictures of us both, we were so still for him and did everything right. But though he was so precise and demanding about his photography, without having to speak the kind of behavior he expected from his sitters, when I asked him to sit for me, I was shocked that he was moving around the whole time and being cute. I think he really wanted to defeat me. But all he did was to raise my defenses sufficiently that I could have gotten a successful drawing out of him if he'd introduced a dog into the picture! Oh, he was shaming, but I just wouldn't stop with sitters who were consciously resisting me, consciously torturing me, and kind of laughing at me while I was trying to draw them, like Roddy. I wouldn't throw down the pencil or do anything like that because I'm a professional, and a much better one than Roddy was, because he couldn't help being a snob and showing his contempt for somebody he didn't like. It was a long time before Roddy stopped being suspicious of me, but otherwise I forgave him. In other ways, he really was a very good man.

And in a way, he would eventually reward you for all you had endured with him: by orchestrating a private audience with your childhood idol, Bette Davis.

That meant his life was not in vain! He set it up, I know, to please us: to please Chris by pleasing me. But he made it happen for me, so I can't complain!

We'll discuss that ultimate encounter a little further on. Did you form any intimate social relationships with other gay men in the film industry?

Oh, yes, with George Cukor and Lenny Spigelgass, a screenwriter, and art and music directors. Chris and I got to know George Cukor very well. We were both *very* fond of him.

Among Spigelgass's many credits were the film adaptations of the musical Gypsy *and of his own hit play* A Majority of One, *both of which starred Rosalind Russell. George Cukor was Hollywood's preeminent "woman's director," working with the likes of Garbo, Crawford, both Hepburns, Bergman, Shearer, Garland. Did you discuss any of them with Cukor? And/or any of his many now-classic films? Just a few that instantly come to mind are* Dinner at Eight, The Women, The Philadelphia Story, Gaslight, Adam's Rib, Born Yesterday, A Star Is Born, *and* My Fair Lady.

Yes, and especially the actresses in them! And bless him, he told us lots and lots, knowing that we would be interested, and me especially interested in the women. Oh, the wonderful stories! But you know, I was so determined not to be seen as a movie fan, I missed all kinds of opportunities to really cross-examine him. Such lost opportunity, so many times, because for years I was just so shamey-faced about being a Hollywood movie fan that I wanted to keep it a secret, so I kept my mouth shut, even though George Cukor was a very good friend.

He was a good friend, but what was it like to actually also be directed by the venerable George Cukor? You and Chris make a brief appearance alongside Candice Bergen and Jacqueline Bisset in a party sequence in Rich and Famous, *Cukor's last film, which was a remake of the Bette Davis–Miriam Hopkins movie,* Old Acquaintance.

Well, it's right at the beginning. If you're three minutes late for the film, you'll miss us, and it's just a second of us on film, but it took an *entire* day! At the end of that day, we were *so* ready to skedaddle! Well, you know, we loved him a lot, and he was always himself, but it was an awful lot for him to take charge of that at his age. But he never lost his way, and he was always fun to be with.

But in your experience, gay men working behind the cameras in Hollywood—even one of such stature as Cukor—were far likelier to befriend you than those more directly in the public eye?

Oh, yes. Of course in those years, Rock Hudson *was* talked about. Queers knew about him, but heterosexuals didn't, really, until his death from AIDS. It took something like that to inform them, although I suppose some of them had heard the scuttlebutt. I knew through lots of my queer friends who were invited to his house and liked him a lot, what fun and how charming he was, though we were never invited. There was always a distance in his behavior if he were at the same party as we were. We never did more than shake hands, and never even had any kind of conversation. And yet he was often present at the Selznicks', and looking sensational.

I imagine you similarly knew non-actors in the industry who stayed closeted for professional reasons?

Yes. There was a man in publicity, and he and his friend were both queer. One worked in the studios and one had his publicity firm, but they wouldn't go to parties together. Ever. They would escort women if they went to the Selznicks' or any other party, but Chris didn't. Ever. He deplored "passers."

How about Charles Laughton? He was your next-door neighbor in Santa Monica and a friend?

Chris was very fond of Charles. Charles was a kind of magic personality to Chris, because when he was a teenager, he had seen Charles acting in the theater in London and admired him, and admired his early movies. It was Laughton's relief to have Chris for a friend, with whom he could totally indulge himself by acknowledging his own queerness. Also, not have to include Elsa, because Elsa only was allowed in the house after his death.

Laughton had been married to fellow star Elsa Lanchester for many decades, but they weren't living together?

She only took residence after his death. She was in a house on Curson Avenue in West Hollywood. Charles didn't want her here; this was for Terry and him.

Terry Jenkins was an aspiring young actor with whom Laughton had found lasting love.

Terry was a very handsome young man, and very sweet, respectable; really very nice. Both Chris and I liked him, and Charles was really in love with him. I think that was the first time in Charles's life, and right at the end of it, that Terry was on hand. And because Charles adored Chris, he bought the house next door to Chris just to have access to him, and to bring his boyfriend. That was the whole purpose of the house, but of course Elsa was very censorious about that! I think it was the first time that Charles stood up to Elsa, saying he was going to have this house and that she could do whatever she wanted. He was really underfoot here all the time, because he couldn't get enough of Chris, but then it was less than a year before he got the illness that killed him. And then wouldn't you know it: Elsa, who was against the house from the beginning, took it over, and she used it for a weekend house for years. Twenty years, anyway.

What was your relationship then like with Lanchester?

I think she retroactively punished Charles by always making clear her dislike of me; that was her revenge on Charles. And she disliked me naturally because she saw me as an obstruction to her access to Chris, though I consciously never asserted that power. But I knew I had it. I could have said to Chris, "I don't want you going over to Elsa; I take it personally," but I didn't do that. I knew that she would rather have him to herself, but occasionally she would invite me formally, just out of respect for Chris, I suppose. We always knew that we didn't like each other—that was unspoken. It didn't occur to her that I would tell him just how nasty she'd been. So Chris knew: he knew all about it from me. I didn't keep it a secret from him, because I knew he would understand, and I knew that he knew that she was half-mad, anyway! She was a very, very unbalanced creature. Well, how unbalanced is it to want to seduce queer men, and yet only *tolerate* queer men, both socially and in her bed? That's really so frustrating, isn't it? I think she took pleasure in tormenting Charles, in knowing that she was keeping him away from the company that he would have indulged himself in much more, if it hadn't been for her. How's that for perversity? And she thought she could charm Chris, and she did, but it was sexual love for Chris: she would have just dragged him into bed if she'd felt he would've allowed it.

After Laughton's death, was she then as much a presence here in your house as he had been?

No, because she made trouble with me. We had a wonderful cleaning woman whom they took on for the Hollywood house they were living in. Dorothy used to tell us all the gossip. They had knock-down fights—screaming, hysterical fights. Dorothy told us in detail, and of course we were all ears! Elsa claimed never to have guessed that Charles was queer. Well, any fool! She took that stance because she could. It was a very good way of handling him: she was the betrayed woman. And they were both almost literally in love with Chris. Dorothy told us that they fought over Chris in the Hollywood house. But still I tried with Elsa: she and Charles were two of my early celebrity sitters. Charles sat for me in his hospital room during his final illness. He was just impossible: he moved the whole time. He was really insufferable, telling me, "Well, I was moving because that was good for you as an artist." I just bit my lip. If he'd understood *anything* about being an artist, he would have sat still. Whereas Elsa sat very well, but smoldering. And what did she do after I did three perfectly good pictures of her, and they all looked like her? She took me downstairs to show me their art collection, which was actually very poor, and finally a drawing that she herself had done, which she told me was better than anything I had done of her that day! Well, it was just not true. But I was young and I just kept my mouth shut. Can you imagine an ego like that? And being exercised on a young man whom she assumed was just the dumbest creature living? But that was always her attitude to me.

When you see her films now, are you able to separate out your opinion of her as a person from that of her as a screen personality?

She was really a personality. I mean, she was really always Elsa Lanchester in movies: she didn't have a range, but she did an awful lot with her identity. She was very insecure, because she really was a Cockney, and she was always conscious of being a personality supported by Laughton, but she had her own career, and she was good. But she also loved Chris, and oh, how she hated me!

Just as Laughton ultimately exerted his independence from Lanchester, as you matured some years into your relationship with Chris but still were quite a young man, you exerted your own sexual independence for a period. Although Chris accommodated this, his private torment inspired him to write the novel that is arguably his masterpiece, A Single Man.

It was very difficult, because it hurt him. Yes, of course it did, but my argument was, "You've had so much more experience than I've had," because I'd had very little sex with guys before him. Knowing I was queer since I was eleven still didn't do anything to help me get over my shyness, my uncertainty of myself, my believing in myself. Oh, if I hadn't met Chris! But then I met him because I *had* to. Yes, it had to be fated. It seemed to me I didn't deserve such a man. Such good fortune to have him as an example, as somebody who showed me the way to live and to not hide, not to be ashamed of myself; how to on occasion flaunt it, use it even for all of its shock value. That was so exhilarating and liberating for me!

You've said about the period leading up to your meeting Chris: "I was just waiting to be told who I was."

Yes! And he was just the *ideal* person. He might be the only person in the world who *knew*, who *could*. And I knew that the things that he said to me weren't just wishful thinking. Every *fiber* of his being was behind it, because he lived it; he knew what he was saying. Words *meant* something to him; they meant an *immense* deal. When he said something, he was just determined to mean it and to express it as fully as he could. That was his triumph. And with all of that, he managed to be modest, as well, and to aspire for something higher.

And through his example and inspiration, so, too, did you. In 1961, you decided to try your wings.

After going for four years to Chouinard—and as I said, I didn't just go there; I practically lived there—I had the idea of going to London to the Slade School. Yes, it was time for me to try my wings, I think, and I used the Slade School as a reason to be on my own from Chris. But my departure was heartbreaking for us both, because when it came right down to it, I was as scared of London as I was frightened of going to art school for the first time here. We just wept buckets before I left, and from the moment I got to London, we were just weeping on the phone; we were so lonely for each other. But I had the greatest good fortune. I had stopped on the way in New York, and because we had been seeing Richard Burton and his first wife, Sybil, here, I went to see *Camelot*, which he was doing with Julie Andrews.

Just a few years prior, Chris had reported in his diary that at a party Laurence Olivier gave for the playwright and actor Emlyn Williams, "Richard Burton got drunk and told Don he was as beautiful as Vivien Leigh!" Despite its drunken delivery, what a compliment to receive!

Oh, yes, it was! Well, we had become good friends when he was making movies here. So I went backstage at *Camelot* to say hello, and there Richard was with Sybil. When I told them I was on my way to London to go to the Slade, Sybil said, "Well, why don't you stay in our house in Hampstead? Richard's got the next three months in the show, and the house is empty!" My plan, when I arrived, was to go to Stephen Spender and his wife's house in St John's Wood.

The poet Stephen Spender was a longtime friend of Chris's. Meanwhile, a wealthy couple named Russell and Edna McKinnon had sponsored your trip. Who were they, and how had their patronage come about?

They were a married couple, presumably heterosexual, but I'm certain he was totally queer. He hired me as a portraitist to do several sittings with him, and I remember she sat for me, too. It seemed to me certainly a marriage of convenience, and the convenience being really just a marriage to make him seem more heterosexual. I think that mattered to him, but he certainly seemed totally queer to me, but without ever referencing anything totally queer. But yes, then he sponsored me, and really financed my trip to London. He certainly paid for my passage there.

And then Stephen Spender had arranged for you to study without credit at the Slade School?

Yes, and really, it was totally unnecessary. I really just used it as a reason to go to London, and a reason to stay there and have a kind of studio there for a while, and the while turned out to be almost an entire year. I arrived in January, and by April, Chris had already come over to stay with me.

What was your relationship like with Spender?

Oh, just really as with all of Chris's friends who became my friends. But I stayed with him and his wife Natasha the first days, and that was absolutely a mistake. It was so depressing, so miserable, that part of London, and the moment I got to the house, I realized they didn't want me there. It was as obvious as it could be. Even Matthew and Lizzie, their children, made it clear to me I didn't fit in, standing in the hall outside my bedroom door and snickering and peeking in. They thought it was just too funny for words, this pretense of mine of being a houseguest. It was so like Stephen to say, "Oh, Donny, come and stay with Natasha and me," and then when I got there say to Natasha, "I don't know how we're going to get rid of him soon enough." Oh, boy, I couldn't get out of there fast enough, and did I start work immediately! And so that Burton house, which I had graciously refused: after the first week, I called up Sybil, a transatlantic call, and asked, "Sybil, is that

offer you made me still good?" She said, "Of course, darling!" And
so I made plans to move up to Hampstead the very next day. I was
so relieved. I was told how to contact Richard's brother, Ifor, and
his wife. I met them in Hampstead, and they took me right across
the street to a dear two-story house with a living room, a dining
room, a kitchen, and two bedrooms upstairs, with a bathroom upstairs and a little half-bathroom downstairs. It was just perfect: I
had a whole wonderful house! And Ifor and his wife, very nice
people, lived right across the street, if I needed any help. So I immediately called Chris and said, "Come as soon as you can!" So
when Chris came over, it was a snug little place for us to live, and
we could even entertain there; we could cook for our friends. And
of course, when the three months were up, what did Richard do?
He went to Rome to make *Cleopatra*, and he met Elizabeth Taylor!
So Chris and I had the house for a year, without rent! Wasn't that
just the greatest good fortune?

Great fortune indeed for you and Chris, but not so much for Sybil Bur-
ton: her husband and Elizabeth Taylor would launch their storied af-
fair during the making of that colossal film, just as your storied career
was being launched from the Burtons' empty house back in London.

It really was, yes: my career officially began there. Hampstead
was right on the Northern line, and it was a direct line to the Slade
School, so I didn't even have to change trains. It took me less than
fifteen minutes to get to school each morning. Of course, I was
going in mid-term, so I wasn't asking for credit. The term came
to an end after a couple of months, but long before it came to an
end, I had started asking everybody I met if they would sit for me,
as I had here. When I was going to Chouinard, I had started doing
sittings only with my friends, and it just seemed a natural progres-
sion to start doing that in London. I sometimes did three sittings
in a day! And getting from sitter to sitter, either on the Underground or a cab, if it was somebody way far out of town. Doing
that on my own the first months before Chris came, yes, that was

a very exciting time. Of course, we were speaking on the phone and writing almost daily, and I was keeping him up to the minute on all of my adventures.

But also during this time, you were at least peripherally attending the Slade, under the mentorship of the painter Keith Vaughan?

He was officially my tutor, but I didn't need a tutor! You know, it was just kind of making it official so I wasn't just kind of visiting in and out. I didn't need or even want tutoring, but he used to look in on me at the Slade. And I was just almost stiff with embarrassment, joining these painting classes late, to use the models, to paint the models. I guess I felt I had to have an official role there rather than just be visiting and asking people to sit for me, which is exactly what the year turned out to be. I think after barely a month of showing up at the Slade, maybe only a few days in the week and finally not at all, I quit going, because I was just calling up everybody I knew there, and asking them to sit for me.

After having developed such an insatiable appetite at Chouinard for working with live models, in London you were able to corral a roster of most remarkable sitters. You've referred to this period as your "boot camp."

1961 was a busy year: I really did work at my craft. I wanted to show Chris that I was really worth his time and trouble, so I went to London with the Slade School as a cover. Well, I've *always* been dedicated to my work, but then I was doing a lot of it *daily*. It wasn't just a couple of days a week; I was *always* at it. It was a real obsession with me: I wanted to be an artist, and I wanted to do portraits of people—and always from life. God knows, nobody else was doing it. Now, it's regarded as "quaint" to work from life! You know, how old fashioned can you get? But that's what I was proposing to do in London, and so I made a kind of outward show of it. I remember in the early months, I often had two sittings in a day—one in the morning and one in the afternoon—

and that was starting out from the house in Hampstead, which the Burtons had loaned to me, and getting on the Tube. As I said, the Slade School was right on that particular Tube; I didn't have to make any changes. I just got on in Hampstead, and in ten, fifteen minutes, I was in London. But I think the Tube only ran until about nine or ten at night, so if I stayed in London later than that, I'd have to take a cab back, and a few nights I did, and that could be very expensive, so I avoided it. But that was all of '61, and I had my first show at the Redfern Gallery there in October '61. It was all the drawings that I had done since I arrived in January.

Among your stellar sitters during that formative year was the formidable novelist E. M. Forster, known as "Morgan" to his intimates, to whom you had been introduced a few years earlier on your first trip to England with Chris.

I didn't dare ask him to sit until Chris came over, because he was very kindly, but he was also strict in his judgment of people: an assessor of behavior of his friends, and I knew that about him. So when I did ask him for a sitting, I went to his flat, and I did a first drawing of him. Of course, I wanted to do two more. I'd just taken what he did, when he sat down, but it wasn't quite what I wanted: I didn't dare ask him for eye contact, so he sat there and he was looking away, and he was kind of slumped in his chair. I did a pretty good drawing of him, but of course, it was a warm-up. But he assumed that the sitting was over, and I was intimidated enough by him that I didn't beg; I was afraid to raise his ire. So I had just that one drawing, which was very unsatisfactory from my point of view, and I showed it to Chris, of course, and told the story also to Joe Ackerley.

J. R. Ackerley was then a daringly openly gay writer and the longtime editor of the BBC's magazine The Listener, *in which he promoted Chris's work along with Auden's and Spender's.*

I knew Joe and his sister, Nancy West. He and Morgan were very good friends, and Joe was one of the few people who could censure Morgan. So I showed Joe the drawing of Morgan and told him, more or less, what I'm telling you now, and Joe went back to Morgan and did the very delicate work of persuading him to sit for me again. Anyway, a second sitting *was* set up, and I did three drawings, but I was so keyed up for it that the first drawing of the second sitting was the best by far of all four. Even though I still didn't dare to ask him to look at me, instead of slumping down, he was up, and held his head up. And when he first looked at the drawing, he laughed, because he thought he looked so imperial! He was actually showing me something that he wasn't aware of showing people, and he saw it immediately in the drawing: he wasn't the kindly old man that he thought that most of his friends would see! The grandeur came out—and that's the best one I ever did of him.

You nevertheless managed to expose what lurked beneath his guarded reluctance.

I always hope that when the two come together that I will be in my best working condition, and be able not to feel the grandeur of my sitter so much that it interferes; that I'll be in prime working state, and be able to do my best work with somebody really famous. It's wonderful when the two can come together.

Your best portrait of Forster graced the cover of the first publication of his landmark novel Maurice *in 1971. Although he had written the book in 1913-14 and later revised it, he had withheld it from publication during his lifetime due to then-prevailing social and legal attitudes toward homosexuality.*

Yes, yes. It's a good drawing of him, and it really looks like him.

In Christopher and His Kind, *Chris observed that "the wonder was Forster himself, imprisoned within the jungle of pre-war prejudice, put-*

*ting these unthinkable thoughts into words." Forster had first shared
the manuscript with Chris back in 1933, and ultimately Chris oversaw
its posthumous publication in the United States, per Forster's wishes.*

Yes, because he didn't trust anybody else. Well, they were very
close, Morgan and Chris, yes, and I think Chris was the one he
trusted most. That's why he gave him that job.

*What do you think of Merchant Ivory's film adaptation, which in itself
was still a pretty bold statement for a feature film to make in 1987?*

Oh, I think it's beautiful. Yes, I think it's great. I've seen it many
times, and I don't think there's anything wrong with it, it seems to
me. Chris made great efforts to make contact with Jim Ivory and
Ismail Merchant, because both he and I had adored their films.
They became really very dear friends, and Jim has still been a great
friend to me for many years now. Oh, he's been very good to me,
and gosh, if I hadn't promised myself I wouldn't fly again, I would
go to New York just to see him. Oh, I love him: I think he's just one
of the kindest and most gentlemanly Americans I've ever met, and
I admire him a great deal. I was very fond of Ismail, too. They were
such a great combination because they seemed so different, but yet
it was clear right away they were really devoted to each other. Jim
is so low-key and soft spoken; Ismail was AH! That's what Ismail
was there for: to do all the dirty work, and Jim could always remain
serene! Ismail had great charm, but I did once or twice have dem-
onstrations of how firm he could be, and it was always about
money. Apparently he had a real reputation for bargaining down
to the last penny, and that came in handy when financing the films.

They produced lavish films often on shoestring budgets.

I know it's very difficult for Jim since Ismail's passing.

*Their longtime creative partner, Ruth Prawer Jhabvala, who won Os-
cars for writing both of their other Forster adaptations,* A Room with
a View *and* Howards End, *has now also passed away.*

And Ruth! All three of them sat for me. I even went east and had all three of them to myself, and Jhab, Ruth's husband. They were another very contrasted couple, but we got along very well together. Jhab was fascinated by the process and by the drawings I did of Jim and Ismail and Ruth, but was *so* disappointed by the two I did of him. I don't know what he was expecting or looking for, but I missed it by a mile! But I guess this means Jim is not going to direct anymore, but he's in his nineties, I think?

He is, and is remarkably still working, recently publishing a memoir and co-directing a documentary film, A Cooler Climate. *And just a few years ago, at age ninety, he became the oldest Oscar winner in any category for his screenplay adaptation of* Call Me by Your Name, *his second effort, after* Maurice, *of bringing a tale of same-sex love to the screen.*

That was great, yes. I just wish I liked that young man, Timothée Chalamet, more. I thought it was an intelligent performance; I think he had real presence and he's photogenic, but there's something about him that I resist. I don't know what it is. It's something to do with his personality: he just doesn't appeal to me. He's the wrong kind of beautiful young man.

Your admiration for the Merchant Ivory team was certainly reciprocated. When the National Portrait Gallery in London sought to commission paintings of Merchant, Ivory, and Jhabvala, James Ivory chose you as the artist. At one time, he and Ismail Merchant had also been interested in making a film of A Meeting by the River, *from the script you and Chris had adapted from Chris's novel.*

That was our most finished script. We worked on that for many months, and we did have a New York stage production, but if Chris and I worked on a stage production, we always had in mind the movie script that would follow it, and that would be our real endeavor: to get it in shape for a movie. And yes, Jim Ivory really wanted to do it.

That film never came to fruition, alas, nor did their later proposed PBS documentary film based on October, *your collaborative book with Chris that collected a selection of your portraiture and his journal entries from one solitary month.*

Yes, and what a shame it didn't happen, but Chris's final illness precluded that. Of course, that would have been very nice for us, because we were both very fond of Jim, and of Ismail, too. Yes, they would've been the ideal people to do it.

Their film adaptation of Maurice *would have also been in development around that time, although it wasn't released until a year after Chris's death. Was he aware that it was in the works?*

I bet they mentioned to Chris that they were intending to make it, but it was too late for Chris even to have anything to do with it. But that would have pleased him. I think he would have liked the film, and their next Forster film, too, with Vanessa.

Their subsequent adaptation of Forster's Howards End *starred Emma Thompson, who won an Oscar for her performance, along with Anthony Hopkins, Helena Bonham Carter, and Vanessa Redgrave, who was Oscar-nominated for her supporting role in that film. You would have first known Vanessa Redgrave through her marriage to your friend Tony Richardson in the 1960s?*

Yes, they were quite a pair. We very seldom saw them together, but a lot separately. Tony, we knew very well and were very fond of, and we were very fond of Vanessa, but she's not a person that I could ever get close to, I don't think. There's something very distant about her whole manner and personality. I haven't seen her in years and years.

Circling back to that formative period for you in London, when you were the right kind of beautiful young man, your passionate dedication to your craft led to your swiftly amassing quite a portfolio.

And that portfolio, by the time August came by, was quite considerable, and I had lots of portraits of well-known people. I had met one of the men who ran the Redfern Gallery, so I took them to show him, and got an offer for a show in October. I've never had a show as successful as that first one at the Redfern Gallery. Because of Chris and all the people he knew in London, the opening was *glamorous* beyond belief! The gallery people were amazed. There were two well-known artists opening at the same time: one in the major room upstairs, and the other one in the room behind that upstairs. I was the basement attraction, but on the opening night, *everybody* was downstairs! The upstairs was deserted! Because of Chris, and because of the famous people I had been working with, everyone was downstairs. I don't think the other two artists ever forgave me! That was embarrassing for me, but what could I do about it? Anyway, I was so delighted that all those people came! Auden came, Forster came, Stephen Spender, Francis Bacon, John Gielgud, all kinds of theater people, and Maugham, who at that age almost never went out where there would be photographs. Well, all of Chris's friends came to please Chris, but also I had done drawings of most of them, so they were coming also to acknowledge that fact and see themselves on the wall.

But what a tremendous benediction of you as a young artist, having those revered figures draw such attention to your work.

Imagine! It was hugely exciting for me. It was like starting at the absolute top. And as far as I'm concerned, nothing to do with my career has ever been as exciting as that first opening night, because I felt the backing of all of those glamorous people, as well as dear friends by that time, who really gave me support. That was wonderful. And I sold lots of portraits. They were all pencil drawings, mostly, and they sold for £25 each. But like a fool, I sold things that I would adore to have now. I sold my best drawing of Forster for £25! But you know, being young and starting out as an artist, sales meant something. That best drawing I did of him was used by the publishing company when *Maurice* was published, but just his head from the drawing—it actually included his hands. It was so early, I didn't even ask him to sign it, but oh, I wish I had that drawing back. But you know, it was exciting, too, to feel some kind of success. As I mentioned earlier, I realized right away with Chris that I had to have an identity. If we were going to stay together, I couldn't be just his young, cute boyfriend; I knew that wouldn't be enough for either of us. So everything was riding on my establishing myself as an artist.

One newspaper review of your work in that show paid particular attention to your portrait of actress Gladys Cooper.

Yes, that would've been London, because she was such an English personality that Hollywood people, in spite of all of her work in Hollywood films, didn't really know or care much about her.

In spite of Best Supporting Oscar nominations for her performances in Now, Voyager, The Song of Bernadette, *and* My Fair Lady.

Gladys made them memorable. Yes, the more unpleasant the role, the more memorable! She was having a good time in *Now, Voyager,* and Bette Davis, of course, would have known she was *real* competition.

Cooper delivers a wonderfully wicked performance in that film as Davis's domineering mother.

I always love Davis's first entrance, looking like Groucho Marx! But it doesn't take her long to transform, yes! I even remember the movie theater where I first saw it in 1942 in Glendale: The Gateway, which has long since been torn down. It had opened in the two Warner theaters—the one downtown and the other in Hollywood—and I didn't get to see it until it was already in the Atwater neighborhood, but I made up for it by seeing it several times.

Gladys was right here in the Palisades for years. She had a house here, and we used to go there for dinners or take her out. She was wonderful company.

While in London, didn't you also briefly work as a fashion illustrator for Women's Wear Daily?

Yes, and that was right up my alley. That was that first year, and within a few weeks, I was making far more money than I needed to support myself quite handsomely. I enjoyed myself, too: it was like having professional models for free! And it was a whole different kind of approach: they made up, and I often did full figure drawings of them. Oh, that was just a perfect experience for me, those first jobs that I did for *Women's Wear Daily.*

How did you get the job?

It was somebody who knew my work and asked me if I had ever done any fashion work. But to me, it wasn't fashion work: it was just a continuation of my portrait work. Lots of my drawings were really fashion drawings that were also working as portraits. But early critics of my fashion work would often say, "Well, it looks just like Margie, but where are the buttons and the zippers?"

So they were recognizable as portraits, but the focus needed to be on the fashion?

Yeah, the seams and the buttons and all of that! But to me, it was just a matter of another ten minutes: "OK, if you want them . . ." and I added them without any struggle at all.

Had you done any fashion work prior to that?

Yes, in downtown L.A. at the May Company department store, I did probably two-and-a-half months of work doing drawings for their newspaper ads. I've got a whole portfolio of those clippings. They were published in the *L.A. Times.*

Chris's diaries also mention his having sent you Vivien Leigh's private phone number during your time in London. This would have been a few years before she ultimately sat for you, but did you contact her then?

I went to a rehearsal of *Duel of Angels*, which she was doing on stage with Mary Ure, thinking I would maybe get access to her to ask her for a sitting. I went hoping I could even draw her without her officially sitting for me, but I was just kidding myself: if I didn't have cooperation, I couldn't do anything that my own principles would allow me to consider a fair try. No, it was just frustrating myself.

And eventually you did *get Vivien Leigh to sit for you, when she was in Los Angeles in 1964 for the filming of* Ship of Fools.

Yes, I did get Vivien Leigh to sit properly. Well, I never got her to *sit* properly, but at least I got her to agree to let me have at her! Of all the restless people I've drawn, she was the most frustrating of all, because she wasn't trying to defeat me: she was trying to *please* me. She just couldn't. She was the most charming, considerate, sensitive, lovely person, but she warned me before our sittings, "I've frustrated some of the best artists of my time," because she genuinely couldn't be still. It was just part of her mental illness. I saw it when that poor woman sat for me, and my drawings were undeniable proof, with nothing approaching the quality of my best work. I had to resign myself to that, but I got a couple of drawings that at least are identifiable as her, and were even signed by her. One is in a bandana, another in a hat. She would do anything I suggested. She even put her hand to her face, propping her head up to keep it still. I thought that might steady her, and it is the best of the drawings I did, with the hat over. For years, drawing people with a hat on was a particular test of my ability, and I often failed, but at least the hat looks like it's sitting on her head. I saw sweat breaking out on her forehead, she was trying so hard. Imagine that wonderful, distinguished, beautiful creature tormenting herself to please *me*?

And when I said I was through, nearly shooting out of her chair like she had come out of like a cannon, just after the effort of being still for fifteen minutes? Oh, to get a really good portrait of Vivien Leigh would have been something I'd be *so* proud of, but nevertheless, considering the conditions of our sittings, I got a couple of things that I would even exhibit, if necessary, but I never put them into any of my official shows, because people who would be very interested in an accurate portrait of her wouldn't like anything that I was able to get. But I adored her. She was probably the only person who frustrated me as a sitter, that I still adored! She was just so charming and so great-looking. At parties and when we got her here for dinner, she was always fascinating, always charming, always nice, and never distant in any way. Just to be in her company was practically ecstatic for me: the voice and everything about her.

Given the heady success of your first show, were you at all tempted to stay on in London to further establish yourself?

How could I? I'm a born Californian, in Los Angeles, and I love it. I'm spoiled. Every other place I've been, I had this standard to compare it to, and California, Santa Monica, always wins. I've been to lovely places all over the world, but I've never been to one that's made me think, even *think*, that I might want to live there rather than here. I've always been at home here, spoiled from my earliest days. If the weather is not as good as California weather, then I'm sulking. And all the years of hearing from New Yorkers and the British, all kinds of people, about how awful this place is, how can I stand it? I always keep my mouth shut. I just say, "Well, you know, I was born here. It's really all I know." But the truth is, it's *not* all I know, but it's all I care about. And it was so exciting for me in 1953, that first trip to New York. *Snow!* Oh! I was just *so* excited, and it was the most glamorous place in the world. I just couldn't wait to get back, and I loved it for years, but now you couldn't budge me for *anything* to move away from Santa Monica.

*You've told me that after Chris joined you in London, you both even-
tually started going to any movie that featured a California beach
scene.*

I did love that year in London, but oh boy, did I miss California
weather. So when Chris came to join me, yes, we both used to go
see Hollywood movies just because we knew they'd been filmed
on the beach. *One-Eyed Jacks*, that Brando film, we went to largely
because a lot of it was filmed on the Malibu beach. In spite of the
period costumes and all, it was unmistakably a California beach,
and Chris and I literally almost wept. It really got to us both. We
both were just so homesick for this place, because we met on the
beach and we always loved being together on the beach, laying in
the sun. If it wasn't on the beach, it was on the roof of my studio.
Chris never regretted leaving England; it was only his friends he
missed. But then Auden was living here, too, and he used to come
and stay with us, or we would go to New York and see him there.
Oh, Chris loved it here, and he loved it immediately. He'd always
wanted to come to California, and it took immediately. He had always been a fan of movies: the idea of Hollywood had excited him,
and he was never disappointed having come here. Well, he decided to spend the rest of his life here. But of course, when I first
saw New York and then London, I thought, "Oh, how wonderful
it would be to live here." And actually, I did live the better part of
a year in New York, with many visits from Chris, who, even
though he didn't like New York, stayed with me. And then London, too, how wonderful it was, indeed—but it was nothing like
California. That year in London was the longest I've ever been
away, but oh, Chris and I were just so *glad* to get back; we couldn't
rejoice enough. The first morning we were home, we drove down
to the beach and went in the water. Oh, such happiness!

*Your first New York show opened just a few months later, in January
1962, at the Sagittarius Gallery, followed later that year by your Los
Angeles debut at the Rex Evans Gallery.*

Don poses with Marilyn Monroe
at the Academy Awards ceremony
in March 1951.
(Photo by Ted Bachardy,
courtesy of Don Bachardy)
© Don Bachardy

ed with Marilyn Monroe and
er acting coach, Natasha Lytess,
the 1951 Oscars.
'hoto by Don Bachardy,
ourtesy of Don Bachardy)
Don Bachardy

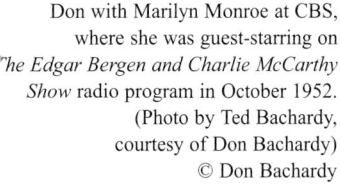

Don with Marilyn Monroe at CBS,
where she was guest-starring on
*The Edgar Bergen and Charlie McCarthy
Show* radio program in October 1952.
(Photo by Ted Bachardy,
courtesy of Don Bachardy)
© Don Bachardy

Don and Ted captured in a press photo with Bette Davis and Gary Merrill
as they arrive at a preview screening of *Decision Before Dawn* in December 1951.
(Courtesy of University of Southern California, on behalf of the USC Libraries Special Collections)

Don's first encounter
with Bette Davis,
December 1951.
(Photo by Ted Bachardy,
courtesy of Don Bachardy)
© Don Bachardy

Joan Crawford signs
Don's program at the 1952
Hollywood premiere
of *Singin' in the Rain*.
(Photo by Ted Bachardy,
courtesy of Don Bachardy)
© Don Bachardy

Don poses with Lauren Bacall
and Humphrey Bogart at the
Academy Awards ceremony
in March 1952.
Bogart would win the
Best Actor Oscar that evening
for his performance in
The African Queen.
(Photo by Ted Bachardy,
courtesy of Don Bachardy)
© Don Bachardy

Don and Ted pay little attention to
Frank Sinatra (left) as they swoop
in on Ava Gardner for a photo
and autograph at the premiere
of *Pandora and the Flying
Dutchman* in January 1952.
(Photo by Ted Bachardy,
courtesy of Don Bachardy)
© Don Bachardy

A press photo captures an "unidentified fan" (Don) getting an autograph from Susan Hayward at the premiere of *David and Bathsheba* at Grauman's Chinese Theatre in November 1951. Hayward's then-husband, actor Jess Barker, looks on.
(Photo courtesy of SuperStock/*Sydney Morning Herald*)

Don and Montgomery Clift
lock eyes at the 1952 Oscars.
Clift was a Best Actor nominee
that year for *A Place in the Sun*.
(Photo by Ted Bachardy,
courtesy of Don Bachardy)
© Don Bachardy

Don with Elizabeth Taylor
at the Hollywood premiere
of *Quo Vadis* in 1951.
(Photo by Ted Bachardy,
courtesy of Don Bachardy)
© Don Bachardy

Don with two stars whose daughters also became stars: (left) Janet Leigh is surprised by Ted's camera as she signs Don's program outside a 1952 Hollywood premiere; (below) Don gets an appreciative look from Debbie Reynolds at the 1951 premiere of *Detective Story*. (Photos by Ted Bachardy, courtesy of Don Bachardy) © Don Bachardy

Chris with Julie Harris, a houseguest during the filming of *East of Eden*, and friend Jim Charlton in Malibu, spring 1954. (Photo by Don Bachardy, courtesy of the Christopher Isherwood Papers, The Huntington Library, San Marino, California) © Don Bachardy

Don, Chris, and Jim Charlton on Zuma Beach in Malibu, spring 1954. (Photo by Julic Harris, courtesy of the Estate of Julie Harris and the Christopher Isherwood Papers, The Huntington Library, San Marino, California)

Don drawing his most frequent sitter, Chris, in December 1962.
(Photo by George Hoyningen-Huene, courtesy of the George Hoyningen-Huene Estate Archives
and the Christopher Isherwood Papers, The Huntington Library, San Marino, California)

Christopher Isherwood, 1962. © Don Bachardy

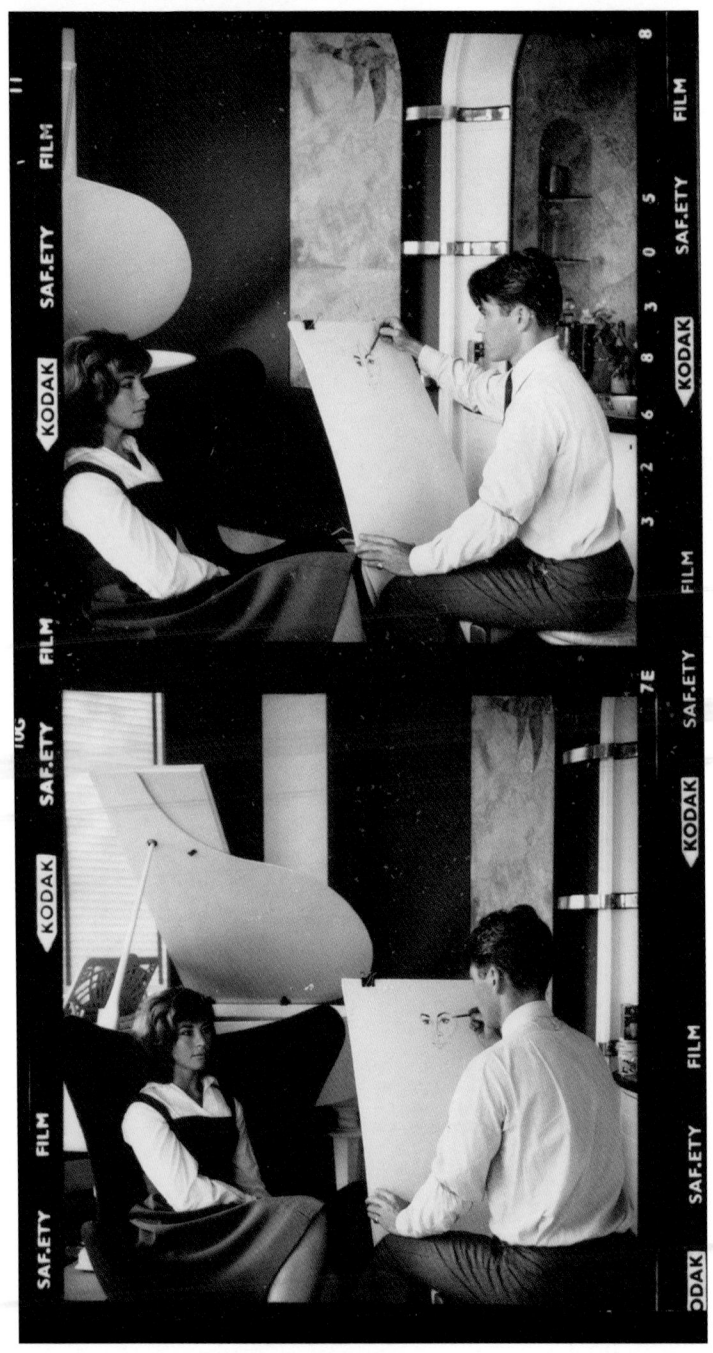

Don drawing actress Nanette Newman near London in 1961.
(Photo by Bryan Forbes, courtesy of Sarah Forbes Standing and the
Christopher Isherwood Papers, The Huntington Library, San Marino, California)

Vivien Leigh, 1964. © Don Bachardy

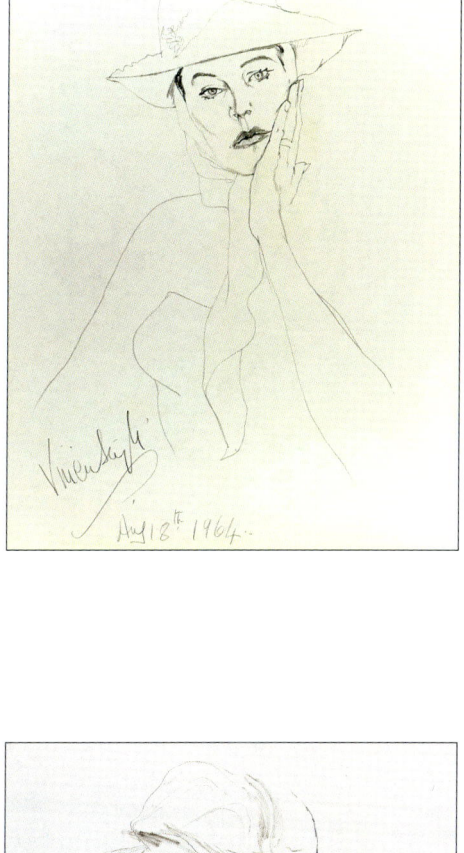

Montgomery Clift, 1964. © Don Bachardy

Marlene Dietrich, 1963. © Don Bachardy

One of Natalie Wood's early portrait sessions with Don Bachardy was documented by *Life* magazine photographer Bill Ray in 1963. (Photos © Bill Ray, courtesy of the Natalie Wood Archive; portrait © Don Bachardy)

Natalie Wood, 1963. © Don Bachardy

Don looking out over the Santa Monica Canyon from atop his studio in October 1967.
(Photo by Dale Laster, courtesy of the Laster Family and the Christopher Isherwood Papers,
The Huntington Library, San Marino, California)

Don with his parents in 1968.
(Photo by Ted Bachardy,
courtesy of the
Christopher Isherwood Papers,
The Huntington Library,
San Marino, California)
© Don Bachardy

Don and Chris at home in the 1970s.
(Photo © Stathis Orphanos,
courtesy of Juli Veee and the
Stathis Orphanos Photographic Archive,
Rare Book and Special Collections
Division, Library of Congress,
Washington, D.C.)

Don and Chris with *Cabaret* star Michael York, photographed by Pat York in Don's studio in July 1972.
(Photo courtesy of Pat York and the Christopher Isherwood Papers,
The Huntington Library, San Marino, California)

Yes, it was the same season, the fall of '62 going into the early winter of '63, and then the same thing the next year, from the end of '63 to '64. Those were the years when my career as an artist was becoming official.

Two of your early celebrity sitters—the pioneering drag queen and muse Barbette, and the legendary writer and satirist Dorothy Parker— both materialized at your L.A. opening and posed for photos in front of their portraits.

Oh, yes, yes! Because we knew Dorothy and Alan early.

Parker was twice married to Alan Campbell, her writing collaborator on the 1937 film version of A Star Is Born, *among numerous other Hollywood screenplays.*

Yes, I had very early exposure to them both. I think I had met them even before I went to New York. They lived in West Hollywood.

What were your impressions of her?

Tragic, but her face really, I think, expressed more tragedy than her life did. I think she was really quite suited to her life, and certainly she and Alan were very well-tuned to each other by the time I met them. Chris didn't feel particularly close to either of them, but there were always good feelings among the four of us.

Was she as sharp a wit in person as in her writings?

Yes, her delivery of her statements was always very good and often surprising. But she and Alan, even when they were sober, were profoundly both personalities who had been drunks. Even when they were perfectly sober, that had already established itself—they hardly needed to drink anymore! But both of them, especially Dorothy, were so patient with me and sat so still. I did some of my very best early work of her especially. But as I've told you, I've always been extra tuned to women. In those early years, they were always my best subjects, the ones that I investigated with my most intimate instruments, always getting more expression out of their faces than anyone else—and probably because my mother was so resistant to that kind of relationship with me. It took me almost ten years to use the authority I'd learned to demand from her and make her sit for me, and until I did that, I had to work it out with other women. But I finally managed it: I've got a very good history of both endeavors. Lots of drawings of women.

Shortly after your return from London, you established your own home studio in what had originally been a carport?

The floor downstairs is the floor of the original garage. It was just a small garage big enough for two small cars, and we both could park in it. I turned it into a studio in '62, of course with help from builders: a one-room studio, and added a toilet, sink, shower—very tiny, but they all functioned. It was a one-room studio from '62 until '76, when we had a second floor put on. Chris was always hesitant about any changes of that kind, but he let me do it. Oh, it's an ideal studio for me. It's exactly right: the right light and space, with all my storage downstairs and all my sittings upstairs. I knew it would work. Yes, we were very happy here... for *a while.*

That's a curious way to phrase it.

It's said at the end of *Long Day's Journey into Night*: "Oh, we were so happy, for a while!" And Chris and I were always happy here. It didn't come to any kind of disappointment, ever. The disappointment was what we both knew what had to come: he would die before me. And we even managed that.

CHAPTER 6

This is a real house

Don and Chris at home in Santa Monica, 1972. (*Photo by Pat York, courtesy of the Christopher Isherwood Papers, The Huntington Library, San Marino, California*)

Let's discuss the domestic journey that ultimately led you and Chris to your now-iconic home in Santa Monica. It began with your expulsion from the Hookers' garden house.

We were living there when we got to know each other, but we were banished from there by Evelyn's husband. It was so painfully embarrassing for her to have to evict us, and why? Because we were queer, and she was the patron saint of queers!

But wasn't their objection more about your age difference?

Well, I looked awfully young, yes, but Evelyn's husband, he was a grumpy old thing. He hated having me there. Chris was OK because he was a scholar working away in their little cottage. It was only a shed when they offered it to Chris. Chris had his architect friend, Jim Charlton, turn it into a very nice little one-room house, very attractive for him, but the Hookers, especially Edward Hooker, took exception to having me living there with Chris. I still was spending two or three nights a week in town with my mother and brother in an apartment there, but more and more, I was around. Evelyn had finally asked Chris that he move out.

Did that damage their friendship?

Yes, it lasted a few years, but Chris didn't hold a grudge. But we had to quickly find another place.

You and Chris then lived somewhat nomadically for the next few years, although always within the Santa Monica Canyon?

Chris had often been in Santa Monica Canyon since he arrived in '39, because Salka Viertel lived here.

Chris's 1945 novel Prater Violet *had been inspired by his work with the Austrian director Berthold Viertel on the 1934 British film,* Little Friend. *Salka Viertel, meanwhile, was a Hollywood screenwriter who co-scripted several films starring her close friend, Greta Garbo. Until their divorce, the Viertels' Sunday night tea parties in their Santa Monica home became a regular gathering place for Hollywood and émigré intellectuals.*

Berthold and Salka had split by the time I came on the scene, and he was living in Germany and had another woman, and Salka stayed in the Mabery Road house here. We saw a lot of her. But yes, we had five houses altogether before this one, all within walking distance here in Santa Monica Canyon. Just rentals, until the last one on Sycamore Road, we bought.

Didn't the designer Tony Duquette have a hand in decorating your house on Sycamore?

He just made it easier for us to get furnishings for it. For instance, there are two chairs in the living room that Tony designed, but they're very conventional, and he probably just claimed to have designed them.

For a time, you had worked for him as an assistant?

Yes. It was really my first job in the art world.

Had you had any previous job experiences?

Yes, at a Ralphs supermarket here at Vermont and Santa Monica Boulevard, just for a few months at the end of my college career. That was a good experience for me. I was a good wrapper, except that there's something in my nature that likes to fit as many things into a given space as I can. I remember a few old people cautioned me not to pack their bags so heavily, because they had to carry them. They'd rather have two than get everything into one.

What was it like for you, then, working for Tony Duquette?

Well, Tony had a real affliction: he was *stingy*. Money was way too prominent in his head, and I worked for him really for nothing, for months and months, and I had to drive all the way into town. He knew he was taking advantage. I was fond of him, but he was a difficult person and really wrapped up in himself completely. He had his own studio then, which had been the film studio of a silent screen actress.

It had been Norma Talmadge's studio. She was a major star of the silent era who was backed by her wealthy husband, Joseph M. Schenck, in their own successful production company.

Oh, yes, she was a genuine star. But it was really my first job in the art world, though Tony wasn't really considered a member of the art world. He had a lot of talent, but it was strictly a theatrical talent. Actually, his wife, Elizabeth, was the one who could draw, but he really subjugated her. She was called "Beegle," and it had more than one application! Because she did get treated sometimes like a dog by him. I got a couple of drawings of him that will tell you all you really need to know about him. They're so like him. He was one of the very pictorial people: he *really* did embody his personality. Everything about him was perfectly designed to tell you who he was. And he was as queer as a coot, not thinking, *thinking, oblivious* to all truth that he was the only one who knew!

Chris's diary makes note of a star-studded birthday party that Duquette threw for Beegle, describing the event as "a sensation. Marion Davies' husband threatened to shoot down the chandelier while Agnes Moorehead was reciting. 'It'll be like Booth and Lincoln,' he said." Later at Pickfair, the once-fabled Hollywood home of silent film superstars Mary Pickford and Douglas Fairbanks, Chris further reported that Davies's husband "somehow or other fired two shots, one of which grazed Mary Pickford's forehead." Do you remember that wild evening?

Yes, and it was Tony using her birthday as an excuse for having a big party for the opening of his studio! It was all about the opening of his studio. Moorehead gave acting classes in the studio after the opening. She was involved in various kinds of productions that Tony devised for her, or she wanted to do and he helped her.

She later appeared in the star-studded 1973 TV adaptation of Frankenstein *that you co-wrote with Chris.*

Yes, I liked her a lot, and I went to her house several times for sittings. I don't think she ever came here; it was somehow an understanding that I would always go to her. In those early days, I think I really preferred it, because my studio was slow to evolve, and finally by the time it was a place where I really preferred to work, my friendship with Moorehead . . . well, she was getting old and taking her leave. But she was really a good sport about the drawings. She really did look *glamorous* in person, with the red hair and kind of really attractive hairdo she almost *never* got to wear in movies. But Marion Davies, I didn't have all that much of an exposure to her. There was one dinner party we went to that she gave at her big mansion behind the Beverly Hills Hotel. Of course, the money came from Hearst, and the houses, too: they were all acquired in the Hearst era. But her later husband—now, that's a relationship that I know almost nothing about. I forgot even that he existed.

Former movie queen Marion Davies had been the longtime mistress of the wealthy and powerful newspaper tycoon, William Randolph Hearst. Shortly after his death, she abruptly married a sea captain who just happened to be a lookalike for her late lover.

I don't think I could tell you a thing about him! I don't even have a mental image of what he looked like. He was just a drear. Do you know who Speed Lamkin was? The writer?

Composer Ned Rorem dubbed him "the poor man's Truman Capote." He and his sister, Marguerite Lamkin Littman, were longtime friends of Chris's and yours.

He claimed to be Marion's friend—and he was; I'm sure he was—but I think she used him largely as entertainment, because he was just full of awe for her and for Hearst and for money, grandness, and all of that. He had already met Chris before I knew Chris, and was always very silent, very humble, and thrilled in front of Chris, as right he was to be in Chris's company. Well, he was a Southerner, and he knew how to behave: manners were something that didn't have to be explained to him.

Getting back to your own now-fabled home: what first brought you to it, given that you and Chris had purchased your house on Sycamore Road only a few years before?

We lived in that house for two-and-a-half years almost, and it was a very nice house, comfortable, but it was in the bottom of the canyon on a narrow street, and kids played in the street all day long. Chris's workroom was on the street, and it bothered him, so that's really the only reason we started looking for something else. That's why this house seemed so appealing: it's quiet here. It's like living in suspended animation: there's life all around but no immediate access, which I've always loved about this house.

Whereas this house is indeed suspended on a side of the canyon, wasn't your last rental house actually atop the canyon, requiring quite an upward climb to get to it?

It was a little prefab house at the top of the canyon, with seventy-five wooden steps up to it! A long stairway up to the house. Of all of the five places we lived in, some very briefly, that first place on Mesa Road was probably the longest. We had lots of parties there: we gave a party for Anna Magnani and Tennessee Williams when they were here doing *The Rose Tattoo*, and I remember we gave another party there during the filming of *East of Eden*, and Julie and Jo Van Fleet and other people from the movie came, because we were on the set a lot and met most of the people who were working on it and in it, including Dean. But one of our early visitors to climb the seventy-five steps was Greta Garbo! I cooked dinner for Greta Garbo. I've dined out on that for quite a few years!

I will gladly take you to dinner just to hear you tell that story again!

Salka Viertel was a big tease. She knew I was a big movie fan, and she used to say, "Maybe I'll bring Greta with me tonight." And I suppose I was salivating. Finally, a date was made, but Salka wouldn't confirm that Garbo was coming. "Oh, I'm not certain that Greta is coming!" I remember looking down from the corner window of the prefab house, down the stairs, and there were *two* female heads coming up the stairs, and so one *had* to be Garbo. Salka's head was gray and Garbo's just dusted with gray, but she still looked very beautiful. She and Chris were about the same age, and both Virgos—Chris an early one: he was slightly older than she—but there she was!

What was Garbo like that evening? Was she personable?

Yes, but she was very low-key. She spoke quietly, and in that deep voice that I remember was thrilling to me, the low register of it. All that "I want to be alone" stuff: well, she was with Salka, and they were great friends, and Chris had known her previously very well, and he was happy to resurrect the friendship with her just for my benefit. But oh, it was just *such* a dazzlement to see her in *color*! Of course, I had never seen her in Technicolor, but her coloring: God, she would have looked great in a color film! She was all in blue: navy blue slacks and blue sweater with a baby blue neckerchief. Her hair was shoulder-length, and she had on almost no makeup, except her eyeliner and a little blue on her eyelids, and a rose-colored lipstick. But still, the effect of seeing her in color was so exciting after all the black-and-white photographs and movies.

What did you cook for her?

Steamed zucchini. That's all she wanted, so we had a big pot of steamed zucchini. It was a cinch! I forget what we had for the rest of us, but that was all that Garbo wanted. She might have had a glass of wine, but I remember standing up with her before dinner in the kitchen. She was always domestically curious: she wanted to see how other people lived in their houses, particularly in their kitchens, so she was out to the kitchen very early after her arrival.

How did the evening then play out?

Chris found her very tedious. She was kind of coy and silly and arch, and he just had no patience for that kind of female behavior. But it was a big thrill for me: oh, it was an evening of *looking* for me! That was one of the luxuries of meeting exciting world-famous people with Chris: I would rely on him to do all the talking, while I did all the looking. I could always relax with Chris, because he was such a terrific talker, and he could always cover any absence of talk from me, so I could just gape at Garbo or Salka or whomever.

Again, it demonstrates how simpatico you and Chris were in relationship with each other.

It does, yes!

Chris recorded in his diary only the basic facts of another extraordinary evening that began auspiciously enough with Lauren Bacall coming to dinner.

I was so worried about making a faux pas by calling her "Lauren." I always had to remind myself, "It's Betty! Betty!" Not the movie star Lauren, but Betty!

Lauren Bacall, whose real name was Betty Joan Perske, was known to her intimates as "Betty." Chris wrote that she was "a very lively do-it-yourself kind of girl."

Bacall was looking absolutely sensational. She must have been into her thirties by then, but oh boy, she looked great. It changed a few years later, but when we first saw her, she looked as good as she did on film. It was really exciting to see her.

Did you ever get her to sit for you?

I asked and asked, but she would say, "Of course. I'm going to San Francisco next week, but after that." And then I would call and get, "Yes, but not right now. In about three weeks, do call." So I would call her and get another delay, and I realized she was never going to do it. After about a dozen tries, I gave it up. We then still saw her occasionally, but I never mentioned it, because I knew she wasn't going to do it.

Nevertheless, she delivered quite a special surprise the evening of your dinner party.

She said, "Bogey and I . . ."—she called him Bogey—"Bogey and
I have a projectionist coming with *To Have and Have Not*, and we're
going to watch it tonight. Would you like to come join us?" Well,
you can imagine the answer to that! And this was after the dinner
party: it must have been ten-thirty before we left the house! And
they were in Brentwood, which means the film couldn't have
gotten rolling until around eleven-thirty, but it wasn't too late for
Betty to call up her next-door neighbors to see if they wanted to
watch it with us. And who were their next-door neighbors? Judy
Garland and Sid Luft! Who came! And Judy was very fat, and all
dressed up in a little satin cupcake hat and a black satin evening
jacket! Now, perhaps they had been out to a party, but somehow,
I don't think so. She was all dressed up just to come and sit up and
watch a movie, and she looked like she had dressed for a premiere!
And she was invited at the last moment! At least there was a
proper projection room to do it in.

Now that is a star! According to Chris's diary, that wondrous evening
happened in early May 1955. Just a little over a month earlier, Garland
had given birth to her son, Joey, the day before Grace Kelly took home
the Best Actress Oscar that Garland had been widely expected to win
for her comeback performance in A Star Is Born.

Yes, it was after *A Star Is Born*, and imagine Betty Bacall just saying, "Judy and Sid live next door. Let's call them up to come over"?
I was in seventh heaven!

Was there much conversation among you all before or during the
screening?

Well, you know, we were just seeing a movie with Judy Garland,
and I can't remember anything she or anybody said. I remember
a few remarks, nothing particularly witty, just a relevant detail or
two. *Why* didn't I come home and write it all down immediately?
I did very occasionally, but later for my sittings, rather than for
just social experiences. But even with the sittings, I didn't write

about everybody. I mostly wrote about the ones who gave me the most trouble!

They certainly make for the best stories. Speaking of which, one of yours involves another unexpected encounter with Judy Garland.

Yes. I had a very good friend named John Carlyle, who was an actor who never got very much recognition. He made brief appearances in a couple of movies, and on TV he played feature parts occasionally. He was a very sweet guy and a good friend, and one of the few in all my years with Chris that I could really enjoy Hollywood gossip with when we were together. He was always with this-and-that celebrity, and then telling me about it. Well, he was really a dear friend, but he *also* was a good friend of Judy, and he often teased me that he was going to try to invite me, too, when Judy was coming. Then one night, in the middle of the night, around two-thirty in the morning, the doorbell rang. Chris and I were in the bedroom, sleeping, and wondered "Who could it be?" and then, "Who's going to answer the door?" Finally, Chris said, "OK, I'll do it," and he got up and went to the door. We always slept naked together, so I think certainly he must have put his robe on to answer the door—I hope so! Anyway, there was a few minutes' pause; I waited, I heard the front door open, I heard an exchange of words, and then a loud *slam*. And I learned after the fact that it had been John and Judy, drunk as skunks! John knew that it would be OK with *me* at any hour of the day or night to bring Judy, *but* he didn't OK it with Chris. He didn't even tell *me* that it *might* happen . . . well, it didn't happen, because the loud slam of the door was final! And the only evidence of Judy's presence on our property: we used to have a trellis over the front door, and we had hanging pots. One of the pots had a plant that sends long tendrils out with little pieces hanging on them, and they droop down. One of those pots, with all of its tendrils, had been stripped bare! It was at the top of the four steps before you get down to the level of the front door, and that's where Chris said he saw another figure standing, waiting up there. John had done the knocking on the door, and it was he who got the door slammed in his face by Chris, so it had been Judy up there stripping that plant! I found a pile of the leaves there the next morning.

In his memoir, Under the Rainbow, *John Carlyle wrote that he "regularly joined Judy in her nocturnal prowling," both of them "tireless in the grip of amphetamines." His inspiration for a wee hours drop-in visit to you and Chris was met with delight by Judy. Their outrage at Chris's inhospitality was expressed in hurling their vodka glasses down from the road into your entryway.*

Ah, yes, I know he wouldn't leave out any detail of that! It was just bad luck. If only *I* had been the one who had gotten up and answered the door! It was just happenstance which of us got up to open the door and deal with whomever, because over the years, there were at least half a dozen people who did that. I can't even think who the others were, but that was certainly the most auspicious. But there was no preparation by John: they just got soused and came. If I had answered the door, I wouldn't have encouraged it, but I would've *gladly* let them in and sat up until six or seven in the morning with them, and then maybe put Judy to bed in the back room or something. I might have even become one of her dearest final friends!

You got a plucked plant instead. Do you also remember their shattered vodka glasses on your doorstep?

No! Well, that's news to me! They were probably too drunk to hit the target! Over the years, there were several incidents of some flying object hitting our roof and waking us in the night, and people going up the street down below and yelling out "Faggots!" or something like that.

So clearly knowing who was in the house, targeting you?

Oh, sure, yes. It got around. Yes, quite a few incidents, and you see, our bedroom is right off the deck here, and we always kept the window open, so it was very easy to hear.

Getting back to John and Judy's far more benign intrusion: how did
your relationship with John Carlyle fare after that ill-timed incident?

Well, that was the end of the friendship between John and
Chris, but John was a good friend of mine and I loved him, so I
went on seeing him, but I always went by myself, and not because
Chris didn't forgive him: Chris didn't care, but John didn't forgive
Chris. I don't think he ever met Chris again in the flesh. He was
afraid of Chris, and no wonder he was afraid: he earned it by bringing Judy that one night. And it really took a lot of soothing from
me to get John to forgive *me*! He was doing it for *me*, anyway, bringing Judy: you could do that with me, because I was jaunty, but not
with Chris! But as well as he knew Chris, he couldn't imagine *any-*
body not wanting to meet Judy at *any* price, at any inconvenience!
It was just fated that Judy and I were not to be friends!

And you never had the opportunity to at least draw her?

No. She would have been very tough. Even Bouché, who almost never failed if given half a chance, got commissioned to do
a sitting with Garland for the *TV Guide*, and the drawings weren't
really good, and I'm sure because she was such trouble. I'm sure
she didn't sit properly. To get a really good likeness, you *have* to
have real cooperation. I'm sorry not to have gotten a sitting with
Bacall, but she was a very shifty character, although charming and
very intelligent and funny, fairly funny. Jennifer Jones said no
right away, and never changed. Bacall said yes, yes, yes, and kept
postponing it. In the end, Jennifer was the kinder of the two: she
just said nothing in the world would make her do it! And it was
much truer of her: it was very difficult—I heard lots—even for studio photographers to get sittings with her in costumes for her
films. She would hardly do any of that, and because of Selznick,
she didn't have to.

David O. Selznick, the powerhouse producer behind Gone with the
Wind, *among other prestige pictures, had not only successfully groomed*

Jennifer Jones for stardom, beginning with her Oscar-winning perform-
ance in The Song of Bernadette, *but also married her after their di-*
vorces from their respective first spouses.

If she didn't want to, he didn't make her. If you inspect the publicity for her films, there are always *very* few photographs of her.
Very few.

You can take some consolation in the fact that she became a friend,
and you had many opportunities through the years to intimately look
at her.

Oh, she couldn't have been sweeter! Yes, both she and David
became very good friends, and we used to go to their movie star
parties. Those parties were just full of Hollywood stars—*every*
major star, it seemed to me!

You must have been just agog!

Oh, yes, I was just goggle-eyed! Well, it was Hollywood high society, and the Selznicks could command anybody.

It must have taken considerable willpower not to outwardly betray
how inwardly starstruck you were?

You see, it was just perfect, because I was with *Chris*. He could
do all the talking, and I could do all the looking and listening, and
I did. That's exactly what I did.

How had your relationship with the Selznicks come about?

Well, did I tell you the first time I met Truman Capote? It was
also in that prefab house. He was at the peak of his social success
as a writer and personality, and he came to lunch one day. I'd
heard so much about him, and I was very scared of meeting him
and being tongue-tied, of not knowing what to say to him. But up
the wooden steps he came, and it just sort of happened immediately: he said, "Oh Donny, I'm so pleased to meet you," and immediately I lost all my self-consciousness. I was so nervous and

worried he wouldn't like me, but because he loved Chris, he *instantly* saw to it that I loved him right away, and he was just irresistible: he knew he could have me, and he was perfectly right! We'd fixed lunch for him, and we sat down at the dining room table at noon and didn't really leave it until after four in the afternoon. He was staying here on that visit with David Selznick and Jennifer Jones, and she was one of my favorite movie stars, so a little bit like Salka teasing me with Garbo, Truman teased me, "Would you like to meet Jennifer?" Of course, my tongue was hanging out! And so, at the end of the afternoon, he said, "Donny, why don't you come with me to Bel-Air, and I'll introduce you?" So I did. Because there was construction going on in their Tower Road house, Jennifer and Selznick were staying at Janet Gaynor and Adrian's house. Jennifer wasn't there yet, but Mary Jennifer, her daughter by Selznick, was in a bassinet; she was just barely six months old. Truman said, "We're going to wait." So we did, and she arrived soon after, wearing a snood, because she'd been doing makeup and wig tests all day at Fox for *Love Is a Many-Splendored Thing*. I was just thrilled to meet her. She was charming; she couldn't have been sweeter to us. And of course, Truman was just laughing at me for being so gaga.

I bet you were! She was at the pinnacle of her stardom then, and would receive her fifth and final Academy Award nomination for that 1955 film, which was also a Best Picture nominee.

I've seen it, of course, a few times over the years, and every time I see it, it surprises me by being better than I remember it. William Holden is so good in it: he's so easy, so relaxed, so believable in the part. And Jennifer is much better in it than I remember, but of course hampered by that wig. That evening I met her, that's what she'd been trying on that day at Fox, was that wig. It's very difficult for an actor to give a good performance wearing a wig! Especially when you know it's a wig, and it has nothing to do with the way they look in other movies; it's always such a mistake, I think.

Speaking of liking something—or someone—better than one has anticipated one would: didn't Chris come to alter his initially poor impression of David Selznick?

Yes, he really rather disapproved of him, from what he knew of his behavior, but there was a very nice side of him, and Chris brought it out. They became really genuine friends after David hired him: he wrote a script for Jennifer about Mary Magdalene. He was very skeptical that he would like David, and to his surprise, he really did. He even thought he was very intelligent, and they had good discussions about the script, working on it from time to time, and essentially they got along hugely well. And that was a relief, because I was hoping to get close to Jennifer! When I first met her, she was really as top a favorite as I've ever had of women in movie stars, and oh, she was so nice to me and looked so glamorous. She was very, very sweet. Right away, we liked each other. After Selznick died, we got even closer to her, and then her third husband, Norton Simon, turned out to be a really sweet guy.

Norton Simon was the billionaire founder of Hunt's Foods and benefactor of the Norton Simon Museum in Pasadena.

We both liked him a lot. Selznick had sat for me in '62, but Jennifer *never*, no. I was *always* on her trail: again and again, I asked her, but finally, when she asked me if I would do a picture of Norton, she said, "If you will, I'll sit for you." I was worried that he'd be very difficult, but he was a good sitter, and I did two pictures of him. One, I think, was one of my best of that period. She was there to see the drawings. When I finished, I said, "Now, Jennifer, it's your turn," and she said, "I'm not going to sit. I only said I would to get you to do Norton." I'd suspected it, but I'd wanted to do a sitting with him, anyway. I had gotten the message very early that it would have been torture for her. A portrait sitting, even with a photographer, for her was *agonizing*, and with me it would've been impossible, and I eventually realized it and stopped tormenting her. Not that she found any difficulty in refusing me: it was like a Southern belle refusing her boyfriends! Even famous photographers like Cecil Beaton seldom got their way with Jennifer as a subject. And Cecil was very bristly: he took offense easily if he were resisted professionally in any way. Though he was very sweet to me, always after he sat, when he saw what I had done, he always tried to persuade me, "Can't you take this out?" Always, always.

And of course, you couldn't and wouldn't betray your own standards by doing so.

And they weren't really unflattering. I even stayed a week with him and his mother in England at that beautiful house that he had in Wiltshire, which was beautifully decorated. I have drawings of his mother, who drove him crazy. She really was pretty well into senility by then, and she was just indifferent to Cecil. *That's* what drove him crazy. He'd had power over her when he was young, and now no more. She was very independent, so he criticized her in any way.

The book Cecil Beaton: Portraits and Profiles *pairs a 1963 portrait of Chris with Beaton's effusive journal entry about finding happy refuge in your home during the filming of* My Fair Lady. *He won Oscars both for his art direction and costume design for that movie. In his diary, Chris recorded the following appraisal you made of an evening spent in Beaton's company: you remarked, "'I like the warmth of Cecil's indiscretion.'" So when he was gossiping about his dearest friends, he at least buttered the knife before sticking it into their backs?*

Yes! He was a very good study, because he had so many different personalities: so many voices that he used for different people in different moods, and he was very verbal. Yes, I got lots of amusement out of him. He really enjoyed saying wicked things, and would sometimes laugh to himself! And of course, he wanted to entertain Chris, but also maintain a kind of rude kindness, and it wasn't always quite possible!

Earlier you described first meeting Jennifer Jones in Janet Gaynor and Adrian's house, but separately you also cultivated a friendship with that famous couple?

Yes. Chris had known Gaynor and Adrian. I didn't meet them for quite a while, but then we became good friends, and Janet even sat for me, in 1962. She was really an early celebrity sitter for me.

Janet Gaynor won the very first Academy Award for Best Actress in 1929 for her work in three silent films: 7th Heaven, Street Angel, *and* Sunrise: A Song of Two Humans. *She was later nominated for her performance in the 1937 original version of* A Star Is Born.

I didn't get to see her in anything, really, because she quit films just as I was being introduced to them. It was years before I got to see her *Star Is Born.* I did see hers before the Garland one, but it was a terrible print of it. The color was so bad, it was like Cinecolor, all awful blue and orange. But a few years later, I got to see the full color. I was stunned! It changed the movie entirely! I was relieved, really, because I'd heard it praised so much, but I couldn't really be objective about it until I'd seen it in real color. It was a long time before I got to see *Sunrise.* I think it's a wonderful film, but again, a very serious case of a performance being almost totally wrecked by an awful wig! Why in hell did she have to have it? I guess her hair was short, and they wanted her to look country. The wig was such a mistake, but it's a beautiful film.

It's widely considered a masterpiece of the silent era, if not one of the greatest films ever made. When you knew Gaynor and Adrian, who had been MGM's leading costume designer in the 1930s and early 1940s, they were already a long-established couple, having married shortly after her early retirement from movies. What were they like in person?

She was exactly like herself: that voice, and yes, she was very friendly. And Adrian, I liked him a lot. He was full of stories, and very relaxed. They were a good couple because they balanced each other in their talk, and their voices were so different: she had that real chirpy voice, and he was much more mellow-voiced and charming.

Theirs has long been alleged to have been a "lavender marriage."

You would have thought that if you hadn't heard anything. They were very much in rhythm with each other, very much. It was a solid relationship that had supported them for years, and they were both very comfortable in it, and I don't think either of them *ever* seriously tested it with any troubling outside relationship, because they respected each other too much. As I said, she was one of my earliest celebrity sitters. It was one of my early tests, and I was able to rise to the occasion. I went to her house in Malibu and did three drawings of her in *ink*. Ink! In India ink, and they're all amazing for somebody my age then. They're such likenesses of her. But she was just *terrific* with me: she took all the poses and held them. She was real professional. So I did bang, bang, bang, three drawings in a row, and I'm so proud of all three of them. Well, women were really what I was good at and provided me with my entrée, and taught me what I wanted from my sitter. It would have been much harder to begin with men, and I knew I had to be just as good with men. It took a long time to equalize the number of men and women who sat for me.

At one hundred years old now, your house certainly dates to Janet Gaynor's Hollywood heyday.

Isn't it startling? And when I first heard it was built in 1925, it seemed like a relatively *new* house! Now, it's quickly become an old house! The house next door that was Charles Laughton's is a kind of twin, built by the same man at the same time, but it's two stories with smaller rooms, and not, I don't think, nearly as nice as this one. Which is almost what they call a shotgun house: you can stand at the front door and shoot a gun through the back door. In this case, the back door is on the side. It's right at the end of the house, but it's on the side.

What was the house like when you first saw it?

We were first shown it by a female realtor who drove Chris crazy. It was very run-down: it was being lived in by a ragtag group of people, four or five people who were just kind of savages, and everything was in terrible shape. The living room and dining room were two shades of hospital green. Our bedroom was pink, and Chris's workroom, which was really meant to be the master bedroom, was baby blue. But I always wanted more than a pint-sized view of the ocean, and so that's what I was thinking about. We didn't say anything to each other until we got rid of the real estate woman, and then Chris said, "Well, what do you think?" I said, "Chris, I think that's the house for us." He said, "You're joking!" I said, "I know it looks awful. They've made a mess of it, but it's solidly built; it's very simple."

And the location and privacy are incomparable.

It had a view, and no neighbors! It was made for us. So Chris said, "OK, I'll trust you." We moved into the house, and before the end of the first year, he declared it was the best of all the houses he'd lived in. His favorite, he said. It turned out to be the perfect house for us: just exactly right.

I would imagine that you repainted it pretty quickly?

I did it all myself; that was the bargain. I said, "Chris, forget about the colors. If you'll trust me, I'll paint the whole thing myself," and I did. Every interior room took three heavy coats of white paint to get the awful colors out. I'd never done painting like that before, but after all, I do claim to be a painter, so I didn't really have an excuse! And because it was our house, I really gave every coat of paint my full attention, so it was a good job, and it really transformed the place. I did it all myself with brushes and a roller and lots of ladders and lots of stiff necks and a stiff back, but it was a proud accomplishment.

The white walls certainly provide the ideal backdrop for your extensive and eclectic art collection, with every wall covered in unique paintings, drawings, photography, and sculpture.

We didn't have any art when we first moved in. We had a couple of prints that Chris had acquired along the way, and some of Bill Caskey's work.

Chris's previous partner, William Caskey, had become a photographer after receiving a "blue discharge" from the U.S. Navy during World War II for his involvement in a gay scandal. Chris and Caskey collaborated on the book The Condor and the Cows, *an account of their travels together through South America.*

He was a very good photographer. We used to have encounters with Caskey in our first year together. I shudder to think of those encounters. Caskey was very witty, but he had decided that I had taken his man away. In fact, he drove Chris out; he was so difficult to deal with. But the collection started by exchanging with my artist friends.

Your living room is the setting of David Hockney's 1968 dual portrait of you and Chris, posing in the flanking wicker armchairs that until only recently were still in place in the room.

It's a very good likeness of Chris. He said that he got it right away, but he was dissatisfied with the painting of me. I had gone to London, and he was impatient to finish the painting, and he wanted me back. But when I did come back, it was already too late, because the paint had gotten very heavy. He painted my face in and out so often that he really couldn't do much more to it. Chris was an easier likeness to get. Almost all you need is to get the eyebrows for Chris.

Do you have favorite pieces in the house?

No, a lot of them I like, and they've become kind of old friends. Many of them have been up for years. It's been fun collecting my artist friends' work: it's my form of interior decorating.

Among your collection is a grouping of pieces by Chris's parents.

There are two portraits by Chris's mother and watercolors by Chris's father, and the house where Chris was born by a professional artist. Chris and I spent two or three nights with his mother and brother in that house.

Chris was born into affluence in 1904 at Wyberslegh Hall, the sixteenth-century house on the Bradshaw-Isherwood family estate in Cheshire, where his brother, Richard, continued to live with their mother, Kathleen, following the death of their father Frank in World War I.

Boy, talk about atmosphere! And it was so cold, we took hot water bottles to bed with us. Rubber ones, I remember, and they were really necessary. Chris was used to that English weather, but hated it. His brother was seven years younger than Chris and looked very like him. He was unmistakably an Isherwood, but he also looked like the village idiot: he had no front teeth, and whatever he was wearing was always full of food stains. Chris was very worried that I'd be horrified and maybe scream in the night, but I got used to it very quickly. For me, he was so interesting-looking because he was much heavier built than Chris, but really the likeness between them was unmistakably very strong. It was also a fascinating experience because it was the real thing, all this historic side of England and old houses, and they were really landed gentry. Chris always spoke of the Windsors as Johnny-come-latelys: who were they? The old British families were so much more genuine—and I met a lot of those people and found out exactly what he was talking about. His mother, too, was quite an encounter.

Chris's mother held to the conventions of her class, relinquishing Chris to the care of a nanny and then boarding school, although, as Isherwood scholar Katherine Bucknell has written, she remained "utterly loyal to both of her notably unconventional sons." How did she receive you?

Of course, I was very young and looked even younger than I was, but she was very nice to me. By that time, Chris had her trained very well. Still, she must have been shocked. I still looked so young.

Although perhaps she had long since ceased being shocked by anything or anyone with which or whom Chris associated. Meanwhile, as Bucknell has further observed, she "epitomized everything against which he wished to rebel."

Yes, and she was smart enough to take it. She had no choice, really, because he was the firstborn son, and Richard clearly had no future but the kind of life he led. He was very intelligent, but just shocking-looking and strange beyond belief, until you got a kind of sense of what he was doing and what it all meant. Of course, I got a lot of briefing and backup from Chris on how to behave. Even Richard began to relax with me, and he was very strange.

His letters to Chris are fascinating: intricately printed on airmail paper filled front to back, in which he discusses Chris's writing and his canvassing of local opinions about homosexuality.

Well, they shared that, yes. Oh, they're wonderful letters, the way they're written.

Was only cosmetic work needed here on your own house, or were there structural challenges as well?

There was nothing wrong with the house; the only structural element we added was the deck. There wasn't a balcony: the two dining room doors opened in, and if you stepped out, you'd drop down about ten feet. So after painting, we ended up getting a carpenter in to make the deck and put in sliding glass for access to the front bedroom. It's not really in keeping with the architecture of the house, but the sliding glass is alright, and the deck made all the difference. I always have breakfast out there, unless it's raining. Even when it was very cold, Chris and I used to just muffle up in our heavy robes and have breakfast on the deck, even when we could see our breaths, it was so cold. Having breakfast with him was just a *wonderful* start to the day, even after years and years, and always out on that deck.

It provides a stunning view out over the canyon to the ocean beyond. The downward view is also a bit breathtaking, when you realize how truly suspended this house is on the hillside. Has your view changed much over your seven decades here in the house?

Yes, it's just gotten fuller. It's been so gradual that I've gotten used to it. It just used to be much greener. There are probably twice as many houses. All the houses on the opposite side of the canyon, at the top, those are all new ones. If it happens gradually, it doesn't really seem very painful.

For many years, you had quite an eccentric neighbor in the reclusive former silent film star Mary Miles Minter, whose seemingly innocent involvement in one of Hollywood's first major scandals—the unsolved 1922 murder of director William Desmond Taylor—had fatally wounded her movie career.

Oh, she was a real crocodile, and her mother was the prime suspect in the murder! Well, just knowing *her* makes her mother guilty!

Didn't she once accuse you of trying to run her down in the road?

Oh, yes, she accused me of drunk driving! One night, she was walking on our dark street, and I was coming home. I had had a couple drinks, but I wasn't the least bit drunk, and suddenly there she was in the middle of the street! Not on the sidewalk, not to the side. I realized it was her and she wasn't in any danger; I saw her in time to put the brakes on. She wasn't carrying any light, and the street was so ill-lit that I suppose it scared her a bit, so she accused me of being drunk. But she was very eccentric. We only went over there once together. She wasn't inviting, no. Chris saw her as a troublemaker, so he avoided her.

He made note in his diary that she did reach out upon learning that he had been the victim of a horrifying home invasion, although she really only wanted to tell him about her own experience of being savagely attacked during a burglary.

I'd forgotten about that—that she'd been intruded upon—but yes, with Chris that was really so utterly bizarre. I was working in the studio upstairs, painting a young man, and I heard a knocking on my door downstairs. The shade was down, but I knew it was Chris, because I could see his blue robe in the crack between the shade and the doorframe itself. So I called out, "Chris? Chris?" No answer. So I went downstairs very quickly, opened the door, and there was Chris standing in front of me, *gagged*. There was not much, but enough blood on his head to really scare me. Chris had heard somebody come in the front door, so he got up from where he was sitting in the back room in his study, and there was this *thug* running down the hallway, who then *hit* him and gagged him and tied up his hands! Imagine! While I was in the *studio* with a young man! We might have both come out and at least have scared the hell out of the guy! But I had no idea until I heard this knocking on my door. That was really one of the worst things that ever happened to us in this house, that whole incident. It was really upsetting for both of us.

Apart from that horrific home invasion, you and Chris crafted an otherwise blissful domestic and professional sanctuary for yourselves. Let's get back to discussing when you first built out your studio.

It started with the original garage building. The ramp came all the way down from the road above, and for the first years, Chris's and my two little cars fit snugly in side by side. That was then converted into a one-room studio for me, with a small bathroom put in. We used to go up on the roof of the garage and sunbathe, and that's how we realized it was the best view from the property. We always intended a second floor. I don't know why we waited so long; it didn't go up until '76, and then it made a perfect studio for me. I store all my work downstairs, and do all my painting and drawing upstairs. Yes, it spoiled me. I really wouldn't want to work anywhere else.

It separates you from your home life yet conveniently maintains your proximity to it.

Psychologically, it helps to close the front door of the house and go into the studio. And sometimes I don't come back until midnight, if I've got two sitters, and then I work by myself at night. Well, it's the perfect studio for me. Not only is the light so much better up there, but I only work from life, so I always have a sitter, and at least I can give them something pleasant to look at while they're sitting. My sitters have told me so often how much it helps.

The ocean view from your studio is spectacular.

It used to be all a series of doors, and then my architect friend Tim Hilton changed it to these two big windows, and that created the whole miracle of the studio. It was a series of improvements, and the final one was a big window on the side, which used to just be a slit. It was never quite right until that last change, which just made it perfect from my point of view.

It certainly opens the space outwards, while bringing in tremendous light. I would imagine that working in your own studio also gives you great freedom: you can spatter paint on the floor without any concern. Indeed, your paint-speckled studio floor could rival any Jackson Pollock painting!

It's been painted many, many times, and when I have it painted white again, it takes really quite a long time to get used to it. The first two or three brush shakings always are difficult to stomach on that pristine white floor!

Well, it's a creative space that is entirely yours, whereas Chris's work-room in the back of the house was his, and you've kept it pretty much as he left it.

Yes, it's pretty much as it was. I just moved his daybed under the windows. He could nap there, and had a bookcase with his po-etry books to protect him from anybody coming in. His desk, which he had made for him in '54 or '55 when we were on Syca-more Road, is hideously heavy; very difficult to negotiate. We had it brought it up here.

It's my understanding that you've slept in this workroom all these years since his passing?

Yes, yes, and think about him at night, too. I had thirty years with him, and it's given me more than thirty years of contempla-tion since he died. And both have been a huge gift to me.

Do you still feel as though you're intimately connected with Chris?

Oh, yes, yes. I know even without being able to give any ev-idence that I've spent all kinds of evenings in my dreams with him in the thirty-plus years since he died. Chris and I always slept to-gether in the front room, which was our bedroom, and we always believed that we had a whole other relationship with each other at night in our dreams. But what a strange experience to live to be older than he was! Because he had always been so remarkable for being so much more experienced than I, that I should actually be able to live to a greater age than he did and ponder it all?

CHAPTER 7

It was exactly what the boy wanted

Don in New York, 1965. *(Photo by Martin Hensler, courtesy of Maina Gielgud and the Christopher Isherwood Papers, The Huntington Library, San Marino, California)*

Let's discuss the formation of "the Animals," the affectionate private personas that you and Chris developed in communications between each other, in which he assumed the character of an old horse and you a young cat.

Well, that was our home-manufactured existence. Just little by little, in the very earliest times together, the animal personas established themselves and never let go: they were very, very expressive of our relationship, and very satisfying and too powerful even for either of us to free ourselves of if we'd wanted to, and we neither didn't.

Chris wrote that your "relationship is really so very very strange. No wonder it gives us trouble. I mean, I often feel that the Animals are far more than just a nursery joke or a cuteness. They exist. They are like Jung's myths. They express a kind of freedom and truth which we otherwise wouldn't have."

Yes! Yes, it was: it went very deep, and it was born very quickly, and just got stronger and stronger until it was just silly to resist it and to pretend that I wanted anything else. I had what turned out to be a dream life for myself, and I had most of it on my own terms. But it was constant work: dedication to balancing all these balls going up in my hands, but I was willing to go to practically any effort to have my freedom and to have my domestic home, as well. Luckily, it only took a few years to realize there was no place like home, if it's the right one—and it was the right one so soon that even *I* couldn't believe that I'd been that lucky, but I was. I've had an *incredibly* lucky life, and I've managed to live out all of my ideas of adventures of one kind and another that I was curious about. I don't think I've really missed much of the kind of adventures I dreamed of when I was young.

In the fall of 1960, you twice traveled on your own to New York for early commissions: one to design a theatrical poster for Tennessee Williams's Period of Adjustment, *and the other for a play that Julie Harris was set to star in,* Little Moon of Alban.

Yes, and I just realized it was really a dead-end road, that I wasn't an illustrator. I did drawings of Robert Webber, Barbara Baxley, and James Daly separately, made a composition out of them, and that was the poster for *Period of Adjustment*, but I don't think it was a very good one. It certainly wasn't right. I'm not really adaptable: I have to have it my way; it can't be for anything else. I'm upset to let it happen: as soon as anyone is expecting to use a work for some purpose, that really spoils my pleasure. I want full rein. I'll take on anybody as a subject, but on the basis that I don't know at the start what I'm going to do; that I don't know whether it's going to be of any use to either of us. And if I can establish that from the beginning of the sitting, then I can usually do something. But if there's a purpose—if it's going to be used for this or that and it mustn't be bigger than so much or smaller than that—then you take my creativity away from me. I want to surprise myself, because the surprise of looking at somebody in the way that I look at him or her is what I build the whole experience on.

What was your relationship with Tennessee Williams like over the years?

Our relationship was based really on his regard for Chris and his desire to please Chris, and I was young enough to take a little bit too much advantage by asking him too often to sit for me, until finally it really was too much for him and he had a kind of hissy fit to find himself again stationed in a chair, made to succumb! You know, he wanted to please Chris a lot, and I knew it, and I overwhelmed him with pleas for sittings, which I knew I would eventually get, because he didn't want to offend Chris. Oh, he was very good to me. He also got me jobs on the films that were being made of his work... not really jobs, but access to the actors who were in them to do sittings with them, that kind of thing.

And he commissioned you to draw his beloved sister Rose, taking you himself to the private mental institution to which she had been permanently committed?

Yes, well, it was of the very important tests that I passed. She was scared of me and trembling, but she sat for me, and I did a *very* good drawing of her, a very good likeness. Just the one drawing, but it was all that was necessary. And that was an achievement I was proud of, too.

So he was pleased with both the encounter and the resulting drawing?

Oh, heavens, yes. I would never have dreamed of asking Chris's brother, Richard, to sit! He was just too, too eccentric to.

Another takeaway for you from that experience, as Chris noted in his diary, was a "very reassuring talk" you had with Tennessee Williams in which he not only confirmed his fondness for you, but "also said that he regards his friendship with [Chris] as one of the greatest friendships of his life."

Well, their admiration for each other's work was really genuine. I certainly know Chris's admiration of Tennessee was totally true and sincere, and I always felt the same about Tennessee's regard for Chris, that it was truly genuine. He adored Chris. I can think of few writers that Chris was friends with that I would say that about. I can verify that Chris felt Gavin Lambert just didn't take enough trouble. He just didn't. A first draft was a finished draft, from Gavin's point of view, whereas Chris never stopped refining until he felt he'd gotten it the way he wanted it. Gavin just wasn't nearly fussy enough.

Gavin Lambert was a British-born Hollywood writer who discreetly infused his screenplays with gay undertones, such as his adaptation of his own novel, Inside Daisy Clover, *for a 1965 film that starred Natalie Wood and Robert Redford. Chris appears in Roddy McDowall's "home movie" footage shot during the filming of* Inside Daisy Clover *on the Santa Monica Pier.*

Yes, we were good friends with Natalie Wood, and knew her through Gavin Lambert. I had quite a few sittings with her over the years: the first one was in '63, and then in '69, and the last one was '77; I think probably just those three. I usually did two if not three drawings in each sitting, but the last work was my favorite, the one I like best of her. And close to the time of that last sitting, Robert Wagner also sat.

Portraits of Don Bachardy
and Christopher Isherwood
by Pat York, 1972.
(Photos courtesy of Pat York and
the Christopher Isherwood Papers,
The Huntington Library,
San Marino, California)

Chris and Don at a January 1977 book signing for *Christopher and His Kind* at the Nicholas Wilder Gallery in Los Angeles, where a selection of Don's portraits of Chris was being exhibited. (Photo © Jack Shear, courtesy of the Christopher Isherwood Papers, The Huntington Library, San Marino, California)

Don and Chris with longtime friend David Hockney and professional soccer player Juli Veee outside the bookstore A Different Light in Los Angeles, 1982. (Photo by Stathis Orphanos, courtesy of Juli Veee and the Stathis Orphanos Photographic Archive, Rare Book and Special Collections Division, Library of Congress, Washington, D.C.)

Don painting Chris in 1984. (Photo © Jack Shear)

Bette Davis, 1973.
© Don Bachardy

Olivia de Havilland, 1977.
© Don Bachardy

Joan Crawford, 1974.
© Don Bachardy

Joan Fontaine, 1976.
© Don Bachardy

Don with Divine and arts journalist
Joan Agajanian Quinn at a party
he hosted with Chris in 1978.
(Photo by Jack Quinn,
courtesy of the Joan Quinn Archives)

Divine, 1978.
© Don Bachardy

Natalie Wood, 1977.
© Don Bachardy

Robert Wagner, 1977.
© Don Bachardy

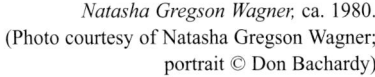

Natasha Gregson Wagner, ca. 1980.
(Photo courtesy of Natasha Gregson Wagner;
portrait © Don Bachardy)

Don draws Katharine Ross on the Connecticut set of *The Stepford Wives* in June 1974.
(Photo by Muky, courtesy of Ron Munkacsi and the Christopher Isherwood Papers,
The Huntington Library, San Marino, California; portrait © Don Bachardy)

Don poses in his studio with a newly completed portrait of Samantha Eggar, January 1982.
(Photo by Samantha Eggar, courtesy of the Christopher Isherwood Papers,
The Huntington Library, San Marino, California; portrait © Don Bachardy)

Don's portraits of the all-star ensemble of Robert Altman's *Short Cuts* (1992) include future Oscar winners *Julianne Moore*, *Frances McDormand*, and *Robert Downey Jr.*
© Don Bachardy

Don and Chris at home in
Santa Monica, September 1979.
(Photo by Wayne Shimabukuro)

Don working on one of his
last portraits of Chris,
December 1985.
(Photo by Wayne Shimabukuro)

Ted Bachardy, 1994.
© Don Bachardy

Tim Hilton, 1993.
© Don Bachardy

Self-Portrait, 2003.
© Don Bachardy

Don backstage with Michelle Williams after a 2014 performance of *Cabaret*. (Photo by Richard Sassin)

Don with Alan Cumming in Santa Monica in October 2014. (Photo by Richard Sassin)

Don with longtime friend
David Hockney in 2022.
(Photo by Richard Sassin)

Don with Joan
Agajanian Quinn at
the Bakersfield Museum
of Art's "On the Edge"
artist panel in 2020.
(Photo by Erin Katgely,
courtesy of the
Joan Quinn Archives)

Don at work in his studio in 2018.
(Photo by Sean Black)

ilda Swinton, 2014.
© Don Bachardy

Mark Ruffalo, 2014.
© Don Bachardy

Reese Witherspoon, 2015.
© Don Bachardy

Don Bachardy in Santa Monica, 2018.
(Photo by Sean Black)

What was she like in person?

She was wonderful. Oh, she was very unpretentious, and she was stunningly beautiful. She was really a top-drawer person: so kind and so responsible and handled her celebrity as though it was second nature, for somebody so young. But then, of course, she'd been a child actor. *Tomorrow Is Forever* was her first film, and she's wonderful in it. It was so much fun seeing her grow up through movies, and then be able to review those movies when she became a big star. She was one of the first of the Hollywood child actors who was always good as a child, but she was even better once she was grown up. She was just lovable: a sweet, genuine, charming young woman. Really, just heartbreakingly sweet, and so natural and friendly and not the least bit grand *ever*. I really admired her. And she sat so well for me.

You must have been acutely affected both by her tragic accidental death and its impact on her husband, Robert Wagner, and their daughters.

Yes, we knew him very well. He was always so sweet. Their daughters sat for me, and he sat for me, too, and was very good about it. I liked him personally, and just couldn't believe that such a dramatic, sensational event happened. They were both drinkers, but I never saw either of them drunk. And they were really good friends. It wasn't just a publicity move: they were really in love with each other, and such dear people. Well, they were a magic couple: so, so beautiful, both of them, and young and romantic and sympathetic and *charming*, and not grand at all, either of them. They were really like children: they had a really charming, innocent quality about both of them, and were always very sweet-natured and fun to know. But oh, what a shocking death! When Chris and I heard about it, we just couldn't believe it. We were really so fond of her. I always feel sheepish when my friends my age die before me; I always wonder what would have become of them. Can you imagine her at my age? She would have been wonderful.

She was the last of the three young stars of Rebel Without a Cause *to meet an untimely death, following James Dean and Sal Mineo.*

I remember seeing it in London. It opened there when Chris and I were on our first trip to England in late '55. And we'd met Dean many times, because of Julie.

Chris observed that a dinner you endured with Nicholas Ray, the maverick director of that landmark film, proved to be "one of our most desperate evenings of boredom."

Because he was drunk! He was just very drunk. And we'd heard so much about him from Gavin Lambert.

Lambert had collaborated on the screenplays for two of Ray's subsequent films, Bigger Than Life *and* Bitter Victory.

He actually claimed that he'd had an affair with Nicholas Ray. Some of it might have been exaggeration. But yes, we met Ray a few other times at parties, but that was the only time we were alone with him. He was drunk when he arrived and drunk for the rest of the evening, and it was really tough-going.

Your longtime friend Robert Wagner played the title role in Ray's The True Story of Jesse James. *Wagner's co-star in that film, Hope Lange, was another of the younger Hollywood set of the late 1950s and early 1960s who became a close friend of yours, and would marry Alan J. Pakula, the producer of* Inside Daisy Clover.

Oh, she was somebody adorable, and one of the most beautiful young women I've ever encountered. We met her very early in her first marriage to Don Murray. She was just like an angel from heaven! Yes, she would look at home with a pair of wings on her back!

Murray and Lange both made their film debuts co-starring with Marilyn Monroe in Bus Stop. *Hope Lange was then Oscar-nominated for her performance opposite Lana Turner in* Peyton Place, *and more than held her own opposite co-star Joan Crawford in* The Best of Everything.

She was such a good actress, I think, but not allowed nearly enough range to prove it. Breathtakingly beautiful when we first met, and I think Don was jealous of her, but I think her next husband, Alan Pakula, nearly worshipped her and treated her as the jewel she was.

Although she would ultimately marry Pakula—the producer, writer, and director who was Oscar-nominated for To Kill a Mockingbird, All the President's Men, *and* Sophie's Choice—*she left Don Murray for a relationship with Glenn Ford, her co-star, along with Bette Davis, in Frank Capra's* Pocketful of Miracles. *Ford would also become a friend of yours and Chris's, and would sit several times for you?*

Including one sitting wearing a cowboy hat, yes!

Among your papers at the Huntington Library, I found some remarkable snapshots, presumably taken by you, of Hope Lange and Don Murray backstage at a 1960 L.A. stage presentation of The World of Carl Sandburg, *which starred Bette Davis and Gary Merrill. Davis is also captured in several candid post-show shots reminiscent of the photos you and Ted surreptitiously took of her nearly ten years earlier at the preview screening of* Decision Before Dawn. *You and Ted had infiltrated that earlier event, but given your newfound connections through Chris, you were now able to include your brother in the intimate backstage access you had for this one?*

Oh, yes, I remember that. Yes, we went together, Ted and I. It was an occasion where Ted and I would be more likely to be together there than Chris and I.

Whereas a theatrical production associated with any of Chris's friends would certainly have seen you in attendance with Chris. Over a heady 1961 Christmastime in New York, for example, you went to see Julie Harris, with whom you both were also staying, in A Shot in the Dark *on Broadway; and, in the company of the playwright himself, were at a preview performance of Tennessee Williams's* The Night of the Iguana, *seeing Bette Davis in another of her rare stage appearances.*

Yes, and Tennessee introduced us to her backstage before the show. That was exciting, yes!

When your good friend Armistead Maupin interviewed you and Chris for The Village Voice *in 1985, he said that he considered Chris, Truman Capote, and Tennessee Williams to have been "the three graces of the older [gay] generation," to which you suggested adding Gore Vidal, but then pointed out that he'd "never really declared himself."*

Well, that's partly Chris, too. He loved Gore as a friend. He loved him, but he was always embarrassed not to be able to praise his work. And of course, Gore couldn't help but notice, but he was too proud to ever put himself on the spot, or put Chris on the spot. He never insisted on a frank opinion from Chris, whereas Chris genuinely loved some of Tennessee's plays, although not so much the stories. But I think it would be true to say he respected Gore as a writer a bit more than Truman. I think he truly loved Truman, as I did, but not as a writer. Even though Gore never wrote anything that I think Chris could wholeheartedly praise, he respected him and admired his absolute dedication. I think Truman would have lived longer if he had concentrated on the work.

Indeed, Chris dedicated A Single Man *to Gore Vidal.*

Chris felt *A Single Man* was his best novel, and that was a sincere act of respect to Gore. And let me say for Truman: that hurt him, because he and Gore were rivals, but he wouldn't let it spoil his friendship with Chris.

Capote and Vidal maintained a legendary rivalry.

Oh, the two of them would not stop! Every time he came to town, Gore would bitch Truman up to the wall, and every time

Truman came, he'd just make such cruel fun of Gore! Well, they both made us laugh. They couldn't have been more wicked about each other, and making Chris suffer for being friends with the other! They were just merciless with Chris! But Chris wouldn't let it get him down: he wouldn't take it seriously. The truth was, he didn't admire either of them enough as writers. I think he felt Truman was a much better writer, but that what he wrote about wasn't interesting to him. So I think he respected Gore maybe more than he respected Truman, but he loved Truman as much as he loved Gore, because he was so entertaining.

What was your own relationship with Truman Capote like over the years?

Truman was just one of the sweetest, wittiest, best people I've known. He was just great company, and I was really *very* fond of him. I knew that he was courting me and pleasing me as a means of getting in Chris's good graces, and indeed he did: he got into *both* of our good graces. I knew it at the time, but still I loved his attentions. He was just so *amazing* in his charm and his wit, and Chris appreciated it just as much as I did. We both loved him.

You've regaled me with some delicious Truman Capote stories, my favorite of which finds you and Chris joining him on a late-night flight...

Oh, the takeoff! We were sent from the airport here to Burbank Airport because of the fog, and it was a night flight, so by the time we got to Burbank and into the air, it must have been two, two-thirty in the morning. It was a very rocky takeoff, and while we were still climbing—Truman was in first class; Chris and I were in tourist—Truman got his safety belt off, came tumbling down the aisle right into tourist class, and leaned over to us and said, "Are my bunnies scared?"

Delivered, no doubt, with devilish intent?

That was Truman, yes! The stewardesses went out of their minds! They had never dealt with anybody like him. He just wouldn't take no!

You and Chris were among the intimate group of celebrity mourners at Truman Capote's memorial service in 1984, with Chris's eulogy later described by John Gregory Dunne as being "the most graceful thing of all." Chris simply said, "There was one wonderful thing about Truman. He could always make me laugh." Chris then began to laugh, and returned to his seat.

I think he was just determined not to be solemn, and not to put on a funereal face. I remember there were aspects of what Chris said that I thought would sound odd to a lot of the people there, just because they were not the accepted tone: that he really was giving Truman what he felt he deserved, which was a personal touch. He was speaking about Truman the way Chris himself would prefer to be spoken about, so it was not the least bit solemn or teary, just because he loved Truman. He couldn't really—and didn't—speak publicly as openly as he spoke to Truman himself, but he was *always* good on those occasions. I never remember feeling that he hadn't hit exactly the right note. He was a gifted public speaker: never rehearsed; never read; always spoke spontaneously. I mean, he would think about the tone he wanted to strike and the points he wanted to make, but he would never compose anything, and that always impressed me. And he was always just right on. I often heard people at funerals afterwards saying, "Oh, what you said was totally unexpected, and how right it was!" He was a very good theatrical performer, and of course, speaking at a funeral is pure theater! You owe it to the audience to surprise them if you can, to make them laugh. Laughter is so refreshing to employ. He even was asked to speak at Merle Oberon's funeral, and he was just perfect! We knew her:

she'd sat for me a couple of times, and we went to her parties. He was surprised to be asked to speak, but then he said, "Why not?" I remember particularly after the funeral saying, "Gosh, you surprised me," and how good he was, and how right. It really did create sparks in the atmosphere, but I can't remember now precisely what he said. I wish I could. He was always wonderfully dependable on those occasions.

It's mentioned in both The Animals *and Chris's diaries that at some point, Gore Vidal was attempting to get you sittings with John and Jacqueline Kennedy?*

Oh, he talked big and bragged about his connections, but both Chris and I felt he was on very unstable ground: that it was more bluster than real content, and that he was talking it up more than it deserved to be. I'm sure he went to the White House and saw them, but I don't think he could ever have effected that kind of event. And anyway, I would rather do sittings with movie stars!

And he did indeed coordinate sittings for you with another power couple: Hollywood superstars Paul Newman and Joanne Woodward.

Separate sittings, yes. Tackling one was quite an effort for me, so I did them one at a time! But they were both very good, she especially. I've still got the first one I did of him, and it looks very like him. She was harder to get a likeness of, but I did because I was determined to, and she was very helpful. Both of them were very nice to me. But having a movie star at my disposal always took tremendous courage for me. I was scared out of my wits sometimes that I would say something wrong or disgrace myself, or that I was biting off way more than I could chew. But if Gore had arranged it with the Kennedys, I certainly wouldn't have turned the opportunity down. But I just never took it seriously: I thought he was just bragging. I was very fond of Gore, but he was trouble for me in so many ways.

How so?

For years, I could be in the same room with him for an hour or more and feel that he wasn't the least bit conscious of my presence. He was rude in that kind of way, but it didn't occur to him to treat me any other way: I was like Chris's beau. I think sex for him was just a kind of something to get over with as quickly as possible. But we actually got to be friends, and I became very fond of him at the end of his life. I know he loved Chris—as capable as he was of loving anybody—and that Chris really meant something to him, that he really did admire him, and so after the first few years of encountering him, I just stopped expecting any kind of recognition and took it in my stride. I have a whole series of pictures of him, from the earliest times through, well, *past* when he turned into a real *toad*. That was shocking, for somebody as handsome and as vain as he'd been in the early years, to really become almost grotesque. Our last sitting together was the best of all, because he was Mr. Toad himself, holding himself upright, and he was very lovable. It was like finally realizing that Mr. Toad was, after all, just another lovable creature—and there *was* something touching about him. Gore was one of the first of Chris's friends that I decided it didn't matter how they behaved to me: because Chris was fond of him, I made up my mind to be a man about it, and to take Gore's total lack of interest in me in my stride. And once I did that, I started to become fond of him. He always called when he came to California: he always wanted to see Chris, and finally, I wanted to see him as much as Chris did. So it was one of the tales that began dangerously and ended surprisingly well.

Whereas your relationship with Lincoln Kirstein played out somewhat in reverse. For an intensive period, you were the object of his affection and attention, and through him gained intimate access to the New York City Ballet. Chris later wrote of you being enraptured by ballet, observing that it "really gets to [Don] as almost nothing else does."

It was true. I was amazed myself. I'd had absolutely no exposure to it before that first trip to New York with Chris, and then meeting Lincoln and seeing a lot of the ballet, by the time I'd started drawing professionally, I was really deeply into it. And in the '60s, especially around '64 to '66, I made a lot of trips to New York by myself, and that was very important to me: a kind of establishing myself, functioning independently of Chris. Lincoln and all kinds of other people helped me do that, and that was very encouraging to me. It was very good for Chris and me, too, because it proved again that I could go away, and *come back*. The first and worst instance of it was when I went to London in early '61: as I said earlier, that was the most heartbreaking departure for both of us that ever happened between us. I knew he thought I was going off for good. That wasn't at all my intention, but in his mind, it was certainly a possibility down the line. But I had to find out what it was like on my own, in a big city, like New York or London, and if I could function without Chris's backing. And I could, because a floor had been established for me to stand on in both cities. I could and did operate, *and* deliver. Yes, I often went alone to New York after the first introductory trips with Chris, because Chris didn't really like New York. As fond as he was of Lincoln and Wystan, he still was very resistant to going to New York. But of course, Chris was so gentlemanly, even with me, that he would never interfere with any excuse I had to go to New York to work.

And for a brief time, you even rented an apartment there?

I did take an apartment once, for half of '65 and some of '66— on West 20th, between Eighth and Ninth. Lincoln actually found it for me. It was a gorgeous floor-through apartment with wonderful light, and with a garden in back which was covered in snow in the winter. I was loaned a bed, and went through almost a junk shop to get just chairs and a table. So that lovely apartment was almost bare, but it was so good to have so little furniture: nothing to worry about or take trouble over. That space, in New York especially, seemed wonderful to me.

So your intention to be there was for purely professional reasons?

To do a ballet portfolio. Can you imagine corralling all those dancers for sittings? In New York, having to travel by subway or taxi, with my big board and bench? Only one or two came to me on 20th Street. And during that year that it took me to do those drawings, of course I went to the ballet constantly, and I just fell in love with it.

I imagine that Chris was characteristically accommodating, even though, as during your London sojourn, you both suffered in being apart?

Oh, yes, and I think Chris was a little cross with Lincoln, without telling me, because he guessed—well, he *knew* that Lincoln had made it possible for me to have a good excuse to go to New York, because that's where all the dancers were. But Chris wouldn't dream of interfering with my career as an artist, since he was the one who made it possible. He came two or three times and spent a month or six weeks with me, but he never wanted to stay in New York longer than that. And I wanted to have a place of my own in New York, but the truth was that I didn't really want it, didn't really need it, and as soon as Chris wasn't there, I missed him. So what was the point of it? It was worth doing for a time, and I got it out of my blood. But when I came back in '66—of course, with trips back and forth—I proved that, when I left, I was coming back—and with the first significant publication of my work.

As with that earlier year in London, this New York period proved just as critical in establishing yourself as a professional artist.

Same thing then. You see, I had this idea that to be an artist, what I needed and therefore wanted was to be on my own and have my own place. But I just needed a few weeks' experience of both to know I didn't want it at all. I much preferred being with Chris; I missed him and wanted him back! I remember crying over the phone early that year I went to London, missing him so much, and I knew he missed me, so he came over and spent six months with me there. He was already too important to me to not have by my side.

For a time, you were folded into Kirstein's unconventional household near Gramercy Park, which included his wife, Fidelma, and the artist-conservator Alexander Jensen Yow. Fidelma was the sister of the artist Paul Cadmus and an artist in her own right, but like her husband, she battled mental health challenges throughout her life.

Oh, poor thing. All those dinners at 19th Street, she would sit at the end of the table talking, talking, with Lincoln, Jens, and I and whoever else, and Fidelma talking, saying, "I know I'm talking too much," and then she'd go on talking, just silencing the table. Oh, God, how we all suffered. She knew that she was giving herself away, and that it was kind of silly, inconsequential talk, but she couldn't stop herself, and nobody would say, "Shut up, Fidelma." Well, she suffered with Lincoln, but then, Lincoln probably had to have a cover, didn't he? It was just that shame and embarrassment. Of course, it was another time, but if he hadn't been such a coward, he could have done it without a fake wife.

Nevertheless, he kept a series of boyfriends coming in and out of the house, which she benignly accommodated.

Yes, yes, including me.

In a letter you wrote to Chris from New York during that period, you made this observation of Lincoln Kirstein: "He will never be able to stop thinking of me as a dear little boy from the west. I don't fit into any of his preconceived ideas about The Artist. He can't explain to himself how I could be any good really. His only way of coping with me is to treat me like a student in need of guidance and so I have to listen to talk about 'form' and 'vision'."

Imagine, after knowing me quite well by that time, having that kind of attitude? Well, I was naturally condescending, too, in writing that, and why not? I understood. I knew nobody took me seriously, including all the people in the ballet company. I was just Lincoln's latest pretty boy from somewhere. They didn't consider me any kind of artist. Well, they hadn't seen my work, really, or they just took one look at me and said, *well, he can't be much of an artist.*

And then Kirstein ultimately choked in approaching his co-founding partner in the New York City Ballet—its venerable choreographer and longtime artistic director, George Balanchine—for his agreement to their producing and selling the portfolios as ballet souvenirs.

Lincoln was such a coward. He knew Balanchine so well by that time, but he was still embarrassed because, well, Balanchine would probably presume what everybody else did: that Lincoln was only doing it not because I was a good artist, but because I was a pretty young man. And of course, Lincoln's total embarrassment about it made it all the more impossible for me to be taken seriously as an artist. But I'm not ashamed of that portfolio: I think those portraits are very competent, and the dancers were surprised, too. When I started doing the sittings with them, I knew that most of them were just expecting some kind of amateur performance, but they got portraits that look like them, that are well-drawn. And I did the whole company: all the featured players, and I've got second and third drawings of some of the dancers. They were really beautiful.

It was a large company. How long did it take you to get to everyone?

It took me a year to get everyone, not because I was unable to work, but because it was so difficult pinning down the dancers. They were doing their seasons all over the country. I think Jacques d'Amboise was the first of them I did, in '64. There might be one or two that are dated '66, but the bulk of the work was done from '64 to early fall of '65. Some of them were done at the theater—I remember Mimi Paul sat for me in her dressing room—but some of them actually came to me, to the apartment I had on 20th Street. Most of them were first drawings, but there were some that I did two of, if they were at all interested. I knew I had got d'Amboise with the first one, but I did do another one of him. I did another one of Mimi Paul, because she was one of the most restless. Patricia McBride was even more difficult than Allegra Kent, just because she also couldn't be still. Melissa Hayden was really one of the best of the dancers, and the most difficult of the sitters. She was the one who really couldn't be still; she was always changing. I don't remember any of the others giving me any trouble. Maria Tallchief was one of the ones I most enjoyed working with, and she enjoyed it, too, and that's why she sat for a second one. I got two good drawings of her; it was very difficult to choose between them. Arthur Mitchell loved his portrait, and why do you suppose he loved it? Because he looked White! I mean, it's perfectly clear that he's a Black man; I just didn't color him in dark. They were all black-and-white drawings, and I didn't bother to make his skin dark. I didn't think about it; it's just the way I worked. The color of it really had so little to do with who he was or what he looked like.

There's tremendous diversity throughout your body of work, the result of your insatiable quest to portray the great variety of the human experience.

Yes, I'm an artist who's really interested in humankind. What artist could ask for a more interesting subject than another human being?

No matter how that fellow human being looks or identifies?

Couldn't matter less. The more difference you can dig up, the more fun it is! Also, it makes for a much less interesting drawing if you cover up all that white paper.

In trying to suggest skin color through shading in a black-and-white drawing?

Exactly. I remember, actually, in my early days, people were so surprised by my drawings of Black people because they were clearly Black people, but with white paper for skin. But I didn't have to color in the skin, make it brown or make it dark in any way; I didn't need to. I just concentrated on the features the same way I treated White people. I think a lot of Black people were surprised how they came out: that I didn't have to color everything in, and yet it was perfectly clear they were Black people. I just draw the features, that's enough. For me, that's where the personality is: it's not in the dark or light, it's in the features themselves.

And even in your later painted portraiture—to which you apply a rich palette of colors, no matter the person's actual skin color—your focus has remained on the features of your subjects.

Since I identify myself as an artist of personality, it doesn't matter what the color is; the color is just a minor consideration. It's the *personality*, you see, that I've always been interested in: how to depict the personality. So the color is just an added tool, just something that makes it easier for me to express more about a given person. And because I work from life, I always have to worry about time and not tiring my sitter, so putting in the unnecessary darker tones just to prove that somebody is Black rather than White, it isn't worth it. And you see, it was in my early experience, too, because we had Black models in art school. I kept a lot of my art school work, and a lot of the male nudes were Black men, though most of them were obligated to wear a covering, a jockstrap. Not all of them, but it always irritated me. I'm very adept at drawing penises. They have every bit as much personality as the face!

They certainly do! There's a quote of yours from Chris & Don: A Love Story *that I find particularly expressive of your philosophy and approach as a portrait artist: you say that "every face has to be im-*

portant. Every face. And when you think, each individual is showing me a face that he is living his entire *life with, so it has to be of* immense *importance."*

I've *never* turned *anybody* down. In fact, what interested me very early were people who I said to myself, now he or she would be very tough to do a likeness of, to bring out what is striking about them, just as people. And so, from the beginning, I promised that I would never turn down anyone who was willing to sit and be still and let me look my heart out. And in fact, I had a whole period when I concentrated on the difficult ones, just the ones who, when I first looked at them, I wondered how would I render that personality, how could I get a likeness of him or her? I searched them out: I searched out the people who I thought were more difficult, just to find out if it was really true, and usually I could do them. It might have taken more trouble at first, but then eventually I proved I could take on *anyone*, if they cooperated. It *has* to be a collaboration: I'm only as good as my sitter, because the more patient they are with me, the more I can do with them, and the more I can bring out.

Just as you've challenged yourself throughout your career in taking on a great variety of sitters, in the late 1970s you also transitioned from drawing to painting your portraits. Why the shift?

Well, I was determined to be absolutely certain of my craftsmanship before I launched into color. So I didn't have to wonder, could I draw that hand, or whatever detail? I would just think about color, and I wouldn't have to worry about the draftsmanship. I knew I could do it.

Meanwhile, those ballet portraits were executed just a few years into your professional career.

I graduated from art school in, let's see, '60, so I became a professional in '61, '62, and it was in '64 when I started those. I was thirty. But it was a good year and a half, maybe two, since the last of the drawings was done before it was published and it got shown to Balanchine. I know it got shown to him, because I have the copy that Lincoln showed Balanchine, and it's full of red pencil notes by Balanchine, and I know it was embarrassing to Lincoln. But as close a friend as Chris was and I became, he didn't quite believe in me enough. He would pay for the ballet portfolio, but he couldn't bring himself to set up a sitting with Balanchine. He couldn't take that extra step, because he really was still in awe of Balanchine. So what consequence could the ballet portfolio have without Balanchine in it?

I would imagine it left the portfolio feeling incomplete, unendorsed.

Yes. I saw the crazy side of Lincoln coming along before it really developed. But of course so many people told me, including Chris: Chris knew he was very quixotic and unreliable, so I had a lot of information to help me navigate the waters.

Chris's diaries make mention of several collaborative projects that Kirstein pitched to him, such as a film of Sleeping Beauty, *but none of them ever came to fruition.*

Lincoln was a mine of ideas and came up with so many, and they were often very good ideas, but he just didn't have the staying power to believe in his own ideas, and eventually everybody found that out about him. It was too bad. Yes, I think there were a couple of other things besides *Sleeping Beauty* that he was very excited about and spoke to Chris about, and Chris said, "Yes, I'd love to do it!" But then when you stop having brainwaves and produce a starting fee—you know, get down to it—well, he never did.

Just as his staying power in supporting your ballet portfolio fell apart just before the finish line.

And of course, Lincoln had to turn on me, because he hadn't put it up for sale. That was why it was printed, but he was embarrassed to do it, and embarrassed to tell me that he was embarrassed; embarrassed that anyone in the company knew, so it was only his bad conscience that he suffered from. I went to New York after it had been published, but nobody had seen it: he hadn't shown people, and he was under pressure. I remember our last meeting in the flesh was at the theater at intermission, or before a performance. There were other people around, and Lincoln was very excited; we had words, and he was so upset. I suppose I told him what I thought of his cowardice then, and all the misleading things he'd said to me. I certainly wasn't scared of him. He was a big man, but I knew he was a pussycat.

Were you tremendously disappointed or disillusioned by that experience?

Well, that my first real job, but no, it didn't matter. I'd done a job, and I knew I'd done it well. I put my heart in there, and did the very best work I could. And Lincoln spent a lot of money: that wasn't cheap to do. But it was too bad: I was sorry to lose a best friend. I loved him, and I never saw him again. But that wasn't hard to effect, because I was here, and he was there.

You hadn't yet embraced your vocation as an artist when you first met the other celebrated artists who orbited Lincoln Kirstein. Now that you were among them as a fellow working artist, what was their reception like to you? Most notably among them would have been Kirstein's brother-in-law, Paul Cadmus, whose Seven Deadly Sins *had so deeply impacted you on your first trip to New York.*

Those paintings tell something about Paul: I do think he had a horror of pretty much most of humankind. It was a thrilling shock for me at first, but it kind of seemed almost too much, eventually. And Paul never encouraged me in any way: he kind of laughed at me, you know, just with his manner. He was very friendly to me: he sat for me, he showed me his work, but he didn't like me, I thought. But I wasn't sure whether he really liked anyone. I think it was really that he didn't like humankind much, that he wasn't kidding about the "deadly sins." I think that it was really a subject matter that he reveled in. He was always sort of laughing at human nature: that he was always finding more proof of his poor opinion of most human creatures—more proof of that than he really wanted—and that he was kind of wanly beleaguered by his own poor opinion of most people.

And perhaps by his own chosen lot in life, as a visual reporter of it all?

Yes, that it was all essentially kind of somber and sad. And yet he was almost saintlike in his behavior: that quick smile of his! He looked almost saintly, until you got to know him better!

When beneath the veneer lurked a harsh critic of humanity, whereas your approach to your work is to demonstrate the tremendous variety of the human experience without judgment.

Yes, yes, yes, it comes down to being judgmental. Yes, I think he certainly was, unmistakably so. And he was that sweet man, but it was more convincing in the early years I knew him. It became a façade behind which the deeper, darker Paul was more and more visible, until it got to the point where I could barely see the sweet version of himself; the other took over to such an extent. I never felt that Paul saw anything to like in me, so I kept my distance from him. It took me years before I dared to ask him to sit for me, and I feel that he just endured the experience without getting anything out of it. I certainly don't think he saw any hope for me or for my work as an artist. But those were the days when I was still trying to believe in myself as some kind of artist, and felt that there wasn't any encouragement from any of the people that I knew in the art world in New York. I felt that in some way, there was an immediate resistance just to anyone from California: that that was the part of this country that showed most clearly what was wrong with it.

As though to say, how could you be any good if you weren't New York School?

Yes, how could you be any good if you weren't somehow unhappy and gray, gloomy, and wan?

Was it challenging to maintain your confidence in your own artistic vision while in the company of fellow artists in that New York scene?

Well, I think I hid behind my own objectivity. I sometimes shocked myself at my own daring! I would really draw anybody who would sit for me. It took a long time to ask Paul to sit, and I knew he hadn't enjoyed it and hadn't thought it was worthwhile—for him. But I saw all of these people from the outside; I didn't really make any kind of meaningful contact with any of them. Jens Yow was the only one.

Alexander Jensen Yow was the longest-lasting of Kirstein's extramarital companions. An artist and photographer, he was briefly George Platt Lynes's studio assistant and designed fashion backdrops for Cecil Beaton before becoming a master conservator at the Morgan Library in New York. He also modeled for both Lynes and Paul Cadmus.

He was a real charming surprise! Jensen had the top floor in Lincoln's house, and he was such a beauty and a darling, too. I always thought he was so sexy, and exactly the right size! And that wonderful voice of his!

He maintained his melodious Southern accent right up to his recent passing at age ninety-six, even though he had left North Carolina for New York some seventy-five years before.

I always think it's such a shame when Southerners study to lose the accent. A genuine Southern accent is always charming. Well, he was so attractive to me, and such a sweet and sensual personality he had! And just his voice, I can hear it now: the Southern twang. Not twang: *flavor.* Oh, I remember him so clearly. We went to the ballet and to the theater together a few times. Jens was always very sweet to me, very nice, and I was very attracted to him, but I never made a pass at him because I assumed he didn't reciprocate, so I didn't want to embarrass us both.

He was wonderfully candid with me, as are you, in describing the ever-swinging pendulum that was Lincoln's behavior, from brilliance to madness and back again.

I think that Wystan Auden was the only person that Lincoln got any kind of nourishment from.

And why was that, do you think?

I think he just had enormous respect for him, but I think he was suspicious of Chris. I think he felt Chris had been contaminated by California. I think he liked him better fresh from England than he did as a Californian.

Kirstein's own passing passions and peculiar prejudices were what moved one into and out of his ever-revolving favors. But as you said, beyond Kirstein, there seems to have been a general skepticism among that New York set of you as a "California artist." Yet you were ultimately confident enough in your own work to ask other artists beyond Cadmus, particularly New York artists, to pose for you?

I waited a long time. I'm always hesitant to work with other artists. I feel it's a test of my nerve! Yes, I would tackle a movie star with much more conviction than another artist.

Didn't Salvador Dalí put you on public trial by sitting for you in a New York bar?

Yes! It was at The St. Regis in New York, and when I arrived, they called up to his room to tell him I was there. "He's coming down." "Why is he coming *down*?" I thought I was going *up* to his apartment to draw him in the peaceful quiet. No! *His* condition for sitting for me was to make a public spectacle of himself!

And thereby one of you.

Yes, but I'll *still* do a sitting with an artist—or with any celebrity sitter, really—and adapt to whatever conditions they force on me, because I consider myself a professional, and if I don't want to do it, I shouldn't be drawing well-known people.

On one heady day alone, you took on sittings with two superstars of the art world: Jasper Johns and Andy Warhol.

Yes, I did three drawings of Warhol, all done in one sitting, on the 29th of January 1970. You'll notice they aren't signed and dated.

He didn't or wouldn't sign them?

And you know why? He didn't want to sign them because he thought I might sell them as self-portraits, and he wouldn't get the money! He was very, very obsessed with money. He was raised poor, and he must have been worth quite a bit finally, but I know he was very obsessed by money. I think it's a terrible weakness. I was disappointed, so I said, "Well, will you sign them on the back?" He hesitated again, and then said, "Alright," and he signed all three pictures in wah-wah writing. He had very precise handwriting, but he did it all illegibly. Now, imagine being that stingy? That mean and petty? A fellow artist, and he wouldn't sign, because he wouldn't get the money? Let me never find myself being cheap like that!

Or a fair-weather advocate of someone's work, as was Lincoln Kirstein.

Lincoln fought with almost everybody, but he was not in control of himself. I don't blame him: he had a passionate temperament, and he couldn't really control it. That's who he was, and he was hopeless to change; he'd have to be somebody else to behave properly. He could be rational and obey his keen intelligence, but when the temperament took over, he was helpless to fight it. So we had that kind of misunderstanding, finally, which I was very sorry about, and because he was upset with me, that meant he couldn't call up Chris and be friends with him anymore. The ballet portfolio debacle was all between Lincoln and me, but it was Lincoln's guilt about that *and* me that was the problem. Chris had no problem: he really was fond of Lincoln. He loved him, I know, and felt deprived of his friendship. In the early years, when we were together with Lincoln, the three of us were very close. It was only when I started going to New York by myself that the trouble began. I very much regretted that, but I think Lincoln was just ashamed of himself, and so that interfered with *his* attitude toward Chris. It wasn't about Chris's attitude toward him. If I'd told Chris what I was up to, it might have sounded to him like I was in jeopardy of leaving him, but because I didn't let it happen, it didn't happen. I had the sense to know who Chris was, and enough respect. I could betray him sexually, but I certainly wasn't going to betray him in any other way. And anybody who knew me at all knew that I was Chris's, and why? Because I never met anybody like him! He was everything to me. He was all the arts, all the movies rolled into one supreme being, and he was always that to me, so physical wanderings were nothing.

Did you ever come even close to being potentially lured away by an emotional entanglement with someone else?

You know, it was just that youthful dissatisfaction and wondering about different destinies, and whether they would maybe suit me better—but even if they might have suited me better, I still would have missed Chris. Even though I imagined briefly that that's what I wanted, I found out very quickly it wasn't what I wanted at all. So I had some ongoing relationships that only made me realize I was kidding myself. Well, you see, I started out with Chris when I was eighteen, so I was thinking, "Well, I must be too young to hit it lucky with the person I want to spend the rest of my life with." But the truth was: I *was* that insanely lucky. I met him right away, and I stuck to him, and I didn't want to give him up!

And there ultimately proved to be no need for your fear of having somehow missed out in playing the field.

Yes, and I played the field enough to realize that's exactly what it was worth. You have a pastime for a while, and then . . . oh so nice to be back home again!

One further early wandering occurred just prior to your year in London, when you were loaned the use of a small house as a first studio by your friend Paul Millard, who was an actor and property investor. You and Millard had a brief affair, which you kept secret from Chris?

Prior to London, in West Hollywood. And that was my fault: he was in love with me, I thought, but I don't think I ever was with him, so I shouldn't have led him on and shouldn't have engaged in that kind of duplicity. It wasn't good: it wasn't anything but tough on Paul and hard on Chris, and finally hard on me.

Trying to balance it all?

Everything. I thought I wanted something more lasting, but the truth was, I was just dabbling. I had been fond of him, but I imagined in finding Chris in the first place—and he just was Mr. Right—that I had to test myself *and* him. And even after those difficult years in the beginning, I realized I was just fooling around, and I really wanted to be with Chris.

You nevertheless enjoyed a relationship with an alternative "Mr. Right"—physically one, anyway—on the occasion of your thirtieth birthday in 1964, when you traveled to Egypt, Greece, and then on to Austria not with Chris, but instead in the company of another particularly beautiful young man?

Yes, I went with Rock Hudson's boyfriend, Lee Garlington! He was *gorgeous*: one of the most attractive young men I've *ever* encountered. Blond, *beautiful* body, tall, and deep voice: oh, all the things that just made me tingle! Oh, I was in love with him instantly! And I got to make a trip to Egypt with him, yes.

Another occasion when Chris, the faithful old "Horse," waited patiently behind while you, the "Cat," went out "mousing" on your own.

Yes, yes, yes. And that was one of the first occasions, and it was just necessary. Lee was a *perfect* specimen of Mr. Right: physically, age, deep voice, gorgeous—just everything. Well, if he was enough for Rock Hudson, he was good enough for me!

After all, one has to have one's standards!

Yes! I have nude drawings of him. Oh, Chris was very patient with me! Chris, of course, knew exactly what was going on. Lee was Southern and had just the most beautiful body. The deep voice, oh. I would say physically he's the most beautiful, sexiest man I've ever had sex with, and that trip to Egypt was just, yes, I was in love with him certainly, but not foolishly. I just was determined to get to him and have him for just a few weeks. And Chris, with all of his experience as a young man? Of course, there was no way he could keep all of his adventures unknown to me, so I used them. I said, "Look, I'm the age you were then, and you're not going to pen me up, are you? Fence me in?"

Could he dare to deny you all he had experienced?

He would if he could have.

But he gambled instead on playing the long game, on being graciously accommodating, hoping you would work it out of your system?

Well, after all, it's all about the person you live with: how well you know him. And I felt he ought to have known me well enough to trust me. To let me wander, but to trust me—and he did. And I proved him right to let me go, and let me come back. I started really early telling him he didn't have to worry about my being spirited away, but of course he didn't believe it, until after years of faithful service, he began to believe it. I just wanted the freedom to sample! My attitude was, and I said to Chris, "You had all that experience when you were my age, and are you going to deny it to me?" But I told him, "I can handle it without breaking up with you," and we didn't break up. Ever. I had lots of temptation, but it was never anything strong enough to move my feelings for him. But it was hard on him: even though I assured him I didn't want to leave him, still I was fooling around with this one and that one, and just being foolish and inconsiderate of the people I was involving with my life. But luckily, I think, most of them knew it right away, because I found out pretty quickly myself.

Perhaps the most serious threat to your relationship with Chris arose from a series of portrait commissions for the casts of works by the playwright John Osborne. That job took you back to London in 1968, and into the intimate company of the director of those plays, Anthony Page.

You see, I was having an affair with Anthony Page: we were sleeping together. I think I even was in love with him, and maybe we might have ironed out something together if it hadn't been for Chris. But that was probably the deepest I got with *anybody* that I was sleeping with while Chris was still alive, because there were all those months I was in England with Anthony and we could spend a lot of time together, which we never could have if he were in town here. And I know Chris worried that somehow I was going to slip through his fingers, and I did fall in love with Anthony, but I knew it never would last. We would have driven each other crazy.

Nevertheless, Chris worried about it, if only privately expressing it in his diary.

That was his nature: he worried.

You can track his faith in your relationship strengthening as the diaries progress and the years pass: he becomes more and more

confirmed and confident in his belief in the permanence of the rela-
tionship.

And you see, we never lost our physical relationship. And it was really more than sex: it was about really being physical in bed together, sleeping.

About intimacy?

Yes, and I know it was as true for him as it was for me: it was the intimacy that mattered. The sex was just the icing on the cake. It was the intimacy that it was all about, and that was always secure, no matter how much temptation I had—and I had a lot. And I invited it: I wanted it and I acted on it. And why shouldn't I? If I could live with him knowing all the experience he'd had, why couldn't he? Well, because it was going on concurrently, and that *is* a difference, but I said he just had to get used to it!

Do you feel, as do many gay men, that we don't necessarily need to sub-
scribe to the heteronormative construct of monogamy in committed
relationships?

We were explorers, we were inventors, and it wasn't frivolous. It was every bit as real as heterosexual sex could be, and to this date, at my ripe age, I've never had sex with a woman, or wanted it or needed it. And for what reason? I've been perfectly sexually satisfied all of my life. I've been so lucky! And I love women: they're really still my favorite subjects. I think I still can give more to a portrait of a woman than I can to a man, or at least every bit as much. It's gotten now that it doesn't really matter, but in the beginning, even when I was drawing movie stars, the first man didn't come around for years. I had to really learn to get the same enjoyment out of drawing men as I did women. But now, it doesn't make any difference.

Did Chris share much with you about his more significant previous re-
lationships?

Well, you see, I questioned him all of the time. I knew he would try to avoid it, but he couldn't lie to me, and I knew it, so I'd be a fool not to take advantage of that. He maybe didn't tell me *all*, but I forced him to tell me *enough*. And if he didn't like admitting it or my asking, I felt I *deserved* for him to be patient with my appetite for experience, and not deny me what *he* had. But yes, I questioned him relentlessly. We spoke often over the years about Heinz Neddermeyer, because Chris was very fond of him, so he told me quite a bit about him.

In 1952, Chris had been reunited with Heinz, now married and with a son, on his first visit back to Berlin since 1933. They would remain in warm communication in spite of Chris ultimately declining to sponsor and financially support Heinz and his family's emigration to the United States.

Yes, and I'm not sure I ever even met him, but I knew Bill Caskey. I met him in those early years, and Billy was *really* dangerous: *really* dangerous for *me*, because Chris was still his property, in his mind. I was a trespasser. The few times I met him, I understood very well that from his point of view, Chris still belonged to him.

And what did or could you do with that awareness of his view?

I just trusted myself and my own estimation of Chris. Billy was very self-defeating, and I think it probably boiled down to feeling guilty about being queer early on. Chris would never dream of it, but he told me enough about Billy and the difficulties that he had. Billy was emotionally damaged before he knew Chris, and he betrayed Chris right and left: I mean, they were deeply involved, but it had nothing to do with faithful devotion, and I think that's what eventually got Chris out.

So there certainly wasn't much to hold one in relationship with him?

I think their relationship really depended very heavily on liquor, so it was always tempestuous. It was a very open relationship for at least a great many of their six years together, and I think it was always tempestuous, even when they were together. They'd split up, but they were still close and occasionally having a night together when Chris and I took up together. Billy was very disapproving, and showed it. I'm sure he gave us six months at the most. I shudder now at some of the evenings I spent with just Chris and Bill Caskey and maybe a mutual friend of theirs, but I did it. And he was attractive, Bill Caskey.

I've seen beautiful nude photos of Chris and Caskey taken in Province-town in the late 1940s by PaJaMa, the photographic collective comprised of artists Paul Cadmus, Jared French, and Margaret French.

I've seen some of those, too. Billy was like Chris: he was short, but he was very masculine, with a kind of gruff voice, and a very witty speaker. Well, I know he must've made terrible fun of Chris taking up with me, but he didn't deter him, and Caskey then got so irritated with Chris that finally he had to go to sea just not to be able to see him, to get it off his mind. So he signed up as a seaman on a ship, and by the time he came back a few months later, Chris and I were a happily married couple.

His absence had certainly not made Chris's heart grow fonder. Whereas with another Bill—Bill Harris—Chris maintained a lasting friendship following a brief romantic relationship?

Oh, yes, a hot romance. Hot, but brief. Bill Harris never fell out of Chris's affection, ever.

Did you ever meet him?

Often. Certainly his beauty had evaporated by the time I met him, but yes, we became quite good friends. Sometimes I was alone with Bill Harris—probably on my later trips alone to New York, I saw him. I was fond of him, but Bill and I couldn't help but feel ever so slightly like rivals. I knew he and Chris had had a big affair before I knew Chris, but that never bothered me. I think, if anything, it was a little bit painful to Bill, who had been a great beauty, to meet me, still at pretty much the height of my beauty, and not feel sad, because he'd lost his own beauty by then. Not his charm, but his beauty. Bill never got over being told when he was young and beautiful that he looked like Marlene Dietrich! And I became very close to his two friends who moved out here, Jack Fontan and Ray Unger.

Jack Fontan's claim to fame was as the "Naked Sailor" in the original Broadway production of South Pacific. *I'm sure you know the story: beautifully sculpted and wearing only the shortest of shorts, he was known to squat spread-eagled during one particular musical number, thus revealing the fact that he never wore underwear. Women and gay men kept the premium front rows sold out throughout the show's long run!*

Yes, I've heard about that!

So you would have known Fontan and his partner, fellow bodybuilding enthusiast Ray Unger, after they moved to Laguna Beach, California, where they established a gym that counted Bette Midler among its members. Fontan had previously been in relationships with Jensen Yow and Chris's former lover, Bill Harris, whom he and Unger ultimately took into their home and cared for through his death from AIDS.

Jack was still very beautiful: a very attractive man, and I even remember we had sex together, Jack and I, and I was very hesitant for fear that it would create a negative condition between Ray and me. I loved Ray as much as Jack, and I didn't want that to happen, but Jack assured me and even Ray assured me, "Go ahead!" So I did. They were very sweet to me and became very good friends, and I used to go down to Laguna and sometimes stay overnight, and of course we talked a lot about all those earlier days in New York. They both knew Lincoln Kirstein and filled me in on a lot of the gossip I had missed at the time. A current theme around that time with Chris, after we'd been living together some years, was my having my own life and my own friends that weren't all dependent on him, and Jack and Ray were the personification of exactly that distinction. They became *my* friends rather than Chris's, because Chris knew it was smart to let me have my own friends. But it hadn't ever been a case of his *not* letting me; it was a case of *my* being afraid to dare to have friends of my own. He wasn't possessive in that kind of way. For many years, he knew or thought that there was always the possibility that I'd find somebody I liked better than I liked him, and I told him I wasn't going anywhere. But of course, why should he believe me, until I'd been around so long that I proved it? We were together for thirty-three years. But oh, I remember in those early years, he'd say, "Oh, you'll meet somebody. You'll find a nice guy." And I'd say, "Oh, yeah? Oh, yeah?" until finally he stopped that.

But yet, in honestly acknowledging that you were still a young man without the wide experience he had enjoyed, he allowed the relationship to open up. Through then writing what became A Single Man, *he explored the consequential possibility that you might be spirited away, never to return.*

Yes, what would his life be like if I did leave him? But you know, that was a way of strengthening himself and believing in himself as capable of living a life on his own. I kept saying "I'm not going anywhere," but it didn't matter: he had to believe it, and finally he did.

Do you think perhaps he finally exorcised it through the writing of A Single Man, *in really examining what it might be like should you permanently leave him?*

Yes. And he always discussed what he was writing. I gave him the title.

You did?

I did. He always asked my opinion. He said, "I haven't found a title yet," and it just popped out of my head. "How about *A Single Man?*" I'm surprised he took it seriously. "Oh, I want to think about that." But that's what it became.

Not only does that title fit the book perfectly, but it's also fitting that you named it, given the inspiration and impetus you inadvertently provided for its writing.

It was his favorite of all of his books. And isn't it miraculous that Tom Ford managed to make a really good film out of it?

He made an extraordinary film of it, well-deserving of the critical praise it received.

I think it's a wonderful film. And the odds were certainly against it: the first film of somebody who hadn't been known in any way as a filmmaker? Wow. The odds were sky high against it.

Did Ford consult with you much during its development and production?

I remember he came one day and sat on the couch and said he wanted to do it, and I said, "Wonderful." I encouraged him in every way I could, and I was on location several times while it was being made. I was always encouraging. He showed me a rough cut of it, and I loved it. Yes, the odds were really stacked against it, and he pulled it off. I loved the film.

And you make a brief appearance in it, sitting alongside Tom Ford's partner Richard Buckley as fellow "professors" in a faculty lounge.

Richard was a very sweet man, but we're in it oh so briefly. I think I saw the film two or three times and found I had missed our appearance every time! I remember the first time I was through it, trying to remind myself which one I was before I'd already disappeared!

At least you're fleetingly visible, unlike your first experience as an unseen extra in The Rose Tattoo.

Oh, that was so *utterly* humiliating, and I was wised up about my childish ambition to be an actor. Oh, I gave up that ambition full-heartedly in favor of having so much more fun, yes!

CHAPTER 8

The beautiful and damned

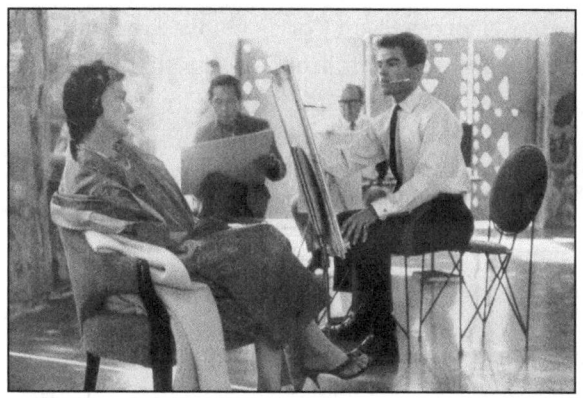

The formidable Mrs. Frank Lloyd Wright poses for Don (and others) at Taliesin in Scottsdale, Arizona, in January 1963. (*Photo by Joseph F. Rorke, M.D., courtesy of Shawn Rorke-Davis and the Christopher Isherwood Papers, The Huntington Library, San Marino, California*)

Given the tremendous impact of movies on the development of your visual sensibility, just as Chris's early moviegoing had influenced his writing, it's no surprise that you two eventually collaborated on writing a number of screenplays.

Yes, we wrote at least six scripts together. Only one of them, the *Frankenstein*, got produced, but as with those things, that's average. You're lucky if you get one in six produced. But our favorite was a version of F. Scott Fitzgerald's second novel, *The Beautiful and Damned*. It was just a perfect subject for a film, and we wrote a screenplay we were so pleased with. It was almost *all* lines that we got out of the novel. You couldn't get more sincere than we. It was oh so makeable, but it never got made. And I know it would make a *wonderful* movie still, but there's no chance nowadays of having anything like that made. Hollywood has made a sharp turn in the kind of movies they produce nowadays. But with just a little bit of help from a good cast and a good director, we knew it would have been a swell film. Of course, my role was really based on how well we knew each other; on Chris's ability to be himself with me. I know I helped him a lot. In frustration sometimes, I would poopoo my input, but he would say, "No, you're wrong. You've really helped me in ways you don't understand." Of course, he was always so kind and sensitive and flattering when he told me I had talent enough to be a writer. I would say, "Oh, you're just putting me on." And that would make him so angry, because he wanted to be believed. But he won out!

Your own talent as a writer is amply evident in your book, Stars in My Eyes, *which collects just a sampling of your celebrity portrait stories.*

Oh, goodness, all of that came out of my journals. The subject matter was what I was after, not the writing. I'm no writer myself, but at least I know enough about writing to know where my real talents are! Well, there were so many sittings I did with Hollywood people who would have been perfect subjects, but I can't explain why I wrote about all of the ones I did and didn't write about the others, which were every bit as interesting to me, and in some cases more so. It was just happenstance, the ones that I did write about. The sooner I wrote about the sittings, the better the material was. I always tried to write as soon as I got home from a sitting, because I knew that writing immediately was always the best. I couldn't really relive it if it was too long before:

if more than a few days had passed, I couldn't fake it. It had to be fresh. But largely because when I work, I have to make appointments with people to sit for me and then I have to write them down in a datebook, those are very helpful in jogging the memory—just as if I have the pictures in front of me, they spark me and I can remember certain parts of the details of the encounter. Even when I look at a work of mine from decades ago, working from life really sears it into my memory, so I can always come up with some detail if I have the work I did in front of me. But why did I stop writing about them? I wish I had gone on, because each were really exciting experiences for me. And here I am, surprised by the clarity of my own memory, because I would have thought before we started talking that I might not have very much to say, and here I am, chattering on. And I have had *wonderful* experiences, acknowledging moments of real *luxury* in my looking, and of saying to myself, "Gosh, I'm here, drawing Joan Fontaine!" That kind of awe—it's still there; it's still exciting just to talk about it! But yes, I think I've got at least ten or twelve volumes of typewritten journals. It was all very messily handwritten for years, on little blue-lined paper in those little notebooks with about nine holes. Most of it was with pencil, and with little arrows writing more things—tiny writing, anyway, and then tinier above. But I did at least take the trouble to make a fair copy of it all, and in the process added material, if it was relevant. A lot of it I could barely decipher, but decipher I did. It's all now legible, and I'm not going to destroy it before I die, so it's there. It'll be of interest, I think, and it's very frank about myself and people I was involved with, but years ago I made the decision not to publish.

And why is that?

Because I have too much respect for writing! I just know it isn't good enough. A lot of it has interest because of *what* I was writing about, and of course there's a lot about my life with Chris.

It's the information rather than the quality of the writing that is of interest, and I know that, but I think it's presumptuous of me after all these years to come on as a writer.

Were you nevertheless disappointed that your screenplay of The Beautiful and Damned *was never produced?*

We did get paid for all of those outlines—we were doing it on spec—but yes, that was the one we were most pleased with. By then, we knew each other so well that we could spend a solid two hours, maybe three hours, every morning working on whatever script; then we'd take a break, go down to the beach, jump into the water, come out and dry off in the sun, go back and have a snack, and then I'd work in the studio and he'd go back to his workroom. And we both said how helpful it was, doing our own work, knowing that the other was doing *his* own work. It was a dream. For many years, it went on.

Another script with which you had much more success was an adaptation of what would be Chris's last novel, A Meeting by the River. *It was produced as a play both in Los Angeles and briefly on Broadway, and more recently was revived in a podcast production featuring Dominic West and Penelope Wilton.*

We did the play and the movie script. Again, I know I helped Chris a lot, but most of the time, I really kept my mouth shut until he asked me for something specific. Occasionally, I could come up with something helpful to him. It was a little bit, I imagine, like being hypnotized by a professional hypnotist: if we were communicating well with each other, it was like being a medium for him. I remember he once wanted a word for a continual movement, something that wouldn't be still, and I came up with the word *inconstant*, which is not a word I would ever think of using, at least not at that time; I've used quite a bit since. And he loved it, because it made him remember there's a line in *Romeo and Juliet* where Juliet refers to the "inconstant moon." I wish I knew what he wanted it for—that, I can't remember. But I know that when he wanted my help, oftentimes his question would come when I was in the middle of something else or I was on my way somewhere, so that if I answered at all, it was spontaneously. It was that hypnotist/medium kind of relationship we had. And sometimes when we were working together, I knew that my role was just that: to be intuitive rather than interfering. Most of the time, I could suppress my impatience if I felt I'd rather be in the studio than sitting at the typewriter. I did sometimes feel that, but I would keep my mouth shut. Anyway, we only worked in the mornings, and we never did it for more than three hours, and sometimes for only two hours or even less. But we did do it steadily, and eventually we were very pleased with the work that we produced. But my input was always based on my knowledge of him, rather than any concrete example. I couldn't point to a single line of dialogue that I could say was all mine, and why should I? Why should I even make that demand? Anyway, Chris was much better at dialogue than I, and that is why I can hear his work in some of those Hollywood scripts he wrote, because I knew the way his mind worked.

What inspired you and Chris to take on reimagining Frankenstein *for a film?*

It was the producer's idea. I thought when the producer brought it up that Chris would not be interested, but I was surprised by how much he wanted to do it, and how much fun he had thinking up the female character, the female creature. I could tell he was having a great deal of fun doing it. Even the typing was fun, and I am a good typist. I could keep up with him because he was considerate in his delivery of the dialogue, what he writing. In those early days, we really established a working rapport. That showed itself in many other ways in our years together.

What inspired your novel approach of making the Creature physically beautiful upon his creation, but then grow increasingly hideous?

Just the poignancy of being beautiful and losing it—that's very heartbreaking and very theatrical, and the kind of thing you can really develop, it seems to me, so much more emotionally. We had a lot of fun doing it. We really had our own terms and always discussed everything, and Chris again and again claimed that my input was equally as essential as his own. And we knew each other so well that we knew how to make each other laugh, and that's *very* important when working together: oh, if you can get the humor going, that's the magic in any script, even writing a tragedy. The humor is so essential.

If you'll pardon the pun, were you pleased with the way your Frankenstein *script ultimately came to life as a film?*

No, it could have been so much better. We had a second-rate director. He was a nice man, and he did his best, but oh, it could have been so much better!

Your director was Jack Smight, best known at that point for having directed the thriller No Way to Treat a Lady, *and for* Harper, *which starred Paul Newman amidst an all-star supporting cast that included your friends Lauren Bacall, Julie Harris, Roddy McDowall, Robert Wagner, and Shelley Winters.*

We had written the *Frankenstein* script for John Boorman. He'd just done *Deliverance*, and he said, "I can do anything I want, and I want to make this a big budget, three-hour film." Oh, we were going gangbusters! And we loved John: it was all for him, written for him, but our producer didn't want it taken away from him! He knew that John Boorman was a powerful director who would make it his! And he was right, but he also knew it would become John Boorman's success, not his, and so he sabotaged it! We worked so well with John, and it could have been the film we dreamed of! But this *jerk* ruined it! I can't even remember his name now. He was the son of somebody or other.

He was Hunt Stromberg Jr. Aside from producing your Frankenstein as a three-hour, two-evening network television event in 1973, he was otherwise known for having transformed actress Maila Nurmi into the kitschy character Vampira in the 1950s.

We always knew that he was just as far from being top drawer as you could be and still function! But it would've been impossible for him to please us, and we took it for granted we would never be pleased, but that didn't keep us from doing everything possible to make it as good as we could. There was certainly no laziness involved: we worked on that as though we were novice writers, and it was our first child. But he just didn't know, so we just had to deal with him on his terms. But we got on with him. That all seems long ago now.

You nearly worked with him again on a subsequent horror film.

The Lady from the Land of the Dead. That was our mummy story, and the other one that got closest to getting a real production going, and it was with Stromberg, yeah. We had a lot of fun!

But back to your Frankenstein: Stromberg evidently had clout enough in Hollywood to assemble quite a stellar cast. It featured Michael Sarrazin as the Creature and Leonard Whiting as Dr. Frankenstein, supported by James Mason, David McCallum, Jane Seymour, Nicola Pagett, Michael Wilding, Agnes Moorehead, Margaret Leighton, Sir Ralph Richardson, Sir John Gielgud, and Tom Baker.

Well, you know, that was his idea, being in the business: to get star names and actors to sell it, and he could get any cast he wanted. But OK, he got a lot of names in it—but oh, it was so badly done. We wrote it, it was really good, we were really pleased with it, and it could have been just what John prophesized: a three-hour film, and a hit. It would have been a smash, because together we were just perfectly attuned. But I've had such a lucky life, why care about one of the few disappointments? We didn't have any kind of director; Chris never had. Tony Richardson might have been that, but Chris knew that Tony would always have to change things to make it his. If we couldn't have John, what we wanted was a wonderful director like William Wyler who could serve a script, who would want a script that was the very best a writer could do so that he could do with that script the very best a director could do in serving it. But Tony would always want to change it—and that's why Terry Southern was a better writer for him than Chris.

Chris collaborated with Terry Southern on the script for Tony Richardson's 1965 film adaptation of the Evelyn Waugh novel, The Loved One.

The very real quality of what Chris supplied Tony with was the structure of the script. Most of the dialogue was made up spontaneously by Terry Southern on the set. Chris spent a lot of time on the set, and he said it was extraordinary: just before turning the camera on, Tony would say, "Terry, give me something here. Tell me what this line should be." Chris said Southern's ability to come up with spontaneous dialogue was really enviable.

So Chris didn't feel pushed out?

He didn't. He knew Tony very well, and he knew Tony was after something other than a real script by Chris. But Chris, doing his best as always, really did construct the script, and I think it shows, as compared to a lot of Tony's other movies of the period. Also, as it was from the Waugh book, I bet Tony would not have gotten as good of a script from Terry Southern had he been the only writer for it. He might have been able to come up with the immediate dialogue on the set, but I bet he wouldn't have gotten as nearly a well-structured script.

Was Chris pleased with the outcome of any of the many films he had a hand in writing?

Oh, he was pleased with a lot of his own work, and together we were very pleased with several of our scripts, because we always wrote them to please *ourselves*. Chris always thought it was so amateur of playwrights who were hired from New York to write a screenplay and felt that they were writing *down*. Chris *never, ever* felt he was writing down, because it would have bored him. He just had to please himself, really: it had to be fun for him, and he could *always* find the fun in *any* writing job. And if I couldn't find it myself, he'd show it to me. He had a lot of movie jobs, which he wouldn't have taken except he had a new young boyfriend, and he felt that the more money he made, the better it might turn out, and so he took things that he wouldn't have ordinarily accepted. But it got to the point where he didn't want to write scripts anymore by himself, so he said if I would work with him, it would be much easier to do it. I'm pretty well-organized; I always have been. That was helpful to Chris. Even in those early years together, I was helping him by organizing manuscripts and things. But it turned out that the most valuable class of my entire school career in Los Angeles was the typing class I took in junior high! That had given me more advantage than anything else I ever learned! Well, our first collaboration: he was finishing a novel called *The World in the Evening*. We would discuss the scene that was going to be written, and then Chris would start reading it out to me, and I could keep up with him. He was very considerate when he would dictate: he would go at a pace, and I could keep up with him. I was a good typist, sixty-plus words a minute, and it was fun. We laughed a lot and had a good time working together. He had this charming way of asking my opinion about all kinds of things, and making me feel like we were doing it together! I think *The World in the Evening* was the book he spent more time on than any other. It was really a transitional book: it was his first book on American material. But it was a big hump: I think he went through seven versions of it over

many years, and the draft that he was doing when we got together
was the last of seven. And my name is in it: at a certain point,
there's a party, and it's being described, and the last names of some
of the guests are mentioned, and Bachardy is among them. Chris
put it in to please me, because I typed the final copy of it. When I
took dictation from him on the final draft of the last chapter of
the book, that's when he put in my name. But I don't think I could
really do dictation at all now. I'm visual: I have to see it—and if it's
just words, I have to see them, too.

You culled the stories you included in Stars in My Eyes *from your journals. Was it because of Chris's example as a dedicated diarist that you
also picked up the habit?*

Yes, I got the habit from him. Chris kept a journal, but he also
kept datebooks, and one of our first collaborations was that he
would let me keep his datebook for him. I mean, he would dictate
it to me: I would write things down, and he would add to it or sub-
tract, but I realize it made it more a difficulty for him than a convenience. Most of my diary-keeping started in the '60s, but it
wasn't until the '80s that I became very consistent. It had a lot to
do with Chris, because it encouraged *him* to keep *his* diary. In the
mornings, when I would be writing my diary, he would be writing
his own. I think it encouraged him to write more, which is really
what I wanted. But it never occurred to me to share my journals
with Chris. He never read any of them. It was a pact we made, very
early, because he knew, and we joked often, about the terrible
things I must be writing about him: the dastardly portrait I must
be making out in my literary description of him!

*But it was your own private space in which to work out the frustra-
tions that invariably bedevil even the best of relationships.*

It was. Well, my frankness is about my *own* bad behavior, not
Chris's, because if anything, he was my victim.

Perhaps the most extraordinary letter included in the book The Animals, *which collects your correspondence with Chris, is the captivating account you sent him of an unforgettable visit to your friend Marguerite Lamkin Littman's family home in Louisiana.*

Oh, Marguerite! Imagine having all that drama? It was so Southern Gothic! The moment I arrive, her father shoots himself? I mean, it was almost a comedy! Well, having that experience and then describing it to Chris, yes, it was a lot of fun to do it, and there was so much to write about! That very first night, BANG! Yes, it was too *Southern* for words! Well, she and her brother, Speed, were *perfect* representatives of life in the South, and the *bizarre* results it could affect! Marguerite was just an *adorable* creature: just so funny, so wise and witty, and a bit gullible at the same time, so it was a *wonderful* combination. And she was just extraordinary looking, from my point of view. I could never really get her to sit quite still enough for the portrait of her that I longed to do which would do her justice. I did several, and some of them are good, but she deserved my absolute best. But somehow or other, *why* it was so difficult is that she didn't believe in her looks. She was a facsimile of how she thought a beautiful young debutante ought to behave. She could have been the real thing, and in fact she became it, just out of willpower, but there was still that question of doubt in her own mind, and that was always interfering with her.

Nevertheless, she parlayed her portrayal of a Southern belle into quite a unique career for herself in Hollywood.

Oh, yes, she became the absolute only verifiable Southern expert of *all* things Southern at the perfect time in the mid-1950s when the South took over Hollywood, and she got a job on every single one of those films. She coached Elizabeth Taylor on *Cat on a Hot Tin Roof*! And was, "Oh, Elizabeth and I are this-and-that..."

Like Elizabeth Taylor, Marguerite later became an HIV/AIDS advocate, founding a British fundraising charity that later merged with Elton John's AIDS foundation, of which she then became a director.

She was also determined to regard herself as a buddy of Tennessee, but I know just from my own relationship with Tennessee that he was reluctant to let her have her way a lot of the time.

Meanwhile, your letter recounting Marguerite's own very Southern family drama could easily rival anything Tennessee Williams ever wrote. Chris himself was so gripped by your account that he replied, "I enjoyed it so much that I quite forgot to feel sorry for anybody. Honestly, this is literature!"

I thought at the time he was maybe just flattering me, but Chris told me that I could have been a writer. But he consciously encouraged me in the direction of art, because he quite rightly guessed that if we were both writers, it would probably produce many more conflicts. And gosh, he was always so sensible, and thank goodness I knew it. In fact, thinking back, I was going to say it was so perceptive of me at that early age to realize how unusual he was, but then it didn't need perception, because he was so utterly charming—and at his very best with young men! And then that awful dilemma of finding my vocation: I would never even have been an artist if he hadn't been there encouraging me. But then it took him three years to get me into art school, and then more important even than art school was when I came home—and it was way downtown, driving there back and forth every day—he would say, "Let me see what you did." And he wasn't kidding: he really *was* so interested. As I say, I would never have believed in myself sufficiently without him. I mean, he paid for it all, sure, but what was even more important was that genuine interest.

Beyond his encouragement and praise for your work, did he ever critique it?

I showed him everything I did. Even on the rare occasions when we didn't agree on my work, years later I remembered I was defending something that he didn't much like, or vice versa, and I almost always realized he was right the first time. He was unusual, yes, in so many ways.

And he reciprocally invited and valued your participation in his own work, such as the guidance you offered during the writing of his 1962 novel, Down There on a Visit.

That's the one I helped the most with.

Whereas you have every reason to be proud of how your adaptation of Chris's novel A Meeting by the River *came to life.*

We did the play and got it produced here in L.A., and even got a Broadway production with a whole week of previews. But the opening night was the final performance; the reviews were so bad. By that time, we were very glad to get out of New York and get home. But we had a very good production here, directed by Jim Bridges.

James Bridges later wrote and directed The Paper Chase *and* Urban Cowboy, *among other major movies.*

Really, both Chris and I said that Jim's production made all the effort of writing the play worth it, because we *did* get to see our work on stage with a great cast and a great talented director.

Among its cast were Laurence Luckinbill, who had previously appeared in the groundbreaking original Off-Broadway production of The Boys in the Band *and its subsequent film adaptation; Florida Friebus, who was best-known on television for her roles in* The Many Loves of Dobie Gillis *and* The Bob Newhart Show; *and a young actor named John Ritter, who would achieve TV stardom just a few years later in* Three's Company.

That was the production here, and then it was a completely different production in New York.

But at least you had the opportunity to see your creation come to life as you had envisioned it.

And that was very satisfying. Jim was a very talented young man and a good friend. He was wonderful to work with, too. We never had a single problem, and did that whole production with him and often visited his movie sets.

Among your papers at the Huntington Library is a production still of you and Chris with Jane Fonda on the set of The China Syndrome.

Yes, because Jim Bridges wrote and directed it. He and Jack Larson were, I think, our best queer friends—they and a few others. Yes, we were very close to both of them and loved them both.

James Bridges's life partner was Jack Larson, a playwright, librettist, and actor best known for his role as cub reporter Jimmy Olsen on the 1950s television series Adventures of Superman.

Oh, yes. I've seen too little of it, and even now after all these years, I'm hungry to see really more of that show.

Prior to his thirty-five-year relationship with Jim Bridges, Jack had been the companion of fellow actor Montgomery Clift.

They'd had an affair, and Jack, of course, was very proud of it! But you know, he was a pretty good-looker at the time, too, so it was perfect. They made a very good-looking couple. But Jim was very attractive, too, especially in the early years. It was awful when Jim was dying, just awful. He *hated* dying. I remember a visit I paid to him in the hospital on his deathbed: it was just so painful, and I don't mean physically painful, but the pain of just having to go, and so young, and he was so ambitious and with more than enough talent to handle all of his ambition.

After Bridges's death at age fifty-seven from cancer, Larson would live on another two decades in their longtime home, the Frank Lloyd Wright-designed George Sturges House in Brentwood.

Oh, that gave Jack such pleasure! Living in that house was like he'd been anointed. Jack especially was just *so*, "Oh, Mr. Wright!" He got the Wright furniture, and he just loved living in that house, but it was a real killer. Two tiny little bedrooms. Chris and I just marveled that they could be so pleased with this *really* uncomfortable house. The Wright chairs were so unbalanced that every time you sat down, you were in danger of tipping! And yet we couldn't say a *word* against Master Wright! Jim was much freer about him when Jack wasn't around, but Wright was still a saint for Jack. Of course, everybody who knew Wright knew not to complain to him, because his answer would always be, "Relax, and enjoy the house." But for Jack and Jim, especially Jack, it was his *dream*. He just couldn't have been more thrilled with it. They kept it as Mr. Wright wanted it. Well, I wouldn't want to do it!

I understand that you had a memorable encounter with the Master himself, Frank Lloyd Wright, and even had a sitting with the imperious Mrs. Wright?

Yes, I did. We made a trip to Taliesin in Arizona earlier than the one I made myself to draw her, when Wright was still alive. And the drinking at Taliesin by the students and the teachers! Wright wasn't present for any of those late-night meetings. We were there because his second-in-command was the brother of our friend, Ben Masselink.

Ben's brother, Eugene Masselink, was a designer and Wright's longtime secretary. Ben wrote several books before becoming a television writer for such shows as Marcus Welby, M.D., Barnaby Jones, Hawaii Five-O, The Six Million Dollar Man, The Incredible Hulk, *and* Starsky and Hutch.

Gene was a nice man, and so was Ben. Ben and Jo Lathwood lived right down on the canyon here. They were pretending to be Mr. and Mrs. Masselink, but they never married. She was a

designer of sports clothes and had a lot of Hollywood clients, like
Janet Gaynor and Anne Baxter, people like that.

*Among the first bikinis to appear on California beaches in the 1940s
were those designed by Jo Lathwood. Coincidentally, Anne Baxter was
not only an Oscar winner and major star, but also the granddaughter
of Frank Lloyd Wright. She appears in one of your early fan photos,
and later sat for you.*

Oh, she was very generous to me, but she was hopelessly ac-
tressy! She had a good heart: I was very fond of her, and she sat
for me so perfectly several times. But you see, she was just so ac-
tressy that it was all so phony, but in a kind of likable, almost innocent way. It was really unworthy of her, but she couldn't drop
the theatricality of her personality: being an actor was the limit of
her expression. And she was always squat, and always a little too
overweight, but earnest. Earnest, and she believed it, too, but it
was always so tinged with theatrics with her. You see it in her
movies; you see it when she goes too far. It works in *All About Eve*
because she was really playing it as herself: even though she was
giving a performance, it was the same performance she gave as
Anne Baxter! She had to have a really tough director to rein her in.
But there are some of her performances I like, and considering her
looks and stature and promise, she had a miraculous career. And
she loved being Frank Lloyd Wright's relative, yes. She was frank
about her association.

*I would imagine that she also approached the experience of sitting for
you as a sort of performance?*

Yes, she *acted* believing in me and believing in art, and so I
knew I had her; she couldn't get away, because she couldn't stop
doing that. And because she regarded herself as an implacable professional, she would stand almost anything; even a painful situation, she'd be brave. When she sat for me, she was *acting*
somebody sitting for a very talented artist, and a lot of the time

there was a strain, maybe twinges of pain, but patience always, and never a harsh word or an unfriendly action. Chris and I both sincerely liked her. She invited us to her house a few times, but she was somehow so silly, her performance of even being just a friend: she was more theatrical in a room with her than she was giving a performance in front of a camera, but yet there was something really sympathetic about her. And dying so young, I never would have guessed. I think she probably would have become quite an effective theatrical personality, because she was *all* about theater and the kind of falseness that makes you an actor, a lifelong actor. I would have been very curious to know her as an old lady.

Chris's friendship with Jo Lathwood and Ben Masselink had predated your relationship, but it then intensified among the four of you?

It thrived especially when I came on the scene, because there was a thirty-year age difference between Chris's and my ages, and Jo was twenty years older than Ben, so that added a kind of simile to the equation and immediately gave us priority to be their best friends. Oh, yes, it brought Chris and Jo closer. They were very good friends and a good encouragement to us.

Circling back to Ben's brother Eugene Masselink: I suspect there's much more to tell about the Taliesin visit he arranged for you?

Oh, yes! Because he was Wright's second-in-command at Taliesin, we were treated very well there and given a big shindig, followed by a night of heavy drinking, which was the custom at Taliesin. They were drunk every night! So of course, Chris and I, being visiting guests, wanted to join in! But the drinking was such that the first morning, we'd been so plastered the night before that we both had major hangovers, and of course everyone was roused to breakfast, and very gung-ho. So here was Chris, his nerves almost to the breaking point, and at breakfast, after maybe just a cup or two of coffee and maybe some mush, Wright, a real sadist, suddenly announced, "And we have a distinguished writer here who's going to tell us all about . . ." some absurd subject, and without any preparation at all, not a *hint* to Chris that he was going to be put in that position. He had to get up, with a major hangover, and talk about a subject that Mr. Wright had picked out of the rafters. He was a real sadist. It was second nature to him to get a celebrity there, and then to humiliate the celebrity if he could—just try to expose him and punish him for being whatever he was. Just instinctively; he didn't even have to think about it. Somebody like Isherwood *dares* to come, even when he's invited? He'll make him *sorry*.

Was Chris able to rise to the occasion?

Chris was a real professional. I knew how terrible he was feeling and what it was costing him, but he just drew himself up and he did it, and you would never have guessed. He was even funny. He really outdid Wright himself, and I felt so proud. Chris wasn't going to weasel out. In front of a student body, most of them nice-looking young men, he didn't want to disgrace himself or turn them off. He wanted to charm them, if he could, and if he'd been given a chance, he'd have been even more charming than he was on that morning. But he did his best, and of course, they wouldn't have realized the difference.

And Wright got a well-deserved comeuppance!

He knew what Wright was up to, his whole sadistic treatment. Mr. Wright would have been just delighted if Chris had made a terrible impression. That's what he was hoping for. He was insufferable, from everything I ever heard about him. Ben, through his brother, told us real stories about what went on at both Taliesins. Oh, well, Wright got the wife he deserved. They suited each other very well, he and the last one. I don't know what the first one was like, except she must have been either a fool or a masochist.

Wright had scandalously left his first wife and their six children for a client's wife, who, along with her two children, was later horrifically mur-

dered by a servant at Taliesin in Wisconsin. *Wright would ultimately divorce his first wife, then marry his subsequent morphine-addicted mistress, before finally ending up with the grand Olgivanna, his third wife.*

He behaved like a real heel. Maybe men have a chance to be much better people now that women are speaking out for themselves. I know the customs were different then, and a lot of women objected, but they were silenced by the horde of women who followed the example of the first Mrs. Wright, or created the example for *her* to follow.

Olgivanna Lloyd Wright later sat for you. Were you summoned back for that sitting, or had you asked for it?

Well, I'd asked for it, and so yes, I went back. And as he'd played a trick on Chris, she played one on me. If it could be set up properly like it was in life, it could be hilarious in a film! I drove to Phoenix especially for the sitting. That was a trip I made by myself, to draw her, and in fact, it's the longest I've ever driven a car, back to Arizona. It had to be prearranged in advance for such-and-such a day at such-and-such a time, and I was led to a quite quiet room with good light to work by. As I was just finishing setting up my drawing board and bench and all my equipment, I heard this *clacking.* I thought it was a wall behind me, but I hadn't realized that it was all made up of door panels, and they were being opened, opened, to a vista of the whole of the next room *filled* with people sitting at *their* drawing benches, very like mine, with their drawing boards set up! You see, the *queen* was so regal, she couldn't sit for just *one* artist, so the whole of Taliesin West had been summoned for the *great* occasion: The Queen Sits Again! And not sit just for Bachardy, but she graciously had allowed all of the students at Taliesin West to be able to gaze at her for as long as it took them to do a drawing! Granted, it could only take less than an hour, because the lady was very strict. So there I was, all set up, and I was meant to draw her with the *entire* student body of Taliesin West practically looking over my shoulder while waiting for the Master to pick up his pen and make the first stroke! Without any warning whatsoever! It was so insensitive of her, and yet so absolutely characteristic of her. She was that kind of sadistic queen: so regal, so phony, so awful, and with a colony of drones all salaaming to her all the time!

Did your nerves get the best of you in that high-pressured situation?

Well, by then I was already a professional, and I couldn't lose my temper or my nerve. I just took it as it came, and I just did one drawing of the queen. Oh, she was so unpleasant with her *graciousness* to her subjects!

Her benediction upon you all!

And I *knew* it wouldn't be a good drawing, because she prevented it by making it a public occasion! But I was *so* humiliated and embarrassed by being put on the *stage* by her. And anyway, who *was* she? Why would I worry about doing one inferior drawing of her? Even *that* was too good for her! Oh, she was so asinine, her behavior. Really, it was very unpleasant observing her. And if you see, if she hadn't played that trick on me, I would have done— with her permission, of course—a second or third drawing, but probably she would have balked at sitting for another, because that would have interfered with her idea of a grand sitting. You don't do it twice.

So while perhaps momentarily gratifying to her ego to impose such needless pressure on a portraitist, how ultimately short-sighted it was of her not to allow you to take your time, and privately, to get the very best of her?

You know, it was stupid of her to agree to sit for an artist and then to program the situation herself, without the artist's knowledge or consent! I had already made the trip to Phoenix to do the sitting, so I couldn't say uh-uh, and just drive home. I think if I'd have known what I was in for, I would never have even made the drawing. She really was *so* superior and gracious and queenly. She was *absurd*.

Mrs. Wright is but one of many challenging sitters you've faced over the years.

Oh, you can imagine some of the challenging people I got to sit for me, or Chris got to sit for me. Charles Boyer was just nasty to me.

How so?

I went to his house in Beverly Hills, and I was kept waiting a good half an hour. Down the stairs he came, and before he even sat down in the chair to sit for me, he said, "I have my toupée upstairs, but you won't need that. You can just draw my hair in." He had it upstairs, but *I* could do the grunt work of making it up in my drawing? Nowadays, I would say, "Couldn't you just make the effort of going back upstairs to put it on?"

Because you draw from life, so only what you can see is what he'll get!

But this was very early in my experiences of working as a professional artist, so I did it—I faked it—and it was *so* against my grain! You know, I was young enough and green enough; I did it. I did two drawings of him. They're both undeniably Boyer, and one of them is even quite good, but it was so rude of him! He wasn't a pleasant man, I'm sorry to say. And when I thought about it, I realized that it's clear in all of his movie personalities that he can be charming, but there is something off-putting about him.

Was Boyer satisfied with the drawings?

He wasn't about to congratulate me or praise me or do anything. It was just adequate from his point of view.

How about Mrs. Wright? Did she ultimately approve of your portrait-under-fire of her?

She did look at it, because I asked her to sign it, and she did. Yes, she passed on it. But she was almost too grand even to . . .

Deign to offer any words of praise.

Yes!

Let's get back to a far healthier and more rewarding collaboration: that between you and Chris. Among your combined papers at the Huntington Library, I've found several early drafts of your film script for Cabaret, *yet the screenplay was ultimately written by Jay Presson Allen?*

Oh, yes, we wrote an entire script, and I think we both had the impression that if it had been shown, if it had been read, if the people who decided . . . but we never knew. It just seemed like we'd never written it, and they'd never read it. And it was so early in the doings that we realized right away that we weren't even in the running, so we just backed off.

Why do you think Chris was passed over? Not only was the film an adaptation of his own source material, but he was a seasoned Hollywood screenwriter!

I think they were actually afraid of Chris, that he would be difficult and make all kinds of demands. We never felt comfortable with anybody in the production, it seems to me now.

What did you and Chris think of the stage production of Cabaret?

He didn't like the idea, because he really didn't like or trust New York theater people. He met many of them before he knew me, and it just wasn't a world that he wanted to frequent. So Chris never saw it on stage. I was going to New York and said, "Oh, Chris, come with me," and he replied, "No, I don't want to see it."

In fact, he opted not to join you in attending Truman Capote's legendary Black and White Ball at the Plaza Hotel in November 1966, just to avoid the temptation of being in New York and succumbing to also seeing Cabaret, *which had debuted on Broadway just a few weeks earlier. But you nevertheless went to both.*

Truman would have been disappointed unless at least one of us was there at the ball, and besides, I wanted to go, yes! I remember I mostly sat on the sidelines with Glenway Wescott, because we were good friends by then. I was happy just to observe it all!

What was your impression, then, of first seeing Cabaret?

I went right away, and I sat there thinking how right Chris was. He would have just hated it. But it was a hit, and it financed us for the rest of Chris's life. And it's still financing me, so, well, there's no tragedy.

Did he see the subsequent film adaptation?

Oh, yes. So the musical was done—he never saw it—and up came the film, but nobody asked him; Harold Prince or whoever, they never even came. The *set designer* came just to consult Chris about his being in Berlin during that period, but nobody else came anywhere near Chris. Nobody.

I find that astonishing.

Well, they didn't want to, because they wanted to do it *their* way! They didn't care about making it as good as possible! No, they wanted *it* to fit into *their* construction. We went to see the preview of it in Westwood. We sat in the first row of the balcony, center seats, and on came the movie, and Liza Minnelli was on the screen maybe three minutes when Chris leaned over and said, "She's no good."

In Chris & Don: A Love Story, *you explain that Chris's chief objection to Liza Minnelli's performance wasn't really that she was "no good," but rather that she was too good: too talented and polished a professional to pull off being the hopeless amateur he had intended the character of Sally to be. Minnelli then materializes in a brief interview in which she gracefully acknowledges that while Chris had his own point of view about the film, he nevertheless "liked that people liked it so much."*

Well, she was a professional and a lady! And he wasn't being vindictive: he wasn't just saying it because he hadn't had any part in the production. But oh, it so easily could have all have happened differently, and we all might have been good friends—for a few years, anyway. But I think she might have been worried about Chris, that he would find fault with her. She was certainly nothing like any of the other versions of Sally Bowles, including the real Sally, whom I knew.

Chris had based the character of Sally on the British journalist and political activist Jean Ross, whom he had met amidst the hedonistic nihilism of early 1930s Berlin, where he was a young expatriate writer and she was working as a nightclub singer in lesbian bars and second-rate cabarets. It was her escapades which formed the basis for his novella Sally Bowles, *which was later republished in his novel* Goodbye to Berlin *and the anthology* The Berlin Stories—*and, ultimately, inspired both* I Am a Camera *and* Cabaret.

Minnelli was just as foreign to the role as any image I could have ever had of it. My conception of the character just locked her out altogether, and that was probably what made her so effective in it. I think she's perfectly good in the film, don't you?

I do, indeed. While her read on Sally may not have exactly matched Chris's vision for the character, audiences and critics at the time were certainly unaware or unconcerned about it, and she won a Best Actress Oscar for what is considered an iconic film performance.

And you know, he only saw the film once more, and he never saw the original production in New York. But *it* wasn't any good: Jill Haworth, the girl who played Sally, just was hopeless. Joel Grey was very good, yes: he really sold that production. It was Harold Prince and him.

Joel Grey would sit for you just days before he added a Best Supporting Actor Oscar to the Tony Award he had also won for his work in Cabaret.

Yes, he did. I never knew him well, but I've got a couple drawings of him—I think one of them, anyway, is good—and we got along, yes. But Harold Prince, for whatever reason, never came close to Chris. Well, he just wanted it his way. Chris was a very agreeable guy: he would work with just about anybody, but they were scared of him, I guess.

The 1972 film adaptation, with director Bob Fosse also winning one of its eight Academy Awards, holds the record for the most Oscar wins for a movie without also claiming the Best Picture prize. Because of the film and its enormous success, I would imagine that you've come into frequent contact with Liza Minnelli through the years?

No, I've only met her once in my life, when Chris and I were in New York just on a visit, and he was asked to appear with Liza at a photo session for a cover photograph for whatever magazine it was, and so he did it. We both went to the session. It was very businesslike. I don't even remember who the photographer was. We were let in; Liza arrived later. We were all introduced—we didn't know each other—and Liza and Chris were then taken by the photographer in front of the camera, and suddenly, after just a handshake and saying, "How do you do?" they were all over each other, Chris and Liza, for the camera! The photographer instructed them, "Pretend like you know each other." You know, that showbiz understanding. Liza was laughing, her hand was over his shoulder, and they were just the best of pals. And then it was over. We all shook hands and said goodbye, and that was it!

Chris noted afterwards in his diary that he "rather liked her. She has a complete manner for such encounters and occasions; she genuinely enjoys them, so it doesn't seem false." Meanwhile, although he was generally dismissive of the film version of Cabaret, *he did find Minnelli's co-star Michael York "not only adorable and beautiful but a really sensitive and subtle actor."*

Yes, he did like his performance. Oh, it was nice to know Michael and be able to sincerely praise him without having to invent any positive attitude!

According to Chris's diaries, he also seemed to have had a particular liking for Michael York's legs?

Yes! And just seeing him from, say, the shoulders up, you would never guess that he had really good legs, but they *were* good!

You and Chris posed for joyfully intimate photos taken in your home by Michael York's wife, the photographer Pat York, and both Yorks in turn sat many times for you. Michael York also narrates Chris & Don: A Love Story. *I take it you developed much more of a long-lasting relationship with them?*

Yes, we were good friends with Michael and Pat. They both sat for me several times. She was very good-looking still when I saw her last, and oh, he was so, so pretty when he was young. I have some very good drawings of him at his peak of beauty.

One of those portraits, a head-and-bare-torso drawing of Michael York from 1972, is featured in your Hollywood book.

He was *very* kind to me, yes, but unfortunately I've had little communication from him the past ten or twelve years. He's got some dread illness, and I was told he was horribly affected by it physically.

He has been valiantly battling amyloidosis, while tremendously raising public awareness about that rare disease.

Yes, it's quite brave of him.

Cabaret *continues to be perpetually revived on stage in New York and London. Michelle Williams, who was Tony-nominated for her turn as Sally in the musical's 2014 Broadway production, later won an Emmy playing Gwen Verdon in the miniseries* Fosse/Verdon, *in which the filming of* Cabaret *was featured as a major plot line.*

Michelle Williams is a very sweet woman. I like her a lot. She called me up especially, wanting to come and talk to me about Chris, because she was doing the production in New York. She'd really taken the trouble to read all sorts of things, and she just wanted to get my opinion and find out about him. I was really very impressed by seeing her in the Broadway show. God knows, I've seen a lot of Sallys, and she was certainly one of the best. I knew she would be. When she was here asking me questions, she really wasn't kidding. I liked her a lot, and I liked her in the show.

Did she sit for you?

No. Isn't that odd? And she's a really nice girl. I don't know why I didn't ask her. I think probably it's just my age, which has interfered with my personality as an artist. I don't feel quite in command of myself anymore. Well, my God, I'm older than I *ever* imagined I would be, and older than I ever imagined I *wanted* to be, so that shouldn't be so difficult for me to understand.

Oscar-winner Emma Stone succeeded her in that 2014 production, although the most successful revival to date of Cabaret *has been the multiple Tony-winning 1998 production, which ranks as the third longest-running revival in Broadway musical history. Its Emcee was Alan Cumming, later replaced by Neil Patrick Harris, and its Sally was the ill-fated Natasha Richardson, daughter of your onetime friends Tony Richardson and Vanessa Redgrave.*

Alan Cumming is a charming guy, and has a face full of that: exactly that charm that he is such an embodiment of. I thought Natasha was OK. She didn't disgrace herself. I think if it's properly played, it's really memorable, that the character does come to life, but as close to life is still my memory of that first performance I saw of Julie Harris's, and it's now so dim that I hardly know what I'm talking about anymore, as well it should be. But Williams, she was, I think on the whole, a successful one. Not an ideal one in any way: she didn't really bring it to life for me, as I think it could be, but her attempt to be Sally was certainly as good as I've seen, and maybe the best so far.

What for you has been missing in the Sallys you've seen thus far?

It has something to do with femininity. I don't think any of the actresses that I've seen who have played her has approached her as a feminine woman. I feel that's somehow where all the fun in it is: in a kind of comic personality that only a woman could realize. I haven't seen all that many, but I don't think any of the ones I've seen has really done it for me. But I did see Julie in *I Am a Camera* before I knew Chris, and I remember being impressed by her in it, without really fully appreciating what was there in the character as written by him, and that came later.

What are your thoughts on the enduring life of Cabaret? *Its most recent revival in the West End won seven Olivier Awards, including trophies for stars Eddie Redmayne and Jessie Buckley. That production, with Redmayne again starring, received multiple Tony nominations when it moved to Broadway.*

You know, *Cabaret* didn't interest Chris at all. It being just . . . a musical? And just because there are queer characters in it, that didn't cut any ice with him. He even would have thought it was irrelevant to be surprised that something about queers really might be of more interest or of less interest. It just didn't really matter to him. But you see, it's the same with me. I mean, I'll draw you, but you'll sit still. If I can't do that, then I'm not the artist I claim to be. If it's human, I'll draw it! That might come back at me!

So no animal portraits for you?

Oh, animals! Oh! And children are so unformed! Children are the most difficult, because they have their likeness, their personality, but it's so delicately expressed, and of course they seldom sit really still enough for me. Because they're more difficult, I want them even stiller. But those who do have that patience and concentration are fascinating, and I've done some pictures of young people I'm proud of.

One particularly accommodating child sitter was Natasha Gregson Wagner, the daughter of your dear friends Natalie Wood and Robert Wagner, who sat for you at the age of ten in her family's home in Beverly Hills.

Yes, and whatever Natalie did to ensure it, she really sat better than any other sitter of that age. It was really something I *very* seldom let myself in for, but for Natalie, I'd be willing to do it.

Natasha recently wrote about that experience: "I remember wanting to please Don and my mom, of course. She told me how important it was for me to sit still, that I was lucky to have my portrait drawn by him. She didn't say it in a way that was condescending; she said it in a way that made me feel that she was entrusting me with an adult responsibility, and I wanted to pass the test! There was action going on around us: my sister Courtney coming in and out; my mom probably casting a watchful eye; Willie Mae, our nanny. We always had a house full of people! Dogs and cats and hamsters, maybe the TV could be heard from the kitchen, certainly the smell of Willie Mae's cooking wafting in and out, [but] all the while, I stayed focused so that Don could draw my portrait. I think I look sad in the portrait (almost a foreboding sense of loss), but maybe what Don saw in my face that day was determination: to be a good sitter. I don't know."

I knew her just briefly as a little girl, but something told me she would be a good sitter, and she was really amazingly good.

Her bravely and beautifully written memoir, More Than Love, *is but one of her many efforts in recent years to bring greater visibility to her mother's incredible legacy. One of your early portraits of Natalie Wood adorns the title page of the family-authorized photobook* Natalie Wood: Reflections on a Legendary Life, *and is also featured in the promotional booklet for* Natalie, *a fragrance inspired by its namesake's favorite natural gardenia scent.*

Yes, I was very pleased about that. And what is the significance of the title of her memoir?

The title is taken from an oft-shared endearment among Wood and Wagner and their children: "I love you more than love."

Ah, yes. Telling someone "I love you more than love": well, that's wonderful, isn't it?

CHAPTER 9

I am a camera

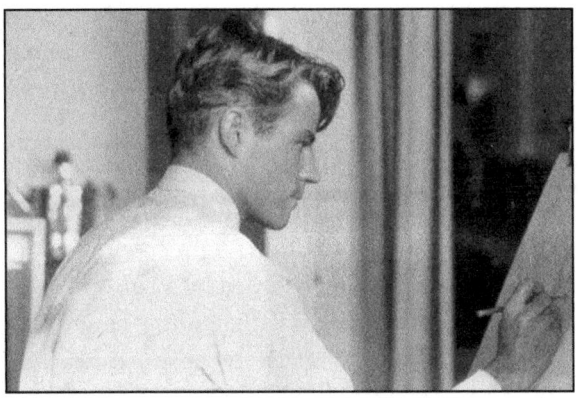

Don at work during a formative period in London, 1961.
*(Photo by Bryan Forbes, courtesy of the Christopher Isherwood
Papers, The Huntington Library, San Marino, California)*

Isn't it ironic that after so voraciously consuming those idealized, Hollywood-manufactured "realities" and personalities while you were young, you developed such an appetite for exposing the truth behind it all?

And how perverse of me to have an appetite for something beyond it! The movies trained me to look, but because I looked at so many movies, I wanted something even more startling than what

251

the movies could give me, and that is *life*. That is the truth, in all of its horror as well as all of its beauty, because the horror is part of the beauty. The horror makes the beauty so extraordinary: it points out the sadness in the eyes, rather than the sparkle, because it's the truth. I have to be after that for what I record, because it can't always be seen by the ordinary camera. Yes, the ordinary camera *can* see it: Cecil Beaton's untouched photographs of people have that same kind of excitement in them, that same truth, and he knew it. So of course, when he would photograph the Queen, the retouchers went at it full time. He wasn't going to send the Queen his un-retouched photos of her. Nobody would like them, either.

The candid photos he took of Garbo in a New York hotel room just a few years after she left Hollywood have that very excitement in them that you just mentioned.

They do, and of course, in those last pictures he took of Garbo, she was still beautiful, especially from a still photographer with knowledge of lighting. You see, more lighting would only tell me more truth that shouldn't be recorded by a conventional portraitist, and Cecil was clever enough with lighting. I knew that Garbo: I saw in life that Garbo, not long after those last Beaton pictures were taken, when I cooked dinner for her. I thought she looked just stunning—and of course, I had never seen her in color! But I hadn't even started art school yet. Had she still been available to me after art school—by which time she was several years older— I would have never had access to her. But she looked wonderful in 1954, in our first house across the canyon.

Chris had known her for some time, is that right?

Chris had known her since '39. He met her for *Saul the Fearful.*

Which was an unrealized film project.

He said when he came to Hollywood, the three people that he dreamed of meeting were Garbo, Chaplin, and Mickey Rooney!

He met Garbo and Chaplin almost immediately, but it took him toward the end of his life to meet Mickey Rooney, even though he worked at MGM and went on the set of Mickey Rooney's films and drooled, I'm sure, watching the cute Mickey perform for the camera. But by then, it was very rewarding, because what Rooney lacked in physical beauty, he made up for with his fantastic energy. Even as an old man, he never lost that energy. There was something so lovable about him. I went to his one-man show a few years after Chris's death, and the energy was just amazing. He was really funny and charming and a really awesome creature, even though he lost all the beauty he had as a boy. He was like nobody else, and Chris worshipped him in all his early films.

Meanwhile, your boyhood idols far outnumbered just three movie stars—and you ultimately met most of them!

If you had told me as a kid—or even as a teenager, when Ted and I were photographing all these people—the number of those people that I would eventually be drawing from life in a real sitting with them, looking them in the eye, I would have said, "My God, I must have died and gone to Heaven," Valhalla, with the experiences I've had. Bette Davis sitting for me? Twice? In her house in Connecticut? Spending the entire day with her, alone with Bette Davis, making me lunch and then dinner as well, before she let me go back on the train to New York? What kind of luck! I must be blessed if such a thing was going to happen to me.

Davis seems to have been the ultimate "get" for you, and potentially the most intimidating, given not only your lifelong reverence for her movie performances, but also her seemingly formidable personality.

I mean, to get Bette Davis to sit for me? *Jezebel* was just out when I was four, and I knew all about that movie and the *Life* magazine full-color page of her in *Jezebel* in that red dress, which was actually *bronze* in the movie, because a real red dress didn't photograph dramatically enough in black-and-white! As a child, that was just *wonderful* information for me, and of course, she was an intense favorite of mine for years. Oh, to get at her!

How did it ultimately come about?

Our first *almost* meeting happened after Chris had met her, and I don't even know how we'd got into the position of inviting her to lunch; I think that he had just done it.

Again, it's incredible how Chris played your "wingman," orchestrating many opportunities for you not only to meet celebrities, but then to also ask if they might sit for you.

Yes! I couldn't have swung it without him, and he wouldn't have bothered to swing it without *me*, because we were a team. He was charming to them to help *me*, because he knew it meant so much to me just to know these people and then get to draw them, so there was no end to his maneuvers to help me with whatever people I targeted for assault. And you see, in his company, he was my guarantee: I wasn't just a young Hollywood besotted fan. "Oh, if he's with Isherwood, maybe that young man has some real promise." So it just opened doors for me that never would have opened. Well, I wouldn't have even had a chance to know what the doors were without him! With my determination and his continual encouragement, yes, we were a real dynamo together.

He must have been so pleased with your ultimate success.

I knew it would please him, and that gave me all the more determination—and how could I better show my appreciation to him? He arrived here from England in '39 and still had an appetite for Hollywood personalities, but it was really at least a good fifteen years later before we got together, and so he'd already had enough of Hollywood, from his point of view. But because he knew those subjects were a real turn-on for me, he went way out of his way to take me to parties that he wouldn't dream of going to, except he knew how delighted I'd be to accompany him, and then went out of his way to invite people to the house, like accosting Bette Davis at their first meeting, but he did so because he knew I'd be so thrilled. But she did agree to come, and we had lunch all ready to go, and she called up at the last moment and canceled. We did then meet her soon after at a Sunday lunch at Charlie Brackett's, and I was thrilled beyond belief.

Early in your relationship, you and Chris had become good friends with the multiple Oscar-winning screenwriter and producer Charles Brackett, who by that point had collaborated with filmmaker Billy Wilder on a host of now-classic films, including Ninotchka, The Lost Weekend, A Foreign Affair, *and* Sunset Boulevard. *So after that first social encounter with Davis at Brackett's, you mentioned earlier that you were next introduced to her by Tennessee Williams backstage at the New York preview of* The Night of the Iguana?

Yes, but then it was years later before we met her again, but I think meeting us again at a dinner party at Roddy's reassured her.

As we discussed earlier, Roddy McDowall was not only a lifelong movie star himself, but also a dedicated film preservationist and historian.

Oh, he knew *everyone* who had ever been in movies who was still living. It was Roddy who asked Davis especially to dinner with Chris and me, and I took it as a special favor to me, because he would have known that I would like to meet her again. He set it up for me so sweetly, and of course I found a moment to ask her, would it ever be possible that she might consider sitting for me? That was out here in California, and she said, "Well, I can't do it now. I'm leaving for Connecticut in a couple of days." But I said I was going myself to New York the next week, so she gave me her telephone number to call her! And I did call her, and we set a date.

For the day after Halloween, 1973.

Going way back in my drinking days—because both Chris and I loved to drink—if I had a sitting the next day, I had to be careful not to drink too much. So usually, I was *very* careful to be in perfect shape for my sittings with well-known people, but oh, it's so typical of life that a few times I went to a sitting and I had a very bad hangover, and I did one of my best pictures! And that was *so* perverse, to produce something that was really among the very best things I've ever done when I had a hideous hangover. But with Davis, I was out *way* too late the night before. *Imagine* not being in *perfect* shape for Bette Davis?

Your ultimate sitter!

I had to catch a midday train from New York up to Connecticut. I remember calling her after I got there to say there'd been no taxis at the train station; I had to wait almost half an hour for a cab. She said, "Well, I've got lunch for you, but it'll keep until you get to the house." And I was wilted when I heard that we were going to have lunch together, because I had all my drawing equipment with me, and it was November, so by two o'clock, the light was already going. But there she was, standing on a porch and *tiny*, all in blue: a blue top and jeans, and in her bare feet. I had certainly expected Bette Davis the power dynamo, but she seemed so much more vulnerable than I expected. She was so polite to me, so gracious, standing at her door when my cab arrived, and she took me in the house, and she *did* have a whole, big lunch set up for me. So I couldn't just pick at it; I had to eat it, and it was the last thing I wanted to do before a sitting. So we didn't get to the drawing for at least an hour and a half, by which time it all had to be by artificial light. But she lasted right through the afternoon, and sat for three pictures—and none of them she liked. She said the second one was "cruel," but the last one, which I thought she might really complain about because it caught her vulnerable look, was the one she chose of the three.

In spite of the challenging circumstances, you nevertheless had Bette Davis all to yourself for the better part of a day, which, as you recount

in Stars in My Eyes, *commenced with her serving you corn chowder
and concluded with drinks and a supper of Stouffer's pot pies.*

Somehow I knew she didn't have that kind of artificial grandeur that so many people who have been in the movie business ac-
quire. I think it's usually kind of expected of them, but she didn't
have that at all. She was very forthright. But I knew none of those
first three drawings I did that day were what I could do, because
she was really too nice to me, in a way; because it was too much
of a social encounter with her. But I was thrilled by that, and of
course, I still wanted a crack at her. So when I asked her for
another sitting, she said, "I'm coming back to California in a
month's time, and if you call me on such-and-such a date . . ." But
when I did, she complained, "Oh! I had a stiff neck for days!" after
our sitting. "I was very good to you. *Too* good." So after she complained about how long and painful the stiff neck was, I said, "Well,
does that mean you're not going to sit again?" But she said, "I'll
give you one hour this time, and that's all. *One hour*, and I mean
it!" And she really kept her word. The second sitting was in the afternoon—a bright California day—in the living room of a house
she was staying in in West Hollywood, and she was in Technicolor,
with blue eyeshadow and that pink-red mouth, all made up and
in a very kind of spiffy, pastel-colored wool suit, with pink and
blue woven all into the jacket, and that classic hairline with the
bangs. That was worth all the frustration in Connecticut!

And was such a contrast to the Davis you'd experienced in Connecticut!

It was really eye-popping! There was very little makeup in Connecticut. And of course, in that second sitting, I was almost trembling, sure that she'd be tough. I probably had sweat on my
forehead, I was working so fast for that fourth drawing, and she
looking at me fiercely, knowing she was intimidating me. We both
knew when the hour was almost up, and she noticed I was working feverishly, and that's when she said, "Look, I'm not going to

throw you out if you aren't finished on time." But by that time, I'd hurried so that the drawing was nearly finished, because I expected that fierce Davis if I went over the hour! Oh, her saying, "One hour, and I mean it!" I knew I'd never get another chance with her, so I was working under *extreme* pressure. And she appreciated it, I know, and that's why she said I could go longer.

And you succeeded in getting the picture.

Yes, because it really was: that was the one. I nailed her. It's much the best of the four pictures. Much the best. She was absolutely looking *very* Bette Davis.

But even in that fourth drawing, like the three that came before it, you were incapable of not honestly portraying what you saw in her face. And as you describe in Stars in My Eyes, *her response to it was remarkably equally honest—not in criticizing your work, but in graciously accepting the face that she, too, saw both in the mirror and on the page.*

I remember her taking a long time, walking very slowly and eventually getting behind me, and there was a *long* pause, silence, before she said: "Yup! That's the old bag." None of those big Hollywood star actresses would *ever* have been capable of saying what she did when she saw her portrait, and that she could say that about herself and not wonk me over the head, and sign it and date it anyway? It was a triumph for both of us, because she knew she was being a good sport, and I knew that she was being sincere: that it really was totally different from the three previous drawings from the first sitting. She saw that it was a much more ruthless version of her, but she liked it because it was stronger. Yes, I knew it was much the best one, and it *had* to be, because showing a picture of her had to be the best I could do. As tough as she was in many ways, she had an amazing ability to be objective about herself.

Unlike a star sitter like Ginger Rogers, who meticulously critiqued your portraits of her.

And coming on as a "fellow" artist! So that she just criticized me right down to the tiniest detail, and I couldn't refuse it because she was a "fellow artist"! Our first sitting had been in Palm Springs. It was a big house, and we were alone in a very big living room, but she was forever making absences. Her mother was also in the house, dying. They were very close, and very involved with each other. But Rogers was *so* tough, and using her persona as an "artist" equal to all other artists. It wasn't about defending her ego or her beauty, which of course it was *all* about. She was relentless, telling me how to correct my drawings, and I was fixing, fixing. I had to fake it, you know! Oh, after those first two failures with her, and going for a last sitting in her house here in Beverly Hills, it was stacked against me. And it was the same situation as with Davis: I knew she was going to be just as difficult or more difficult, but somehow, she was ready for it and very fresh. I could really see her kind of pull herself up, and then look at me, with that face, that big red mouth, and she was in just a little softer, black sweatshirt. It was perfect for me. I knew it was my last chance, and I really met the challenge: I knew it would be just the one drawing; it had to be fast; and I could just feel it working. That I was full of confidence, the more I did, the better I saw it becoming. But I was even afraid to show her, finally, when it was finished. She had been so picky the first time, but now she was silent. She knew it was good. Even in her own image of herself, she could see that it was fair. That really is one of my most miraculous achievements in a sitting with a movie actor, and it's still one of my favorite drawings of a movie star. I also remember Merle Oberon, who was very concerned about how she was presented. That was the condition. I was sent to do a portrait of her for an ad for Oleg Cassini: she was wearing one of his dresses, so it had to be a full-length picture of her. But by doing that commission for him, I then had access to her, and she did agree to another sitting that was just for me. At both the Cassini sitting and the two later ones with her, she would get up every ten or fifteen minutes to inspect what I had done. If she saw one hint of perhaps not the happiest signs of a flattering drawing, she would ask, "Oh, could we start again?" But I had asked for it, so I couldn't complain. Sure, I started again. A photographer takes his portraits away: they're in his camera, and from three hundred exposures, he chooses maybe half a dozen to show Merle Oberon, if she's the subject, and of course they will all be retouched by then. I don't even know what *I* think when I first finish a drawing, but after her interrupting me every fifteen minutes, I was too rattled just trying to keep the whole portrait together and get her back into the same position. I often ask myself, *how can I complain?* I chose this; it's what I really wanted to do.

How do you handle the vulnerability of those moments in which a sitter is unpleasantly surprised by the honesty of your portrait?

Or turning to me in amazement, asking, "Do I look like that?" And what can I say? Because there it is: nobody else did the drawing or painting. I have to admit to it: my sitter *must* look like that to me.

I'm sure you've had to quickly craft some delicately diplomatic responses.

Gosh, I've been doing it professionally since 1960. That's over sixty years.

I know that Joan Fontaine, for example, gave you a particularly trying time—a completely opposite experience of that which you had when her sister, Olivia de Havilland, later sat for you.

Yes, and I do use that as an illustration of my own attitude. The sitting with de Havilland was just perfect. She was just indefatigable: she sat without moving for nearly two hours, and I was able to get both of her hands in. Only my belief in her cooperation could have made me dare to include even one hand and most of the other one, too. But Fontaine was exactly the opposite: as uncooperative as de Havilland had been in the other direction. It was so frustrating. Even with the best cooperation from Fontaine, she couldn't look nearly as good as de Havilland. What I saw in de Havilland as an old lady was that old control of herself: she really had the reins still very tight in her hands. She'd go just so far and then draw the line, and turn into the sweet de Havilland. She was really a formidable personality, and such control, such willpower. And to be so many things almost at the same time, I'm sure her whole life was a kind of performance. Oh, she had an iron will. No wonder she lived to one hundred and four—and even at one hundred and four, she still looked like de Havilland. I could see in photographs of her that she was identifiable. Whereas with Fontaine, when she sat for me, something already had happened to her mouth being pulled up in one corner; it hadn't weathered well. She was, I think, one of the most beautiful of the female stars in her first years, and she still actually looked very good, but her mouth had already collapsed: it had caved in, and couldn't be saved by all the lipstick on earth. I couldn't help but draw it; there's no way I could make it the mouth that I knew she wanted it to be. That one drawing I did of her sealed the bargain: there *was* no bargain between us.

As you write in Stars in My Eyes, *while Fontaine interrogated you about your background and approach, you managed to feverishly complete a first drawing which she coldly told you she "loathed" and wished you would destroy. You then dared to begin a second drawing, after she had repositioned herself into a three-quarter angle she preferred to the "broadened" full face you'd disagreeably captured in your first drawing.*

And I did begin again, and under maximum pressure, but finally she made it clear I had to stop, and she couldn't get out of the room fast enough. I was still putting my work in my bag, and she was already zipping down the hallway in that way she moves in her films when she's in a hurry, yelling back, "Let yourself out!" just as rudely as she could manage. I think she was furious. It was the bum's rush, if I've ever had it!

Have such challenging encounters with difficult stars then colored the
way you see them on screen?

But whose films are those now that I watch with much more
attention than I gave to de Havilland? It's Fontaine! I think her
movie work is very, very interesting. When she's good in movies,
she's absolutely like nobody else. She had a real range: she tried
all kinds of things, and went through periods of one look after
another. It's all of interest to me. Somehow, my interest hasn't
abated in her; it's as strong as ever. I watch her with much more
appetite than her sister, because I think she's more extraordinary.
But I still don't forgive her for wrecking my sitting—and out of
sheer perversity! She hoped to wreck it. I could just feel her self-
destructiveness saying, *Aha!* But yes, some of those people who
really behaved badly and meanly, I still see their movies. I don't
take it personally. I'm a good sport in that way. I've been so lucky
that I can't be a bad sport about the failures. And it's the best way
to get to be tough, working under *any* condition. There have been
some other people, too, whose behavior was so humiliating that I
was even sorry for them. They were so busy making it clear that
they wanted nothing to do with me, but as long as I had the pencil
or paintbrush in my hand, I just kept working, and sometimes I
could even do a pretty good picture. And some people have actually *smiled* while they're sitting badly for me, because I've betrayed myself by showing a suffering look of trying oh so hard to
do my best while they were fighting me every inch of the way. But
it was actually very good for my character, because I'm basically a
very shy person, and just to *begin* to ask people to sit for me—and
finally ask world-famous people to sit for me—has always been a
struggle, and I've always had to assume a personality that really
isn't mine: one that won't let anybody into my head. It made me
really tough. Sometimes I wanted to come home and cry on
Chris's shoulder, but I just wouldn't, because when I decided to
be a portrait artist, I said words to myself that I'd never blame a
bad drawing on my sitter.

It must take a level of conscious restraint not to edit when a celebrity is sitting for you.

I'm too much of a professional: I'm too dedicated to what I do, and I've proved it to myself again and again that I can do fair portraits of people I have the *least* respect for. But the more I work, the more I want to include everything I see, because that's the difference between life and photography. If I'm really under pressure, I do leave some things out, but it's usually not the unflattering things, just because they are what gives it character, and what keeps it from being a Hollywood glamour shot.

In her frustration and fury over your one completed drawing of her, Joan Fontaine had finally given you just such a glamour photo of herself—taken from her favored angle, of course—to more "accurately" work from.

And yet her sister was exactly the reverse: Olivia de Havilland was patience itself. She came here one afternoon, and sat without moving a hair. She was *powerful*: I felt her belief in herself, and there was something very polished about her look. She really had taken trouble: she was a star, and she was determined to look that way. She was wearing a blouse with a nice bow and makeup; hair very freshly styled and very still, almost too still; and wasn't the least bit worried, just determined to do her best. And in fact, she was so good, so still, that by about an hour and a half, I remember being afraid she might think me too cruel, and I said, "Your concentration is wonderful; I'm so enjoying this, but if you're tired, we could take a break." And she said, "No, that's not necessary. Just tell me when you're through." Just as cool as could be, and absolutely in charge. I copied everything I could, and it's one of my very best movie star drawings. I think that drawing is a real achievement. It looked exactly like her, and it was elaborate, with hands in: one up here, and the other on the bottom of the drawing, which is something I very seldom get to do with Hollywood actresses. But it was really so much of a likeness that it disturbed her.

It caught something perplexing about her, and she saw it immediately: it was as though one side of her lip was forming a snarl. "I have to think my way back to what it was I was thinking about that comes through in the drawing," she said, "and creates the expression I don't recognize." All beautifully stated, so interested even at her own expense, but I knew she didn't like it, because it told too much about her. Well, it's just that the expression was one she didn't *want* to recognize, and she'd let herself lose control for maybe ten minutes, and Bachardy went in with his drill!

It's likely that Fontaine and de Havilland would have also instantly spotted the cracks your portraits revealed in each other's armor. Their infamous feud was already long-established by the time each of them sat for you.

Oh, with Fontaine, there was really a tigress struggling to get out. No, if there was any struggle, it was to keep it down, rather than lose her graciousness. With de Havilland, it's the kind of portrait that really subtly tells too much about her. Oh, she recognized it, but she was smart enough to know, at the same time, it was a good drawing; she couldn't really demean it. Yet, it was cold. And if you think of her in films, she was almost always lovable, except for *The Dark Mirror*, playing the good twin and the bad twin. She's just hilarious as the bad sister! She really put her heart into it. I'd read somewhere later that she regretted that film. She gave it too much!

And there again perhaps revealed too much of the underside of her own character, just as her real sister saw hers betrayed in the "dark mirror" of your portrait of her. I'm sure you followed the news of de Havilland's unsuccessful lawsuit against the producers of the TV series Feud, *with its ironic title referring not to her own sisterly strife but to the infamous rivalry between Joan Crawford and Bette Davis? De Havilland objected to its semi-fictional portrayal of her by Catherine Zeta-Jones. You were included as a character in the final episode of that series,*

which rather loosely recreated your sitting with Bette Davis, as por-
trayed by Susan Sarandon, as a means to illustrate her grappling with
being aged and alone.

Ah, well, if I'm going to lose my virginity, I don't want it to be
to Susan Sarandon! But yes, I saw that, and I have no complaints.
I had no idea about it until I saw the show. Somebody must have
read *Stars in My Eyes*, although it wasn't quite, "That's the old bag."
I suppose they wouldn't have believed it—that of all those big Hollywood stars, the women, that Davis was the only one of them
who could have made a remark like that. Whereas Joan Crawford
was all teary and graciousness when she sat for me.

Please do tell the story!

My sitting with her took place in her New York apartment. It
was in the morning, probably ten or ten-thirty, and she opened
the door herself, which was a very rare experience in those days
with movie people. She had her hair pulled back in a bun,
bleached streaks in it, and was looking so powerful; that face was
so strong, and I thought, "Oh, goody, I can really concentrate on
her face!" She was in a hideous smock, but luckily, I thought,
"Well, at least I don't have to record *that* in all its color." She said,
"I'm not quite ready." She led me into the living room and said,
"I'll be with you in a few minutes." And so I set up using two dining room chairs, with one facing me and my drawing board
propped on the back. Usually chairs like those were a lifesaver, because most people had them in their house or hotel room. It was
really tough if I had to find something else to balance my board
on, but I even triumphed over that problem several times. She reappeared in maybe ten minutes or so, and oh, my heart sank! She
had put on a great big bubble wig! Oh, the shock of it! But she
was so vulnerable, really shattered. You saw it in her eyes—they
were really painful, frightened eyes—that she was tremulous, un-
certain. So I was so careful with her, awed by her, but I think now,
if I had had the sense to do it, I could have coaxed her out of the

wig, and I bet she would've sat without it. I might have been able
to talk her into that, because drawing that wig just *killed* the sitting. With just the hair pulled back flat—even though it was not
fixed in any way, just because she knew it was going under the
wig—I could have worked so much faster without that hairdo to
cope with and just concentrated on the face, which, even in those
vulnerable days for her, was still very strong. With those heavy
eyebrows and the big red mouth, yes, it was very exciting. But it
was so early in my experience of doing sittings with big stars that
I was always polite and desperately afraid to ask for what I really
wanted, but most of them were very good to me. I've often
wished I could have had another crack at her. But it's funny that
people have such a comic vision of her now as kind of being so
powerful. She was the absolute reverse. She was one of the most
vulnerable stars I worked with.

*On screen, Crawford was a scenery-chewing, face-slapping diva in
shoulder pads and arched eyebrows. Unfortunately, her off-screen
image has become inextricably associated with Faye Dunaway's wire
hanger-wielding portrayal of her in* Mommie Dearest, *the camp
classic movie adaptation of Crawford's daughter Christina's tell-all
memoir.*

She really was almost trembling. That powerful, overwhelming
personality that so many of her fans expected was just kind of a
performance. It was really too late to get at her, but I did two drawings: very quickly a first one, which in a way is better than the
more elaborate second one, because I only indicated the big wig,
and concentrated on her face. But the first one was too much like
her: to have shown that would have been brutal. When I asked her
to sign it, she signed "With love," and then a big "Joan," and an
even bigger "Crawford." I swallowed hard and said, "Well, will you
sign the other one, too?" I was really hoping to try to stop her from
making it an autograph to a fan, but she did the same thing: she
signed it, "Thank you, Don, dearest friend. With love, Joan." When

I asked her to add the date, that kind of threw her. She added the date, and then just couldn't stop, so she grabbed the pen again and added, "Still with love!" Lots of love in the dedication right about, but *still* with love! Love overfloweth! Now, it's just more authentication for the pictures, but it ruined them. What I wanted then was a picture I could show of her, but a picture of her with an autograph to a *fan* on it, hanging with my portraits of other movie stars, would have made her look foolish.

I know you then respectfully withheld the drawing from exhibitions of your portraiture during her lifetime. Chris's diary reports that he fielded a post-show call from Crawford's secretary about the exclusion of the picture in one such show, but left it to you ". . . to call her and explain. The real reason is that Joan signed it all over with loving words and a huge signature, absurdly and fatally upstaging the drawing."

One of her devotees who knew about the sitting came up to me somewhere in New York at a party, saying, "I saw your show. Why isn't Joan in it?" Because I knew in a room full of other Hollywood actors just with the date and their signature, it would have made her look like an ass. I was protecting her, but he was infuriated. He was just too busy huffing and puffing to hear the truth.

In spite of Crawford's overexuberance, I would imagine that sittings with cooperative celebrities can become truly collaborative, fulfilling experiences.

One of my first I wish I had written about was a sitting in London in '61 with Deborah Kerr, when she was making *The Innocents*. She set aside a whole afternoon for me, and I did *four* pictures of her! She must have sat nearly four hours. I got all good likenesses of her—and they were all different from each other—in that one afternoon, because she was a *perfect* collaborator. Oh, she was *so* kind to me, and she wasn't kidding: she was available to me like no other celebrity. I was still so nervous about doing sittings with world-famous people like she was already at that time—she was a major star—but she let me spend the whole day with her at her house, which was completely silent—no help, nobody but her, no special charm, just Deborah Kerr, just being very sensible and very contactable. No stress, no "when is this going to be over?" She kind of took it in her stride, and you know—well, you *do* know—it's not easy to sit for me, and yet I had the nerve to ask her for a *fourth* drawing? I've thought since, how insensitive of me, and yet she never let on that she was finding it difficult in any way. She somehow made it OK and didn't complain, and was so sweet to me, so nice. I was at the time amazed at how wonderful the working experience had been, but it didn't occur to me for a long time that there was something really genuine in her, something really touching. I've been wonderfully lucky a lot, because of Chris, in being able to meet so many of the female stars, but almost queen of all the women in every sort of score that I could rack up was Deborah Kerr. What a sweet and smart and good woman she was, and *very* sophisticated. I *love* seeing her work now—as though knowing her really taught me how to interpret her. I didn't really get on her boat until really quite late in my life, and now I want to see all of her movies again. She's risen several notches on my list of the movie actors I like best. I was just floored recently by again seeing *Bonjour Tristesse*. That film is very much better than I thought when I first saw it, and she's just amazing in it. I like a lot of Preminger films, but I think that's one of the best.

You've mentioned that Angela Lansbury was similarly accommodating in your first of many sittings with her.

She was my first: my very first real Hollywood movie star sitter, and that was a real treat, because I was a devoted fan of hers. She was doing the stage play of *A Taste of Honey*, directed by Tony Richardson, and that's how I got her. It played here before it opened in New York; Tony used the performances here in preparation for New York.

And through Tony Richardson, you were commissioned to draw the cast?

I was, yes, and I think at least six of my drawings were framed and hanging in the lobby of the theater in New York. I was still going to classes at night, but I had graduated from art school. Dora Bryan, who did her part in the film, also sat for me, but that was in London.

Thereafter, Angela Lansbury became a frequent sitter of yours.

Yes, she was *very* available to me. I think I probably did more drawings from sittings with her than of any other movie personality of that period, because she made it so easy. I've also got lots of drawings of her mother, Moyna Macgill, who was adorable.

And was an actress in her own right. Without a word of dialogue, she deliciously steals her one scene in Vincente Minnelli's The Clock *from stars Judy Garland and Robert Walker.*

Oh, yes, at the lunch counter! And have you ever seen *The Strange Affair of Uncle Harry?* I think that's her best movie. She has a really good part, a suitable part for her. It was as much a thrill to work with her as it was with Angela. Angela was a very good sport, but I knew that it gave Moyna a real charge to be looked at, and that made it all the more pleasurable for me. Moyna loved the attention, and because I was young and eager, I kept doing drawings of her, and I got so confident with her that I would say, almost with certainty, she was the first of my Hollywood subjects that I dared to try color with. I hadn't *dared* to ask any of the other movie people I'd been doing sittings with to sit for a color work. I was very scared that I'd discourage myself, that I wouldn't be able to do it, but it really turned into such a good experience that I gave up black and white almost completely. And so some of my earliest color portraits are either of Moyna or Angela. Oh, Angela was very nice to me, very nice, and she appreciated my paying attention to her mother, but I would've done it anyway! And because it pleased her, it made it all the more enjoyable for me. She never thanked me personally, but I had very strong feelings that she was grateful that I was taking Moyna off her hands for an afternoon. It was Angela who got me a job for *The Manchurian Candidate*: a drawing of her that was used in advertising; at least in the Hollywood magazines, *Variety* and *The Hollywood Reporter*, there was a full page. Yes, that was really nice for me. And her husband, Peter Shaw, was a very nice man.

I would imagine that the time pressures some early celebrity sitters put upon you—not to mention some of the impromptu locales in which you needed to set up at their convenience, before you established your own studio—ultimately served to further hone your dexterity as an artist?

When you're a portrait painter, it's no good to only do portraits of people who aren't going to be recognized by the public. How else can they know that I can get a good likeness, if none of my subjects are somebody they've seen? So that usually means actors, movie actors, and that just lays on much more pressure, because of course they have a lot more people after their time, so I have to do it on *their* terms rather than on mine. When I was young, I handled all of that quite successfully. I could work under terrific pressure sometimes, but I was always determined to get something or other out of it. I didn't often fail, if I had just a little bit of cooperation.

As we mentioned earlier, in those early days, you also often had little to no control over the environment.

Oh, yes: setting up in New York theater dressing rooms quite often, or here in movie studio dressing rooms. I remember John Houseman had to be precisely an hour. I had done a sitting with him previously and a sitting after that, but oddly enough, that very pressured one done in an hour was the best one I did of him. But I'm guilty of responding to that very pressure that I now find so difficult to deal with, and it's much easier now that most of my sittings are here. In fact, I think I've only once worked away from the studio in the last couple of years. I have everything I need out there. During those early days of working in people's living rooms, there was always the danger of spilling paint on the carpet, or doing something like that.

Did that ever happen?

No, I never damaged anybody's house; I would remember if I did. I had to be sure I was as professional and as quick as I could be, and would just adapt if it were somebody I knew other people were after. In those early days, when I was often working in people's houses or apartments, of course their phones rang. Occasionally they would say, "I can let the machine take that," but sometimes they got up. I remember going to Warren Beatty's house to do my sitting with him, and he was a very good sitter once I got him sat down: he was very still, and he loved being looked at. I know that now, automatically: the sitters who not only can be looked at but really enjoy it, and he was one of those. I did three pictures of him in that sitting, and I was in his house for hours and hours because after each one, he would disappear. I could hear him in the other room on the phone—he was a big telephone personality. It was a good thirty minutes, maybe forty minutes or more, before he reappeared and then again sat perfectly for me for maybe an hour and fifteen minutes, and then the same thing happened after the second picture. But all three pictures of him are pretty good ones, and he was at the peak of his beauty, too.

Whereas I know that Barbara Stanwyck proved particularly challenging in a different way during the brief sitting she allowed you in her home.

I didn't dare tell her my minimum request was for an hour and a half, so I told her an hour. We didn't know each other, but I had been on the set of one of her movies, *Cattle Queen of Montana*, toward the end of her career. She was a real warhorse: always good, always dependable, but I do like her showier performances more, like in *Clash by Night*. But she liked doing westerns and getting into men's clothes. *Cattle Queen of Montana* was shooting at RKO, and I had gone to the still room to get some stills of somebody I wanted, and instead of leaving the way that I had come into the still room, I went into the studio itself where all the soundstages were, because I knew she was making *Cattle Queen of Montana*. At that time, she was a big favorite of mine, so I watched some of the filming, then chose a moment when she was sitting in a chair on the set to approach her and ask for an autograph. She was so cold and so suspicious, being approached on the set. I really saw it in her eyes: should I have him thrown out? I remember the tone of her voice, and the very few words she said to me rang very suspicious, but she decided that I might be the son of some studio executive, so she gave me the benefit of the doubt—but it wasn't very willingly. Even in her own house, she was very cool, very businesslike. She'd asked on the phone when she agreed to sit, how long would I take? I said an hour, because I was afraid she'd balk if I said any longer. Well, she took me at my word. She invited me at precisely the hour, and how to impose my word? The doorbell promptly rang at one hour after I'd arrived: it was some assistant of hers. She had programmed him to come at exactly the hour! And when the doorbell rang, she said, "May I?" in a rather sinister tone. Could I deny her? And that was the end of the sitting. I wonder if I had said it would take an hour and a half, whether she would have agreed to that, and the doorbell would have rung a half an hour later? That, I don't know. She might well have said, "That's too long."

She might well have. But nevertheless, even under such extreme pressure, your resulting portrait is unmistakably Stanwyck.

Well, I was lucky to have anything at all! I had guessed there might be a lot of resistance, so I did that drawing of her under a high fever. Oh, she was really a pro. She was all fixed up by the time I arrived, but of course we didn't even get down to the drawing for at least ten or fifteen minutes, so I had 45 minutes. She was very still. We knew the hour was ticking away, but even though it was after the experience with Davis, I didn't expect Stanwyck to be generous with her time. Stanwyck was like a metronome, with the minutes ticking away. I bet she was counting them while she was sitting for me. But I had anticipated such a scenario, and I was working so fast, I actually got one of her hands in the drawing. I always tried to get at least a hand in if I could, and I'd drawn the line of the sleeve, and I got the hand in, very characteristic of her, when the doorbell rang at exactly sixty minutes. I could have gotten the other one in, too. But I got her to sign it.

In spite of a particular "fix" she directed you to make.

She said, "There's something wrong with the mouth, but of course you'll fix that later." The mouth *was* twisted up, but it wasn't as though *I* had invented the twist! I didn't recognize it either, but it was there, so how could I avoid it? I knew what her mouth *ought* to look like, but if I had her sitting for me, I *had* to draw it. I was going to draw what I could see!

Again, Bachardy went in with his drill!

But I couldn't explain *that* to her, that I can't make anything up—just as I can't avoid including anything that I see, even though I know it's going to be a problem. Something very strange *had* happened to her mouth, and she didn't look much like Stanwyck even to *me* anymore. I could have done things to make her look more like Stanwyck, but I just wouldn't do it, because to me, that's the responsibility of working from life. So the drawing really doesn't look like her, but it looks like her *on that day*—and it looks like her as an old lady. She really had stopped looking like Stanwyck. Part of it was plastic surgery: I *knew* she'd had some of it done. But I had to draw her as she looked, and I had to do it very fast. That was my only chance, and I knew it. For years, that first drawing was just the warm-up, but give me a chance! Let me do a quick one, a half-an-hour one, even. But there was no way I could have squeezed a second sitting that day, and I knew I might call her a dozen more times, and she would never do it again. She was a strict mistress, and she prided herself on her own strictness. God, how unlikable! But of course she'd say, "Why should I want to be likable?" She wasn't losing a thing! But I was invited to have a drink with the friend who rang the doorbell, and I agreed.

And then she began interrogating you.

She was probing. Who exactly was I? She was doing the sitting because of Walter Plunkett, who was a very sweet guy, a very nice man.

And a prolific and celebrated Hollywood costume designer, mostly notably for Gone with the Wind *and* Singin' in the Rain.

I had done a drawing of him that lasted about two hours—and he was an old man at that time. The older you are, the harder it is to sit for a long time without a break, yet he had his hands in a kind of difficult position, careful not to move them. He was just an ideal sitter. That one picture I did of him, I knew I'd never be able to do a better one, because he cooperated to such an extent. Then at the end of our sitting, he asked me if there was anyone in particular I most wanted to get as a sitter? Without hesitation, I said Stanwyck. I no sooner had gotten home when the phone rang. It was Stanwyck calling to set it up!

Yet another venerable costume designer, Edith Head, who remains the most awarded woman in Oscar history, both sat for you and then similarly offered to connect you with one of your most wished-for Hollywood subjects?

Edith Head, we liked each other a lot. She wanted to help me, and she said, "Is there anyone in Hollywood you haven't had a sitting with that you'd like to?" I knew the sky was the limit, because she was so distinguished. So what was the first thing out of my mouth? Without hesitation, my mouth preceded me: "Alfred Hitchcock!" She said, "I can arrange that. He's a very good friend; we have dinner once a week." And indeed, she gave me a number, and that very day when I got home, I called it, and Alfred Hitchcock came to the phone. I said, "I'm calling because I've just been with Edith Head, and she gave me grounds to hope that you might consider sitting for me one day. I'm an artist, and I'd love to do a portrait of you." You know, *he* drew that absurd caricature of himself.

His trademark self-portrait, done in just nine ink strokes, which opens the well-known title sequence to the long-running television anthology series, Alfred Hitchcock Presents.

Yes, so I knew he would sit, and I knew he'd be still. And indeed, he said, "Of course I'll sit for you. She's already told me about you, and I'd like to do it and I *will* do it. I'm just finishing up this film I'm working on, and it's going to be another two or three weeks at the most. And when it's done, I'll call you, not you call me. I'll call you and we'll do it." And I knew he meant it. But the movie happened to be *Family Plot*, his last movie. He got sick as soon as it was over. Chris and I did meet him three times in the flesh at parties, and each time, we had a wonderful conversation with him. He was very accessible, a wonderful talker, very entertaining. And of course, I just admired him no *end*: everything about him was lovable, from my point of view. I'm so glad I at least got to see him and talk to him in person.

Which, for sure, was consolation for not getting a sitting with him, although you can certainly take added comfort in having gotten to many of your childhood idols—Bette Davis in particular!

I would have been so surprised as a kid to be told that Hitchcock would be the biggest disappointment!

You drew veteran star Mary Astor, whose long Hollywood career had started in silent movies of the 1920s, a few years after she appeared as a villainess in an episode of Alfred Hitchcock Presents, *and not long after her final film appearance in 1964, in support of Bette Davis in* Hush . . . Hush, Sweet Charlotte.

Oh, I adored her. That was really one of my best encounters. She really became a friend, and acted just as though she weren't a movie actress, really. She was just so friendly. I think I got really closer to her than any of the actresses I knew, and that really meant a great deal to me. I even visited her in hospital during her final illness. I think she really regarded me as a friend.

How had you met her?

By writing her a letter! And she wasn't *anything* to me when I was a devoted moviegoer in my youth. I mean, I had nothing against her, but she had no particular pull for me. So I didn't get to see *The Maltese Falcon* until after I knew Chris, because it was *his* talking about John Huston and how much he liked that film that made me excited to get at it, and then it was even *better* than I'd expected, after all Chris had told me. I had already seen Astor in *The Great Lie*, but her performance in *The Maltese Falcon* is even better.

And she made those films back-to-back, winning a Best Supporting Actress Oscar for shamelessly stealing The Great Lie *out from under its conspiring star, Bette Davis, who had not only lobbied for Astor to get the part, but then worked with her on recrafting the script.*

You have to give it to Davis: she knew that Astor was *more* than competition, and it whetted her appetite. Her role in *The Great Lie* is *nothing* compared to Astor's.

After which Astor was unfortunately relegated to mostly playing mother parts, notably in Meet Me in St. Louis *and* Little Women.

Oh, all the mother roles! *Mother* roles!

Which is rather ironic, considering that her career had astonishingly survived a very public sex scandal just a decade earlier!

And it really gave her a big charge to her movie career! She started getting really wonderful parts!

Astor later wrote two candid, bestselling memoirs about her "life on film." Louise Brooks, the iconic silent star who similarly found renewed acclaim late in her life through her writings about cinema, stands out as another of the truly one-of-a-kind encounters you've had with Hollywood legends.

She was a real encounter. There she was, all by herself, and at my first sight of her, I wouldn't have even known it was Louise Brooks. I had seen *Pandora's Box*, of course, and another one of her films, and she was like nobody else: that look she had was really original, that tight bob. I can see any of those films of hers: there's no end to their interest for me, and she's a personality in them, on film, like nobody else, but she was a very difficult personality. She wanted to meet Chris, so after our sitting, I took him to her, and he found her very difficult. She challenged him: she was very smart, she was a big reader, and she even read his books. But she was the kind of person who, because she was nervous *about* him, she expressed her nervousness *at* him by challenging him. He didn't warm to that, particularly from a woman, but he also had very good manners.

She later softened her vitriolic assessment of your drawings of her, but what do you think of them?

The only criticism *I* have with them is that they're all too much alike, but I had no choice. When I do three drawings, I suggest that for the first one, the sitter is looking away; then the second one, I say, "Look at me"; and then there's no rule about the third. But in the one of her where I *must* have said, "Look at me," she's *not* looking at me—or the effect of the drawing doesn't show that she's looking at me. I think she didn't want to; I think that was her choice. I know I asked her to.

You navigated a quite intimidating encounter all on your own with Katharine Hepburn.

The only famous celebrity sitter who made me do it out of doors. She took walks every day in the hills above Beverly Hills. We were quite near the Selznick house up there, and she just sat down at the bottom of a tree trunk, and I had to set up my gear in the out of doors. That was very tough for me. It's so distracting being outside, with the light coming from different sources, but I said I would do it because I knew it had to be her way. But even though the three pictures all looked like her, and the last two were remarkably good, considering the circumstances, she would only sign the second one, which was not the best, because she looked serious. She looked maybe even a little unhappy. You wouldn't think an actress would be so eager to look like a drama queen! But it was only that one, which isn't as good, that she signed, and I told you her remark about it when she saw it?

No, what did she say?

"Fair! Just fair!" Oh, she was very pleased with herself, but she wouldn't know a good portrait of herself if it knocked her out—if her head went through the canvas or paper! But I still proved myself to myself, even working out of doors.

But you've found that some of your best work has actually been created under such varied pressure as exacted by the likes of Hepburn and Stanwyck and others?

Yes, in those days. Now it would be *very* tough, working under that kind of strain. But I'd been doing it under such a variety of conditions, as you can imagine. Working with celebrities and under excruciating circumstances quite often, it was the best education I could've had. It was very good training, because I was so determined and so hungry to succeed that I never complained, and always managed to get something or other out of the situation. Even working in underlit houses, apartments, with really almost no light at all sometimes.

Backstage in dressing rooms, too, as with your childhood idol Alice Faye during her Broadway turn in the 1974 revival of Good News.

Oh, how awful that production was! There was something so coarse and almost amateur about it, or it was so for a particular kind of low taste that everything was canceled out; any kind of real amusement was dead on arrival. And oh, Faye really took me over the ropes—but it wasn't severity with her, it was just kind of *inattention.* She didn't really mind sitting in the slightest; I think she just felt that it wasn't expected of her to be malleable. I wouldn't have done that in a dressing room, for a start, and while she was performing! She made me work in her dressing room at the theater on a matinee day, and was always listening for her cue, so I don't suppose I got more than ten or twelve minutes in a stretch, and then she'd be off to get on stage, and then she'd come back, put on another costume, and redo her makeup, and maybe she'd sit down for another ten minutes or maybe five minutes and I would pick up the drawing, and then she'd go off again, completely unaware of any suffering from me. But of course, it meant a lot to me, so I would've agreed to anything and was ready for anything, because she and Bette Davis had the claim on my earliest and most indelible impressions of any of those movie women.

And you'd started drawing early on by copying their pictures from movie magazines, so theirs were faces you already knew incredibly well—although sanitized versions of them.

And the face was still Alice Faye's, unmistakably, with her one eyebrow raised, and I did a drawing of her that couldn't be anybody else. She had a very big head for her body: it just seemed enormous to me, with this big sort of pudding of a face, swollen by age, but it was nevertheless Alice Faye. By that time, I'd really had so much experience, and I'm so obstinate by nature that if I'm bound to do something, I'll go to extremes if it's necessary. So if I had to be patient and put up with the kind of treatment that Faye gave me, I did it. And certainly having done drawings of both Davis and Faye from movie magazine pictures of them, it was all part of a pattern. And also, I had endless encouragement from Chris. He knew what these Hollywood people meant to me, and he was always interested. As I told you earlier, he'd been a movie devotee in his teens, so he understood it all, and he gave me that scrapbook that he had kept, which was mostly *Photoplay* magazine's pictures of movie actors.

Who had been some of his favorites?

Agnes Ayres.

Rudolph Valentino's leading lady in The Sheik.

I think Vilma Banky was a little prettier than she. Ramon Novarro was another favorite of Chris's.

Novarro became Valentino's successor as the screen's leading Latin lover during the late 1920s and early '30s, although in reality he was gay, and would ultimately be horrifically murdered in 1968 by a pair of hustling brothers.

He was on the same ship that took Chris and me to Europe for my first time, and we saw him walking on the deck with relatives.

And wasn't that ship the ill-fated Andrea Doria, *on which you sailed from Gibraltar to Naples? It famously sank the following summer.*

Yes, on the *Andrea Doria*! We'd been on the old tanker *Saturnia* for the Atlantic crossing, and suddenly this lavish luxury ship! But we didn't meet Novarro—or if we met him, it was just like fans, and he very much like a movie star. He was a great star. Oh, I love silent films. Chris did, too. We saw many of them together—and most of them Chris had seen when he was young!

Do you have a favorite silent film or filmmaker or star?

Oh, Harold Lloyd was very lovable. I knew him through two queer friends who got to know him well. I was very pleased to know Lloyd, but in fact, I didn't really have a full knowledge of him—or at least as deep a knowledge as I have of him now—because I got introduced to his work *after* I met him, so without that illumination then, I never had a chance to talk to him about it in a deeper way. But one time we went to Harold Lloyd's house and he showed us films, and he was wonderful. He treated his career with great dignity. He made *terrific* films. Some of them make me cry, they're so funny, they're so good. Oh, his movie personality just goes right back in my heart. I just love it. It was too early for me even to dare to ask him to sit, but oh boy, do I wish I had.

Besides Louise Brooks and Janet Gaynor, which other silent stars sat for you?

Lillian Gish did, twice! She was very precise: a sweet, business-like, ladylike performer always, and a perfect sitter. That's why my pictures of her are good. We met Gloria Swanson once in her house, and I knew that it was nothing doing there. I did get Ina Claire to sit. She was a houseguest of George Cukor's, and he set it up. She did it for him, but that was fascinating for me, and I did a pretty good picture of her. I knew everything was riding on that one sitting: I knew I'd only get her to do one, but she was very nice to me. I remember we also met von Sternberg.

Josef von Sternberg was an innovative Austrian-American director whose magnum opus, 1930's The Blue Angel, *launched a little-known German actress named Marlene Dietrich into international stardom. The two would subsequently collaborate on six additional Hollywood films that showcased Dietrich's stylish sexual ambiguity.*

There was a showing of two of his very best Dietrich films at UCLA, and Chris stopped him in the aisle, and he spoke to us for a few minutes. He was *very* grand. I remember Chris saying to him,

"That's a wonderful film." He said, "I know." And he was right! But by then, von Sternberg wasn't doing anything in Hollywood, and what he had done at the end of his career were just real cheap productions, although *The Shanghai Gesture* is my favorite Gene Tierney film. I told you about my telephone conversation with Gene Tierney, didn't I? Because I asked George Cukor if he would persuade Tierney to sit for me; I got her phone number and called her, and she said, "I've had my portrait painted! I don't need another!" She was very imperious, very indignant to be even brought to the phone.

Did she think perhaps that the painting of her that features so prominently in Laura—*which was actually a blown-up studio photograph smeared with oil paint—sufficed as her one and only official portrait? Another wasn't needed?*

Maybe, yes! It was her star-making performance, but *The Shanghai Gesture* is still my favorite Tierney film. Have you noticed how that film is built on almost close-ups alone? I think Darryl Zanuck hoped that von Sternberg would do for Gene Tierney what he did for Marlene Dietrich, so von Sternberg did his best with all those close-ups of her, and that's what makes it as enjoyable as it is. I get goosepimples looking at her in that film. But I don't think the public liked Tierney for years, starting out being treated like an exotic. It was Zanuck's idea to make a star out of her, but it just took a bit longer for her to be approved of. It really took until *Laura*.

Proving that the von Sternberg-Dietrich formula was specific to that particular pairing. Speaking of Dietrich, remarkably you got her to sit for you.

Chris's agent was Hugh French, who was a good friend of hers and was probably in business with her. He had a beach house in Malibu, and he gave a midday party on a Sunday, a little lunch. We'd been two or three times before and were invited again, but this time, with no preparation, there was Dietrich, in a sun hat and pedal pushers and a button-down shirt, and with almost no makeup except for eyeliner and pencil and lipstick—otherwise, it wouldn't have looked like Dietrich, but she looked great. I asked her if she would sit for me, and she kind of went, "Hmm?" So I sent samples of my drawings, photos of maybe four or five people she would recognize—movie people—and about three days later, the envelope came back, and I opened it. There were the photographs, but no note, nothing. I wailed to Chris, "She's not going to do it!" But then I closed the flap of the envelope and saw there was a scrawl on it: "I'll call you. M." And she *did* call just a few days later. I said, "When are you free? How can we arrange this?" And she said, "Tonight? I'm free." Of course, when Marlene calls and says, "I'm free," you drop everything! I was really afraid to make too many demands and make her feel that it was going to be too difficult, so I said, "Well, Chris and I have two people coming for dinner. I'm doing the cooking, and you're welcome to join us." And she agreed! I had to go into Beverly Hills to pick her up, but my own car, a Karmann Ghia, was out of order, so I had to use Chris's little black Volkswagen Bug. Imagine picking up Dietrich in that? But I drove into Beverly Hills at five o'clock, and went into an apartment in one of those streets between Olympic and Wilshire Boulevard. There had been a party there. It was after the party, but there were still three or four guests—she was sitting on the middle of the sofa with people on each side—and I took one look at her and realized why she had called me. It was the total Dietrich job: she'd obviously been at the beauty parlor all day and was fitted for the dress, so if she was going to host a party, she would rather knock off two or three obligations at one time! If you go to that trouble, you don't waste it on one person: you make as many dates as you can! I've noticed celebrities doing that. So here she was, just fixed up in this sumptuous white Balenciaga suit with white material embroidered with a white thread, very delicate, and of course the face painted on perfectly and the hair newly done—I mean, as *different* as could be from the Dietrich I'd met at Hugh French's beach house! Oh, if I could have gone to work that very Sunday afternoon, taken her away in a room! That's how I got Charlotte Rampling: she was in a beach house, and when I arrived I saw it was full of people, so I persuaded her to go into one of the empty rooms, and had her all to myself. It was for only one drawing, so it had to be right, but it looks exactly like her. And she was just a major interest to me: that personality! She's charming, intelligent, and just super looking and so talented. Those first films of hers were just so exciting for me, and she was just terrific in person; just more exciting even than on the screen. I've got that one drawing of her, but I wish I'd had my way like that with Dietrich.

Instead, you got the full iconic Dietrich look.

Well, if she hadn't been Dietrich, *nobody* could have told me the woman I had met at the beach was the same as the one who was fixed up in that elegant white suit and looking, even up close, just super good. So what did I do? Well, I *had* to do it: open the door to this broken-down Volkswagen and pile her in! But you know, her great friend and mine, Marti Stevens, said, "Oh, you know, Marlene's a *mensch*, but she's really a good sport," and it was true. But one thing I did note was that obviously my driving was a bit too fast, because she rather clung to a handle on the glove compartment! No matter how much I slowed down, it never was quite enough! But I drove her all the way to the house, and she was charming with us and our two friends, both artists, Bill Brown and Paul Wonner. I had called them up to prepare them. I said, "We have an extra guest tonight: Marlene Dietrich's coming." They said dubiously, "Oh yeah, and who else?" But they were delighted, and she and Chris got on very well. And then she took over at dinner: she stood at the end of the table, filling all of our dishes from the big pot of food I had cooked! It was a paprika stew, and while she was dishing it, I saw one little bright pair of orange spots go right onto her white suit. I didn't dare tell her! I could have included it in the drawing I did of her, but I didn't, of course.

So your portrait of her was then also done during that already heady evening?

Yes, and when we finally got at it after dinner, it had to be ten o'clock, and by artificial light. The studio then was just the one little room which had been the garage building, with just one little architect's lamp to light her, but I knew of course that all she wanted was that one light to give her the butterfly shadow under her nose. So that's what I gave her, and that's what she responded to, but imagine my one shot at Dietrich being so compromised by so much else going on? But nevertheless, I did three pictures of her, and one is surprisingly good. The second one is not bad, either, and the third one I don't like much, but I did three, and I always produce. If given a chance, I can do it. But also, that was in 1963, when I was twenty-nine.

So your stamina was at its peak.

And my appetite. And I knew, by all the odds, it was my one crack at doing a sitting with Marlene Dietrich, so I agreed to anything.

Was she pleased with the results?

She didn't like them all, but she signed two of them. But you know, when I've got a subject like that, with all of the pressure that's created by the circumstances, it just can't ever be simple. And especially with a subject like Dietrich, who was known primarily for her beauty, her face, that Dietrich look, but already she was in her sixties, so that was very delicate. But I was young enough to just accept any conditions she made. Of all Hollywood actresses who sat for me, of course there was no way of having my way with most of them. Just the fact they agreed to sit for me always meant

I had to be ready for anything. Most of them were professional enough to sit still, but there was always someone who threw me off by moving—or if the determination was strong enough, could defeat me—and I can work very fast, but it's really hit or miss. But in the early years, I would just accept *any* behavior, without even imposing a wish for silence or stillness.

How did you fare with Myrna Loy, who was once voted "The Queen of Hollywood" to Clark Gable's "King"?

Oh, now there, she was just a dream, and with a face I knew so well from films—and it was even better with age. She was one of the most intelligent, most sophisticated of all the Hollywood people I've worked with. I just adored her. She wasn't any kind of a favorite of mine because of all that *Thin Man* stuff, but she just had the perfect, sophisticated attitude to a sitting of a movie star: she was every *inch* Myrna Loy; every inch a professional. She held the expression and the atmosphere that she established from the very beginning: the mood that she was in, she held it, and without any kind of nonsense. And that turned out lovely, because she was just a lovely creature: a true synthetic personality who understood really everything that was going on, and that rarely happened in that situation with a movie personality.

You never got to her longtime screen partner, William Powell?

No, no, he was already sick. I think she would've set up a sitting with him if I'd wanted to—and of course, I would've grabbed the opportunity—but he was already failing, and she probably realized he wouldn't be up to the severity of the situation.

You did, however, get to both halves of another legendary Hollywood pairing: Ginger Rogers and Fred Astaire. We've discussed your appraisal of and by Miss Rogers, but how did you fare with Mr. Astaire?

I went to his house, and he was so *beautifully* turned out: he was a *wonderful* dresser, with the perfect jacket, perfect shirt, tie, *every-*

thing just ideal—but the only thing was: his face. What he really wanted to do was give me the Astaire smile—and he would've been willing to try to hold it for an hour or more, once he'd seen the first drawing I did of him—but it's the first drawing that is *leagues* better than the second one, when he was trying to give me what *he* was hoping to see.

There's a haunting vagueness and vulnerability in the first face he gave you, not unlike that of Henry Fonda's in your portrait of him.

You know, Fonda was an amateur artist, so I was the *real thing* from his point of view, so he treated me like a *master* and gave me a sitting for the ages! It probably took me every minute of two hours, and I know he was straining: everything that was going on in his face showed how difficult it was for him, but he was holding it for me. He was just the best sport I could *ever* have hoped for. He was old and almost had the shakes, but he held still for two hours—and I saw this sick face coming at me and thought, "Oh, he's going to hate it!" But you know, if it's a case of doing my best work and maybe hurting the feelings of my sitter, or don't do my best work and fake it a little bit so that it's not as stark as it looks, I've always chosen the starkness—while saying to myself, almost shaking with someone like Fonda, "He's going to hate it. He's going to see that I've done something that he would've hoped I would not do." But he was enough of an artist himself to realize that *I* was a good enough artist to get what he was giving me, and it came out looking *so* like him, so faithful to what he'd given me that even though it did hurt his feelings, he signed it with aplomb and said, "I love it." He was really just that one in a million who really understood it from all views, and why it came out the way it did; that it was a good picture, if not a flattering likeness. Just thinking about it makes me want to cry, because he was sick: he was dying; it was toward the end of his life, and it was all in his face. But I've so often thought about what fulfillment I've had in my life, just meeting these people who were so deeply in me, and getting to see them in person and record what it was like. Oh! Who could've *dreamed* I would ever get that satisfaction out of my life, the way it began and the way it ended? It was exciting in every respect—even when some of them were so nasty to me, like Charles Boyer, that was all part of it. Even Joan Fontaine: "Let yourself out!"

CHAPTER 10

We were both extraordinary

Don and Chris in photos taken of each other on Don's fortieth birthday, May 18, 1974. *(Courtesy of the Christopher Isherwood Papers, The Huntington Library, San Marino, California)* © DON BACHARDY

Certainly with A Single Man, *but then increasingly in interviews and explicitly with his 1976 memoir* Christopher and His Kind, *Chris began to speak more directly and openly about being gay.*

Oh, he lusted after it. I think his relationship with me made him just all the more determined not to back down, not to cower; to speak up and make no bones about it. And how could he do otherwise? It was a sort of energy for him: it galvanized him. And he deplored any hesitation in his earlier years to make the most of any opportunity to be as queer as he could, and to just speak openly and drag it into every possible conversation! I mean, he wouldn't let anybody get away without talking about it. The more heterosexual the interviewer, the more he would rub his or her nose in it, because he knew that was something he could really defend: he could really speak up about it.

You gave Chris the title Christopher and His Kind, *as indeed you suggested the title for* A Single Man.

I had a natural appreciation of words that I was totally unaware of, and that was part of the bond between Chris and me. So on that unconscious level, Chris and I had a communication that I don't think he probably had with any of his other partners. I don't know where it came from; it's just part of the inevitability of our finding each other.

Chris considered his "kind" to mean not just his fellow homosexuals, but anyone with whom he felt a rapport.

Well, it was deeper than sex. It took me a long time to believe in Chris's idea of me. Chris always wanted to test his work on me before anyone else. It took me a long time to understand and believe that he wasn't putting me on: that he wasn't buttering me up. That he was being genuine: that he could be interested sincerely in the opinion of a person thirty years younger than he was. I realized that it was something even more basic than sex: that we just could tune to each other. I'd be willing to say it was more an astrological combination, both of us being earth signs: that despite our totally different backgrounds, we connected at exactly the right time, even though it had nothing to do with the average kind of connection. I was even more resistant of that idea than Chris, but eventually I could take it seriously that Chris didn't want to work with me just because I knew how to type, because he would sincerely ask me questions. He'd want to know, was this word better than that? Do you have any ideas about this situation? As soon as I realized he wasn't kidding, yay! It was fun! It was a game. A game! A game that we both equally enjoyed.

Just as you and Chris were partners both in life and work, from the 1950s on you were also united in being boldly out—indeed, becoming one of the first openly gay celebrity couples, which placed you in the vanguard of the burgeoning gay liberation movement of the 1960s and '70s.

Well, I mean, because of the age difference and the burgeoning frankness about queerness, how could we not? What other explanation could we give? We were just a couple, that's all, and we were devoted to each other. But for me, all of that also came from paying attention to Chris, and really quite rightly, because he was in at the beginning of so much of it when he first came here, and was never hiding, always speaking out, never not giving it top-drawer attention. Chris *really* cared. It was made extra exciting for me because he was really hoping, with all of his heart. He was really a totally positive personality, and he had no patience for people who give up or surrender for less than what they want. The freedom of queers to be who they are and live their lives the way they want to meant a *great* deal to him. Yes, he realized he was working for the cause, and he had more satisfaction in his life, he told me, than he expected he would. I think if he had lived longer, he would have felt even more encouraged. That was major on his agenda.

That post-Stonewall effort to end LGBTQ+ discrimination and to advance societal acceptance wasn't sudden permission for Christopher

Isherwood to add his voice to the choir. In spite of the constant risks, he'd bravely lived his entire life openly and proudly as a gay man.

Yes, and he did when it was just as shut down as it could be. And imagine then taking on somebody of my age, and traveling with me and not hiding me away? He knew so many distinguished queer friends who didn't dare appear in public with their partners.

Much less a much younger one!

Chris took me everywhere. He was only afraid of taking me places where he feared I might be bored! Oh, I think we shocked far more people than we realized, but we just weren't looking for it—because if you look for it, you're bound to find it. The important thing was that we carried ourselves without shame. We *weren't* ashamed. He taught me: be what you are, and make it something to be glad about. And we both did feel that, so we couldn't lose: no experience could shake us, because we knew we were right. And he would accept invitations from almost any queer organization. Even if he didn't know much about them, he wanted to find out. He was curious. But I remember several times when he wanted to speak to this or that queer group that he was chastised for not coming out sooner, not coming out bolder—not throwing, I guess, everything to the winds. Yes, a lot of the gay crowd thought it was *tardy* at best: why hadn't he been at the front years before, you know, waving a flag? But there are some people you just cannot please, who are just determined to be militant, and if there's not a cause to be militant about, then they'll create a cause.

When anyone with any real awareness of how Christopher Isherwood had always openly conducted his life, well before the bold declaration of Christopher and His Kind, *would take a far more respectful, if not reverential, view toward his courageous and pioneering advocacy.*

Considering his age and where he came from and all, yes, he was determined to be proud of himself as a queer, because he *was*! He was. It was as much a definition of him as it became for me, too. Being queer has brought me *everything* of value, of real value, in my life. Without that, I don't think I could have enjoyed *anything* nearly so much, and I don't think I would have been courageous enough without him to feel that way. That was his strength—part of it, anyway. But he was a wonderful example to me in so many ways: just in teaching me how to stand straight and have good posture, and speak up for myself. All of his lessons are the most important things I've learned.

Did you ever discuss together the real risks of being openly gay during that fearfully buttoned-up period in midcentury America?

Oh, certainly. We realized we were living in *very* dangerous world, yes.

The FBI had investigated Chris during the Red Scare, at a time when the government's position was that homosexuality, then considered socially "deviant behavior," made one who was so "afflicted" potentially susceptible to blackmail by Communists. Although the FBI's interrogation of Chris ultimately came to nothing, was he ever ostracized professionally or socially in Hollywood for being gay?

Oh, there were certainly people who didn't like us, didn't like us appearing as a couple. I'm sure there were people at the Selznicks', at those big movie star parties, who murmured in the corner: the women as well as the men, or the men as well as the women. We were aware of their disapproval, certainly.

Do you think his being so open so early on limited his opportunities in Hollywood?

Yes. That didn't bother him. It was an effective way of making money, but he knew if it dried up or changed, he'd find something else.

He was indeed a well-established and successful novelist long before he came to Hollywood, and certainly during and beyond his time work-ing there as a screenwriter.

Yes. He really had belief in himself: he knew who he was, and he just wasn't about to be ashamed. He only criticized himself if he didn't give something every ounce of his energy.

You and Chris agreed to be profiled for a 1984 People *magazine article that, at that time, was groundbreaking for its frank portrayal of you as a happily committed and creatively collaborative same-sex Holly-wood couple.*

That explains what appealed to them about it: that it was news; that it would make news in itself, whatever queer couple they chose. Of course, they chose us because of Chris being a public fig-ure. They had the sense not to make it offensive to the queer set: politically, we were becoming much more powerful than we had ever been before, and they knew better than to offend us by saying anything offensive, even about me. I knew exactly why they were doing it: they knew it was controversial, even as late as it was. Be-fore that, I mean in the '50s, *Time* magazine made the distaste for queers more than obvious when Chris's books were reviewed. I kept all the ugly specimens of it. But that was before we became a political force, and that only began in the '70s.

Did you suffer any negative fallout from being so nationally "outed" by that People *article?*

No, not to me, and I don't remember being offended by it. I thought it was kind of only medium daring. I thought they played it very safe.

In an interview you and Chris gave your friend Armistead Maupin the following year, you mentioned that some closeted friends had re-acted fearfully to a cover story on you in the LGBTQ+ magazine The Advocate?

I think that was more established people close to Chris's age than any of my friends, and Chris was such an outspoken personality that it really took a lot of pressure off me.

In the decades since Chris's passing, you've certainly witnessed quite an evolution in societal acceptance of the LGBTQ+ population here in the United States, with some significant legal protections now in place, and certainly far more mainstream cultural visibility.

I think it's a pretty good show on the whole. There's still some resistance, and signs of it show up every once in a while, but they seem much more surprising nowadays because so much freedom has been established, and people are ready to be so much more outspoken than they were just not all that many years ago. But a lot really happened, a lot of that kind of stuff, before Chris died, so he knew that we were going to survive it and be stronger than ever. And he was giving it everything he could to encourage the cause. He always identified himself as a queer *long* before most people, *very* few, spoke out as early and as loudly as he did, because he wanted to. And he was such a good spokesman for us. I never missed a public appearance of his if I could help it, because he had *real* magic; he was wonderful. He never disappointed. If he had been recognized sooner, he could have become a major star of the cause. He was just the perfect tone for that kind of encouragement that queers needed to be taken seriously.

Do you think that you and Chris would have had an easier time as a publicly out gay couple today, even with the age difference between you two?

Yes, it's so much easier. In the '50s, even my brother once said to me, "Everybody knows you live with an old man, and I think it's disgusting!" Now, this coming from somebody who slept with older men! I don't think Ted saw any irony in it at all. He just said it to hurt me, because I had offended him in some way—or maybe just out of jealousy.

How did your relationship with your brother shift once you and Chris were established?

I did feel uncomfortable about Ted, because I thought I had to keep him out of my life with Chris. When he was crazy, he wasn't in control of himself, and he would come down here and make scenes. He once kicked the carport door in. When he was the Ted that I chose to believe was the real Ted, or the one I preferred, certainly, he was always apologizing for his bad behavior when he was Ray—and yet he wasn't in control of Ray.

Was Ray another identity and actual personality that Ted assumed?

Oh, yes. Ray Deland was on his checking account, as well as Ted Bachardy.

Was Ray a presence throughout the rest of Ted's life?

He would show up sometimes three times in a year. That was rare. I think the longest run without Ray appearing was two-and-a-half or three years, but he always came back. There would be a long silence, and then Ted would be in some hospital for maybe weeks and weeks. I would sometimes go visit him, by myself. It was always understood that there was some limit to our social recognition of him. It would have been awkward even if Ted and I had been on the best of terms, to be a group of three: Chris with Don and his *also* queer older brother, Ted? Ray was a convenience in that sense. Ted had to understand that while *he* may have been socially acceptable, Ray never was. I told him so. I said, "I don't want Ray in my house, because he's a troublemaker and a noisemaker and a scene maker." If I had made him welcome in this house at any time, that would mean Ray might show up at the height of his mania and make an ugly scene. I didn't want to expose Chris to that; he didn't deserve it. Ted was really *my* problem. I wanted to keep him away from Chris, just as I wanted to keep him away from *me.* I couldn't bear Ray: Ray knew exactly how to raise my hackles, and I would warn Ted every time I would hear Ray begin to appear.

I could hear it on the phone and would say, "Chris, I heard the first sounds of Ray today," and within two or three days, Ray would be in complete power. Ted would be a memory.

What would those periods be like? Was there any consistency to Ray's behavior?

He would show up at six in the morning and be pulling flowers out of the gardens of our neighbors. When we were young, Ted was the beauty; I was just the gap-toothed younger brother. But then, of course, Ted lost his looks much before I did, not only being four years older, but also because he didn't know how to take care of himself. He was bright enough and sensitive enough to suffer dumbly, almost like an animal, and not be able to express himself. And of course, here was I, having sittings with Bette Davis. I couldn't *not* tell him: I owed it to Ted, in spite of Ray, but I also knew that telling it to Ted must have hurt his feelings. It must have been painful that I could tell him about her, but I couldn't introduce him to her. In fact, Ted rarely was in this house on a social basis. Chris and I would give dinners with our queer friends, but we wouldn't invite Ted when we had mixed couples. It was dangerous to give Ray that kind of encouragement. Ray was always behind the scenes, that potential, and because Ray was a mean bitch, if he found out we were giving a dinner party for Bette Davis, he would show up. He wouldn't have any hesitation to come down with cymbals crashing!

Did Ted—and Ray—have any significant romantic relationships?

Oh, yes, yes, he lived with several young men, and the last one for many years. Yes, considering the ups and downs of his early life, he did. And it took a long time, but the period between breakdowns got longer and longer. There were a few ugly recurrences, and he would always have to hit bottom before he could get enough spring back, but yes, he got through it finally. But he was really a real handful for everyone who knew him.

What was your relationship with him like after your parents and Chris were gone? You two had been so simpatico in your youth.

Oh, we'd been so close that, yes, I got angry at him and we had fights, but we still couldn't stop being friends, brothers. We loved each other and couldn't deny it, and he had sort of a miserable life at times that I could really feel sorry for him. But then when he was crazy again, I'd want to kill him sometimes. To repeat the banality of a breakdown like some he had was just *awful* for everyone concerned, and when he'd be at his craziest and show up at the house with a big bag full of movie clippings to go through with me, I didn't enjoy that.

But did you feel that you needed to humor him?

Yes. You know, for a while, I'd say, "Ted, I never want to see you when you're in that state. You know how I hate it, and I don't want you affecting Chris with it," and he'd say, "Yes, I know," and he'd be ashamed of himself, but then I'd feel like such a villain that I'd have to make it up with him. So it was up and down, but in the end, it was pretty even keel for a few years. There was a period when maybe once a week or every other week, we'd take our mother out together to a movie and a meal.

So your communion with your mother and Ted over movies and movie stars continued through the end of their lives?

Oh, yes, and his eye was very similar to mine. We liked usually the same actors, certainly most of the women. We had special favorites that were fun to talk about. And in his last period, yes, I saw him regularly, but our last meetings were just that he wanted to come down in the morning and go through a big bag of all his latest movie clippings. He had a sad ending, so alone. My last visit to him in the hospital was so painful. But I had been very lucky to have Ted, because he had really looked after our mother, who was failing almost exactly during the same time that Chris was, and so much so that I really didn't get to see much of her, because I was home taking care of him. So she took against me at the end of her life, but I didn't want her to know that Chris was claiming the major part of my concern because he was also leaving my life, and so of course he was also getting my real attention. But it made me very grateful to have my particular brother during that, because he just naturally looked out for our mother. He took her over full-heartedly, and of his own accord. She was living alone in a two-story apartment, and I know he went every day. But the very fact that Ted was so attendant to her—and he did it with real devotion; she was very dependent on him—put into sharp focus my difference from him: it put into relief my absence. So that by the time she got into an old people's home, she was very sullen and offended, I know, by the fact that she hadn't seen me nearly as much as she'd seen Ted. But I just couldn't handle two—and the truth is, I felt much more responsible for Chris than I did for her. But it was a choice, actually a conscious one, but my mother couldn't know that or appreciate it. I couldn't tell her she was second in line! Chris died before she did, but I knew she wouldn't forgive me. But Ted made it possible for me to know that at least she was in loving, good hands. He took huge trouble with her, and I know enjoyed looking after her, like I enjoyed looking after Chris. I mean, for the last six months he was alive, Chris was at home here in bed—not all the time, but most of the time, finally. He hated the idea of dying in the hospital, and I was so worried that I would not be able to keep him from it, but I did. It was a relief to both of us that I could keep him home, and I did everything myself, because we both wanted it that way. We hardly saw anybody else. I only occasionally left him alone. Well, I never left him alone; I'd always find somebody to be in the house with him, but that was really rare. I felt much more that looking after him was my responsibility, and one that I really wanted to fulfill, because he had allowed me to have such a wonderful life. So I didn't even really feel it was an obligation; it was really something I wanted to do, and I knew how to do. And I don't know really how I got through it, but I did. Because I had to.

You were able to care for Chris and ultimately become his heir through a unique legal protection that many same-sex couples secured long before legalized civil partnerships and marriage equality: in 1977, Chris adopted you. Chris wrote of that experience, "Yesterday morning we went through the adoption ceremony in Santa Monica, before Judge Mario Clinco. It was done in his chambers, not in the courtroom, quickly and politely, with no awkward questions asked. He said 'good luck' to us both when it was over, which made the ceremony seem like a marriage."

Yes, that's typical of his humor! Chris never, ever entertained the idea for children, nor did I. I'm a born queer. It never was of interest to me even to imagine how I might have handled it, feeling guilty in so many ways in not being able to supply essential information. But there was one specific advantage to the adoption: was it for inheritance? Yes, I think it was. Even so, I had to pay heavy taxes when he died, but it would have been worse if we hadn't done that.

Although uniquely expressed, you and Chris shared a gift of observation. Does his signature "I am a camera..." quote hold any particular resonance for you as a portrait artist?

"...with its shutter open, quite passive, recording, not thinking." Yes, of course I know exactly what he was talking about. Well, you see, without realizing it, Chris and I were perfect for each other, because we *both* were fascinated by people. He had a literary interest: he *heard*. He heard how they talked, how they expressed themselves, and I looked at them. Well, I *was* recording, not thinking: that's what I do in the studio in my sittings. I'm tuned in to the visual to such an extent that it takes over, because it's always an identification with the person that precludes anything literary, certainly. So he was a wonderful person to meet people—famous people, Hollywood actors, writers—with, because he could talk to them, entertain them, while I was eating them up with my eyes, and really getting insights into them just because they were opening up for Chris in a way that I could never have done by myself. And it got to the point where, when Chris was writing about somebody we both knew, he would ask me how would I describe that person? And so it was a perfect balance, because I can remember my *own* curiosity: I was learning about this world that I wanted to belong to, so I was always alert. The very fact that he would question me later made it all the more indelible. So I would save up things to tell him, and it was fun telling him. He was always such a good listener: he loved listening, and it really vividly affected our intimacy together. His interest in *my* point of view was something I'd never had before, and I thought, can it be worth anything? But if he thinks so, maybe it is, and maybe I should be as alert as I can be. And we were off to the races.

It seems only fitting, then, that you and Chris ultimately shared even the experience of his dying. You devotedly nursed him through his final months, but with his encouragement, you also approached this deeply personal experience as an artist would.

Being alone with him, day after day, and concentrating on him in that way I only do when I'm working—I mean, not only looking at him, but identifying with him—it really did seem like we were doing it together. So the last six months of his life, I was drawing him. Of course, I knew he was slipping away, but as ruthless as I am when I am working, it was also the most intense way of being with him, of looking at him. That's really what I needed: that intense closeness, being with him. That was my farewell to him: just getting him in my head so that I could never get him out—and I never will.

Nevertheless, both as his life partner and as an artist, that must have been incredibly challenging.

Oh, yes. He was always a perfect sitter for me, but in those last months, last weeks, he was restless, moody; he was unfocused; he was sleeping. I was really doing it by his presence: I knew the face, the head, so well, that I only needed a second, as it were, to do each feature, because I knew him in my mind, but his *presence* was still powerful. I think it's certainly the best work I've ever done, and in a way, it *had* to be, because it was he who had made me an artist. His encouragement was what had made it all possible.

One gets a palpable sense of his energy receding, leaving across your last drawings of him.

That's a quality you can only get from life. Even if the drawing is crude, if I can get that life, that animation, that's the whole point. It's the living creature. You know, I had no idea when I was doing all of those sittings with him, and even the last sittings with him, what those pictures would mean to me after he was dead. With the two pictures of him hanging in my studio, I've really had moments when I feel him with me. I look at those pictures and imagine painting them, and feeling from him what I was getting in his eyes. It's really like having him again for just a moment. I've regretted every picture of him I've ever let go of; I sold so many of him, but I just didn't know at the time what they would mean to me later.

You must have felt yourself in such a vacuum when he died.

Well, it was almost a relief. We were both dreading it so much that I think both of us, by the time it happened, had fortified ourselves. I didn't shed a tear for an entire month. I don't think I dared to; I didn't really think about it. In fact, I wondered, "Why don't you cry? Why don't you show some kind of...?" But I did have a big, big bawl about a month later. Suddenly, it just hit me, wondering how I could be without him, but the answer was: I *wasn't* without him. I knew him so well that I wasn't without him— and I've never been without him since. He's a part of what created me. We lived in each other, so if I was alive, he was still with me, because he'd inserted himself *into* me. I was part of him. We had a very physical relationship, always sleeping in bed together—and not just together, but really intimately entangled, wrapped up in each other, because that's where we felt at home. I knew him intimately like I will never know anybody else in my life. Even after thirty years, we were physically intimate.

As well as emotionally and intellectually intimate. If ever two have truly become "one flesh," you and Chris were the embodiment of it.

And we showed that a thirty years' difference, what did it matter? Pooh! We found each other, and we made something wonderful out of it for ourselves. Yes, that was a great, great strength between us.

And it still continues to feed you.

I love thinking about him, I love remembering him, but I don't have to make the effort, because I really incorporated him into myself. I've not become him, but I've become strong like him. And oh, that gives me such exhilaration to be able to say that, and believe it! And to know that he knew it, and now I know it. So that's why I can go on without him, because he's such a part of me.

Nevertheless, after having crafted and shared a life with Chris for over three decades, what was it initially like for you trying to navigate a life on your own?

Well, I'll tell you exactly how I handled it: it was real dedication to the work in the studio, and then to reading Chris's journals at night. I know I've told you that I never read any of his diaries while he was alive, even though he never hid them from me. I knew always where they were kept: they were in perfect view, accessible to me, and on many occasions when I was alone in the house, sometimes for a week or more, I could have—and I think so many partners *would* have—betrayed him, but I didn't. It wasn't until the day he died, and without any acknowledgment to myself of what I was going to do, but that night, after his body had been taken out of the house, as I passed through his workroom on my way to bed, I picked up the latest volume and began reading it. I worked back in time, and it was an amazing experience for me, as he'd guessed it would be, as many of the entries in the late journals were addressed, "Don, I know you're going to be reading this after I'm dead." And indeed I was—and reading and rereading and re-reading; getting it really into my head. And it was so intimate: I read very slowly, savored every detail, often read pages again and again, and that's what really got me through that first year without him. It was perfect therapy for my state of mind when he was gone from my life, a *perfect* celebration of our time together, to read all those volumes. I never wanted it to stop. But I soon realized he had never been gone. He would just keep on playing his part, whether he was alive or not: playing a part in my head. And I was able to view all the years with him from every aspect I could think of, and I'm really still doing it, still living with him so intimately that I sometimes forget that he's not with me, because he's *become* me. And there was nobody before or since who has ever entered that most intimate chamber but him.

During that same period, you also lost a number of friends and models to AIDS, so many of whom still vibrantly live on in your portraits of them. One of the most hauntingly beautiful of these paintings still hangs in your studio, that of your close friend Rick Sandford. He looks remarkably like Timothée Chalamet in that particular portrait.

Oh, I think Rick would be pleased to hear that, yes! A lot of people think it's a portrait of a woman. Rick didn't look the least bit like a woman, but that picture somehow manages to look both like Rick and a good-looking lesbian!

Which is especially ironic, considering that he ultimately became a gay porn actor!

I think Rick and I only had sex in our very first encounters, but he was a very close friend of both of us. He was a bridge like no-body else across gaps that age might have created, because he was not only as devoted to moviegoing as we were, but read as much or more than Chris did, so they always had something to talk about. Often I would just be listening to the two of them discussing a book that I myself hadn't read, and I was so delighted. Chris was, too, because he never lost his interest in young men—and the more beautiful they were, and the more open they were to talking about their lives, the better from his point of view. But we saw as many or more movies with Rick than we saw by ourselves. Rick was up for anything: his curiosity had no bounds, so I knew I could suggest anything to him. Yes, that's where he and I really connected much better. We were very considerate about the movies we saw with Chris: we didn't take him to Betty Grable or Alice Faye movies! He'd suffered enough of those with me alone!

Do any of your portraits of others lost to AIDS come immediately to mind?

Oh, yes. There was a pretty young boy who'd sat for me several times at the height of his beauty, but he was an early victim of AIDS, and he called me up especially to offer himself as a sitter, knowing that his beauty had already been ravaged. And so that was an invitation to me not to do any soft-pedaling: he encouraged me to put in everything I could see, and I did. It was, anyway, a part of my basic attitude to my work, but he was saying, don't be ashamed to tell everything. So I took him up on it, and it's a shocking comparison. There was only a year or two at the most between our sittings when he was so beautiful, but once he got AIDS, it was just all downhill. I think we did two sittings, so I probably have at least four or five late pictures of him.

Do you know what his intention was in not only allowing you to do that, but in actually requesting it?

He wasn't somebody who even suggested I only ever show one of the beautiful pictures I did of him. I think he was intelligent enough to know his beauty wouldn't last, and he wanted it recorded—and instead of being ashamed of what AIDS did to him physically, he was intelligent enough to know there was a value in recording his decline. I guess he perceived he knew me well enough as an artist to know that I wouldn't shrink from it; if given that license, I would make full use of it—and did. Whereas most young men, that was the last thing they would have thought of doing. I thought it was so protective of him to know that telling me I had license would make it all the more irresistible to work with him. I didn't have to worry about shocking him by my own recording of what he truly looked like—and he was devastated, physically, by the comparison: you would hardly have known it was the same young man.

How courageous of him. That must have been such a challenging yet extraordinary experience for you, both personally and as an artist?

Yes. Well, the one difference was: among the early pictures are nudes; none of the late pictures are. He didn't suggest it, and neither did I. But that became my most sensitive relation to that period, the most heartbreaking example. Of course, there were so many friends who were struck down, but he had the sense and the urge to want to share it with me, and to know that I wouldn't shrink from it. I suppose I could do a book full of my sitters who died of AIDS, but that young man was just a particularly touching example. And so I didn't flinch: I didn't have to worry about hurting his feelings, and he knew that. He welcomed it; he realized he was doing something for the cause. Yes, that was his way of sharing it.

You've since become a longtime supporter of various AIDS charities, and have donated your work to fundraising efforts.

Yes, always to that cause. Oh, certainly, glad to. And I still do.

Meanwhile, you've previously cited Chris's illness as the reason you yourself didn't contract HIV. Can you explain why you've thought this?

Yes, because I was home taking care of him. If it hadn't been for my devotion to Chris, and if he hadn't been in need of my attention to him personally, I would certainly have died of AIDS, because I never took precautions. And once the epidemic started, it would have been too late, anyway.

Were you surprised at all to find that Chris didn't mention much about HIV or AIDS in his later diaries, even though you were both losing friends during that period, and indeed you were non-monogamous as a couple?

Oh, we certainly talked about it. I mean, everybody, all of us talked about it, of course, but I think he was too close to his own death to want to get into it. It was difficult enough coping, because he was somebody who had such an appetite for life, for experience, like very few people I've known. But also, he was beyond it, and I didn't realize to what extent until after he was dead, when I read his diaries.

It must have been so heartening to discover that even after his passing, you could still remain in dialogue with Chris, just by reading his diaries.

Yes, exactly, and that of course had not only occurred to *me*: as I just said, *he* addressed entries *to* me. Yes, it was like he was still holding my hand.

CHAPTER 11

What an artist would do

Don in an undated photo by Stathis Orphanos. *(Courtesy of Juli Veee and the Stathis Orphanos Photographic Archive, Rare Book and Special Collections Division, Library of Congress, Washington, D.C.)*

You've discussed the necessity of creating a body of work that portrays publicly recognizable faces as an essential demonstration of your ability.

As I say, when you're a portrait artist, it's no good to just do portraits of people who aren't going to be recognized by the public. How else can they know that I can get a good likeness if some of my subjects aren't famous people they've seen?

Have you found through the years that the recognizability of celebrities in your portraits can pull focus from the artistry behind the portrait? That viewers get more invested in identifying your sitters than in also recognizing you, the artist who has so effectively rendered the likeness and evoked the essence of that subject?

But that's always been part of my work. If I do a picture of a person from life, I want it to be as good a likeness as I can make it. I mean, it's just instant: I wouldn't know what else to do with it. My approach as an artist to the work that I do is just to make it as accurate as I can, regardless of who my sitter is. All that is essential to me is to have a live model, and if I've got that, I know what to do.

Again, as you say in Chris & Don: A Love Story, *"Every face has to be important."*

Years ago, I decided that a responsibility of the profession was to be interested in *everyone* who sits for me: to find a way of drawing or painting that person that interests me. That's my job, and I love doing it, so it hasn't changed. What *has* changed is more distraction from the outside just keeping me out of the studio, but once I get in there, I know exactly what to do. And I still love doing it, and it's every bit as challenging as it ever was. I don't make any more demands beyond asking my sitter to be as still and as patient as possible, and cross my fingers and hope they won't fall asleep. You'd be surprised, maybe, but about one out of three starts succumbing to sleep within the first half hour.

And how do you handle it when that happens? Alert your sitter somehow?

"Just turn a little this way." Even if they've moved out of position, they're still conscious enough, most of them, to remember what they were doing before they began to get out of it.

Well above and beyond your celebrity portraiture, you've now amassed thousands of portraits of "everyday" sitters.

Oh, yes. The famous people I've drawn are not even ten percent of all of the work I've done. I do everybody, but no matter the sitter, I always instinctively can only give my best, like Chris could only give his best to his writing. In that same way, both of us understood how to do what we did, and so from the beginning, I always tried just as hard with the "unfamous" people I worked with to make my pictures as like them as I could. And of course, that was the best practice I could give myself for the occasions when I had somebody world-famous sitting for me, and the night before was dreading the sitting, wondering how I could ever get myself in shape to face that person—and then was trembling at the sight of them, and often holding my pencil with a shaking hand! Yes, but what good training not only for my art, but for my character! It was like going into the lion's den.

Time and time again. Did working with celebrity sitters ever get easier for you over time?

Well, I gained confidence in my own ability, and though I was still scared, still awed, I knew I had a better chance of proving myself to whomever it was. Even now, I always hope that I will be in my best working condition and able not to feel the grandeur of my sitter so much that it interferes; that I'll be able to do my best work with somebody really famous. It's wonderful when the two can come together. But my routine then was always to not put all of my eggs into one basket, but to do three drawings, if I could, working very quickly. The first one was a warm-up; the second one was zeroing in; and then the third one was, I hoped, the coming together of everything—and it often worked that way. Then eventually I got to the point where I could dare myself to switch to pen and ink, which is totally unforgiving: you put a wrong line down, and it stays. I gave up pencil because I ruined a few good drawings with bad cans of spray fixative, which you have to use with pencil. But that was in the mid-'70s, and I had been doing it for fifteen years, so yes, I was skilled enough. That's when I did my very best drawings, those ink drawings, in the late '70s, early '80s. Those were one per sitter, because it sometimes took me more than two hours without a break. At least with three drawings, in two or three hours, there would be breaks in between, but still that's maybe an hour or nearly an hour for each drawing. That's an awful lot to ask of a sitter, but then the difference between me and most other portrait artists is that the professional portraitist does maybe thirty or forty sittings of an hour each. I do a very intense three or maybe four hours, and then it's over—so if my sitter can bear it, it's an ordeal, but it only happens once!

That's certainly the trade-off. Do you actively pose or direct your sitters? Or find that you have to put them at ease somehow, so that they'll allow more of their authentic selves to show through?

No, they can't help but let themselves show through, because there they are. They're in that chair, on that marble stand, and there's nothing else to do but be themselves. And even if they're embarrassed or shy, they can't hide. Often I'm as embarrassed as they are, and if I didn't have a brush in my hand to protect myself, I wouldn't *dare* look at them like I look at them. It's a little bit like a kind of public execution! You know, I've only been thinking about this in recent times: my sitters often expect to be posed, but all I really want from them is stillness, and if I can get them to look me in the eye. I started suggesting that to them, because I found that if they looked me in the eye, they picked up from me what it was I was after—which was attention and stillness. So if I could persuade them, or if they got it right away, it was a participation. Because I began to realize, it's the most perfect form of collaboration: it's a back-and-forth, and what I'm doing with eye contact is using my sitter's energy to help me. It's coming to me, and then I'm giving it to what I'm doing. So that eye contact is now just a basic of what I do. And if you have eye contact, you no longer have to tell somebody what to do, because if they'll allow it, that's real communication—and soon there's a back-and-forth established so that my sitter, almost by the end of the sitting, knows as well as I what it's all about. And that's how I do it.

Instead of signing your work, as most artists do, you instead ask your sitters to sign their portraits. Why is that?

I started asking my famous sitters to sign and date my pictures because I thought nobody would believe me that I hadn't copied a photograph. Of course, once I started working from life, I could recognize just by looking at a drawing of anybody whether it was done from life or not. But the average person looking at a portrait of somebody famous, if they knew it was done by a twenty-one-year-old, would say, "Well, he must've copied it from a photograph." But I realized years later that it was perfectly appropriate to have my sitter's signature on the piece, because it's a collaboration. A photographer can't ask his sitters to sign, because the photo has to be printed, and by that time, the sitter is gone. He could maybe ask them later to sign it, but I can ask them right there and then.

But yet you rarely also sign your work?

In the earlier days, I would sign them if I exhibited them, but now, unless a gallery person, like my dear Craig Krull, especially asks me to sign them, I consider my sitter's signature and date to really be what authenticates them as my work. I like to think of my signature as being redundant. I hate adding it, since the sitting itself is all in one go, if my sitter can manage it without a break, and then he or she signs it and dates it. So that's all of a piece. But then, even if I wait until that evening before I put my name on it, it always seems like breaking the precedent of the picture itself. But I've done it so many times, and I know it's an objection that most people would not understand, but I'd rather do it my way! Also, when I do a picture of my artist friends and then ask them to sign and date it, they always insist I put my name on it; otherwise, people will think it's a self-portrait!

I would imagine that you likewise never revisit a completed portrait to tweak anything.

No. If my sitter comes again, I do a whole other sitting. I've always done that over the years. I call them repeat offenders. There are certain friends I have a whole series of.

So would you say, then, that you prefer drawing everyday people?

You know, everyday people. They make me dread the celebrities. Even if the celebrities are kind and patient and reassuring, it's always a challenge. But with somebody who has the time, with nobody else begging for them to sit, grabbing their attention, yes, it's less strain on me.

And given how routinely the celebrity is being looked at, do you find you sometimes have to work through and beyond a conditioned glaze they might give you? Or that some approach the sitting as a sort of performance, and turn on their public persona when it's the real person behind it that you're after?

That's true to a certain extent nowadays, but when I started, it was a little bit different: there were still more artists working from life. Now, there are none of us left. I only know two artists who work from life, really. Although David Hockney does work from life sometimes, he also works from photographs, and totally from photographs in his pictures of people. Divine, for instance, sat for me, but the upshot of it was that it was all in order to get to Hockney! I was just boot camp for David: he knew that I knew David, and the dream of his life, he announced, would be to sit for Hockney. So what did I do? I invited David down to share Divine with me at one of our sittings. Of course, Divine was thrilled. So then David invited Divine to sit for him for one of his big oil paintings, in his studio, and invited me, tit for tat, to come and join him, to share Divine. So I gave them a good hour head start before I arrived, and what did I find? The dream of Divine's life was to sit for David Hockney, but there, in a chair on the dais, was Divine...

asleep! And David, brush in hand, was huffing, waiting, wondering how to rouse Divine! I guess he had already tried to waken him. So there Divine sat, snoozing. Finally, he roused, and what was it that roused him? There was a stand down the boulevard, and they were frying potatoes, and he woke up and went, "Potatoes!" and was out of that chair! So much for the dream of his life! So now I'm not longer a conduit to David. Everyone who calls me in order to get a crack at him, I tell them David made me vow not to give his number out.

It's fascinating that Divine would self-sabotage the "dream of his life."

I think that was his thing. He wasn't at all a good sitter. He'd been sleeping for me, too, but I thought, well, for *David*, he'll perk up. So when I went to David's, I said to myself, "Now, maybe I'll get something really good of him—he won't *dare* sleep!" But there he was. I somehow managed to do a couple pictures of him that I liked, but for somebody who asked all these favors and then to go to sleep?

Your Divine portraits date late in your period of exclusively drawing in pen and ink, not long before you transitioned to predominately painting your portraits from a vibrant color palette. What drew you in that direction?

Oh, just as you said earlier, to challenge myself; just because it was there. And of course, that made it much, much more difficult, because it takes time to mix color. With black and white, it was just looking at the sitter and then at my drawing, going back and forth. With color, I had to look away to mix it, and that was agonizing and time-consuming. With black and white, it was just that back-and-forth. But just because it was more difficult, I had to do it. And so I did it in my own way, which was using the white of the paper: making the negative spaces work, which I know other artists deplore. But if I covered the whole sheet with color, it would just take way too long, and I had my sitters maybe for a couple of hours at most. I had to find a quick way of doing it, so there's almost always a lot of the white. In recent years, I've started working on prepared color grounds: just an arbitrary one-color, or maybe two colors, and then I have to use opaque paint to cover some of that, or maybe just a thin coating of one color. It makes a difference; it makes it more of a painting. But you see, because I want to do it all in one go, in one sitting without a break—even three pictures in one sitting, each of them without a break—I have to take shortcuts. I have to. And since working from life is essential, I have to consider my sitter's comfort. Some people can do it, but for others, it's very tough. But here I am with more than sixty years of experience, feeding on people. I often feel like a vampire!

In the midst of a sitting, what determines the choices you make from your color palette? Is it just an intuitive process?

I keep it as simple as possible. I have one magenta, one orange, actually two yellows—and I really only use one of them lately—a green, and a blue. It's amazing, with experience, what you can do with a basic palette. I can almost dip into each color without looking, because I know the placement on my palette, so it cuts down time, usually. And I rarely have to sacrifice getting a true version of the blue or the orange—it surprises me it can be done. Also, I think there's something about the versatility of acrylic; and using water, I can extend the range of a basic hue. But it's a case of necessity creating a way: if time is of the essence, I find the best way of handling it, if I can.

While in command in your studio, the two variables with which you must still grapple are the amount of time and attention a sitter can give you.

In the old days, as I said earlier, I used to prefer to work with people in their homes, where they lived. But yes, I really hate leaving my studio now, because in my studio I can drip paint on the floor, and also, I have my own way. The light is wonderful, and it's slightly easier to intimidate people! But actually in the early days, it was the other way around, because by working with people in their houses, it forced them to be more gracious than maybe they might be if they were strictly doing me a favor, because I was a guest in their house. So they couldn't say, "You've had enough of me!"

Unless they let the prearranged ring of a doorbell say it for them, as did Barbara Stanwyck! You certainly traveled widely in the past for your work.

If I could swing it, I would like never to have to leave home again. I have everything here I care most about, and it's so necessary for me to work in my own studio. That's really what keeps me going.

And you're still occasionally exhibiting your work, most recently in shows dedicated to your portraits of women and your self-portraits. As your oeuvre now encompasses thousands of portraits, how do you select which to include in an exhibition?

Now it's just the simplest it's ever been, but I don't think I've ever done an exhibition without some compromise, because I *have* to show some portraits of famous people who are recognizable. As I say, how will the ordinary looker at my work know that I can get a likeness? And if I make any money, it's usually off commissions. But now, I just choose works that I think are good paintings and drawings.

Earlier, we discussed the dismissive New York art world view toward your work as being that of a "California artist." Have you felt supported here in the L.A. art scene through the years?

Oh, I don't have to feel supported, because I've *always* generated my *own* work ethic: I do it for *myself.* I don't even want to show my work anymore. I'm not interested in having exhibitions now, because I'm just interested in stimulating myself, feeling that determination to work and to be motivated on *my* terms to do the work *I* want to do, and to try to avoid hurting people—but if I must, I will, in order to keep from doing something that bores me as an artist. Yes, even if I have to hurt people's feelings. I can usually tell by doing just one picture of somebody whether they're going to be able to go on with me or if that's it. But I've been through everything that a portrait artist can experience, so I know what I want, and I don't waste time on wondering, "What am I going to do today?" I can just look at somebody and motivate myself right then and there. Just to let *any* kind of intention, other than working, creep in ... well, I just made up my mind *years* ago, *anyone* will do as a sitter. What I won't do is work again with somebody who moves around or falls asleep or tells me how sad they look in my pictures of them.

You've also dealt with the occasional sitter who has tried—out of vanity, but always in vain—to direct you. In a 2009 oral history interview for the Smithsonian's Archives of American Art, you cited as a then-recent example the model and actress Lauren Hutton, who began her sitting by showing you professional photos of herself, as though to guide you as to how you might best ...

Please her! But my first and really *only* thought is to please *myself*! At my age, I can't *still* hope to please my sitter! And if I have any kind of reputation as an artist, I just don't have to go through that routine of working with people who expect to come out happy with a smiling portrait.

Or, as you stated in that interview, working with people who essentially tell you, "this is what I want to look like, not, I want you to tell me what I look like. I would love to hear that."

Yes, indeed.

Hutton at least allowed you to draw her from life, unlike the larger-than-life Mae West, who proposed another approach quite contrary to her famous signature line, "Come up and see me sometime!"

Yes! Well, Chris and I "went up" to see her at her beach house near here, and when I asked her if I might also *draw* her sometime, she said, "Sure!" And then directed me to a closet in which there were stacks of different 8x10 glossies of herself, and told me to take as many as I liked to work from! Of course, I couldn't and wouldn't just work from photographs, but she was quite old by that point, so I feigned being agreeable and took some of them anyway, which pleased her.

After your tenure with the Rex Evans Gallery, you were subsequently represented in L.A. by Irving Blum, followed by Nick Wilder and James Corcoran. You're now represented by Craig Krull. Various stars appear in photos documenting your many openings at galleries and in other L.A. spaces through the years. At your 1973 exhibition at Barnsdall Park, for example, you're pictured with Julie Harris, Elsa Lanchester, John Huston, Leslie Caron, and Roddy McDowall.

And that's a long trek from the west side. It's really the other side of Hollywood, more than halfway downtown, so it was good of them to come that distance.

Paulette Goddard is among the glitterati seen in photos of your open-ing at the New York Cultural Center the following year.

Oh, good for her! I'm really crazy about Paulette Goddard. Just the sound of her voice! She has one of the most distinctive voices ever. And I was so lucky—I got to spend hours with her because Anita Loos was a dear friend of ours, and *they* were dear friends, so Anita brought us together, knowing how much I was thrilled by the thought of meeting Paulette.

Was she as sharp and vivacious in person as her screen personality?

Oh, yes, just that wonderful voice and such a sense of humor al-ways. She was really fun. It was always just a fun, casual context, and that really delighted me. And she was really one of the major inter-ests of my moviegoing early years. She's good in everything, playing a half-breed in *North West Mounted Police*! And in a film that's a long-time favorite: *Hold Back the Dawn*. I'm not a fan of Charles Boyer, but Goddard and de Havilland counteracting are such good foils for each other in that. She's a perfect balance for de Havilland.

Among your personal photos is a color snapshot from 1957 of you and Chris with Goddard and her fourth husband, the novelist Erich Maria Remarque, along with Swami Prabhavananda and photographer Florence Meyer Homolka.

Oh, yes, Paulette is wearing a lavender dress. That was taken in our previous house, the first house we bought, at the bottom of the canyon here, and Paulette and Erich came there and we had dinner with them. Then when I was in New York, I always saw as much as I could of Anita, and when Paulette was there, that was even more wonderful. But of course, doing portraits of a star like Paulette Goddard can be very hazardous. Oh, what I might have done with her! I didn't even put my good drawing of her in *Stars in My Eyes*, just the one I write about, and that really hardly looks like her to me. Gosh, I really did do better with her than that implies. I did three in our first session, but I don't even have a photograph of the best one of them, and I couldn't include the other two pictures from the first session, either, because I didn't even have them. I'd sold one of them. Just as—fool that I was—I let my best portrait of Montgomery Clift go! I only have a photograph of it now, and God knows where it's got to, if it's even still in existence. Oh, madness! Well, it's too painful!

Paulette Goddard appears in photos with you, and separately with Andy Warhol, at the opening of that New York Cultural Center show. Warhol is seen with his ubiquitous tape recorder in hand.

Oh, yes, yes, if there was an opportunity for him to further his ambitions, he was always there!

Did you ever visit his legendary studio, The Factory?

Yes. I don't have any particular memories of it, except for the time one of his studs was roaming around while we were talking, and he said to him, "Hey, come over here and stand behind the counter and take your dick out, and we can get some photographs." Photographs weren't taken, but it was kind of surprising! And so they were all-purpose, those people who were kind of vaguely employed there, and usually there were two or three of them wandering around when I was up there.

A number of Warhol's so-called "superstars" sat for you, including such colorful stars of his underground films as Joe Dallesandro, Viva, Holly Woodlawn, and Candy Darling.

Candy Darling was really one of the nicest and most charming of them. She sat for three pictures. I was much faster in those days, and yet the portraits look more detailed than the ones now that I devote a whole session to. But after two—one full face, the other three-quarter—she noticed something in the first picture: it was a slight shadow under her chin, indicating her Adam's apple. So for the third picture, she managed to get a pose that covered it! I suppose it seemed mysterious to her why I had included it. If she had asked me to leave it out, I would have complied, certainly, but since she didn't, there it is!

Warhol shared your reverence for the Golden Age of Hollywood—so much so that he crafted his own de facto movie studio with his own stable of performers. Among his staggering number of scripted and improvised movies were hundreds of portrait films that he called Screen Tests. *What did or do you think of his moviemaking?*

Oh, I think some of those films that he made are very entertaining. I did see most of them, and there was always something entertaining about all of them, I thought. None of them were difficult to get through. There was always something going on; some personality of interest behaving interestingly.

Meanwhile, remaining steadfastly based in L.A. has kept you in prox-
imity to the mainstream Hollywood movie industry—and occa-
sionally a direct part of it. Another film in which you appear—or at
least a part of you does—is the 1975 cult classic The Stepford
Wives, *directed by your friend Bryan Forbes. Your hand—substitut-*
ing for that of actor William Prince, who plays an artist in the
film—can be seen working on a portrait of the film's star, Katharine
Ross.

I drew all the wives, yes. Really having known Bryan previously
is what got me that job: it was he himself who wanted me and saw
to it that I was hired. I never believed in him as much of a director,
at least not for films, but as far as I was concerned, he was very
easy to work with, and he and his wife were two of my earliest
commissions in London, really early on.

Your most significant participation in a mainstream movie was as the
cast portraitist for director Robert Altman's 1993 film Short Cuts.
How did that unique job come about?

It was through one of the producers, Mike Kaplan, whose baby
the whole project was, really. He got me the job and facilitated me
as official recorder of the cast. In every way he could, he just
couldn't have been more thoughtful and helpful, and a very nice,
sweet man he is.

And all of the performers were contractually obligated to sit for you?

Yes, it was an ideal movie job, if I'd *designed* the role I wanted
most to play in the production of a movie: a large cast, many famous names, lots of women as well as men, and just anything I
asked for was, "Of course, of course, whatever." Yes, and then
watching more of the filming than I ever had of anything else, and
it was such a varied cast, it was always interesting. I didn't personally like Robert Altman very much, and he was very uncomfortable with me, but then he was uncomfortable with so many other

people. But he was really a *man's* director, and I could just feel that, watching him direct women. I don't think he was nearly as good with them or as comfortable.

Some incredible women are included in the impressive ensemble cast of that film, including future Oscar winners Frances McDormand and Julianne Moore.

Oh, Moore was the most eager and amenable of all of the women, and hence I did more pictures of her than anybody else. But she was *much* the most difficult of all of the women in the film to get a good likeness of.

Why is that?

Because she's pretty in a way which was almost paralyzing for me: no single feature of hers is in any way odd or idiosyncratic or identifiable. But I think she's a very talented performer and couldn't have been nicer to me, and took more trouble to please me as an artist than anybody else on the film.

Her lengthy resume of diverse, critically acclaimed performances in-cludes a supporting role in the film adaptation of Chris's novel A Single Man.

She's not a one-note, no: she can handle all kinds of characters. She's really a dedicated actor, and has all the essential equipment, I think, for the job. Oh, and McDormand! She's the homely one, yes, and very relaxed: just exactly who she is, and brings that to all of her performing. Always easy, always on the button, giving an in-telligent performance. I think she's the only one besides Moore who I did more than two or three drawings of. She was really en-gaged in the experience.

How about Lily Tomlin, another member of the Short Cuts *ensemble?*

Ah, yes, I liked her, too. Very droll!

Among the notable men in the cast of Short Cuts *is Robert Downey Jr., whose star has certainly soared even higher in recent years.*

Oh, sure, yes. Oh, he was one of the easiest and most relaxed and likable of the males involved.

How about screen legend Jack Lemmon, who also appears in the film?

Well, that was our second time around. We'd had a sitting in my first year as an artist in London in 1961. I can't remember how it transpired—I didn't even know him—but he sat for me, and it was very important, because that was my first show, and who could be more recognizable than anybody else in it than Jack Lemmon? It really is a face, and he was a perfect sitter and really enjoyed it and took an interest in it, and he really wanted to be friends. And we might have got there; I don't know why we didn't. But for *Short Cuts*, I don't think he had any memory at all. He wore a hat that he wears in the film, and he was like a zombie: never a quirk, never a movement. I think he must have been on some very strong whatever you call it—pacifier—and just with the juice drained out of him. It comes across in the two drawings I did of him. And when I referred to our first sitting, he said, "Oh, yes. Oh, yes. Yes." I don't think he had any inkling, any *key* to remember what we'd done together.

What was the sitting with Robert Altman like?

Oh, I was kind of dreading it. He was as heterosexual as you can get, and the kind of man that just doesn't go with queerness. I mean, there was no prejudice: I didn't feel anything like it, but no real access, either. I was really dreading it, but he sat perfectly for me. If he hadn't been so accessible, I was afraid I would have failed, but he really was, and my portrait of him turned out to be one of my favorites of the whole lot, I guess just because I was dreading it, just because I found it difficult to do. But it looks exactly like him, and it's a fair version of him. It's one of them I like best.

Another man's man of a director, John Huston, not only sat for you, but also supportively showed up at one of your L.A. gallery openings.

Chris knew him far better than I did, and he was very interesting. Of course, he too was totally heterosexual, and that made more of a divide. He had such armament in his personality to keep out people that he didn't want to communicate with, but he could only do so in a kind of makeshift way.

Huston and Altman joined a stable of other high-profile filmmakers who figure in your oeuvre. Another was William Wyler, who received a record twelve Academy Award nominations for Best Director, two of them for movies he made with your favorite star, Bette Davis: The Letter *and* The Little Foxes. *He also directed her Oscar-winning performance in* Jezebel, *your longtime favorite of her films.*

Oh, yes, and they had a heavy affair, too. I'm sure she wore him out!

What was it like for you, getting him to sit?

He was very lovable and very old when I drew him, and that made him particularly sympathetic. He was, I think, very mellowed by it, and I could relate to him on that ground, about his being much older. It was really just that one sitting, but I was full of admiration for him. *Jezebel* is as close to a perfect film as you can get.

While a sitting with Alfred Hitchcock ultimately eluded you, you did manage to ensnare François Truffaut, the influential French New Wave filmmaker whose 1966 interview book, Hitchcock/Truffaut, *was a groundbreaker in the very genre we're exploring here with our own book-length interview.*

Yes, but his Frenchness made him much more impenetrable for me. He was very likable, and we got along very well, but he didn't speak much English, and I don't speak any French. Chris could make much more contact when they were together than I could with him. But I felt very sympathetic towards him, and that's why I'm pleased with the drawings I did of him, because they allowed me to get into him. He was a truly talented and unique personality.

A true auteur, like Hitchcock and Orson Welles.

Yes, yes. Chris got to meet Orson Welles long before he and I met, in the very early days when he was in town here, but I never even got to see him alive. I would love to have known him. I love his personality, love his work, and know how fascinating he must have been. Chris had encounters with him, not many, but he made real contact with him, I know.

Meanwhile, you did get to know the controversial director Roman Polanski, who sat for you in 1968 at the behest of his then-wife, Sharon Tate?

Ah, because she came to me. I don't know how she found out about me—we didn't really know each other—but she contacted me, came to my studio, loved my work, and said, "I want you to draw my husband." I was intending to ask *her* to sit for me, and I'm really sorry that never happened, but I knew he had to come first. But he and I got along great: he was just terrific; not the least bit pretentious. He himself knew how to draw pretty well, and he sat perfectly for me. I did three drawings of him, and they were all good, because he cooperated so well. He was really likable and nice to me and treated me like a sort of artist comrade, and is about that high!

While small in stature, Polanski was then commanding an enormous amount of attention following the release of his first American film, Rosemary's Baby, *then a blockbuster and now considered one of the greatest horror movies of all time.*

Yes, he was. But I was using *him* as a prelude to *her*!

It was almost exactly a year after your sitting with her husband that Sharon Tate and their unborn child were murdered by members of the Charles Manson Family.

Oh, we just couldn't believe it! It sounded just too *bizarre* to believe. Oh, that was *so* hard to accept with her—and to *know* somebody that such a thing happened to? It was just *so* shocking. It really just hit us both, Chris and me: really, it was just unbelievable. She was a *lovely*, charming, sweet young woman! And I was just warming up, after the sitting with him: they loved the pictures I did, so it was just a *cinch* that she would sit for me, and I was just waiting for the right moment to ask her. She was really genuinely sweet and really friendly and a likable, nice young woman. And that murder room: that's where I drew him! And my picture of him was on the wall in the murder scene! Isn't that awful, though? It witnessed it!

Your portraits of Vincente Minnelli must surely be counted among the very best of your work. After Minnelli and his wife expressed their displeasure with your first masterful but somewhat shocking drawing of him, which captured him with bulging eyes and a gaping mouth, you were invited back for a second sitting. The resulting second drawing has since found its rightful home in the National Portrait Gallery in Washington, D.C., but in Stars in My Eyes, *you write that "the first drawing is still my favorite. Partly because of its stare and open mouth, it isn't quite like any other drawing of mine, and it reveals a delicate sensitivity in Minnelli which, to me, is essential to his character. Also, the drawing has a lot of what I care most about, a real aliveness. In this case, it's startling."*

I tell you that my two Vincente Minnellis, I think, are really good. Those are my *best*. One of them is an expression of a particular ability of mine, and the other expresses another ability. They're quite different, but they're both utterly him, and I think maybe they're the best things in *Stars in My Eyes*, from my point of view.

*With your brother Ted, you had gatecrashed the 1951 Hollywood pre-
miere of Minnelli's movie musical* An American in Paris, *which was
inspired by the music of George Gershwin. In* Stars in My Eyes, *you
describe the uneasy experience of a sitting with another quintessential
American composer, Aaron Copland. Given your access through Chris
and Lincoln Kirstein to many of the major players in the arts during
that period, would you have met and/or drawn any of the other leading forces in midcentury American music, such as Samuel Barber or
Gian Carlo Menotti or Leonard Bernstein?*

I knew Menotti less than Barber, but when I knew them, I
hadn't really become an artist yet. That was all in the '50s. I drew
Copland the one and only time, and only one drawing, and I knew
I only had one crack at it. And that always makes me very tense,
but I'm happy to say I managed even under extreme pressure working with him. He laughed at the drawing I did of him! But he
signed it anyway. His laughter was all about seeing what he didn't
want to see! But he was a good sport: he wouldn't let the prima
donna in him interfere. And musicians, more than any other art
form, just have their asses lit like none of us! For music lovers,
their objects of devotion are just gods! The music world is not very
attractive to me largely because of that, but I don't know or care
enough about music to mind it.

*Nevertheless, you and Chris enjoyed a close friendship with the Russian
composer Igor Stravinsky, his wife Vera, and his young colleague Robert Craft.*

Stravinsky was really my first star sitter of magnitude. By that
time, Chris and I both adored Igor and Vera, and Bob Craft. Chris
took me to see them, and they were very sweet to me. I never in any
way felt anything but accepted. We really loved them, all three of
them, and would even see them when we went to New York. And
after Igor died, we always saw Bob and Vera whenever we could. But
oh, that first sitting with Igor: we were invited to dinner, and I had

to have had the sense not to have anything to drink, because Igor sat on the sofa after dinner and I did four drawings of him, and they were all among the very best work I'd done up to that point. So that tension, with the odds riding on it, that made me know I was a professional, that I could do it. I wouldn't shrink; I wouldn't give in to my fears of my own incompetence; I would just do the best I could. Yes, I thought very highly of those first four drawings.

How about Leonard Bernstein?

I knew Bernstein, but we only met in New York. I remember him coming up to me at some formal occasion in New York—we were both in tuxedos—and very jollily, he said, "Well, we've *both* managed to keep our looks! I congratulate you." But he paired us together! After Lenny had gone, the friend I was with said, "But he's much older than you, isn't he?" He had to be at least fifteen years older than I was, but there he was, thinking me an equal, and still up there looking as good as I was for my age! And imagining that he was flattering me at the same time!

A composer and conductor, he was a titanic figure in twentieth century American music, perhaps best known for his collaboration with playwright Arthur Laurents, lyricist Stephen Sondheim, and choreographer Jerome Robbins on the perennially revived Broadway musical, West Side Story. *I was once in Arthur Laurents's New York brownstone and spied three works by you lining the stairwell: portraits of the prima ballerina Nora Kaye, actress Geraldine Brooks, and Arthur Laurents himself.*

And he chose the wrong portrait of himself, of course, as he chose the more flattering one! I did good ones of Nora Kaye, yes, and why Geraldine Brooks, I forget. She was a nice girl, and I did several drawings. I didn't even remember his having a picture I did of her. But yes, he sat for me a couple of times. Robbins sat for me, early: I have at least three drawings of him from the early '60s.

Let's touch upon some of the mainstream music artists with whom you've crossed paths through the years. Barbra Streisand sat for you in 1964, just as she was on the brink of superstardom.

It was so lucky that I caught her early in her career. Now, well, she would never consider *ever* sitting for me again. I think she's actually a very unpleasant personality, and just that kind of attitude that is the worst for me.

Elton John was well beyond the threshold to stardom when you drew him in 1972. What was the experience of his sitting like for you?

He was very, very sweet to me; very nice. It was in the quiet of a house that he was staying in in Malibu. I had him all to myself, and I did, I think, three drawings, all pen-and-ink drawings. He sat very well, and they're pictures I'm really pleased with. It's almost an ideal example of what I consider a successful day's work. But it was my only encounter with him.

Chris's diary makes mention of your having met David Bowie after one of his concerts, although he never posed for you?

No, no, I don't think he would ever have behaved, but yes, we met him, Chris and I. I remember being in his dressing room, but I can't even remember now if I asked if he'd sit for me, or if I just assumed it wasn't going to happen.

Whereas a post-concert party for Linda Ronstadt did yield you a sitting, a few days after you and Chris had sat up talking with her and Carole Bayer Sager until two in the morning.

And I could have done better. That was the only chance: the only picture I ever did of her.

You had more opportunities with Michelle Phillips of The Mamas and the Papas. Two exquisite portraits of her from twenty years apart are featured in your Hollywood book.

Yes. It was Michelle who contacted me, because she liked my work, and she was a very nice woman and so pretty. She was really one of the prettiest young women I've ever known.

Moving on to another category of your celebrity sitters: among the many literary greats who have sat for you, certainly Chris, your tireless champion and most frequent portrait subject of all, ranks at the very top of the list. As we've previously discussed, close writer friends like Truman Capote, Gore Vidal, and Tennessee Williams also repeatedly sat for you, as have Armistead Maupin and Edmund White. Let's touch upon some notable others with whom you've connected outside of your intimate orbit. You wrote Chris from New York in early 1964 about a lively sitting with the legendary James Baldwin.

Oh, I loved him! He was such fun and had such a lovely face, just full of humor and enjoyment. Oh, drawing somebody like him, eye-to-eye contact, that was such a great pleasure for me! He was really a *lovable*, lovable creature, and just so alive, his face. He was every bit as adorable as he looked.

You wrote Chris about similarly clicking with the poet Marianne Moore, who sat for you wearing her trademark tricorn hat and black cape.

Yes, we really hit it off, but there were only those two sittings, really: it had to be all created and lived in our brief time together. And we couldn't have been more distanced in age or gender or experience, but judging how unlikely we could connect so intimately with only two or three meetings, that was lucky for me.

You similarly found an instant rapport in a brief encounter with another poet, James Merrill, wistfully observing in Stars in My Eyes *that your "liking for Merrill made me want to please him," while he kindly tried "to satisfy my wish to be of interest to him."*

Now he was somebody I *really* connected with, and it was all really based on the one sitting and one drawing I did of him. But we connected so profoundly that not only is the drawing good, but I think the experience for us both was memorable, and all just really based on that one encounter. It's one of my best single portraits.

You forged more lasting friendships with the poets Frank O'Hara and Joe LeSueur and artist/writer Joe Brainard in New York in the 1960s?

Well, they were much more my compatriots. Merrill was from another kind of life. They were people I could really identify with, whereas Merrill had the remoteness of coming from lots of wealth and style and things that I could only guess about. But considering that, we did we really appreciate each other, I think, and I'm sorry that it couldn't have included Chris. But of course, being writers, it probably would've been much more difficult for them to get together, because that's very different territory.

Speaking of different territory: not long ago, you revisited the official portrait you were commissioned in 1984 to paint of former California Governor Jerry Brown. Given that your characteristic style diverges sharply from that of typical political portraits, your Brown portrait at first proved controversial, with state lawmakers voting to banish it to a far-flung stairwell at the State Capitol in Sacramento. It has since become a popular attraction among visitors to the California State Capitol Museum.

Well, they've had that portrait for a long time. I had never seen it hung in the federal building, so I thought it was high time. When they first got it, they hung it in a stairwell. I thought it was probably a decision to keep it from contaminating the portraits of the other governors, because it *was* in a totally different style. They had four other portraits of recent governors hanging next to mine, and they were all in quite different styles. I guess they've just gotten used to it.

While not an "official" portrait, another high-profile political figure and former film star, Nancy Reagan, sat for you shortly after becoming California's First Lady in 1967.

Yes, and I realized that I got her just in time. I went to the house that they were living in in Pacific Palisades. On my way into the house, I remember going past Reagan doing a session with four other men, talking and so forth, and she was alone in the house. I did two pictures of her. For the first picture, she just sat still and looked at me, and I went to work, hoping that I'd be able to persuade her to sit for a second one, but not knowing. But because the first one wasn't at all what she was expecting, I got to do a second picture of her, and it was a perfect example of a perfect change in a personality. I mean, she took the first picture I did of her as an example of *exactly* what she didn't want—which was a serious, probing, revealing portrait of her—so I only got the second one because she was determined to give me a transformation like I've seldom seen: the warmth, the melting *loveliness*! And just like that, still with the determined stillness and looking me in the eye and not flinching, but just giving me exactly what she most wanted. So that's what I gave *her*.

Her Hollywood training served her well for a continuing public life.

And I wouldn't be the least bit interested in showing publicly the second picture by itself, because it *has* to be paired with the first, because they are different as day from night. The melting personality she gave me for the second one would just break your heart, if you didn't know where it came from!

Have you seen the popular official portraits of former President Barack Obama and First Lady Michelle Obama?

They're just so uninteresting as paintings, as art, but that's so often the case with official portraits. It's people who don't know what *anyone* looks like, asking somebody to paint it who can't see, or won't see. Well, that's really painting your preconceptions rather than painting a picture of the person you're looking at. And you know, they always work from a fistful of photographs. Well, they're kidding themselves! They're not looking sufficiently. That encounter with a living person, *that's* what it's all about. Copying a photograph isn't about anything. It's just about what you do with it when you're alone.

Versus what can be collaboratively achieved in the intensive exchange between you and your sitter in a live sitting.

Yes, yes! It's a challenge. It's always a challenge, and there's no easy way of doing it. Everybody is a new challenge. But why are portrait artists just failing to realize that, and instead just doing one quick sitting in which they take lots of photographs but don't even pick up a brush or a pencil, and then they just work from the photographs? It's just making a travesty out of the situation.

So why not just consider themselves portrait photographers and skip the extra step?

Yes, yes, that's exactly it. But there's so little work being done now in portraiture that interests me at all. I don't even have to know the artist or his or her work; I just need a couple of seconds, and *instantly* I know whether the work was done from a photograph or not.

Whereas the vibrancy of your work instantly telegraphs that it's been done from life, even if you don't necessarily produce happy, smiling portraits of your subjects.

Well, it's a problem in that stillness becomes only a synonym for sadness, because nobody can sit there smiling for even ten minutes, or five minutes, holding a smile. So there's no getting around my sitter saying, "Oh, I look so sad!" But that means portraiture is all about flattering people. It's *not*, if you're really interested in it! It's about digging for the personality, and if you just draw people looking like they're feeling happy, then you're missing the whole point! But you see, everybody hopes it's going to be flattering and wants it to be, and feels really that they failed *me* if they look sad!

But they haven't failed you at all. In working from life, you're able to not only render an accurate likeness by looking at your sitter, but also more deeply into your sitter.

There is an energy going between us, and if one can really connect with it . . . well, it's done wonders for me. It's done whole pictures for me. Well, that's the whole point of working from life. As a kid, I always copied photographs, and of course that element was so often lacking. So that's what was so *delicious* about working from life, was seeing everything that the photograph hadn't shown me. And actually getting sittings with Bette Davis and Alice Faye, whom I had drawn endlessly from photographs as a kid? But I would leave out anything in order not to hurt their feelings? Well, how could I possibly? And the only way that Faye defeated me was by making the conditions of the sitting so intolerable that to be able to do anything at all, I would have defied *any* other artist to do half as well as I did with what I was given! In little increments, drawing under the worst conditions in a dressing room with bad lighting, and waiting and watching her from the wings while she was performing, then rushing back to the dressing room to be ready for her when she came off. I remember consciously saying goodbye to any quality expectation in what I did of her. I did include those portraits in *Stars in My Eyes*, and I consider that very brave of me, not because of anything to do with her feelings, but because I hate showing work that I feel is inferior or is below my standard. And if it's below my standard, like the Faye drawings are, it's because she wasn't giving me a chance.

Nevertheless, what a heady experience it must have been for you, getting to draw both of your childhood idols, Faye and Davis, from life!

Yes, imagine! And there are other people in the book, like Charlotte Rampling, who wasn't nearly the subject then that she is now for me. I could have done so much more with Rampling. She was already somebody truly remarkable for me, but I have much more interest and admiration for her now than I did with that drawing. I think she's one of the most fascinating movie women I've known and watched in movies. So often, the movie may be bad, but she's almost always remarkable. But there are also others in that book where only one picture is the only picture I ever did. Henry Fonda—I could have done better, but still, considering the pressure, I'm not ashamed of it. The only picture of Mia Farrow, too: she seemed to me not as interesting as the others. I think Maggie Smith is a miracle of a one-drawing version of her, and it's such a good drawing in all other respects, and so detailed for a single drawing. I like my drawing of Peter Pears, even though it's so anguished. And the Alec Guinness: something tells me that even if I'd done more drawings of him, there was something between us that would have always been there. For a one-time chance, I do think the Laurence Olivier is remarkable. But only if he hadn't that condition of the eye that people get who look into klieg lights—it bleaches the outer rim of the iris, and eventually makes the eyes look like they've got huge pupils. My drawing would look twice as much like Olivier if the pupils were all black. You would much more quickly say, "Of course it's Olivier."

Nevertheless, your drawing is unmistakably Olivier.

And it had all the earmarks for failure. I knew he was old—it was difficult for him to sit for long, he didn't look like himself, his hair was almost gone, the eyes were faded—but what made it possible was *his* determination. He sat perfectly for two hours, at his age, without even moving his hand! He was just amazing. I felt *willed* by him to do it. That's how it happened: he was just the *epitome* of a professional, and I know he gave that kind of professionalism to everything he did that meant anything to him. And everything was present: all the tension and the pressure of knowing one picture and one picture only, and then that was it. Maximum pressure. And you know, when I draw somebody, I can't do it if I don't like them. And I would even go further than that: drawing for me is an act of love, and so it has to include *everything* I know and feel about the person, even if it's a stranger to me. But there can't be any "no entry" signs on them as my sitter. I have to go everywhere I can—and I can't see anything and not put it in. If I see it, it deserves to be in the picture I do. But I just can't believe that *any* one picture of anybody I've worked with can be all-inclusive, or even as inclusive as I would like it to be.

And of course, Don, it's all in your perspective. Your appraisal of your work won't necessarily always compare to how your sitters or others perceive it.

I used to take it really so seriously. Well, I took real pride in my work, and it was agony to fail. I felt so bad for years about missing my one chance with Ingrid Bergman, but I look at that drawing now, and oh boy, did I get her! I got something remarkable in that. It's not by any means what I might have done, but it does tell something about her—to me, anyway. But it's not the lush Bergman; it's not the vivacious Bergman. She was really like nobody else, and in a way, I was bound to fail, because everything about her had to do with expression and movement, and there she was, sitting still. Poor thing, she didn't have a chance to look like Ingrid Bergman, and I drew her like she looked! And she didn't recognize herself. Oh, she knew it was she, but she didn't recognize herself, because she was looking for the Ingrid Bergman on the *screen*. And that's who *I'd* hoped to record, and instead I only got the Ingrid Bergman in life, sitting still, doing something she really didn't want to do. And I don't say it often, because it sounds like an excuse, but how *can* people look their best when they're doing what they have to do if they come to a sitting with me? They have to sit still and be bored maybe for two full hours without moving. Well, who is going to look anywhere like themselves in their vivacity? So it's a losing game to begin with.

But a winning game in other ways, given all you ultimately reveal beyond the faces your sitters think they're showing you.

But I bet you most of the sitters would say it's not worth the trouble, and why show that part of me if you can't show the best? So it's unfair to them. But then I say, well, OK, I failed them and I hurt their feelings, but they'll recover.

And ultimately you can't predict or be held accountable for how they'll perceive the work. We all see ourselves through our own particular filters.

And I've never done anything but the best I could. I can't do it any other way: I give *anything* I do *all* I've got. It's often not enough, depending on what I'm doing, but it's always all I've got in a sitting. So if I ever find I'm not giving it my all, I would have to stop immediately. And occasionally, I *have* stopped: I'm a dogged creature, but occasionally I've felt that I didn't have it in me, or wouldn't or couldn't have it in me, on a particular occasion. But that's happened very rarely.

And as long as you still find fulfillment in working, why stop, indeed? It's still working "for the work itself, not the fruits thereof," just as you always have.

I've never lost the magic of it. I lie in bed at night and wonder sometimes, how could I have looked at him or her like I did? How am I going to look at her or him tomorrow in the only way I know how to look? Even what I do really becomes secondary to the excitement of looking—of having, as it were, a license to look. A license to, *ooo!* And if I'm quick and don't give myself away, I can really look, and it's never failed. If I can make that connection— just be allowed to be so close and to really look—even holding a pen or brush finally becomes just an excuse: I always get something magical out of it. I just know in some way, I was born to have that experience. After all these years, I can't get enough of it. I can't give it up. And I never change the size of my paper. I used to work on a different piece of paper, a different surface, with each drawing. I now just have two surfaces that are very hardly distinguishable for me. It doesn't matter. The experience is still shocking to me.

It's wondrous that you still find such magic in it, such surprise.

And I mean, what can it possibly be for? Except my own craving for the experience.

I daresay your sitters get something out of it, too—those who allow themselves to open up to the experience.

Every once in a while, people tell me, "You'll never know what it's been like for me." It worries me, and at the same time, it reassures me that it's not all one-sided: that I'm not just some kind of ghoul who doesn't know when to stop.

Meanwhile, you have your own appraisal of the work.

I know pretty soon after the sitting, and I rarely change my mind about my work. The big test is the night of the sitting. I usually go out to the studio and look at the day's work, and that's when I really know for sure what I think of the day's work.

As you have with your portrait of Ingrid Bergman, have you often found yourself reevaluating earlier work you may have been dismissive of at the time of its creation?

Well, I can't fool myself. I'm only interested in doing my very best, and the failures are agonizing. I've felt bad about that Bergman drawing since I did it. What adds to my feeling bad about the drawing is wondering, why didn't I do a second one on that day? Again, I think it was my awe of her, but why? Well, she does hold a very particular and very high place in my regard for movie personalities, but I don't really understand why I didn't do a second drawing. I think she would have welcomed it. I think even though that one took a long time and disappointed us both, I've always felt if I'd asked could I do another, she would have said yes. And it might have been even worse, but it might have been much better. The one I did with Bergman really is the most hurtful of my celebrity sittings: I can't think of anybody I minded more not doing my best with. But I did look at it just the other day, and it *does* tell you something very real about her. She had so many sides to her, but she really was somebody who was at her very best in her vivaciousness: laughing and moving and charming. That's when she was her most remarkable, because it was so genuine. You didn't feel she was *ever* acting; it was because that's who she was. Chris and I did have another *wonderful* encounter with her. Marti Stevens—do you know of her?

She's an actress and singer, and daughter of the film executive Nicholas Schenck.

Yes. She was in *The Constant Wife*, the last theater production that Bergman did. She knew that Chris and I adored and admired Bergman, so she had the four of us together at a dinner after the theater at her house, and we had a *wonderful, wonderful* time. Bergman was absolutely at her best, just loving it and performing and carrying on. Really, it was just a perfect occasion for both star and devotees. We all loved it, yes. She was really wonderful, and that's what I missed recording in my picture of her. But still, we did have that wonderful time with her.

Your Hollywood book includes some of the abstract pieces you were doing for a time?

I didn't give up my sittings; I just added to it these abstract pictures. I quite enjoyed doing them: it was such a luxury to be able to work alone. Being a portrait artist who only works from life, for years I've always had company when I worked. After more than thirty years of that, I was delighted to be able to paint without having anybody else in the studio.

Your recent Nudes *book features another aspect of your portraiture.*

That was a blissful period for me. I had a patron who, for a good two-and-a-half years, sent me male models, nude models. I once had two weeks of all-day sittings with beautiful men. There was always a changeover. Sometimes my favorite ones got two days in a week, or a sitting two weeks in a row, but mostly it was somebody new every day. He paid for them all, and that was a great working period for me. It was just gravy for me. I'd usually start at twelve-thirty, and sometimes the sittings went on past ten-thirty at night. I would never do that to amateur sitters, but since these guys were paid so well by my patron, I felt I could work them harder, especially the ones that I had already worked with and I knew were professional models.

When working with such intensity, how did you stave off any fatigue?

All of my life, I've been blessed with good energy; I've always relied on it. But at my age, I'm slower now. It takes me twice as long to do a picture as it used to, but I still very much enjoy working. I need it. I want it as much as I can. Most of my artist friends, or at least many of them, have had assistants in the studio. I've never had an assistant, and never wanted one. I'd rather do it all myself. I've learned that if you want it done right, you do it yourself.

Back in 1960, Chris predicted that your having received the praise of both Bouché and Beaton would stand as "the greatest triumph Don will ever have in his life, perhaps—because it was the first and because it's doubtful if the praise of any two people will ever again mean quite as much to him as [theirs] did." Now, over sixty years later, let me ask you: was Chris correct?

Oh, no! I've achieved much more significant satisfaction from my work. Getting it published: that *One Hundred Drawings* book that Twelvetrees Press did really encouraged me a lot, and then the beautifully produced book of my male nudes, that means a great deal to me. And also the *Hollywood* book: that's far more satisfactory, although some of the reproductions of the black-and-white drawings are nearly invisible, and that shouldn't be nowadays. It could have been, should have been much better, but anyway, it's still a book that means a lot to me. But *Stars in My Eyes*—I *hate* that book! The look of it, the typeface, the design of it, the quality of the reproductions. But with the *Nudes* book: everything I do is portraiture, and even those are all portraits, but just full-body portraits. I didn't change anything about my approach; I just put more detail of my sitters in: full-figure rather than just head and shoulders. My patron, at my request, sent me not just young beauties, but some middle-aged men, Black men, a great variety, and it was made all the better.

Not with such a concentrated output, but you've occasionally drawn or painted nudes throughout your career. We discussed earlier that you had first worked with nude models as an art student.

Oh, yes, at Chouinard, but they were mostly women then, very few male models—and what few men there were, they were always wearing a posing strap, and middle-aged, unattractive, uninviting characters. So it took a long time to really get into male nudes, but it was because I was saving them until I could draw well enough to really record them properly. But I'd never drawn a nude figure before art school.

That double standard still holds true, alas. Prudish yet prurient Americans still can't seem to separate art from sex when it comes to depictions of full-frontal male nudity.

Well, it was almost considered kind of distasteful: no, we don't want to see nudes of *men*! Women, yes, maybe. But oh, that just fired me up: if I couldn't get them at school, I was determined to get them on my own, either here or at my artist friends' houses.

It's been estimated that your entire body of work to date encompasses some seventeen thousand portraits.

It's insane, that number! Imagine if you had told me that before I started out? But if we count all the work I've done, all the three or four pictures in a sitting, then that multiplies it. Yes, even letting on the list people who were just the tiniest famous, it's a *huge* number, with quite a number of them also sitting more than once. Oh, if I had been told that before I began as an artist, it would just seem too unbelievable to be possible! And in a positive way, considering any of the negative explanations. Yes, even if I never do another sitting, I've got a *huge* collection. I *have* kept a *great* deal of my work. I at least had the sense to do that, because in the early years, I would throw away something that wasn't up to snuff. In later years, since so much of it *isn't* up to snuff, if I start throwing anything away I may be in danger of throwing *everything* out! So I don't want to take that truly drastic step. But in the old days, my creative instinct was nonstop: it just kept generating daily, this appetite. And then in later years, I really had to satisfy it, in desperation, by doing self-portraits. I just had the urge to do *something*, use my ability in some way, and now I feel like I'll be *very* surprised if I do another self-portrait. I've just kind of run that into the ground.

How do you source your sitters these days?

The same way I've always done: just calling people up, or meeting people at parties. There are still artist's models, but nowadays they're usually all photography models, and I rarely work with professional models. I've been very lucky with getting people to sit. I really don't care at all whether it's a nude or a clothed sitting, or color or black-and-white. I just want to keep working.

And as you just mentioned, you've sometimes jumped in as your own sitter. Have your frequent self-portraits revealed anything surprising to you about yourself?

Oh, doing something that I've done for so many years again and again and again, I might surprise myself just by the quality of the picture, or just finding *any* kind of spark to make it as fresh as I can. Lighting, angle—just whatever it is. But working with myself, I can only do that up to a certain point. As long as I have a sitter, I can always get myself sufficiently interested to work, just because that's what I do. I decided that years ago.

And as you once told The Observer *in London, the entirety of your work is about self-portraiture anyway, in a sense. "I'm an unconscious mimic, and I instinctively impersonate my sitter. I'm psychologically in costume when I work," you said, "and what I produce is a self-portrait from inside someone else's skin."*

I've always had a talent to record people in a way that is identifiable to other people. Not only do I identify with them inwardly, but I'm also able to produce an outward bit of evidence that I had them inside me, or at least had them in my eyes. And it's a lovely experience I have when I'm working, and it's really working for my sitter, too: on those rare occasions when I can be exerting my utmost attention, and at the same time relaxing, feeling confident that she and I, or he and I, can really keep going under what we're generating at the moment. And it's its own reward: if I can get into that relationship with my sitter, then I could conceivably go on working indefinitely, though I know neither of us could bear it physically or psychologically. But I'm equipped: nobody is going to throw me off my balance, my intention, unless of course they've made me really dislike them; then it's sealed up, and then I have to get them out as soon as I can.

Meanwhile, you've often also sat for portraits by other artists and photographers. What's that process been like for you, to just be fully the sitter?

Agony—that I really don't want to do it. I avoid it now as much as I can. But I have a young friend, a very good artist named Peter Macauley, who is a *very* sensitive and accomplished portraitist. He does pictures from life, and he's very good at it. I think he's done the best likeness of me that *any* artist has *ever* done. I really think it's quite remarkable.

You've told me that you and he periodically engage in intensive portrait sessions with each other.

Yes, we do pictures of each other, and when he's here, I want to spend all day, every day at it, if he's available, just because I admire his work and he's charming and nice-looking, so it's a pleasure for me. The only drawback is that I wish it was just all me drawing and painting *him*, but I have to be a good sport and pose for him, too. That's a waste of time, from my point of view. I mean, I'm interested in his work, but not in pictures of *me*! But in Peter, I've finally found somebody young enough, attractive enough, and talented enough that I can actually take pleasure in being whatever kind of mentor he wants to use me for.

And he certainly seems passionate enough.

Yes, and that's to me what having talent is: it's not only being able to do it, but *wanting* to do it.

He, like you, is a rare commodity these days, given that he works from life.

Yes. It's really thinning out, young artists who are prepared to go through the difficulties of working with live models. So it's the first time I've been able to play the role of mentor. Well, we're really just two artists together, so it's a very nice and unusual relationship. I like encouraging him, and I think he likes being encouraged. Well, he's encouraged *me*, so I've gotten a lot of incentive from knowing him. It's enjoyable for me, and as I say, the first real experience of mentorship from the other end.

CHAPTER 12

A single man

Don in his studio, 2014. (*Photo by Jason Loper; 1983
portrait of Christopher Isherwood* © DON BACHARDY)

*After a period of mourning Chris, you became involved in a relation-
ship with a much younger man, the architect Tim Hilton. I'm sure the
irony wasn't lost on you of now being the elder in a relationship with
nearly as wide an age gap as had existed between you and Chris.*

It was a delight, because I had a chance to play Chris's role. Tim
is twenty-six years younger than I am. It's not the thirty-year age

difference between Chris and me, but it's clearly serious. So much of it was so illuminating for me, and I found myself over and over talking in my head to Chris, "*That's* how you were feeling in this situation, in that situation! *That's* what you minded. That's what was difficult!" Because I could really identify with him in a way that I never could before, until I was playing his part. And how could I not play it as well as I possibly could? Of course, I wasn't nearly as good at it as Chris, but he was inspiration for me *daily*. And Tim could be a difficult person. I guess who isn't, who's worth the effort of making the effort? But I never felt responsible for him, though I felt maybe inadequate to handle him. And it was tough for Tim, knowing about Chris and suspecting, how could I really believe in him after knowing somebody like Chris for so long? We talked about that. But I think he guessed what he was in for, and with all the experience I'd had with a man so much older than I was, he realized what it was cooking up to be between us. And what a fascinating switch, to be able to play Chris's role with a young man! It certainly was full of surprises and interest. Yes, it was no end of fascination to me, and it's still cooking.

So through your relationship with Tim, do you feel you also inadvertently expanded your relationship with Chris?

Oh, it really did. In a way, I couldn't have picked a better person for the job, because Tim was every bit as difficult for me as I was for Chris. I mean, it wasn't all roses with Chris: we had terrible fights, and I suffered and he suffered, and we got into terrible states, but we couldn't stay in them for long. I was *very* difficult. Oh, so many times I remembered situations between Chris and me which I didn't really fully understand until I was in Chris's role with a much younger man, and finding it very difficult myself. Especially in the early years with Tim, repeatedly I was making these discoveries harkening back to Chris and saying, "*That's* how he felt!" about some situation that had occurred between the two of us. "*That's* what it was like from his point of view."

So you were not only gaining understanding of Chris's perspective on various challenges you two had encountered, but then had the opportunity to practically apply that understanding to similar difficulties in this new relationship?

Yes, that was very, very informative. It took me a while to use Chris in that kind of a way, but it was just so natural, because so much of the troubles that Tim and I had couldn't help but remind me of myself with Chris, and then I had his example. I realized I could think myself out of whatever predicament I was in, because if I thought about Chris, I could conjure him and make him tell me what to do about Tim. Chris was my inspiration, because I was so often thinking as much about him as I was about Tim while I was sleeping every night with Tim. Chris and I always slept very intimately together, and the same with Tim. He and I were very intimate, very close physically always, and still are.

But ultimately your romantic relationship wasn't sustainable?

Somehow, Tim and I managed a pretty good ten years. It was really impossible, finally, but I was absolutely crazy about him, and I still love him very much. We're still very close: we speak to each other every day. He's an Oregonian; always wanted to go back to Oregon, and did finally go. But we still spend a lot of time together—I go up there, or he comes down here—and we talk on the phone every day, usually several times. Well, I have so much to think about. It's really the first time in my life I've been really alone, living alone, since Tim, and I'm enjoying it. I'm not feeling abandoned or lonely. I really don't. I have so much to think about, so much to review, and I still have an appetite for my work.

And you're hardly isolated: you often have a sitter, and you remain very active socially.

Yes! Chris never lost his interest in the world, either. He loved our domestic life together, but he was always a man of the world, too.

It's certainly exhausting to consider any given month's worth of activities recorded in his diaries!

And as I said, it never occurred to me to let him read *my* diaries, until he was dead. Isn't that dumb of me not to? Well, I mean, I just quote him, record all of his wit. I think it would have made him laugh! But he couldn't do that. Of course, he knew always that I would read his, and oh, boy, those journals were a lifesaver. That's what really kept me going, because not only was he in my head, but I was daily reading all those diaries, and eventually getting through the material about our own lives together.

Which must have been a bittersweet experience, both in fondly recalling the good times, but also in gaining insight on his views of your challenges. Were there any passages that surprised you?

I think he would have been much more shocked to read my diaries than I was to read his because, being an amateur writer, I lose my cool more than he ever did. There was only one page that he'd torn the bottom half off of, and the next entry explained why, and it was something he'd written about one of our fights. He wouldn't say what it was, but it was distasteful to him.

So after the fact, either in the moment or in the light of morning after having written it, he decided he had to excise it?

Yes, he had a great sense of responsibility. He took being a writer very seriously. He wouldn't allow himself to betray his own principles for long.

You mentioned earlier how meaningful words always were for him. With your encouragement, he once attempted to write about your relationship, about the unique and long-lasting love you shared, but ultimately, he found he couldn't do it?

He couldn't do it. It was too important to him, in a way. Just to write candidly about our intimacy was to betray it in some way for him. Whereas I readily betrayed it: I'm far franker about my behavior in my own diary than he is about my behavior in his! And that seems to be as it should be.

As indeed you've generously and candidly been in conversation with me.

Well, I love being with you, I do! It's been fun for me. I don't *ever* remember speaking as frankly as I've spoken to you about my work and my attitude, or talking so frankly about my famous sitters, and largely because so few people have ever been interested enough for me to even consider trying. And the memories are still surprisingly fresh. But the movies: I was such an avid moviegoer that it really defined my life, and all through the years, they come back to me much more easily because each of the years had specific films that I remember, and I saw them often enough that they're still with me, and they've become really valuable as memorable joggers of other things that I was doing when I saw such and such a film. Oh, for years I tried to hide my movie-premiere-crashing obsession, because it didn't match with my new life. It was really the greatest story never told: it's about Hollywood, and also about movie fans and the kind of magic that can happen. Imagine, Hollywood still at its height of influence, and these two young inventive fans tracking stars?

And then one of them ultimately gaining almost unlimited access into their intimate society? As well as getting to look at them up close in private one-on-one portrait sittings?

That's really having it every which way, isn't it?! The Greatest Story Never Told!

And now it has been told—although not all of it, by any means. Your life and work carry on.

You know, apart from those brief periods in London and New York, I'd never lived alone. I was still living with my mother and brother in an apartment in Hollywood when I got to know Chris, and I moved in with him almost immediately, into that little

garden house he was living in in Brentwood, in the garden of Evelyn Hooker and her husband. And after Chris and then Tim, I was-
n't sure I was up to living alone here. But thank goodness I found
I was, and in fact, I very much enjoy living by myself. And it's a surprise, because I didn't know that I had the equipment for it.
There's never a day that I don't know what to do with myself. I
think it would have been just awful to find out that I was one of
those people who would rather be with somebody, *anybody*, than
nobody. That always seems to me a sad state to find oneself in: *anyone* for company. But as you say, I spend many of my days with my
sitters, intensely with them, looking at them in a way that I never
look at people ordinarily; I'd be embarrassed to.

*To this day, you're still also actively engaged with your first and long-
est lasting passion: the movies. Are there any current directors or performers whom you particularly follow?*

Oh, yes. Of course, my head is getting very slow on the pickup,
and I'll probably think of half a dozen people later. Ryan Gosling
is somebody whose movies I usually see. Oh, the power of movies,
it's as strong as ever, and it's growing, really. If only the product
was as good as it used to be, but then, how often has that syndrome occurred?

And you are certainly a devotee of Turner Classic Movies.

Yes, and bless TCM! I used to *disdain* movies on TV, because
they were broken into by commercials. How *dare* they! Movies I
really wanted to see again? It was intolerable! Chris and I both
scorned TV, because we couldn't bear that interruption. I don't
think we even had a set until '65 or '66, and it was just out of sheer
snobbery. Occasionally, if I heard about a TV show with somebody
in it I was interested in, I would go to my parents' apartment in
Hollywood to watch it with them. They had a terrible set: very
tiny and ugly, with bad visuals. But I was snooty—until they
started really showing the old movies, and then I had to cave in.

So, really, it wasn't until TCM, with no commercials, that I became a TV watcher, but I've maintained my scorn for practically every TV show. I've never seen *I Love Lucy*, and it seems every once in a while, when I get a peek at it somehow, it seems *so* overdone. I actually have a picture that either Ted or I took of her.

Of Lucille Ball at a premiere?

Yes, and then I met her at the very end of her career. It was at a party: she came late, and was sitting out on the front porch. And you know how front porches are usually lit: not for flattery. And she had no makeup on, and she looked like the oldest person I had *ever* seen! I could *just* tell it was Lucille Ball. I was very close to her, and really, without makeup, she just looked like how one is supposed to look at the end of a century!

Yet presumably still clamped under her trademark red wig?

Yes, so clamped under the wig, pulling up the scalp. Well, of course, it must be terrible to be at a party in the evening, when you've had that done to you during the day. But *everything* was collapsed. She was *just* identifiable as Lucille Ball, but I was thrilled.

Did you speak with her at all?

A little bit. I listened to her, mostly. As I've said, that was the wonderful aspect of meeting all of these people with Chris, because he could do all the talking, and I could do all the looking! Well, he really was hardly interested at all, but he knew how interested *I* was. He would really charm these people, just for my benefit, and do it in the *best* possible way.

You've nevertheless navigated many encounters with movie people on your own through the years. Many of your portraits of them are collected in your aptly titled book, Hollywood. *We've covered many of them, but another I'd like to call your attention to is your haunting 1969 drawing of Jane Fonda, which is paired in the book with your poignant portrait of her father, Henry Fonda, which was drawn ten years later.*

I had gotten her early, in '63, and she was looking just wonderful. She was early in her career, and full of youth and glamour and voluptuousness. I did, I think, three pictures of her, but then about six years later, she agreed to sit again, when she was making the dance marathon film *They Shoot Horses, Don't They?* She had a hangover and didn't have a hairdresser there to get her hair right, but nevertheless, she came and sat. Her hair was lank instead of being set in the '30s hairdo for the film; it wasn't right, and she looked forlorn, but I just lapped it up. It was the kind of drawing, a version of herself, that no movie actress wants to see! She was in a down mood, but she didn't try to cover it with a smile or anything. And so I just went to town, and I did a really poignant drawing of her: just one of the pictures that I'm most pleased with of *any* of my portraits of celebrities, in which she just was herself for the occasion and didn't worry about it. It's a beautiful drawing.

Like her father, she brought her own brand of authenticity to the sitting, but how did she respond to the finished portrait?

I knew it wasn't going to be flattering, but I let myself go, and she didn't even scold me. She saw that I'd given her *exactly* what she was feeling like. She was a *really* good sport about it, and I've always been *so* grateful to her, but it ended my access to her. Never again! It was a betrayal of her, and I knew it wouldn't please her, but there was no way for me to do anything but record it in every way, even though I knew doing it would probably offend her, and I guess it did. But she was such a good sport that she signed it anyway.

Let's talk about a few of your contemporary celebrity sitters. In 2014, W Magazine commissioned you to paint Oscar winners Tilda Swinton and Marion Cotillard.

Oh, I liked Swinton enormously. Bright. I liked her really a lot. There's something very droll about her, and precise. Yes, she made a very strong impression on me. I don't think my two drawings of her did her justice. They don't have magic for me, but I liked her personally a lot. With Cotillard, there was a real distance between us. Just from my vagueness about her now, I know that we never really connected.

Mark Ruffalo, who plays Bruce Banner/The Hulk in the Marvel Cinematic Universe, was receiving accolades for his performances in the television adaptation of Larry Kramer's The Normal Heart *and the movie* Foxcatcher *when he also sat for you in 2014.*

Oh, I liked him. He's very easy, very. He has charm, and he's good company, yes.

Although your studio very much remains a thriving workspace, the history it holds is head-spinning to consider. So many notable people have come directly there for their sittings with you over the years.

Well, if I get a major commission, and if I'm going to do really my best work, again I want to do it where I'm most comfortable and most likely to be impervious to any difficulty. It's *my* choices that are paramount in that way: it's how *I* feel about the sitting, not how my sitter feels about it. But you know, I mustn't make too many conditions. Why? Because that's the way of losing sitters, because if I make it too difficult, they just begin to be intimidated. And so I always try to make it as easy as I can, but also on *my* territory if I can manage it. But there are *very* few famous subjects who will say, what is best for *you*? What demands can make you feel that you're capable of doing your best work? What conditions? Where, what time of day, what kind of light, black-and-white, color? Nobody's ever asked me that, and I've never demanded it, because that's a way to lose a sitter.

Particularly a prize sitter.

Yes, but I'm an artist, and I have to be given a real chance! But very few people understand that, and if I start making conditions, it just seems more and more impossible for them to please *me*.

If the opportunity presented itself, would you still make yourself available to a star sitter?

I'm still such a sucker, I couldn't resist, but I would go into it worrying. But what I might well do: along with doing the sittings, I did have that ten-year period in which I did lots of abstract work. Some of it is not bad, but when I review it, I get very few encouraging responses from within myself. Nothing I look at makes me say I have to get back to that somehow, and I won't promise I won't, but so far, it's not been an attractive enough possibility to get me going. So I think now I'm probably going to find some way of doing an abstract version of a *portrait*. I'm not quite sure how I'll do it; it'll be a challenge for me. I might use my early clippings of movie stars from movie star magazines, maybe find something in there, but I won't try for a likeness; I'll just try to capture the pleasure I used to get from looking at those clippings, with that real appetite for looking. Avoiding a likeness will be the difficulty if I use real movie people from period clippings, but in some way, I don't want to expose their presence. I want to do it in a kind of way it would be very hard to guess how I did it.

Exploring that potential new creative path would certainly bring you full circle back to where your career as an artist truly began: as that young boy who pored over pictures of movie stars in fan magazines, and who then began to train his hand and his eye by translating those pictures into his own early portrait drawings.

And getting over my self-consciousness, and not really getting over it still. And I know that this is all my mother's gift to me, which is both pleasurable and painful. Sometimes I still get chills remembering the sittings with some of these people, and not even necessarily Hollywood personalities, but sometimes just with somebody I know well, or somebody I just met.

It's evident throughout Chris's diaries how predominantly present and forward-thinking he always was. At one point in the early 1970s, he struggled to backfill a "bald patch" in his journal-keeping from the late 1940s.

Yes, I remember it was a long period of sort of piecing together all of those years that he hadn't kept his journal. I think part of it was his new life with me: his intention was just to close the door on the past, and just concentrate on the new life here with me.

Although his reflective efforts did spark new expressions about his past through the memoirs Christopher and His Kind *and* My Guru and His Disciple, *as well as his biography of his parents,* Kathleen and Frank. *Whereas you seem to have embraced the past, and indeed remain in constant relationship with it, even while you're continuing to experience and express anew.*

I still have a pretty good memory. The things that I'm slipping up on are all about what happened last week. My memories of the '60s are better than from last week! But now my old man's brain is really playing classical tricks on me of forgetting, and I used to have such a sharp memory. For years, it was very good, and Chris always relied on me because he knew he could. I remembered names of people I had only met once. But now, I just hate what's happening to me, this encroachment of age/brain deterioration. That is the most maddening thing about my old age. Well, it is a worry, you know, but what can I do about it? I try to stay alert, because life isn't really worthwhile without my memory, at least it seems so to me. Chris—the last three years were very blank with him. His memory had been so sharp.

Was his a gradual ebbing away, or a more rapid decline?

I probably noticed it, of course, sooner than others would and did, but in the last year, it was very noticeable. I realized before I even noticed it that he'd stopped keeping his journal, and I knew that meant something was up. And I think it was that he had forgotten the events of just the previous day, so there wasn't enough to write about. But he himself didn't suffer. For one thing, I didn't make a big thing about it. I'd seen people humiliate their nearest and dearest by exposing their loss of memory. I couldn't do that. I oppose it when people do that kind of thing in front of me.

You spoke earlier of feeling that you're still in continual communication with him, even after nearly four decades of being apart.

Oh, I incorporated him into myself *years* ago. He's very much alive inside me, and I know *exactly* how to connect to him. He's been sustaining me for many, many years, and he's still keeping me going. I might even go so far as to say I'm still living just as a means of pleasing him, because he didn't want me to give up. If there's any possibility at all of an afterlife, I'll see him again. He'll be waiting!

And will likely eagerly say to you, "Let me see what you've done," just as he would when you'd come home from art school.

Yes! Oh, in those early years in art school, he was *so* enthusiastic, and as I've said, that's really what allowed me to be an artist. I never would have done it without his interest and backing and enthusiasm, and he knew that. And it pleased him to do it: he wasn't doing it just to please me; he was doing it because it pleased *him* so much.

You've now surpassed the age Chris lived to, by nearly a decade.

Yes, he died in '86 at age eighty-one, and I've also lived longer than any of my family: longer than my parents and Ted. Of course, I'm more than a bit worried about my own exit, but there's no use worrying about it. But time passes so much more quickly! I guess that's because I forget a lot. That telescopes the time.

How well are you coping with the other vagaries of age?

I've really been in good health all of my life. My only worry is that if I do get something wrong with me, I won't have any equipment for dealing with it, because I've just expected good health, and had it almost all my life. I've hardly been sick in my life, knock on wood. Well, my old arthritic thumbs don't help.

Does that affect your work?

Not yet. And my hands are further disfigured by Dupuytren's contracture. It's a growth that starts in the middle of the palm and gradually sends out feelers into the fingers. In its advanced state, it can pull fingers into claws. I don't feel it at all, except the lumps. It's not painful.

What can be done about it?

It's a very complicated surgery because of all the nerves in the hands, but I don't want to chance it, because I don't want anything to interfere with my work.

Did it develop from your working so intensively with your hands all these years?

I don't think so. Dupuytren's contracture is strictly hereditary, but there's no incidence of it in my family, that I've heard of, on either side. But I knew of it because about ten years before he died, Chris got it in one of his hands, and he'd never heard of it, either. It pulled in his little finger; it crooked the end of it. I first noticed it in my hands six months after Chris died, and I've always regarded it as a little reminder. A kind of, *guess who?* A sort of wry remembrance. So I've actually always felt sort of kindly towards it.

You're still incredibly fit, the result of keeping up your longtime weekly regimen of working out with a trainer. In fact, you became a regular gym-goer very early on, long before it was in vogue for anyone but dedicated bodybuilders.

I started when I was twenty-one. At that time, Harvey Easton's gym was still the only gym in L.A. It had been the only gym already for years before I met him, and it continued on for a year or two more before there were more gyms, so it was really an experience, going to that second-floor gym of his on Beverly Boulevard.

What inspired you at twenty-one to dedicate such effort into sculpting your body?

Well, I wanted a good-looking body, and I got one. In just three months, I really did build myself a very attractive-looking body, from that *gym* point of view. Chris was *stunned*. Sometimes his boy-friends had the same idea I did and had gone to Harvey's gym—even Bill Caskey, who had been with him for years—but Chris said, "I could never see any change in their bodies until *you*! You trans-formed yourself!" I got all the effects of going to a gym that could possibly be realized in three months, because I *really* worked at it.

Your remarkable physical transformation is evident in the many beef-cake photos various appreciative photographers, including Chris, took of you through the years.

Of all the people who photographed me once I'd gotten my gym body, his pictures are the ones I like best. I went to the gym at least three times a week when I was going to art school. I got an hour-and-forty-five-minute lunch, and that was enough time for me to drive to Harvey's gym, do a full workout, have a bite to eat, and drive back for the afternoon session at Chouinard.

You and Chris were never teetotalers, but did you ever smoke? Smok-ing was certainly glamorized and ubiquitous in movies of the 1930s and '40s, and was an essential part of your childhood idol Bette Davis's brand.

No, I never did. Up until I was coming to the age of around eight or nine, I often sat on my father's lap in the evening. His chair was right next to the radio, and often I was sitting up on his lap, inhaling his smoke, finding it so glamorous then, and I think, why didn't I smoke? I once, in my very late teens, tried one cigarette, and I said to Ted, "Well, that wasn't bad," but I never smoked another. Thank

God I didn't. I suppose why I didn't smoke is that my mother never smoked. But she never complained of my father smoking: never any noise about his bad breath or anything like that, and I wonder why not? But isn't it funny: *I* never thought of objecting, either!

Your good health stands you in good stead for your continuing travels with Tim. You two are intrepid road-trippers, trekking cross-country to his architectural conferences and even on a cross-border adventure driving deep into Mexico?

That was a wonderful trip. I loved it. We got right down as far as we could go, and then we turned around and did it again, using a completely different route. I don't think we revisited anything we'd been to on the way down, so it really was a thorough examination and a wonderful trip. I enjoyed it hugely. We've had some of our best times together on these car trips. Of course, if you can manage to maintain civil relations in a car, you can do it anywhere! I mean, because that's certainly intimate enclosure. But oh, I remember family trips I made with my parents in the front seat and Ted and I in the back, and just always the chilling experience of locking with my father's eyes in the rearview mirror! That was always sobering and intimidating. He was usually the enemy in all family situations. But indeed, he did finally get to enjoy the movies we all saw together, and he did drive Ted and me to our early premiere adventures quite often before Ted had his own car, so he did come around a little bit.

Your avid moviegoing with friends continued unabated until the recent Covid-19 shutdowns of movie theaters. How did you cope with being homebound?

Oh, it was really a nuisance, and to me, really, I hated all the quarantining. I think that was the longest absence from a movie theater for me since I was, what, five or six. In the old days, that would have really been tough to bear, but here I am with television now, so I don't ache for movie entertainment. On Turner, there's always something to see, so I hardly noticed a ripple in my life. And I really spend a lot of time alone now—much more time alone than I've ever spent in my life. But as I said, it doesn't bother me; I'm not afraid of my own company. I always know what to do with my time. People who have time on their hands and are desperate for some kind of distraction, I always feel so sorry for them. How awful it must be not to be able to bear one's own company. I love being at home. My house is just perfect to spend an entire day in. I don't mind the least bit being actually a total homebody.

In 2021, your longtime home and studio were designated a Historic-Cultural Monument by the City of Los Angeles.

I'm delighted, really, because we stand for our community, Chris and I, and it's an achievement for two well-known queers to get into the kind of snobbery that Santa Monica is capable of—that they would nevertheless let us in. But it doesn't matter *why*; it's to be *famous*. It's always interesting on what *terms* the fame has come, but fame is fame is fame! I mean, it might be for burglarizing banks or whatever, but to hit the headlines is always some kind of recognition, anyway! Leaving an impression!

You of anyone has certainly left one!

It's such satisfaction because, as I just said, really what counts is the *fame* itself. Yes, however you got famous makes a big difference, of course, but nevertheless by that time, before you've even examined how it happened, you get on the list, and you can never be taken off. And yes, it may be on a list that would horrify some people, but it's still fame of a sort. As a kid, well, I thought fame meant movie star fame, and there would have been no equivalent to that that would have satisfied me then. But nowadays, I see that fame is fame: whatever inspired it, it happened. And so, of course, the question is: OK, if you're determined to enter history, does that mean that being famous for *anything* is better than being not known for anything? In some cases, no, of course not—if you're a murderer or something as bad or worse—but other kinds of fame, yes. I was even very sensitive for years about being known as any kind of movie fan, so I hid it as well as I could when I was meeting these movie people with Chris, because I thought if I got exposed, I would be forbidden. But I don't know if it ever really filtered down into any recognition that was negative. Maybe so, but it doesn't really matter to me now. I've really had a fantastic life. All kinds of dangers, and all kinds of fulfillments. Lucky me, yes. I hope it lasts! But I'm getting to the end of the road! And so, I hope I get there without anything bad happening, besides death, but what can be worse than death? Nothing's worse than death, yes!

You've truly embraced three interconnected identities throughout your life: that of movie fan, Christopher Isherwood's partner, and artist. But how do you hope to be best remembered?

As Chris's boyfriend. I loved being his boyfriend. It was a real role for me to play for him and for the world, too.

In an interview you gave some years back, you said of your relationship, "We were both extraordinary."

Yes, and really, it was mutual fulfillment. We were *exactly* what the other wanted, and we didn't even know it; we didn't intend it. It happened to us both, and it was, I think, a surprise that we could realize such satisfaction with each other by just being who each of us was, naturally. And we were surprised to find that the other was so *ideal* and so exciting and forgiving and intuitive about the whole situation! And to share that with somebody, and to have it?

Yours is truly a "local boy makes good" story—only in your case, the locale has been L.A., Hollywood. You truly went from being one of Norma Desmond's "wonderful people out there in the dark" to becoming a star yourself.

That's what makes it a unique point of view: a real movie fanatic getting himself into this position of seeing it from a totally different angle, living with somebody even more distinguished than the movie people he worshipped as a kid, and meeting literary people. I would never have dreamed. I've had these premiere pictures for decades, but I've shared them with very few people. In the beginning, I would have trembled at the thought of doing so. Just framing the picture of me with Marilyn Monroe, which has been hanging in the house probably twenty years now—that would only have been shown to members of the innermost circle for years. That's just what makes certain things worth telling, finally.

If you could time-travel back to tell your teenage self what a richly fulfilling life he was going to have, do you think he would believe you? That he would someday not only be routinely engaging socially with the movie stars he so admired, but would also be co-creating with them as a fellow artist?

What I wouldn't have believed is, "All this is true, but I still didn't manage to be a major movie star?" It took a long while for that ambition to be seen as what it was. What I wouldn't have been able to understand is how any alternative would have been considered preferable: that the life that I have, in fact, led would ever seem to me worth the sacrifice of the image of myself as a movie star. That is the wonderful reward of being able to identify with others, without becoming them: being able to appreciate the very people that I identify with in a way that I never could, had I become one of them. To be able to see them in three dimensions, without becoming one of them, is my reward in old age. I had to become an old man in order to sacrifice the ambition.

Source Notes

Introduction

They are the most famous gay couple: Christopher Harrity, "The Enduring Love and Exquisite Observations of Don Bachardy," *The Advocate*, Sept. 29, 2014.

There's a brilliant wide-openness about his mouse face: Christopher Isherwood, *Diaries: Volume One: 1939-1960*.

One of the most attractive myths: Stuart Timmons, Christopher Isherwood interview transcript, 1979.

a story about L.A.: Eve Babitz, *Slow Days, Fast Company: The World, the Flesh, and L.A.*

1. I was just waiting to be told who I was

Although Faye was a major star: William Hare, *Pulp Fiction to Film Noir: The Great Depression and the Development of a Genre*.

one of those young kids: Leslie Caron, quoted in *Chris & Don: A Love Story*, documentary directed by Guido Santi and Tina Mascara.

2. A fated, mutual discovery

a psychologist noted for her pioneering work: Myrna Oliver, "Evelyn Hooker: Her Study Fueled Gay Liberation," *Los Angeles Times*, Nov. 22, 1996.

the strange sense of a fated, mutual discovery: Isherwood, *My Guru and His Disciple*.

3. Everybody wanted to meet me

I have known Don Bachardy: Glenway Wescott, *A Heaven of Words: Last Journals, 1956-1984*.

faint praise dressed up in verbiage: Isherwood, *Liberation: Diaries, Volume Three: 1970-1983.*

had no identity: Isherwood, *Diaries: Volume One: 1939-1960.*

with a live ocelot draped over his shoulders: Author interview with Ed Newell, April 5, 2020.

4. I was all eyes

the precise truth as you see it: Elia Kazan, letter to Christopher Isherwood, April 8, 1955.

a ghastly, shattered expression: Isherwood, *Diaries: Volume One: 1939-1960.*

5. The right kind of beautiful young man

who outed themselves before the draft board: Author interview with Bernard Perlin, 2011; Jack Drescher, "Out of DSM: Depathologizing Homosexuality," *Behavioral Sciences,* Dec. 4, 2015.

'the high priests of queerdom': Don Bachardy, quoted in William J. Mann, *Behind the Screen: How Gays and Lesbians Shaped Hollywood, 1910-1969.*

as beautiful as Vivien Leigh: Isherwood, *Diaries: Volume One: 1939-1960.*

the wonder was Forster himself: Isherwood, *Christopher and His Kind.*

6. This is a real house

'It'll be like Booth and Lincoln': Isherwood, *Diaries: Volume One: 1939-1960.*

the poor man's Truman Capote: Ned Rorem, *A Ned Rorem Reader.*

a very lively do-it-yourself kind of girl: Isherwood, *Diaries: Volume One: 1939-1960.*

regularly joined Judy in her nocturnal prowling: John Carlyle, *Under the Rainbow: An Intimate Memoir of Judy Garland, Rock Hudson & My Life in Old Hollywood.*

'I like the warmth of Cecil's indiscretion': Isherwood, *Diaries: Volume One: 1939-1960.*

both of her notably unconventional sons: Isherwood, *Diaries: Volume One: 1939-1960.*

epitomized everything against which he wished to rebel: Isherwood, *Diaries: Volume One: 1939-1960.*

7. It was exactly what the boy wanted

They express a kind of freedom and truth: Isherwood, letter to Bachardy, March 11, 1963.

one of the greatest friendships of his life: Isherwood, *The Sixties: Diaries, Volume Two: 1960-1969.*

one of our most desperate evenings of boredom: Isherwood, *Diaries: Volume One: 1939-1960.*

the three graces of the older [gay] generation: Armistead Maupin, "The First Couple: Don Bachardy and Christopher Isherwood," *The Village Voice*, July 2, 1985.

the most graceful thing of all: George Plimpton, *Truman Capote: In Which Various Friends, Enemies, Acquaintances, and Detractors Recall His Turbulent Career.*

really gets to [Don] as almost nothing else does: Isherwood, *Liberation: Diaries, Volume Three: 1970-1983.*

a dear little boy from the west: Bachardy, letter to Isherwood, June 17, 1965.

every **face has to be important:** Bachardy, interviewed in Santi and Mascara's documentary, *Chris & Don: A Love Story.*

the ever-swinging pendulum that was Lincoln's behavior: Author interviews with Alexander Jensen Yow, 2017-2021.

Jack Fontan's claim to fame: Author interview with Yow.

8. The beautiful and damned

I quite forgot to feel sorry for anybody: Isherwood, letter to Bachardy, June 21, 1958.

liked that people liked it so much: Liza Minnelli, interviewed in Santi and Mascara's documentary, *Chris & Don: A Love Story.*

She has a complete manner for such encounters and occasions: Isherwood, *Liberation: Diaries, Volume Three: 1970-1983.*

a really sensitive and subtle actor: Isherwood, *Liberation: Diaries, Volume Three: 1970-1983.*

I remember wanting to please Don and my mom: Natasha Gregson Wagner, email to author, Sept. 13, 2023.

9. I am a camera

to call her and explain: Isherwood, *Liberation: Diaries, Volume Three: 1970-1983.*

the most awarded woman in Oscar history: Kelcie Mattson, "The Most Nominated Woman in Oscars History Won Eight Awards," *Collider,* March 4, 2024.

a blown-up studio photograph smeared with oil paint: Otto Preminger, *An Autobiography.*

10. We were both extraordinary

Chris considered his "kind": Roger Austen, "Christopher Isherwood Interview," *Conversations with Christopher Isherwood.*

Yesterday morning we went through the adoption ceremony: Isherwood, *Liberation: Diaries, Volume Three: 1970-1983.*

I am a camera with its shutter open: Isherwood, *Goodbye to Berlin.*

11. What an artist would do

***Every* face has to be important:** *Chris & Don: A Love Story.* Directed by Guido Santi and Tina Mascara, interview with Leslie Caron. Zeitgeist Films, 2007.

this is what I want to look like: Bachardy, quoted in Susan Ford Morgan, "Oral history interview with Don Bachardy, 2009 May 21–October 7." Archives of American Art, Smithsonian Institution.

the first drawing is still my favorite: Bachardy, *Stars in My Eyes.*

liking for Merrill: Bachardy, *Stars in My Eyes.*

the greatest triumph Don will ever have: Isherwood, *The Sixties: Diaries, Volume Two: 1960-1969.*

I'm an unconscious mimic: Bachardy, quoted in Peter Conrad, "Christopher Isherwood remembered: 'Chris always loved young men, and I was certainly young,'" *The Observer,* Oct. 16, 2010.

12. A single man

We were both extraordinary: Bachardy, quoted in Jeffrey Masters, "Don Bachardy on His 33-Year Love Affair with Christopher Isherwood," *The Advocate,* May 2, 2022.

Bibliography

Books

Babitz, Eve. *Slow Days, Fast Company: The World, the Flesh, and L.A.* New York: New York Review Books Classics, 2016.

Bachardy, Don. *Hollywood.* New York: Glitterati Incorporated, 2014.

———. *Nudes.* Santa Monica, CA: Craig Krull Gallery, 2017.

———. *One Hundred Drawings.* Los Angeles: Twelvetrees Press, 1983.

———. *Stars in My Eyes.* Madison, WI: The University of Wisconsin Press, 2000.

Carlyle, John. *Under the Rainbow: An Intimate Memoir of Judy Garland, Rock Hudson & My Life in Old Hollywood.* New York: Carroll & Graf Publishers, 2006.

Hare, William. *Pulp Fiction to Film Noir: The Great Depression and the Development of a Genre.* Jefferson, NC: McFarland & Company, Inc., 2012.

Isherwood, Christopher. *Christopher and His Kind.* New York: Farrar, Straus and Giroux, 1976.

———. *Diaries: Volume One: 1939-1960*, edited by Katherine Bucknell. New York: HarperCollins, 1996.

———. *Goodbye to Berlin.* London: Hogarth Press, 1939.

———. *Liberation: Diaries, Volume Three: 1970-1983*, edited by Katherine Bucknell. New York: Harper Perennial, 2012.

———. *Lost Years: A Memoir, 1945-1951.* New York: HarperCollins, 2000.

———. *My Guru and His Disciple.* New York: Picador, 1980.

———. *The Sixties: Diaries, Volume Two: 1960-1969*, edited by Katherine Bucknell. New York: Harper Perennial, 2010.

Isherwood, Christopher and Don Bachardy. *The Animals: Love Letters Between Christopher Isherwood and Don Bachardy*, edited by Katherine Bucknell. New York: Farrar, Straus and Giroux, 2014.

———. *October.* Los Angeles: Twelvetrees Press, 1981.

Mann, William J. *Behind the Screen: How Gays and Lesbians Shaped Hollywood, 1910-1969.* New York: Viking, 2001.

Plimpton, George. *Truman Capote: In Which Various Friends, Enemies, Acquaint-ances, and Detractors Recall His Turbulent Career.* New York: Anchor Books, 1998.

Preminger, Otto. *An Autobiography.* New York: Doubleday & Company, 1977.

Rorem, Ned. *A Ned Rorem Reader.* New Haven, CT: Yale University Press, 2001.

Schreiber, Michael. *One-Man Show: The Life and Art of Bernard Perlin.* Berlin: Bruno Gmünder, 2016.

Wescott, Glenway. *A Heaven of Words: Last Journals, 1956-1984,* edited by Jerry Rosco. Madison, WI: The University of Wisconsin Press, 2013.

Interviews and Correspondence

Austen, Roger. "Christopher Isherwood Interview," *Conversations with Chris-topher Isherwood,* edited by James J. Berg and Chris Freeman. Jackson, MS: University Press of Mississippi, 2001.

Bachardy, Don. Letter to Christopher Isherwood, June 17, 1965. Christopher Isherwood Papers, the Huntington Library, San Marino, California.

Conrad, Peter. "Christopher Isherwood remembered: 'Chris always loved young men, and I was certainly young.'" *The Observer,* Oct. 16, 2010, https://www.theguardian.com/books/2010/oct/17/christopher-isher wood-don-bachardy-diaries.

Harrity, Christopher. "The Enduring Love and Exquisite Observations of Don Bachardy." *The Advocate,* Sept. 29, 2014, https://www.advocate.com/ arts-entertainment/art/2014/09/29/enduring-love-and-exquisite -observations-don-bachardy.

Isherwood, Christopher. Letter to Don Bachardy, June 21, 1958. Christopher Isherwood Papers, the Huntington Library, San Marino, California.

———. Letter to Don Bachardy, March 11, 1963. Christopher Isherwood Papers, the Huntington Library, San Marino, California.

Kazan, Elia. Letter to Christopher Isherwood, April 8, 1955. Christopher Isher-wood Papers, the Huntington Library, San Marino, California.

Masters, Jeffrey. "Don Bachardy on His 33-Year Love Affair with Christopher Isherwood," *The Advocate,* May 2, 2022, https://www.advocate.com/ people/2019/4/22/don-bachardy-his-33-year-love-affair-christopher -isherwood.

Maupin, Armistead. "The First Couple: Don Bachardy and Christopher Isher-wood," *The Village Voice,* July 2, 1985, https://amanidreamtup.blog spot.com/2008/11/first-couple-don-bachardy-and.html.

Morgan, Susan Ford. "Oral history interview with Don Bachardy, 2009 May 21–October 7." Archives of American Art, Smithsonian Institution, https://www.aaa.si.edu/collections/interviews/oral-history-interview -don-bachardy-15735.

Newell, Ed. Interview by Michael Schreiber, April 5, 2020.

Santi, Guido and Tina Mascara, directors. *Chris & Don: A Love Story*. Documentary. Los Angeles: Asphalt Stars Productions/Zeitgeist Films, 2007.

Timmons, Stuart. Christopher Isherwood interview transcript, 1979. Christopher Isherwood Papers, the Huntington Library, San Marino, California.

Wagner, Natasha Gregson. Email to Michael Schreiber, Sept. 13, 2023.

Yow, Alexander Jensen. Multiple interviews with Michael Schreiber, 2017–2021; a selection was published as "Intimate Companion: A Conversation with Alexander Jensen Yow" in *The Young and Evil: Queer Modernism in New York, 1930-1955*. New York: David Zwirner Books, 2020.

Acknowledgments

Composing these acknowledgments is an uneasy task, as "thank you" is a phrase that seems pitifully inadequate to express my gratitude to Don Bachardy for so graciously and generously opening his home, his heart, his memories, and his reflections to me. The extensive time I have been privileged to spend in his extraordinary company these past ten years, both in collaboration and in friendship, has been nothing short of magical. Far more eloquent words of appreciation will no doubt come rushing in after this book has gone to print, but for now, *humbled* and *honored* are the meager placeholders that come immediately to mind—as does that too simple phrase, *thank you.*

The friendship, encouragement, and advice of Tina Mascara have been steadying supports for which I am eternally grateful. I am tremendously lucky to also have a tireless champion in my indefatigable agent, Mitchell Waters at Brandt & Hochman, and in my editor, John Scognamiglio at Kensington Publishing. Their steadfast belief in this project and dedication toward its publication, despite the headwinds it has faced, have been sustaining forces. I also thank Katherine Bucknell for her thoughtful input and help in shaping the manuscript, and Sarah Chalfant and Rebecca Nagel at The Wylie Agency for their constructive guidance.

I am awed by the collective talents of Scott Heim, who masterfully copy edited the final manuscript, and the incredible production team at Kensington—Barbara Brown, Ann Pryor, and Stephen

Smith—who so beautifully brought this book to life and out into the world. My tremendous thanks to them all.

I am so very honored and deeply grateful to Tom Ford, Joel Grey, Ian McKellen, Liza Minnelli, Robert J. Wagner, Edmund White, and Michael York for dedicating such time and consideration into crafting such special statements in support of this book. Simon Callow and James Ivory went above and beyond in generously contributing the longer, beautiful reflections on their friendships with Don Bachardy that open this book. I am beyond grateful to them both, as I also am to Natasha Gregson Wagner for the many extraordinary kindnesses she has extended me, both in aid of this project and in friendship.

For their kind assistance, I thank Bradford Bricken at The Cartel, Helen Hicks at Aevitas Creative Management, Alex Jankovich at Innovative Artists, Alexandra Nourafchan at Tom Ford, Nick Pourgourides at Casarotto Ramsay & Associates Limited, Jerry Rosco for the Estate of Glenway Wescott, Lisa Schiek at Fade to Black, and Victoria Varela at Varela Media.

I am forever indebted to the Andrew W. Mellon Foundation for its invaluable support of this project through a fellowship at the Huntington Library, Art Museum, and Botanical Gardens in San Marino, California, where I had the heady and privileged experience of spending intensive research time in the Christopher Isherwood and Don Bachardy Papers. My work was further advanced at writing residencies I was honored to receive at The North Dakota Museum of Art/McCanna House, The Kimmel Harding Nelson Center for the Arts in Nebraska City, and The Desert House at Joshua Tree, California. I'm so very grateful to Matthew Wallace and Laurel Reuter, Sara Ammon and Sara McNeilly, and Claire Jackel at those respective residencies, and to Mia Bloom, Steve Hindle, Juan Gomez, and Natalie Serrano at the Huntington.

For their generous assistance in securing image selections for the book, my heartfelt thanks go out to Stephanie Arias and Mina Marciano at the Huntington Library, Art Museum, and Botanical

Gardens; Indira Berndtson at the Frank Lloyd Wright Foundation; Manoah Bowman and the Natalie Wood Archive; Logan Esdale and the Van Vechten Trust; Maina Gielgud; Phyllis Green; Fredda Harris and Jenny Harris at the Anna L. Weissberger Foundation; Grant Hayter-Menzies; Erin Katgely and Joan Agajanian Quinn at the Joan Quinn Archives; Joshua Lynes and the Estate of George Platt Lynes; Ron Munkácsi; Åsa Rönngren at the George Hoyningen-Huene Estate Archives; Shawn Rorke-Davis; Seth David Rubin; Francesca Rubino and the Estate of Julie Harris; Matt Severson at the Margaret Herrick Library, Academy of Motion Picture Arts and Sciences; Yuriy Shcherbina at the USC Digital Library; Jack Shear and Taylor Zartman at the Ellsworth Kelly Studio; Sarah Standing and the Estate of Bryan Forbes; and Mark B. Stein and Marcy Taylor for the Estate of Dale Laster.

Special thanks go out to Marlys Ray and the Estate of Bill Ray; Juli Veee and the Estate of Stathis Orphanos; Mark Manivong at the Library of Congress; Sean Black; Samantha Eggar and Jenna Stern; Val Holley; Richard Sassin; Wayne Shimabukuro; and Pat York.

I am immensely blessed to have such a devoted cheerleading squad in beloved friends Dana and Ricky Abt; Ivan Ashby; Don Bacigalupi and Dan Feder; Carolyn Beckett; Linda Francavilla; Andrew and Anne Fredericks; Sherry Gillen; Jon-Michael Hernandez; Marcy Just; Jeanine Kirpec; Mary Macziewski; Martha Paull; Hope and Mary Rogers; Julian Scates; Amy Short and Madeleine Reber; and (especially) my bestie, Amy Maute, and brother Bruce Schreiber. My thanks, too, to Tim Hilton and Peter Macauley for their supportive friendship. Above all, I am forever grateful to the extraordinary elders from whom I have learned so much: Bernard Perlin, Orest Daszo, Ed Newell, Alexander Jensen Yow, and, again, Don Bachardy.

My work on this oral history brought me frequently to Los Angeles, while back home in Chicago, my continuing research, transcribing, and editing pulled me into untold hours of solitary work.

Jason Loper, my husband and stalwart champion of twenty-five years, withstood these separations with loving support, and helped me navigate the many challenges I faced in bringing this book to fruition with sensitive yet sensible guidance. I love you so much, Mister. Here's looking at our next twenty-five years together, and beyond. And here's looking at you, my love.